G. F. (George Farquhar) Graham, J. Muir Wood

The Popular Songs of Scotland with Their Appropriate Melodies

G. F. (George Farquhar) Graham, J. Muir Wood

The Popular Songs of Scotland with Their Appropriate Melodies

ISBN/EAN: 9783337181529

Printed in Europe, USA, Canada, Australia, Japan

Cover: Foto ©Thomas Meinert / pixelio.de

More available books at **www.hansebooks.com**

THE POPULAR
SONGS OF SCOTLAND
WITH THEIR APPROPRIATE MELODIES

ARRANGED BY

G. F. GRAHAM, A. C. MACKENZIE, J. T. SURENNE,
T. M. MUDIE, FINLAY DUN, H. E. DIBDIN

AND

SIR GEORGE A. MACFARREN

𝔍llustrateð by Critical anð other Notices

BY

GEORGE FARQUHAR GRAHAM

AUTHOR OF THE ARTICLE 'MUSIC' IN THE SEVENTH EDITION OF THE
ENCYCLOPÆDIA BRITANNICA

REVISED BY

J. MUIR WOOD

WITH ADDITIONAL AIRS AND NOTES

J. MUIR WOOD AND CO., 42 BUCHANAN STREET, GLASGOW
WOOD AND CO., EDINBURGH
CRAMER; CHAPPELL; NOVELLO, LONDON
MDCCCLXXXVII

PRELIMINARY NOTE.

The present volume contains the popular songs of Scotland; not those only which are usually sung at the present time, for they unfortunately are few, but in addition a large number which, though now seldom heard, ought on account of their quaintness, their wit, or the beauty of their melody, to be ever held in remembrance. To a large extent they have been extracted from the earlier collection known as "Wood's Songs of Scotland," edited by George Farquhar Graham, whose illustrative notes were a leading feature of the work, and who, it may be mentioned, was selected on account of his learning and musical ability to write the article Music in the seventh edition of the Encyclopædia Britannica. It is scarcely necessary to say that wherever in these notes he expressed his own opinions they have been scrupulously adhered to in the present edition; but quotations and remarks from other sources have had to be reconsidered, and frequently to be set aside, in favour of more recent and accurate information.

Of all the annotators of Scottish Song the most copious was Mr. William Stenhouse, who supplied the "Illustrations" for Messrs. Blackwood's re-issue of Johnson's Museum; that great repository of Scottish music, for which Burns did so much, and which he predicted would make the publisher famous for all time. In many ways Mr. Stenhouse was well fitted for the work which he undertook, being a zealous antiquary, no mean musician, and indefatigable in the prosecution of his self-imposed task. Having, however, to gather his materials from a very wide field, it is not surprising that he should have frequently fallen into error. David Laing and Charles Kirkpatrick Sharpe—who in revising added considerably to his notes—pointed out and corrected many of his literary and historical blunders, while G. Farquhar Graham did the same in regard to many of his musical mis-statements. ,It is at best doubtful whether Mr. Stenhouse was able to decipher the Lute tablature of the Skene MS. his references to it therefore are usually erroneous. Even his quotations from the "Orpheus Caledonius" are seldom correct; and, with regard to Playford's "Dancing Master," he cannot have seen the rare edition of 1657 which he so often quotes, for, with two or three exceptions, the airs he refers to are not included in it, though they are to be found in the enlarged edition of 1718, which he probably possessed. Mr. Stenhouse had besides a notion, not uncommon in the earlier part of the present century, that England possessed little if any true national music; a tune therefore which was current in both countries, he contended must be of Scottish origin, and only imported into England since the "union of the crowns." This belief was to some extent fostered by the want of any collection of English airs that could be referred to; for Ritson's is an Anthology of lyric poetry set by learned musicians, rather than a collection of national melodies, though it does contain a small modicum of real folk-music; and Dr. Crotch, in his "Specimens of various styles of Music," is equally meagre, and often not at all correct in his ascriptions of nationality to the tunes. In Scotland, on the other hand, during the previous century, numerous collections had appeared, in which was included every tune well known in Scotland, whether really Scottish or not. To these uncritical collections Mr. Stenhouse was in the habit of appealing in corroboration of his otherwise unsupported assertions, as if an error could be turned into a truth by mere iteration. Unfortunately his erroneous opinions have by frequent quotation been so widely spread that it may now be difficult for the actual facts to obtain a hearing.* In making this statement, it would be manifestly unfair to Mr. Stenhouse to omit that by his zeal and perseverance he gathered together a mass of antiquarian matter bearing on the songs, their writers, and the incidents on which they were founded, that could not now be collected by any amount of industry : many of those from

---

* It is unaccountable how so scrupulously accurate an editor as Mr. Scott Douglas should have accepted Mr. Stenhouse's erroneous statements regarding the airs of many of Burns's songs without making any attempt at verification. Stenhouse's blunders are the only blot on a work otherwise excellent and beautiful, every page being marked by painstaking and good faith.

whom he obtained his traditional information having passed away before his work could be given to the world. Since that time much has come to light in regard to the national music of all countries. In particular, the publication by Mr. William Chappell, F.S.A., of that marvel of research, "The Popular Music of the Olden Time," has not only shown the wealth of melody possessed by England, but has caused a more critical inquiry to be made into the music of our own country. The result of this has been to show clearly that some of our favourite airs are certainly English, while to some others Northumberland may have as good a claim as Berwick, Roxburgh, or any other of our southern counties. While this may be candidly admitted, we still assert our right to include these airs in our Scottish collections, on account of the beautiful poetry written for them by our own countrymen, and with which they are much more associated than with the original English verses, now indeed known only to the antiquary. The celebrated work already mentioned—the Scottish Musical Museum—contains a considerable number of English airs in each of its six volumes, while in the first half volume at least a third are not of Scottish origin ; a fact which Johnson, the publisher, thus explains in his preface. He says, " It was intended, and mentioned in the Proposals, to have adopted a considerable variety of the most musical and sentimental of the English and Irish songs ;" as, however, this did not meet with general approval, it was abandoned after not a few plates had been engraved for the purpose. This ought to be borne in mind when charges of ignorant appropriation are brought against him. In the present work no attempt has been made to eliminate the English airs ; they have been retained in some cases for the purpose of pointing out that notwithstanding the Scottish words they are really English ; in others—as in "The Banks of Doon "—because the Scottish poetry has saved the English air from oblivion, which its own words never could have done. In every known instance the English origin of an air has been acknowledged ; the numerous additions which have been made to the work will be found, however, to be entirely Scottish ; these are mostly modern, but among them are a few worthy relics of the olden time, which have been gathered up after a century of neglect.

In order to maintain the previous high standard of excellence, the arrangement of the accompaniments to these additions was confided to that excellent musician, the late T. M. Mudie, and more recently to A. C. Mackenzie, of whose musical triumphs his country may well be proud. With regard to the notes, all have been carefully revised, many have received considerable additions, while others have been entirely re-written ; dates have been scrupulously verified, and where necessary corrected. To place the airs in strict chronological order, however desirable it might be, is in the present state of our knowledge quite impossible ; but it has been thought advisable to avoid mixing up the ancient style with the modern ; the airs therefore which are known to be old have been placed earlier in the volume than others which have appeared at a more recent date. At the same time it should be borne in mind that first appearance in print or manuscript cannot always be held to determine either the age or even the nationality of a tune.

Besides the additions already mentioned, a four-part arrangement of a few of our airs will be found as an Appendix to the volume. These airs were on two occasions, by special command, sung before the QUEEN at Balmoral by Mr. H. A. Lambeth's Select Choir. As a distinctive name, therefore, this has been called the Balmoral Edition.

J. M. W.

January 1884.

INTRODUCTION.

THE plan of this Work was suggested to the Publishers by a perception of the want of a really cheap Collection of the best Scottish Melodies and Songs, with suitable Symphonies and Accompaniments, adapted to the Melodies ;* and with such information regarding the airs and the verses as might be interesting to the public. No work combining all these desiderata had appeared ; although no National Melodies have been so long and so extensively popular as those of Scotland.

Of the actual state of National Music in Scotland prior to the 15th century, authentic history affords no distinct traces, although it appears that both poetry and music were highly esteemed in the south and east of Scotland, and on the English Border, as far back, at least, as the 13th century. No. III. of the Appendix to Mr. Dauney's work upon the Skene MS., 1838, contains curious matter regarding musical performers and teachers of music in Scotland, from 1474 to 1633. It is entitled " Extracts from Documents preserved in the General Register House at Edinburgh." 1. Extracts from the Accounts of the Lords High Treasurers of Scotland relative to Music. 2. Extracts from the Household Book of Lady Marie Stewart, Countess of Mar, Edinburgh. 3. Extracts from Accounts of the Common Good of various Burghs in Scotland, relative to Music-schools, &c. In these Extracts we find named Scottish and English pipers, several harpers and *clarscha* players, fiddlers, &c.; with Italian and French performers upon the lute and other instruments, also singers, male and female. The fees given to the performers and teachers are stated, and it is evident that music was held in high esteem, and in all probability was considerably cultivated by the Court. We quote a few lines :—

" Jul. 10. 1489.—Item, to Inglis pyparis that cam to the castel yet and playit to the King, . viij lib. viij s.
" Apr. 19. 1490.—To Martin Clareschaw, and ye toder ersche clareschaw, at ye Kingis command, . xviij s.
" May.—Till ane ersche harper, at ye Kingis command, ... xviij s.
" Aug. 1. 1496.—Giffin to the harper with the a hand, ... ix s.
" Apr. 19. 1497.—Item, to the twa fithelaris that sang Graysteil to ye King, ... ix s.
" July 21.—To the menstrallis that playit before Mons† doun the gate, ... xiij s.
" Jan. 1503.—Item, to the four Italien menstralis, ... vij lib.
" Jan. 1507.—Item, that day giffin to divers menstrallis, schawmeris, trumpetis, taubroneris, fithelaris,
    lutaris, harparis, clarschearis, piparis, extending to lxix personis, ... x lib. xj s.
" Feb. 16. 1508.—Item, to Wantonnes that the King fechit and gert hir sing in the Quenis chamer,‡ . xiij s."

Unfortunately, no Musical MSS. containing Scottish airs have come down to us of an earlier date than the 17th century. We have, therefore, no positive proof of the actual existence of any of our known airs until that time, although we have no doubt that many of them existed in a simple and rudimental state long previously. We say in a simple and rudimental state—for we find that the ancient versions of our airs that have been preserved in the MSS. which we shall presently notice, differ in a remarkable degree from their modern representatives, occasionally presenting the more rude outline which an after age moulded into more perfect form, but more frequently disclosing melodies possessed of a charming simplicity, which the lapse of time has altered only to destroy. In this respect the music of Scotland is singularly at variance with a statement of Mr. Bunting, regarding National music generally, and that of Ireland in particular. In his preface to " The Ancient Music of Ireland," 1840, Mr. Bunting says:— " The words of the popular songs of every country vary according to the several provinces and districts in which they are sung ; as, for example, to the popular air of *Aileen-a-roon*, we here find as many different sets of words as there are counties in one of our provinces. But the case is totally different with music. A strain of music once impressed on the popular ear never varies. * * * * For taste in

---

* See TONALITY, p. 164.   † The famous piece of ordnance called " Mons Meg."
‡ In order to form a correct estimate of the actual sums paid to these musicians, we must bear in mind that the items are stated in Scottish money, the value of which was only one-twelfth of money sterling; and we must also take into consideration the prices of various articles of food about the same period. From the household book of James V., 1525, we learn that the cost, in Scottish money, of a beeve from grass, (merta herbalis,) was thirty shillings ; a sheep, five shillings ; a boll of wheat, twenty-two shillings ; and a gallon of ale, twentypence. Thus, although the Italian minstrels got but 11s. 5d. sterling amongst them, each man received the value of a sheep and an ox.

music is so universal, especially among country people and in a pastoral age, and airs are so easily, indeed in many instances so intuitively, acquired, that when a melody has once been divulged in any district, a criterion is immediately established in almost every ear ; and this criterion being the more infallible in proportion as it requires less effort in judging, we have thus, in all directions and at all times, a tribunal of the utmost accuracy and unequalled impartiality (for it is unconscious of its own authority) governing the musical traditions of the people, and preserving the native airs and melodies of every country in their integrity, from the earliest periods." This assertion is not by any means borne out by a comparison of the ancient airs of Scotland, as preserved in MSS., with the traditionary versions of the same airs ; and further inquiry would incline us to the opinion that the same discrepancy exists in the music of all countries that have any ancient MSS. to place in juxtaposition with the modern airs as handed down by tradition. Sufficient proof of this, in as far as Scottish music is concerned, will be found scattered through the Notes appended to the airs. To these we refer for many particulars respecting our national music, which it is unnecessary here to repeat : we prefer occupying our limited space with some account of the various ancient MSS. which are alluded to in the course of the work, as well as of the principal modern editions of the Songs and Melodies of Scotland.

ANCIENT SCOTTISH MANUSCRIPTS CONTAINING SCOTTISH MELODIES.

SKENE MS.—Belongs to the Library of the Faculty of Advocates. Supposed by the eminent antiquary, David Laing, Esq., to have been written about thirty or forty years after the commencement of the seventeenth century. Translated by the Editor of this work; and the translation published, with a Dissertation, &c., by the late William Dauney, Esq., Advocate, in one vol. 4to, at Edinburgh, November 1838. It contains a number of Scottish airs, besides foreign dance-tunes. Mr. Laing says, that the collection was formed by John Skene of Hallyards, in Mid-Lothian, the second son of the eminent lawyer, Sir John Skene of Curriehill.

STRALOCH MS.—Robert Gordon of Straloch's MS. Lute-book, dated 1627-29. A small oblong 8vo, at one time in the library of Charles Burney, Mus. Doc.; then in that of the late James Chalmers, Esq., of London, after whose death it was sold with his other books and MSS. In January 1839, it was sent by Mr. Chalmers to Mr. David Laing of Edinburgh, for his inspection, and by Mr. Laing to the Editor of this work, who had permission to copy it. He made extracts from it, which are now in the Library of the Faculty of Advocates, Edinburgh. Robert Gordon of Straloch, in Aberdeenshire, was a distinguished person in his day. There is some perplexity occasioned by the difference of designation bestowed upon this gentleman by different writers. The late Mr. William Dauney, in the Appendix to his Dissertation upon the Skene MS., &c., calls him Sir Robert Gordon of Straloch, when referring to the MS. Lute-book of 1627-29. Mr. David Laing, in his Illustrations to Johnson's Museum, does not give him the Sir; though in the preface, p. xxi, he calls him Sir Robert Gordon. We learn the following particulars of him from the Straloch papers, printed by the Spalding Club, in the first volume of their Miscellany, edited by their Secretary, John Stuart, Esq., Advocate :—Robert Gordon was the second son of Sir John Gordon of Pitlurg, and was born in 1580. Soon after his marriage in 1608, he bought the estate of Straloch, ten miles north of Aberdeen, the title arising from which he retained through life, although he succeeded to the estate of Pitlurg, by the death of his elder brother, in 1619. He devoted himself chiefly to the study of geography, history, and antiquities; and so celebrated was he for his attainments as a geographer, that in 1641 he was requested by Charles I. to undertake the execution of an Atlas of Scotland. This he completed in 1648, with the assistance of his son, James Gordon, parson of Rothiemay. It is the far-famed "Theatrum Scotiæ,"—a work which is still considered one of the most accurate delineations of Scotland and its islands. Although chiefly known as a geographer and antiquary, Robert Gordon was much employed in various negociations between the contending factions in the time of Charles I. and the Commonwealth; in proof of which, we find among the Straloch papers letters from the Marquis of Argyll, George Lord Gordon, the heroic friend of Montrose, and Lord Lewis Gordon, afterwards third Marquis of Huntly. As Sir John Gordon, his father, was knighted only by James VI., his title of course died with him, and we do not find that his son ever received any title as a reward for his services. His testament, dated 1657, commences, " I, Mr. Robert Gordon of Straloch, considering with myself my great age," &c. He died in August 1661.

ROWALLAN MS.—A MS. Lute-book, written by Sir William Mure of Rowallan, who died in 1657, aged 63. It was probably written about the same time as the Straloch MS., and was lately in the possession of Mr. Lyle, Surgeon at Airth. Its contents are chiefly foreign dance-tunes, with a very few Scottish airs. Sir William Mure was distinguished as a scholar and a poet. See "Historie and descent of the house of Rowallane," from the original MS. by Sir William, edited by the Rev. Mr. Muir, Glasgow. 1825; and, "Ancient Ballads and Songs," by Thomas Lyle, 1827

LEYDEN MS.—Belonged to the celebrated Doctor John Leyden. It is now in the possession of Mr. James Telfer, Schoolmaster, Saughtrees, Liddesdale. It is written in tablature for the Lyra-viol, and was sent, in 1844, to the Editor of this work, with permission to transcribe and translate from it. The transcript he made from it, of all the tunes in tablature, is now in the Library of the Faculty of Advocates, Edinburgh. Its date is uncertain, but cannot be earlier than towards the close of the seventeenth century, since we find in it, "King James' march to Ireland," and "Boyne Water," both relating to events in 1690. It contains a number of Scottish tunes, some of which have been referred to in the Notes of this work.

GUTHRIE (?) MS.—A number of Scottish and other tunes, in tablature, discovered by David Laing, Esq., in a volume of Notes of Sermons preached by James Guthrie, the Covenanting minister, who was executed in 1661, for declining the jurisdiction of the King and Council. See Mr. Dauney's Dissertation, pages 139-143. It is very doubtful when these tunes were written, and whether they were written by the same person who penned the rest of the volume.

BLAIKIE MSS.—The late Mr. Andrew Blaikie, Engraver, Paisley, was in possession of two volumes written in tablature, each containing a number of Scottish airs. One of these volumes was dated 1683, and the other 1692; the latter in tablature for the *Viol du Gamba*. The former was lost, but contained, with few exceptions, only the same tunes as the later volume. Both MSS. were written in the same hand. See Mr. Dauney's Dissertation, pages 143-146.

CROCKAT MS.—This MS. Music-book is frequently referred to by Mr. Stenhouse in his Notes on Johnson's Museum. It is dated 1709, and belonged to a Mrs. Crockat, of whom we have not been able to learn anything. The volume is now in the possession of Charles Kirkpatrick Sharpe, Esq.

MACFARLANE'S MSS.—"A collection of Scotch airs, with the latest variations, written for the use of Walter M'Farlane of that ilk. By David Young, W.M. in Edinburgh. 1740." 3 vols. folio. Belongs to the Society of the Antiquaries of Scotland. The first volume was lent many years ago, and was never returned.

Besides these MSS. there are a few others, which are mentioned by Mr. Dauney, pages 146, 147, of his Dissertation. One, dating about the beginning of the eighteenth century; and another, 1706, in the possession of David Laing, Esq.; a third, dated 1704, belonging to the Advocates' Library; and a fourth, 1715, the property of Mr. Waterston, stationer in Edinburgh. It is probable that several old music-books in tablature may still be hidden in the repositories of Scottish families of rank; and we would entreat the possessors of such books to rescue them from oblivion and destruction, by sending them to some public library for preservation. We are convinced, that many such books in tablature have been lost or destroyed within the last two centuries, through carelessness, and from ignorance of their value.

PRINTED COLLECTIONS OF ANCIENT AND MODERN SCOTTISH MELODIES.

OUR limited space prevents us from giving a complete list of these Collections. The reader will find their titles and dates given by Messrs. Laing and Sharpe in the Introduction to Messrs. Blackwood's edition of Johnson's Museum, Edinburgh, 1839. We shall confine our list to a few of the most important modern Collections, accompanied by such remarks as may seem appropriate.

JOHNSON'S MUSEUM.—This is the earliest very extensive modern Collection of Scottish Melodies and Songs. It was published at Edinburgh, 1787-1803, and consisted of six volumes 8vo, containing 600 melodies with songs adapted to them by various authors; and among these, Robert Burns, the most distinguished of all Scottish song-writers. A new edition of the work was published in 1839 by Messrs. Blackwood of Edinburgh, containing a Preface and Introduction by David Laing, Esq., and very valuable Notes and Illustrations by him and by C. K. Sharpe, Esq., in addition to the Notes, &c., written by the late Mr. William Stenhouse. The music and poetry were reprinted from the original plates engraved by Johnson. To each melody in Johnson's Museum, there was nothing added in harmony, except a figured-bass for the harpsichord. The harmony intended, was merely indicated in the usual vague and arbitrary manner, by the arithmetical numerals;* and there were no introductory or concluding symphonies added to the melodies. The kind liberality of the Messrs. Blackwood has enabled the Publishers of this work to avail themselves of those valuable Notes and Illustrations above referred to; and thus to render this new Collection much more interesting than it could otherwise have been.

NAPIER'S COLLECTION.—The next Collection of Scottish Melodies and Songs was that published by William Napier, in London, in two volumes, folio. The first volume, dedicated to the Duchess of Gordon, was published in 1790. It contained eighty-one airs with songs, and the airs were harmonized by four pro'essional musicians,

---

* See Graham's Essay on Musical Composition for remarks on the absurd imperfections of figured-basses. A. & C. Black, Edinburgh. 1838.

viz., Dr. S. Arnold, William Shield, both Englishmen; Thomas Carter, an Irishman; and F. H. Barthelemon, a Frenchman, and eminent violinist. The harmony consisted of a figured-bass for the harpsichord, with a violin accompaniment. There were no introductory or concluding symphonies. The second volume was published in 1792, dedicated to the Duchess of York, and contained 100 other Scottish melodies and songs; the whole of the airs harmonized by that great composer Joseph Haydn. In this, as in the first volume, there were no symphonies; and there was only a violin accompaniment printed along with the voice-part, and the harpsichord-part with its figured-bass.

URBANI'S (PIETRO) COLLECTION.—He was an Italian singer and music-teacher, settled for some years in Edinburgh. He died at Dublin in December 1816, aged 67. About the close of last century, he published " A Selection of Scots Songs, harmonized and improved, with simple and adapted graces," &c. The work extended finally to six folio volumes, and contained upwards of one hundred and fifty Scottish melodies, with their respective songs. The Melodies were harmonized by Urbani, with an accompaniment for the pianoforte; the harmony filled up in notes for the right hand; and the first four volumes have, besides, accompaniments for two violins and a viola, all printed in score, along with the voice-part. Each song has introductory and concluding symphonies. The sixth volume is dated 1804. The *second* volume was entered at Stationers' Hall in 1794; so that the *first* volume was probably published in 1792, or 1793, or even earlier. The want of the date of publication, in almost every musical work, is a very absurd omission, and often causes much difficulty and perplexity to the musical antiquary. Urbani's selection is remarkable in three respects; the novelty of the number and kind of instruments used in the accompaniments; the filling up of the pianoforte harmony; and the use, for the first time, of introductory and concluding symphonies to the melodies.

THOMSON'S (GEORGE) COLLECTION.—The Editor of this large and handsome work, in folio, was George Thomson, Esq., late of the Trustees' Office, Edinburgh—still living in a wonderfully vigorous old age. It appears that Mr. Thomson projected his work in 1792—that he began his correspondence with Robert Burns in September 1792, in order to obtain songs from that remarkable man; and that their correspondence ended in July 1796, the month and year in which Burns died. Mr. Thomson engaged Pleyel, Kozeluch, and Haydn, at different times, and latterly Beethoven, Hummel, and Weber, to harmonize the melodies, and to compose introductory and concluding symphonies for them. In Mr. Thomson's work, the right-hand part for the pianoforte was written by the composer, with the harmony filled up in notes, as it ought to be played. This was a great improvement upon the former very uncertain system of figured-basses; which were a kind of musical short-hand, fitted only for the use of the most skilful harmonists and practical musicians. Separate accompaniments, &c., for violin or flute and violoncello were added to Mr. Thomson's work. The Editor of the present Collection lately requested Mr. Thomson to furnish him with some information regarding the dates, &c., of the different volumes of his work. Mr. Thomson was so obliging as to write to him as follows:—

" 26th October 1847. All that I can undertake to do, or which appears to me necessary, is to show you the date of publication of each volume or half volume of my Scottish Airs and Songs, as entered at Stationers' Hall—for which see next page—making six volumes folio, for the voice and pianoforte, with separate symphonies and accompaniments for the violin or flute, and violoncello—each volume having an engraved frontispiece, besides smaller engraved embellishments; the symphonies and accompaniments composed by Pleyel, Kozeluch, Haydn, Beethoven, Hummel, and Weber;—the songs written chiefly, above 100 of them, by Burns, and the rest by Campbell, Sir Walter Scott, Professor Smyth, Joanna Baillie, &c.

" Note of the dates of publication of Mr. George Thomson's Scottish Airs and Songs, in six vols. folio:—

" Vol. 1.—The 1st Book or half vol. of Airs and Songs, 25 in number, entered at Stationers' Hall June 1793
                2d Book of do.; together, a vol., ...   August 1798.
" Vol. 2.—The 3d and 4th Books of 50 Airs and Songs,   .   .   .   July 1799.
" Vol. 3.—The 5th and 6th Books of 50 do., ...   July 1802.
" Vol. 4.—The 7th and 8th Books of 50 do., ...   June 1805.
" Vol. 5.—The 9th and 10th Books, 33 do., and 32 do.,   .   .   August 1818-1826.
" Vol. 6.—The 11th and 12th Books, of 50 do., ...   September 1841.
" I published also an edition of these Airs and Songs in six vols. royal 8vo, intended for persons who might wish for copies at a lower price than the folio." (1822.)

WHYTE'S (WILLIAM) COLLECTION.—Published by William Whyte of Edinburgh, in 1806, in two volumes, folio. The first volume, dedicated to Lady Charlotte Campbell, contained forty Scottish melodies, harmonized by Joseph Haydn for the pianoforte, violin, and violoncello, with introductory and concluding symphonies to the melodies. The second volume contained twenty-five melodies, also harmonized by Haydn.

SMITH'S (R. A.) COLLECTION.—This work, edited by Mr. R. A. Smith—who was for some years precentor of St. George's Church, Edinburgh—and by some other persons not named, consists of six vols. 8vo. The Advertisement to volume sixth is dated January 1824. It contains ancient and modern Scottish Airs and Songs. The accompaniment for the pianoforte is printed in notes as it is to be played. There are no introductory or concluding symphonies.

SCOTTISH SONGS

SCOTTISH SONGS.

THE FLOWERS OF THE FOREST.

OLD AIR.

ARRANGED BY G. F. GRAHAM.

ADAGIO.

I've heard them lilt - in' at the ewe milk - in', Lass - es a - lilt - in' be - fore dawn of day.

Now there's a moan - in' on il - ka green loan - in', The Flowers of the Fo - rest are a' wede a - way.

At bughts in the mornin', nae blithe lads are scornin',
Lasses are lanely, and dowie, and wae;
Nae daffin, nae gabbin, but sighin' and sabbin';
Ilk ane lifts her leglin, and hies her away.

At e'en in the gloamin', nae swankies are roamin'
'Bout stacks wi' the lasses at bogle to play;
But ilk maid sits drearie, lamentin' her dearie,
The Flowers of the Forest are a' wede away.

In har'st at the shearin', nae youths now are jeerin',
Bandsters are runkled, and lyart, or grey;
At fair or at preachin', nae wooin' nae fleechin',
The Flowers of the Forest are a' wede away.

Dool for the order sent our lads to the Border,
The English for ance by guile wan the day;
The Flowers of the Forest that fought aye the foremost,
The prime of our land lie cauld in the clay.

We'll hae nae mair liltin' at the ewe milkin',
Women and bairns are heartless and wae;
Sighin' and moanin' on ilka green loanin',
The Flowers of the Forest are a' wede away.

"THE FLOWERS OF THE FOREST." The earliest known copy of this fine melody is that, in tablature, in the Skene MS., preserved in the Library of the Faculty of Advocates, Edinburgh; and which appears to have been written in the earlier part of the seventeenth century. The copy above printed, (by permission,) is from the translation of the Skene MS. made for the late Mr. William Dauney, Advocate, by the Editor of this work, and which appeared in Mr. Dauney's Ancient Scottish Melodies. The old ballad, a lament for the disastrous field of Flodden, has been lost, with the exception of a line or two, incorporated in Miss Elliot's verses. Its place has been well supplied by the two lyrics which we give in this work, adapted to the ancient and the modern versions of the air. The earliest of these, that beginning "I've seen the smiling," (see pp. 4, 5,) was written by Miss Alison Rutherford, daughter of Robert Rutherford, Esq., of Fernylee, in Selkirkshire, who was afterwards married to Mr. Cockburn, son of the then Lord Justice-Clerk of Scotland. The second in point of time was that which we have given above. It was written by Miss Jane Elliot, sister of Sir Gilbert Elliot of Minto, and was published anonymously about 1755. "From its close and happy imitation of ancient manners, it was by many considered as a genuine production of some old but long-forgotten minstrel. It did not however escape the eagle eye of Burns. 'This fine ballad,' says he, 'is even a more palpable imitation than Hardiknute. The manners are indeed old, but the language is of yesterday. Its author must very soon be discovered.'"—*Reliques*. It was so; and to Mr. Ramsay of Ochtertyre, Sir Walter Scott, Bart., and the Rev. Dr. Somerville of Jedburgh, we are indebted for the discovery. See Blackwood's edition of Johnson's Musical Museum, in 1839, vol. i., Illustrations, p. 64 *et seq.*, and p. 122 *et seq.** Also Dauney's Ancient Scottish Melodies p. 152 of Dissertation, *et passim*.

* To save room, future reference to these "Illustrations" will be abbreviated thus :—"Museum Illustrations," adding the volume and page

THE FLOWERS OF THE FOREST.

MODERN AIR.

ARRANGED BY T. M. MUDIE.

$\textbf{C} = 76$

ADAGIO
MESTO.

I've seen the smi - ling of For - tune be - guil - ing, I've felt all its fa - vours, and found its de - cay: Sweet was its bless - ing, kind its ca - ress - ing, But now 'tis fled, 'tis fled far a - way; I've seen the fo - rest a -

dor - ned the fore - most, With flow - ers of the fair - est, most plea - sant and gay, Sae bon - ny was their bloom - ing, their scent the air per - fu - ming, But now they are wi - ther-ed and a' wede a - way.

I've seen the morning with gold the hills adorning,
And the dread tempest roaring before parting day;
I've seen Tweed's silver streams
Glitt'ring in the sunny beams,
Grow drumlie and dark as they roll'd on their way.
O fickle fortune! why this cruel sporting?
O why thus perplex us, poor sons of a day?
   Thy frowns cannot fear me,
   Thy smiles cannot cheer me,
For the Flowers of the Forest are withered away.

"THE FLOWERS OF THE FOREST." In our Note upon the old air, we have already mentioned Miss Rutherford, the authoress of these verses. She was born in 1710 or 1712; married Patrick Cockburn, Esq., of Ormiston, in 1731, and died at Edinburgh in 1794. Sir Walter Scott recounts the following anecdote of her :—"Mrs. Cockburn was a keen Whig. I remember having heard repeated a parody on Prince Charles's proclamation, in burlesque verse, to the tune of 'Clout the Caldron.' In the midst of the siege or blockade of the Castle of Edinburgh, the carriage in which Mrs. Cockburn was returning from a visit to Ravelstone was stopped by the Highland guard at the West Port ; and as she had a copy of the parody about her person, she was not a little alarmed at the consequences; especially as the officer talked of searching the carriage for letters and correspondence with the Whigs in the city. Fortunately the arms on the coach were recognised as belonging to a gentleman favourable to the cause of the Adventurer, so that Mrs. Cockburn escaped, with the caution not to carry political squibs about her person in future. In the 3d and 15th bars a simpler form of the melody is offered as worthy of consideration.

WILL YE GO TO THE EWE-BUGHTS, MARION?

ARRANGED BY G. F. GRAHAM.

go   to   the   ewe - bughts,   Ma - rion,   And   wear· in   the   sheep   wi'   me ?   The

sun   shines   sweet,   my   Ma - rion,   But   nae   half   sae   sweet   as

thee!   The   sun   shines   sweet,   my   Ma - rion,   But

† To gnaiuer in with caution.

nae   half   sae   sweet   as   thee !

O Marion's a bonnie lass,
    And the blythe blink's in her e'e ;
And fain wad I marry Marion,
    Gin Marion wad marry me.

There's gowd in your garters,[2] Marion,
    And silk on your white hause-bane ;
Fu' fain wad I kiss my Marion,
    At e'en, when I come hame.

There's braw lads in Earnslaw, Marion,
    Wha gape, and glow'r[3] wi' their e'e,
At kirk, when they see my Marion ;
    But nane o' them lo'es like me.

I've nine milk-ewes, my Marion,
    A cow, and a brawny quey ;[4]
I'll gi'e them a' to my Marion
    Just on her bridal-day.

And ye'se get a green sey[5] apron,
    And waistcoat o' the London brown ;
And wow but ye will be vap'rin'
    Whene'er ye gang to the town

I'm young and stout, my Marion ;
    Nane dances like me on the green :
And gin ye forsake me, Marion,
    I'll e'en gae draw up wi' Jean.

Sae put on your pearlins,[6] Marion,
    And kyrtle o' the cramasie ;[7]
And soon as the sun's down, my Marion,
    I shall come west, and see ye

2 " At the time when the ladies wore hoops, they also wore finely embroidered garters for exhibition ; because, especially in dancing, the hoop often shelved aside, and exposed the leg to that height."—R. CHAMBERS.   (See Traditions of Edinburgh, vol. ii. p. 57.)
3 Stare.   4 Heifer.   5 A home-made woollen stuff.   6 Ornaments of lace, (fil perlé, hard twisted thread.)   7 Crimson.

" WILL YE GO TO THE EWE-BUGHTS, MARION ?"   The song and the air appear to be both old.   The song is marked in Ramsay's Tea-Table Miscellany (1724) as an old song with additions.   It cannot now be ascertained who wrote the song, or who composed the air ; but it seems very evident that the air has been hitherto wrongly given in its notation in all printed copies ; and there is no existing ancient MS. containing the air to which we can refer.   The printed copies of the air give an unrhythmical melody, not suitable to the beseeching expression of the song.   The prominent word and name "Marion," (pronounced as two syllables, "Maron,") is associated with short and jerking notes, which, besides being ill suited to the words, throw the melody into an irregular rhythm.   In the present edition, the air is reduced to regular rhythm, without changing one of the sounds of the received melody ; while it is believed that the original melody is thus restored in its true supplicatory accentuation and emphasis on the word " Marion."   Any good singer who tries the present set, will at once perceive the improvement in point of expression and of rhythmical construction.   As to this point, we are willing to abide by the opinion of all the best-educated musicians of Europe.   That there was extreme carelessness and ignorance on the part of the persons who noted down our old Scottish melodies in MS. books, we are prepared to prove from the oldest MSS. of our airs existing.   In many cases appears barring at random, without the slightest regard to the true rhythm and melodic structure of the airs ; and with no indication whatever of the relative duration of the sounds indicated by the letters of the old tablature.   In cases of this kind, rational interpretation must be used.   It does not follow, that because an air is wrongly noted, or tablatured, by ignorant writers, the air is wrong in its true and original form.   In Thomson's Orpheus Caledonius (1733), we find an air under the title of " Will ye go to the ewe-buchts," bearing a remote resemblance to the generally received air, and which affords a proof of the strange transforma-tions that old Scottish melodies have undergone in passing through the hands of different editors.   It is in a pseudo-major key, while all the other old sets we have seen are minor, and is by no means so vocal or melodious as our version, but agrees with it in rhythm.

    Dean Christie, in his beautiful volume of Traditional Ballad Airs and Ballads (1876), gives both a major and a minor version of the melody as sung in the north to the " Lord of Gordon's three daughters," a ballad believed to relate to the times of Mary of Scotland.

O WALY, WALY.

ARRANGED BY T. M. MUDIE.

$\mathbf{p} = 63$

ANDANTE
MESTO.

wa - ly,[1] wa - ly   up the bank, And   wa - ly,   wa - ly   down the   brae, And

wa - ly,   wa - ly   yon burnside,   Where   I   and   my   love   wont to   gael

I   lean'd my   back   un - to   an   aik,   I   thought   it   was   a trus - ty tree; But first it bow'd, an' syne it brak: And sae did my true

love to me.

O waly, waly, but love be bonnie
A little time while it is new;
But when it's auld it waxes cauld,
An' fades away like the mornin' dew.
O wherefore should I busk[2] my heid,
Or wherefore should I kame my hair?
For my true love has me forsook,
An' says he'll never love me mair.

Now Arthur's Seat shall be my bed,
The sheets shall ne'er be press'd by me,
St. Anton's Well shall be my drink,
Since my true love has forsaken me.
Martinmas wind, when wilt thou blaw,
An' shake the green leaves aff the tree?
O, gentle death, when wilt thou come?
For o' my life I am wearie.

'Tis not the frost that freezes fell,
Nor blawin' snaw's inclemencie;
'Tis not sic cauld that makes me cry:
But my love's heart 's grown cauld to me
When we cam' in by Glasgow toun,
We were a comely sicht to see;
My love was clad in the black velvet,
An' I mysel' in cramasie.[3]

But had I wist, before I kiss'd,
That love had been sae ill to win,
I'd lock'd my heart in a case o' gold,
An' pinn'd it wi' a siller pin.
Oh, oh! if my young babe were born,
An' set upon the nurse's knee,
An' I mysel' were dead an' gane,
An' the green grass growin' over me!

1 An exclamation of distress—Alas.   2 Dress, arrange, adorn.   3 Crimson.

"O WALY, WALY." In Mr. Robert Chambers' Scottish Songs, there is a Note upon "Waly, waly," from which we give the following passage:—"This beautiful old song has hitherto been supposed to refer to some circumstance in the life of Queen Mary, or at least to some unfortunate love affair which happened at her Court. It is now discovered, from a copy which has been found as forming part of a ballad in the Pepysian Library at Cambridge, (published in Motherwell's Minstrelsy, 1827, under the title of "Lord Jamie Douglas,") to have been occasioned by the affecting tale of Lady Barbara Erskine, daughter of John ninth Earl of Mar, and wife of James second Marquis of Douglas. This lady, who was married in 1670, was divorced, or at least expelled from the society of her husband, in consequence of some malignant scandals which a former and disappointed lover, Lowrie of Blackwood, was so base as to insinuate into the ear of the Marquis." Her father took her home, and she never again saw her husband. Her only son died, Earl of Angus, at the battle of Steinkirk.

The air is beautiful and pathetic. It is undoubtedly ancient, and though its date cannot be ascertained, must be considerably older than the ballad mentioned above. The simplicity of the original has been spoiled by several flourishes introduced into it by tasteless and ignorant collectors. M'Gibbon, Oswald, and others, have much to answer for in the matter of pseudo-embellishment of our finest old airs. We have removed from "Waly, waly," the absurd trappings hung about its neck by these men.

TAK YOUR AULD CLOAK ABOUT YE.

ARRANGED BY T. M. MUDIE.

♩ = 63

ANDANTE
PARLANTE.

mf

In win - ter, when the rain rain'd cauld, An' frost and snaw on ilk - a hill, An'

mf   *f*

Boreas, wi' his blasts sae hauld, Was threat'ning a' our kye to kill, Then Bell, my wife, wha

f

lo'es nae strife, She said to me, right has - ti - ly, Get up, gudeman, save

f

Crummie's life,   An'   tak your auld cloak a - bout   ye.

8vi

My Crummie is a usefu' cow,
  An' she is come o' a gude kin' :
Aft has she wet the bairns's mou',
  An' I am laith that she should tyne;
Get up, gudeman, it is fu' time,
  The sun shines in the lift sae hie;
Sloth never made a gracious end,
  Gae, tak your auld cloak about ye.

My cloak was ance a gude grey cloak,
  When it was fitting for my wear ;
But now it's scantly worth a groat,
  For I hae worn't this thretty year.
Let's spend the gear that we hae won,
  We little ken the day we'll die;
Then I'll be proud, sin' I hae sworn
  To hae a new cloak about me.

In days when gude king Robert rang,
  His trews they cost but half-a-croun ;
He said they were a groat o'er dear,
  An' ca'd the tailor thief and loon :
He was the king that wore the croun,
  An' thou'rt a man of laigh degree;
It's pride puts a' the country doun ;
  Sae tak your auld cloak about ye.

Ilka land has its ain lauch,[1]
  Ilk kind o' corn has its ain hool :
I think the warld is a' gane wrang,
  When ilka wife her man wad rule:
Do ye no see Rob, Jock, and Hab,
  How they are girded gallantlie,
While I sit hurklin i' the asse ?[2]
  I'll hae a new cloak about me !

Gudeman, I wat its thretty year
  Sin' we did ane anither ken;
An' we hae had atween us twa
  Of lads an' bonnie lasses ten :
Now they are women grown an' men,
  I wish an' pray weel may they be;
An' if you'd prove a gude husband,
  E'en tak your auld cloak about ye.

Bell, my wife, she lo'es nae strife,
  But she would gnide me, if she can ;
Au' to maintain an easy life,
  I aft maun yield, though I'm gudeman :
Nocht's to be won at woman's han',
  Unless ye gi'e her a' the plea ;
Then I'll leave aff where I began,
  An' tak my auld cloak about me.

[1] Law, custom, privilege.—*Jamieson.*   [2] Ashes—by the fire.

"TAK YOUR AULD CLOAK ABOUT YE." England and Scotland have each a version of this ballad, but there is this great distinction between them, that while the latter has been sung time out of mind, the former has long ceased to be a living thing. Indeed it may be doubted whether it ever was generally known. Surely if once spread among the people, so excellent a song would have been heard of in some way. Yet we do not find a line of it, nor an allusion to it in the large collections of black-letter broadsides—the Roxburgh, Bagford, and others—nor yet in the Drolleries of the Restoration ; not even in D'Urfey's Pills and the numerous "Merry Musicians" and other song-books of Queen Anne and the early Georges. With the exception of one stanza embalmed in Othello, all knowledge of the ballad in England had entirely disappeared ; and but for the accidental preservation of Bishop Percy's folio MS., an English version of it could not have been even surmised. That it was not printed in Scotland before 1728 is quite true, but as it was not known in England either then or for a century before, it must have been floating about in Scotland probably from the times of James VI., handed down by tradition, and of course modernized in the process. Late as is the date of Allan Ramsay's version, it is nearly forty years earlier than that which Bishop Percy printed in the *Reliques.* He there points out that the folio MS. copy is not without corruptions, but that these had been removed by the aid of the Scottish edition. These corruptions chiefly allude to going to court ; they spoil the story, and their faulty rhymes show they are mere interpolations. As a comparison of the two versions would require more space than we have here at command, we close with a quotation from Mr. Ebsworth, the highest authority upon such subjects :—"Tak thy auld cloak about thee, claimed as being Scottish, scarcely possesses external evidence to warrant the assertion. That it was originally a northern song, *i.e.* one that was sung and popular in the northern counties of England and the southern counties of Scotland there need be no question. In literature and folklore, in ballad legends and romances, the whole of the ancient Northumbria held common property."

THE SOUTERS O' SELKIRK.

ABRANGED BY FINLAY DUN.

$\wp \cdot = 66$

ALLEGRO
MARCATO.

It's up wi' the

Souters o' Sel-kirk, And down wi' the Earl o' Hume; And here is to

a' the braw lad-dies, That wear the sin-gle sol'd shoon.

It's up wi' the Sou-ters o' Sel-kirk, For they are baith trus-ty and

THE SOUTERS O' SELKIRK.

leal ;   And   up   wi'   the   lads   o'   the   For - est,[1]   And   down   wi' the

Merse[2]   to   the   deil.

f

It's fye upon yellow and yellow,
And fye upon yellow and green ;
But up wi' the true blue and scarlet,
And up wi' the single sol'd shoon.
It's up wi' the Souters o' Selkirk,
For they are laith trusty and leal ;
And up wi' the men o' the Forest,
And down wi' the Merse to the deil.

[1] Selkirkshire, otherwise called Ettrick Forest.

O! mitres are made for noddles,
But feet they are made for shoon,
And fame is as sib to Selkirk,
As licht is true to the moon.
There sits a souter in Selkirk,
Wha sings as he draws his thread,
There's gallant souters in Selkirk,
As lang's there's water in Tweed.

[2] Berwickshire, otherwise called the Merse.

"THE SOUTERS O' SELKIRK." Mr. Stenhouse quotes as follows from Sir Walter Scott :—"The song relates to the fatal battle of Flodden, in which the flower of the Scottish nobility fell around their sovereign, James IV. The ancient and received tradition of the burgh of Selkirk affirms, that the citizens of that town distinguished themselves by their gallantry on that disastrous occasion. Eighty in number, and headed by their town-clerk, they joined their monarch on his entrance into England. James, pleased with the appearance of this gallant troop, knighted the leader, William Brydone, upon the field of battle, from which few of the men of Selkirk were destined to return. They distinguished themselves in the conflict, and were almost all slain. The few survivors, on their return home, found, by the side of Lady-Wood Edge, the corpse of a female, wife to one of their fallen comrades, with a child sucking at her breast. In memory of this latter event, continues the tradition, the present arms of the burgh bear, a female, holding a child in her arms, and seated on a sarcophagus, decorated with the Scottish Lion ; in the back-ground a wood." See Border Minstrelsy. Sir Walter Scott and Mr. Stenhouse, by documentary evidence, refute Ritson's assertion that the Souters of Selkirk could not, in 1513, amount to eighty fighting men ; and also Dr. Johnson's Aberdeen story, that the people learned the art of making shoes from Cromwell's soldiers. Scottish Acts of Parliament are quoted relative to "Sowters" and "cordoners," *i.e.*, shoemakers, and the manufacture and exportation of boots and shoes, long before Cromwell was born. Also, it is shown that the appellation of "Souters" is given to the burgesses of Selkirk, whether shoemakers or not, "and appears to have originated from the singular custom observed at the admission of a new member, a ceremony which is on no account dispensed with. Some hog-bristles are attached to the seal of his burgess ticket ; these he must dip in wine, and pass between his lips, as a tribute of his respect to this ancient and useful fraternity."—Stenhouse. Mr. Maidment, in an exhaustive review of the whole of the evidence (Scottish Ballads, 1868, i. 117), agrees with Sir Walter Scott that the "Souters" were present at Flodden, and that the song relates to that rather than to any football match, "for which neither place nor period can be assigned."

The air has all the rough energy of the Border. It is not found in any Scottish collection earlier than that of Adam Craig, 1730 ; Playford, however, gives it as a "Scotch Hornpipe" in Apollo's Banquet, 1690.

O THOU BROOM! THOU BONNIE BUSH O' BROOM!

AIR, "THE BROOM O' THE COWDENKNOWES."   ARRANGED BY J. T. SURENNE.

O thou broom, thou bon - nie bush o' broom! I leave my land and thee, Where

thou and free - dom flourish'd ay, Where Sco - tia's sons are free! The

In - dian vales are rich and fair, And bright is their flow' - ry bloom; But sad their flowers, and myr - tle bow - ers, With - out my na - tive broom!

O thou broom, thou bon - nie, bon - nie broom!

When wilt thou, thou bonnie bush o' broom,
Grow on a foreign strand?
That I may think, when I look on thee,
I'm still in loved Scotland!

But ah! that thought can never more be mine
Though thou beside me sprang,
Nor though the lintie, Scotia's bird,
Should follow wi' its sang

Thy branches green might wave at e'en,
At morn thy flowers might blaw;
But no to me, on the Cowdenknowes,
Nor yet by Ettrick-shaw.

O thou broom, thou bonnie bush o' broom!
Sae sweet to memory;
I maist could weep for days gane by
When I think on days to be.

"THE BROOM O' THE COWDENKNOWES." This is a very ancient and beautiful air of one strain. The song, to which the tune was originally united is, with the exception of the chorus, supposed to be lost. With regard to the melody given in this work, it is necessary to remark that in the Orpheus Caledonius (1725) and the older Scottish collections the air begins on the second note of the scale, while in Playford's Dancing Master (1651) it begins on the fifth, and in Watt's Musical Miscellany and some other works, on the keynote itself. There is no doubt that the commencement on the second of the scale brings out a more pathetic expression, and a passage more characteristic of some peculiarities of Scottish national melody. That commencement has therefore been adopted in this work, while the more usual commencement has not been rejected, but is given at the ninth measure, where a second, and, in our opinion, more modern version of the air begins. The last two measures are an addition sometimes introduced to make the air end on the tonic or keynote. The beautiful verses here given to the air are by Robert Gilfillan—(1849).

Mr. Chappell (Pop. Music of the Olden Time) suggests that the air is probably the same as "Brume on hill," which Laneham, in his letter written on Queen Elizabeth's visit to Kenilworth, 1575, mentions as one of Captain Cox's "Bunch of ballads." But as there is no extant copy of "Brume on hill," evidence of identity is meanwhile wanting. The same name is given in The Complaynt of Scotland (1549) to one of the songs sung *in ports* by the shepherds and their wives; from which we think it may be inferred that "Brume on hill" was a setting of the words in the scholastic style of the time, rather than a melody. Among other proofs that the air is English, Mr. Chappell points out that the oldest song to|it is a black-letter broadside (Roxburgh Ballads, i. 190), called "The Lovely Northern Lass," but the title adds, "To a pleasant Scotch tune called The broom of Cowdenknows;" and the burden or refrain is—
"With oh! the broom, the bonny bonny broom, The broom of the Cowdenknowes,"
which clearly shows that though the English ballad is really the earliest song extant to the air, yet there was a still earlier Scottish song which supplied the refrain; for we cannot suppose an English ballad-writer to have known anything of the Cowdenknowes. The air as given by Playford, 1651, is so tame, so common-place, that it seems impossible to believe that version could ever have enjoyed any popularity with ballad-singers. Its sole redeeming bit of character is that it closes on the second of the key, "*like a Scotch tune that never comes to any reasonable ending*," to quote an opinion of that notable housewife, Mrs. Poyser.

I'LL NEVER LEAVE THEE.

ARRANGED BY T. M. MUDIE.

Why should thy cheek be pale,

Shad - ed with sor - row's veil? Why should'st thou grieve me?

I will nev-er, nev-er leave thee. 'Mid my deep-est sad - ness, 'Mid my gay-est glad - ness, I am thine, be - lieve me; I will nev - er, nev - er

leave thee.

Life's storms may rudely blow,   Ne'er till my cheek grow pale,
Laying hope and pleasure low;   And my heart-pulses fail,
I'd ne'er deceive thee;   And my last breath grieve thee;
I could never, never leave thee!   Can I ever, ever leave thee!

"I'LL NEVER LEAVE THEE." This beautiful air is unquestionably very old. Sibbald (Chronicle of Scottish Poetry, vol. iii. p. 275) is of opinion that the modern version of it is a little corrupted, and that the original air was intended to be sung to one of Wedderburne's Spiritual Ballads, (before 1549,) beginning.—

"Ah! my love! leif me not!
Leif me not! leif me not!
Ah! my love, leif me not,
Thus mine alone!'"

Although Mr. Stenhouse agrees in this opinion, we doubt whether its truth can be established by any existing evidence. (See "Low doun in the broom.") Mr. Stenhouse's words are:—"This (Sibbald's) opinion appears to be correct, for this identical tune is mentioned in Geddes' 'Saint's Recreation,' written in 1673, as appears from the approbations of the Rev. William Raitt, and the Rev. William Colvill, Primar of the College of Edinburgh, both of which are dated in August 1673. This work was afterwards printed in 1683. Several of Geddes' pious songs are directed to be sung to popular tunes, and he vindicates the practice in the following words:—'I have the precedent of some of the most pious, grave, and zealous divines in the kingdom, who, to very good purpose, have composed godly songs to the tunes of such old songs as these, The bonnie broom, I'll never leave thee, We'll all go pull the hadder, and such like, without any challenge or disparagement.' See Museum Illustrations, vol. i. pp. 93, 94. In Mr. William Dauney's Dissertation, p. 88, there is a longer quotation from Geddes. The following passage of that quotation is too curious to be omitted:—"It is alleged by some, and that not without some colour of reason, that many of our ayres or tunes are made by good angels, but the letters or lines of our songs by devils. We choose the part angelical, and leave the diabolical." The set of the air which we publish is chiefly taken from that given by Francis Peacock, No. 15 of his "Fifty favourite Scotch Airs," dedicated to the Earl of Errol, and printed in London about 1776. It is, in our opinion, much superior to the ordinary versions, which have been corrupted by the insertion of embellishments altogether destructive of the beauty and simplicity of the ancient melody. Peacock was a dancing-master in Aberdeen, and a good player on the violin and violoncello. As the words usually sung to the air do not conform to it in their accentuation, and require besides an addition to the second strain, at variance with the rhythm, we have substituted other words written for this work by a friend of the publishers.

B

BONNIE WEE THING.

ARRANGED BY J. T. SUREENE.

$\text{e} = 108$

ANDANTE
AFFETTUOSO.

Bon - nie wee thing, can - nie wee thing, Love - ly wee thing, wert thou mine;

Fine.

I would wear thee in my bo - som, Lest my jew - el I should tine.

Wish - ful - ly I look and lan - guish, In that bon - nie

face of thine; And my heart it stounds with an - guish,

:S: Finish with the first strain.

Lest my wee thing be na mine. *Ritornel.*

p

In the following stanza the first four lines are sung to the second part of the air. and the burden or chorus to the first part.

Wit and grace, and love and beauty,
In ae constellation shine !
To adore thee is my duty,
Goddess of this soul o' mine.
Bonnie wee thing, caunie wee thing,
Lovely wee thing, wert thou mine ;
I wad wear thee in my bosom,
Lest my jewel I should tine.

"BONNIE WEE THING." Mr. Stenhouse informs us that " These verses, beginning ' Bonnie wee thing, cannie wee thing,' were composed by Burns, as he informs us, *on his little idol, the charming lovely Davies.—Reliques.* The words are adapted to the tune of ' The bonnie wee thing,' in Oswald's Caledonian Pocket Companion, book viii." See Museum Illustrations, vol. iv., p. 320. In the MS. Lute-book of Sir Robert Gordon of Straloch, dated 1627-9, there is a tune called " Wo betyd thy wearie bodie," which contains the rudiments of the air, " Bonnie wee thing." That lute-book was sent to the Editor in January 1839, in order that he might translate and transcribe from it what he pleased. The original has disappeared since the sale of the library of the late Mr. Chalmers of London, to whom it belonged. What the Editor transcribed from it he has sent to the Library of the Faculty of Advocates, Edinburgh, for preservation.

We subjoin a translation of the air " Wo betyd thy wearie bodie," above alluded to :—

AN THOU WERE MY AIN THING.

ARRANGED BY A. C. MACKENZIE.

1. An thou were my ain thing, O I would love thee, I would love thee; An thou were my ain thing, How dear-ly would I love thee. 1. Then love thee.

First time only.

Close of every stanza.

Symphony after each stanza.

1st, 2d, 3d, and 4th times.

Last time.

2. Of
3. To

1 Continue from the top of next page, where all the other stanzas begin.

f appassionata. *mf* *p*

1. I would clasp thee in my arms, Then I'd secure thee from all harms, For a -
2. race divine thou needs must be, Since no - thing earth - ly e - quals thee ; ' With

ritard. *a tempo.* *f* Finish with the refrain.

bove [all] mor - tals thou hast charms, How dear - ly do I love thee.
an - gel pi - ty look on me,' Who on - ly lives to love thee.

ritard. *a tempo.*

To merit I no claim can make,
But that I love, and for thy sake
What man can do I 'll undertake,
So dearly do I love thee.
An thou were, etc.

The gods one thing peculiar have,
To ruin none whom they can save,
Oh ! for their sake support a slave,
Who ever on shall love thee.
An thou were, etc.

My passion, constant as the sun,
Flames stronger still, will ne'er have done,
Till fate my thread of life have spun,
Which breathing out I 'll love thee.
An thou were, etc.

"AN THOU WERE MY AIN THING." The earliest known version of the air has been found in the Straloch MS., written by Robert Gordon in 1627. It consists of a single strain of eight bars, and has two florid variations. Like many of the airs given in these old lute-books, it is stiff and unvocal ; this may be partly attributed to its having been written for an instrument where harmony is a feature quite as much as melody, and partly to the taste, or want of taste, of the writer. A century later (1725) we find a better version in the Orpheus Caledonius. So old did Thomson, the editor of that work, believe the air to be, that he ascribes its composition, as well as that of six other tunes, to David Rizzio. He withdrew this statement in his second edition ; but such is the vitality of the absurd fiction, that we occasionally find it gravely quoted even in our own times. There is not a shadow of proof that Rizzio either did or could compose anything. If he did, it would be in the style of France or Italy, and it may be doubted whether Queen Mary herself would have appreciated any other music. We must not forget that she quitted Scotland when little more than five years of age, and returned Queen-Dowager of France, a widow of nineteen, with all her tastes formed, and every association and recollection connected with a more civilized country than her own.
The words appeared in Ramsay's Tea-Table Miscellany in 1724. The letter X is affixed to them, but the author remains unknown. Ramsay added several stanzas, but they are never sung.

JOHN ANDERSON, MY JO.

ARRANGED BY T. M. MUDIE.

= 96

ANDANTE
A PIACERE.

John An - der - son, my jo, John, When we were first ac -

quent, Your locks were like the ra - ven, Your bon - nie brow was

brent ;[1] * But now your brow is bald,[2] John, Your locks are like the

f

* Sometimes sung, " But now you 're turning auld, John."

snaw, But bless - ings on your fros - ty pow, John An - der - son, my

jo.

John Anderson, my jo, John,
We clamb the hill thegither,
And mony a canty² day, John,
We've had wi' ane anither ;

¹ High, straight, smooth.   ² Bald.   ³ Cheerful, happy.

Now we maun totter down, John,
But hand in hand we'll go,
And we'll sleep thegither at the foot,
John Anderson, my jo.

"JOHN ANDERSON, MY JO." This air must be very old. It occurs under the same name in the Skene MS. ; but the set there given (see No. 7 of Mr. Dauney's edition of that MS.) differs considerably from the modern sets. In the latter, the first two bars throw the air at once into a minor key, and the next two bars pass to the subtonic of that key ; while the former has a remarkable vagueness of key in the first two bars of the melody. This vagueness of modulation in the set given in the Skene MS. savours of some old Romish Church chant, and seems to attest the greater antiquity of that set. The air is thus shown to have been known and popular in Scotland under its present name for two centuries and a half, yet there seems to be a doubt whether it did not come to us from the South, and originally as a quick tune. If so, it has suffered no damage in the transplanting. In the first edition of Playford's Dancing Master (1651), it appears as Paul's Steeple, a name which Mr. Chappell connects with the destruction by lightning of that tallest of spires in 1561, and also with a ballad written on the occasion, which, he says, "seems intended for the tune." The words of this ballad can no doubt be sung to the air, but it requires a good deal of the ballad-singer's coaxing to do so. The tune was also, and perhaps more generally, known in England under the name of "The Duke of Norfolk," from a song frequently sung at harvest-homes, and which is shown to have existed at least as early as 1620. The version given by Mr. Chappell (Popular Music of the olden time, 120), though far from being identical with that of the Skene MS., yet bears so great a resemblance to it, that no musician would deny they had sprung from the same source.² As to the assertions that the words of John Anderson are to be found in Bishop Percy's ancient MS., and that the tune is in Queen Elizabeth's Virginal Book, they are equally unfounded. Mr. Stenhouse first made these statements, and his copyists have repeated them without examination.

The stanzas written by Burns for Johnson's Museum in 1789, are those which we give to the air. Other additional stanzas have been published ; upon which Dr. Currie makes the following just observation :— "Every reader will observe that they are by an inferior hand, and the real author of them ought neither to have given them, nor suffered them to be given to the world, as the production of Burns." It is certainly far short of literary honour and honesty in any man to attempt to pass off, upon public credulity, his own spurious verses as the produce of a great poet. Burns has suffered much injustice of this kind.

AY WAKIN', O!

ARRANGED BY T. M. MUDIE.

Ay wa - kin', O! Wa - kin' ay, an' eer - ie; Sleep I can - na get For

think - in' on my dear - ie. Ay wa - kin', O! Lane - ly night comes on,

A' the lave[1] are sleep - in', I think on my bon - nie lad, An' bleer[2] my een wi' greet - in'.[3]

Ay wa - kin' O! Wa - kin' ay, an' eer - ie ; Sleep I can - na get l'or

think - in' on my dear - ie. Ay wa - kin', O !

Ay wakin', O ! &c.
When I sleep I dream,
When I wake I'm eerie;
Rest I canna get
For thinkin' o' my dearie.
Ay wakin', O !

Ay wakin', O ! &c.
Simmer 's a pleasant time,
Flowers of every colour ;
The water runs o'er the heugh,
And I long for my true lover.
Ay wakin', O !

¹ The remainder.   ² Inflame.   ³ Crying.

"AY WAKIN', O!" Allan Cunningham, in his Songs of Scotland, vol. ii. p. 231, says of "Ay wakin', O!"—
"This song is the work of several hands, and though some of it is very ancient, it has been so often touched and
retouched, that it is not easy to show where the old ends or the new commences. Most of the chorus is certainly
old, and part of the second verse." The words we have adopted are part of those given by Mr. Stenhouse, in vol.
iii. pp. 206, 207 of the Museum, as "all that is known to exist of the original verses." We give also the four lines
added by Burns to the old words. They offer some variety to the singer, who must, however, repeat, before
and after them, the four lines, "Ay wakin', O!" &c., in order to suit the music. Mr. Stenhouse gives also a
version of what he calls "the ancient air," though he does not tell us where he found it, and, consequently, offers
no proof of his assertion. He says: "In Mr. George Thomson's Collection of Scottish Songs, the air of 'Ay
wakin', O!' is enlarged so as to finish on the key note, and the time changed from triple to common. The time,
however, is far better in its native wildness and simplicity : both Tytler and Ritson were of opinion that this air,
from its intrinsic evidence, was one of our oldest melodies, and I see no reason to differ from them." The form
which the air has assumed within the last thirty years has now taken possession of the popular ear, and we shall
not try to displace it. The latter part of the air must remind the reader of the conclusion of "Gala Water,"
which will be found in a future page. In May 1795, Burns wrote for Mr. George Thomson a song "On Chloris
being ill," to the tune "Ay wakin', O," beginning—"Long, long the night," and which appears in an altered
form in Mr. G. Thomson's Collection.—The following is what Mr. Stenhouse gives as "the ancient air:"—

ALAS! THAT I CAM' O'ER THE MUIR.

ARRANGED BY T. M. MUDIE.

A - las! that I cam' o'er the muir, An' left my love be -

hind me! My hon - nie love, ay true to me, But true love could - na

bind me! I left my love, an' far a - wa' I

Oh warldly gear![2] how mony vows,
How mony hearts ye've broken!
The want o' you, the wish to hae,
Leave room for nae love-token!

Yon blythesome lark that 'boon[3] his nest
His hymn o' love is singin',
Nae warldly thocht has he; the lift[4]
Is but wi' true love ringin'.

O had I but my true love taen,
My bonnie love, tho' puir;
This day I wadna sae lament
That I cam' o'er the muir!

I now maun dree[5] the fate o' them
Wha'd sell their love for gain;
Maun tine[6] true love for dreams o' gowd,
An' live an' dee alane!

---

[1] Timorous, affrighted.   [2] Wealth.   [3] Above.   [4] Atmosphere, firmament.   [5] Suffer, endure.   [6] Lose.

"ALAS! THAT I CAM' O'ER THE MUIR." "This air is of undoubted antiquity. Burns says, 'Ramsay found the first line of this song, which had been preserved as the title of the charming air, and then composed the rest of the verses to suit that line. This has always a finer effect than composing English words, or words with an idea foreign to the spirit of the old title. When old titles convey any idea at all, they will generally be found to be quite in the spirit of the air.'—*Burns' Reliques*. This conjecture of Burns turns out to be amazingly correct." See Museum Illustrations, vol. i. pp. 18, 19. "It appears, however, that Ramsay was scarcely so fortunate [as to recover the first line of the old song.] What he found was something much less poetical—'The last time I came o'er the muir'—but a poor substitute for the impassioned ejaculation, 'Alas! that I cam' o'er the muir;' and therefore not very inspiring to the genius of the poet, who has certainly not educed from it any thing more than a very namby-pamby sort of ditty."—Dauney's "Ancient Scottish Melodies," p. 253. Referring to the Skene MSS., Mr. Stenhouse says, "In these collections, the identical tune of 'The last time I cam' o'er the muir,' occurs no less than twice, and one of the sets commences with the two first lines of the old song,

' Alace! that I came o'er the moor,
And left my love behind me.' "—*ibid*. pp. 18, 19.

Here there are two mistakes. We have found the air in this MS. only *once*, and very far from being "identical" with the tune in Johnson's Museum, upon which Mr. Stenhouse's Note was written. This, with several other references which Mr. Stenhouse makes to tunes in the Skene MS., proves that he could not translate any of these tunes in Tablature, although he writes as if he had read and understood them.

Mr. Dauney's judicious remark on Allan Ramsay's song has induced the Publishers to give to the air new verses, which have been written for this work by a friend.

WAE'S ME FOR PRINCE CHARLIE.

AIR, "THE GYPSIE LADDIE."

ARRANGED BY T. M. MUDIE.

= 60

ANDANTE.

p

rall.

A wee bird cam' to our ba' door, He warbled sweet an' clear - ly, An'

aye the o'er - come o' his sang Was "Wae's me for Prince Char - lie!" Oh!

when I heard the bon - nie, bon - nie bird, The tears cam' drap - pin' rare - ly, I took my ban-net aff my head, For weel I lo'ed Prince Char-lie.

Quoth I, "My bird, my bonnie, bonnie bird,
Is that a sang ye borrow,
Are these some words ye've learnt by heart,
Or a lilt[1] o' dool an' sorrow?"
Oh! no, no, no," the wee bird sang,
"I've flown sin' mornin' early,
But sic a day o' wind an' rain—
Oh! wae's me for Prince Charlie!

"On hills that are, by right, his ain,
He roves a lonely stranger,
On every side he's press'd by want,
On every side is danger;
Yestreen I met him in a glen,
My heart maist burstit fairly,
For sadly changed indeed was he—
Oh! wae's me for Prince Charlie!

"Dark night cam' on, the tempest roar'd
Loud o'er the hills an' valleys,
An' where was't that your Prince lay down,
Wha's hame should been a palace
He row'd him in a Highland plaid,
Which cover'd him but sparely,
An' slept beneath a bush o' broom—
Oh! wae's me for Prince Charlie!"

But now the bird saw some red coats,
An' he shook his wings wi' anger,
"Oh! this is no a land for me;
I'll tarry here nae langer!"
He hover'd on the wing a while
Ere he departed fairly,
But weel I mind the fareweel strain
Was, "Wae's me for Prince Charlie!"

[1] *Lilt*—tune.

"WAE'S ME FOR PRINCE CHARLIE." James Hogg, the Ettrick Shepherd, in his Second Series of Jacobite Relics, pp. 192, 193, gives this song, and the air, "The Gypsie Laddie." He ascribes the words to "a Mr. William Glen, about Glasgow." It appears that this William Glen was a native of Glasgow, and for some time a manufacturer there, and that he died about 1824, in a state of poverty. He was the author of several other songs and poems. The air is given in Johnson's Museum, No. 181, under the title of "Johnny Faa, or the Gypsie Laddie," to the words of an old ballad beginning, "The gypsies cam' to our Lord's yett." On this Burns observes, that it is the only old song which he could ever trace as belonging to the extensive county of Ayr. This song is said to have been founded on a romantic adventure in an old Scottish family. Mr. Stenhouse, in his Note upon the song, (vol. ii. p. 175 of Museum,) gives a traditional history of the ballad. Mr. Finlay, in his "Scottish Ballads," Mr. William Dauncy, in his "Ancient Melodies of Scotland," and Captain Charles Gray, R.M., in his "Cursory Remarks on Scottish Song," all treat the story of Lady Cassillis' elopement as a malicious fiction, and produce proofs of its falsehood. The date of the air is not known, but it appears in the Skene MS. under the name of "Ladie Cassilles Lilt;" though the set there given has undergone considerable changes in the hands of modern editors, especially in the second strain.

WHY SHOULD I, A BRISK YOUNG LASSIE.

ARRANGED BY G. F. GRAHAM.

♩· = 80

ALLEGRETTO
CON ENERGIA.

Why should I, a brisk young las - sie, Be forced to wed a feck - less[1] auld man? Hoast - in'[2] an' hirp - lin',[3] a la - mi - ter[4] bo - die! I'll die far ra - ther than gi'e him my han'!

Kirk or mar - ket, aye he fol - lows me, Gap - in', glow'rin',[5] till I'd fain han!⁸ Then at our in-gle-neuk⁷ ilk-a day hav'rin';⁸ I'll die far rather than

gi'e him my han'!

A' my kin are like to deave⁹ me
'Bout house an' hame, an' siller an' lan';
Deil tak' the siller an' lan' a' thegither!
I'll die far rather than gi'e him my han'!

My ain jo is young an' bonnie,
An' tho' he's puir, he's aye true to me;
I'll ha'e nae man but my ain dearest Johnnie,
An' ne'er the auld man, altho' I should die!

¹ Feeble.	² Coughing.	³ Limping.	⁴ Cripple.	⁵ Staring.	
⁶ Execrate.	⁷ Chimney-corner; fireside.	⁸ Talking foolishly.	⁹ Deafen.		

"WHY SHOULD I, A BRISK YOUNG LASSIE." The air is No. 48 of Mr. Dauney's edition of the Skene MS., and bears the title, "I will not goe to my bed till I suld die." The air is spirited, and worth reviving; and the only liberty taken with it has been to reduce the extreme instrumental leaps in the Skene MS. to a vocal condition. The old words being lost, the verses here given to the air were written by a friend of the Publishers. The old title suggested the present verses. With regard to the irregularity of the rhythm, or rather metre, in these stanzas, the writer quotes thus from Moore:—"In the Preface to the fifth volume of 'The Poetical Works of Thomas Moore,' collected by himself, 1841, the following passage occurs:—'Those occasional breaches of the laws of rhythm, which the task of adapting words to airs demands of the poet, though very frequently one of the happiest results of his skill, become blemishes when the verse is separated from the melody, and require, to justify them, the presence of the music to whose wildness or sweetness the sacrifice had been made. In a preceding page of this preface, I have mentioned a Treatise by the late Rev. Mr. Crowe, on English versification; and I remember his telling me, in reference to the point I have just touched upon, that, should another edition of that work be called for, he meant to produce, as examples of new and anomalous forms of versification, the following songs from the Irish Melodies, 'Oh the days are gone when beauty bright,' 'At the dead hour of night, when stars are weeping, I fly,' and, 'Through grief and through danger thy smile hath cheered my way.'"

In addition to Mr. Moore's remarks, allusion may be made to the irregular versification of the ancient Latin ballad-mongers—reciters and singers of Ballistea, whence our term Ballad—and even to the Latin hymns of the earlier Christian poets. We may also refer, *passim*, to the remarkable and now very scarce work on Music, written in Latin by the blind Spanish Professor of Music at Salamanca, Francis Salinas, and published there in 1577: especially to a passage in that work, page 356, where he gives a specimen of singular Spanish versification, together with the music sung to it. The words are "Perricos de mi señora, No me mordades agora." On this he makes the following observation—we translate:—"I have not found versification of this kind among either the Greeks or the Latins; nor do I think it is to be found among the French or the Italians. But it is credible that it was introduced among the Spaniards—together with many other customs and words and songs—by the Arabians, after they took possession of Spain, which they occupied for more than seven hundred years."

MY LOVE SHE'S BUT A LASSIE YET.

ARRANGED BY G. F. GRAHAM.

♩ = 138

ALLEGRETTO
SCHERZOSO.

My love she's but a las - sie yet, A light - some love - ly las - sie yet; It scarce wad do To sit an' woo Down by the stream sae glas - sy yet. But there's a braw' time com - in' yet, When we may gang² a - roam - in' yet; An' hint wi' glee O' joys to be, When

fa's the mo . dest gloam - in' yet.

She's neither proud nor saucy yet,
She's neither plump nor gaucy³ yet;
But just a jinkin',⁴
Bonnie blinkin',⁵
Hilty-skilty⁶ lassie yet.
But O her artless smile's mair sweet
Than hinny or than marmalete;⁷
An' right or wrang,
Ere it be lang,
I'll bring her to a parley yet.

I'm jealous o' what blesses her,
The very breeze that kisses her,
The flowery beds
On which she treads,
Though wae for ane that misses her.
Then O to meet my lassie yet,
Up in yon glen sae grassy yet;
For all I see
Are nought to me,
Save her that's but a lassie yet !

¹ Fine.   ² Go.   ³ Large, expanded.   ⁴ Shyly gamboling; dodging.
⁵ Looking, or smiling kindly.   ⁶ Thoughtless'y playful.   ⁷ Marmalade.

"MY LOVE SHE'S BUT A LASSIE YET." The song given in Johnson's Museum, and written by Burns, with the exception of the three lines which are old, is not exactly suitable to the more fastidious taste of the present day. Therefore, James Hogg's song, with the same title, has been chosen in preference for this work. It was first published in the Edinburgh "Literary Journal," and afterwards in the collection of "Songs by the Ettrick Shepherd," Blackwood, Edinburgh, 1831. It appears that the air to which Hogg's words, and the older words were sung, was also used as a dance-tune, under the name of "Lady Badinscoth's Reel." Charles Kirkpatrick Sharpe, Esq., in his Note on No. 225 of Johnson's Museum, says, "The old title of this air was, 'Put up your dagger, Jamie.' The words to this air are in ' Vox Borealis, or the Northern Discoverie, by way of dialogue between Jamie and Willie,' 1641.

        "'Put up thy dagger, Jamie,
        And all things shall be mended,
        Bishops shall fall, no not at all,
        When the Parliament is ended.
        Which never was intended
        But only for to flam thee,
        We have gotten the game,
        We'll keep the same,
        Put up thy dagger, Jamie.'

" ' This song,' says the author, ' was plaid and sung by a fiddler and a fool, retainers of General Ruthven, Governor of Edinburgh Castle, in scorn of the Lords and the Covenanters, for surrendering their strong holds.' "

C

MY JO JANET.

ARRANGED BY T. M. MUDIE.

$\checkmark = 92$
ALLEORETTO
SCHERZOSO.

Sweet Sir, for your cour - tes - ie, When

ye come by the Bass, then, For the love you bear to me, Buy me a keeking glass, then.

Keek in - to the draw - well, Jan - et, Jan - et, And there ye'll see your bon - nie sell,

My jo Jan - et.

Kecking in the draw-well clear,
  What if I should fa' in, then?
Syne[1] a' my kin will say and swear,
  I drown'd mysel' for sin, then.
Haud[2] the better by the brae,[3]
  Janet, Janet,
Haud the better by the brae,
  My jo Janet.

Good Sir, for your courtesie,
  Coming thro' Aberdeen, then,
For the love you bear to me,
  Buy me a pair o' shoon, then.
Clout[4] the auld, the new are dear,
  Janet, Janet,
A pair may gain[5] ye ha'f a year,
  My jo Janet.

But what if dancing on the green,
  An' skippin' like a mawkin',
If they should see my clouted sheen,[6]
  Of me they will be taukin'.
Dance ay laigh,[7] an' late at e'en,
  Janet, Janet,
Syne a' their fauts will no be seen,
  My jo Janet.

Kind Sir, for your courtesie,
  When ye gae to the cross, then,
For the love ye bear to me,
  Buy me a pacing horse, then.
Pace upo' your spinning-wheel,
  Janet, Janet,
Pace upo' your spinning-wheel,
  My jo Janet.

[1] Then.   [2] Hold.   [3] Bank.   [4] Patch.   [5] Suffice.   [6] Shoes.   [7] Low.

"MY JO JANET." This air can be traced from the Straloch MS., 1627, through the Skene MS., 1640 (?), the Leyden MS. (1695?), the Orpheus Caledonius, second edition, 1733, to our own times. Its early forms, though somewhat bald, have both the 4th and the 7th of the scale, and these not merely as passing, but as essential accented notes. As the lute, for which these MSS. were written, can, like the guitar, produce every semitone of the scale, there is really no reason but choice why it should have been otherwise. We give these old versions below. From the allusions in the song to Aberdeen and the Bass of Inverurie, the words have evidently been written by some one connected with that neighbourhood. Allan Ramsay printed them in his Tea-Table Miscellany, 1724, but they are believed to belong to the previous century. Johnson, from some scruple of delicacy, omitted the last stanza.

In December 1793, Burns wrote his comic song, "My spouse Nancy," to the tune of "My jo Janet."

"THE OLD MAN."—(Straloch MS.)

"LONG ER ONIE OLD MAN."—(Skene MS.)

"ROBIN AND JANET."—(Leyden MS.)

GREEN GROW THE RASHES, O!

ARRANGED BY J. T. SURENNE.

♩ = 104

MODERATO.

mf *cres.* *f* *fz*

There's nought but care on ev'-ry han', In ev'-ry hour that pass-es, O; What

sig-ni-fies the life o' man, An 'twere na for the lass-es, O. Green grow the rashes, O!

fz *f fz*

Green grow the rash-es, O! The sweet-est hours that e'er I spend, Are

fz

spent a-mang the lass-es, O!

The warldly race may riches chase,
An' riches still may fly them, O ;
An' though at last they catch them fast,
Their hearts can ne'er enjoy them, O.
Green grow, &c.

Gie me a cannie hour at e'en,
My arms about my dearie, O ;
An' warldly cares, an' warldly men,
May a' gae tapsaltcerie,* O.
Green grow, &c.

For you sae douce, wha sneer at this,
Ye're nought but senseless asses, O ;
The wisest man the warld e'er saw,
He dearly lo'ed the lasses, O.
Green grow, &c.

Auld Nature swears, the lovely dears
Her noblest work she classes, O ;
Her 'prentice han' she tried on man,
And then she made the lasses, O.
Green grow, &c.

* Tapsalteerie—topsy-turvy.

"GREEN GROW THE RASHES, O!" The first strain of the air is found in the Straloch MS. (1627) with the same name, and again a second time, slightly altered, under that of "I k'st while (until) she blusht." Both are dance tunes. They disappear for a century, and are then found—lengthened and embroidered—in Macgibbon's and Oswald's Collections as slow airs. This may show us how much uncertainty there is in regard to the true age of our melodies. Many of them appear for the first time in the middle of last century, which in style have all the marks of age, though there is no trace of them at an earlier date. A good song, superseding very silly or very indecorous words, is often the means of sending an air down to us which otherwise would probably never have been heard of.

The song is so well known, that it is scarcely necessary to say it was written by Burns. Mr. Stenhouse believes that it was the first he contributed to Johnson's Scottish Musical Museum. It appeared in the first volume of that work, 1787.

The assertion made by Mr. Stenhouse, that this air was formerly known under the name of "Cow thou me the rashes green," we believe to be altogether unfounded. He seems to have jumped to the conclusion, that because "rashes" were mentioned in both names, therefore the airs must be identical. We can, however, prove the contrary ; for we have found in a MS. of the sixteenth century, now in the British Museum, the words, "Colle thou me the rysshys grene," set twice over to different music. Airs these cannot be called, for they are altogether destitute of melody ; they appear rather to be single parts of a piece intended for several voices. We need scarcely add that they bear not the slightest resemblance to our Scottish tune.

ADIEU, DUNDEE!

ARRANGED BY G. F. GRAHAM.

$\curlywedge = 92$

ADAGIO.

pp

A - dieu, Dun - dee! from

Ma - ry part - ed, Here nae mair my lot maun lie; Wha can

bear, when bro - ken heart - ed, Scenes that speak of joys gane bye!

A' things ance were sweet and smil - ing, In the light o'

Ma - ry's e'e: Fair - est seem - ing's maist be - guil - ing, Love, a -

dieu! a - dieu, Dun - dee!

Like yon water saftly gliding,
When the winds are laid to sleep:
Such my life, when I confiding,
Gave to her my heart to keep!

Like yon water wildly rushing,
When the north wind stirs the sea;
Such the change, my heart now crushing—
Love, adieu! adieu, Dundee!

"ADIEU, DUNDEE!" The air is found in tablature in the Skene MS., already referred to in this work. See Introduction, *et passim*. The late William Dauney, Esq., Advocate, who published the translation of the Skene MS., with an able Dissertation, etc., was one of the best amateur singers and violoncello players in Scotland. Soon after the publication of that work he went to Demerara, where he held the office of Solicitor-General. Universally esteemed for his abilities and his amiable manners and character, he had the prospect of rising there to higher honours, when the fever of the country cut him off prematurely on 28th July 1843. He was born on 27th October 1800. Before he left Scotland, he requested Mr. Finlay Dun and the Editor of this work to harmonize for him some of the airs from the Skene MS., to which words were to be written by two Edinburgh gentlemen. Three of these airs were accordingly published in 1838 in that form. "Adieu, Dundee!" was one of these. It is now reprinted by permission of Mrs. Dauney, and of Lord Neaves, Senator of the College of Justice, who is the author of the expressive and appropriate verses written for the old air at the request of his intimate friend the late Mr. Dauney.—G. F. G.

This old version of the air is much simpler than that given by Playford in the Dancing Master of 1686, or rather in the 1688 appendix to that edition. Mr. William Chappell, whose opinions on the subject of national music are of the highest value, believes the air to be an English imitation of the Scottish style, which had doggerel verses beginning

"Where gott'st thou that haver-meal bannock?
Blind booby, canst thou not see?"

These lines, however, require more notes than are found in the simple early version; the latter has besides the old Scottish peculiarity in the third bar of at once going down a full tone below the minor key-note, instead of softening the transition, as is done in Playford's, as well as in the modern version. The present writer is therefore inclined to believe that the air is really Scottish, and that having become somewhat familiar to English ears by the residence in Scotland (1679-82) of the Duke of York (James II.) and his suite, it was thereafter used as a vehicle for some absurd verses in the usual licentious style of those times. Any one who may still take an interest in such matters, will find the song in D'Urfey's "Pills to purge Melancholy," vol. v. p. 17 (1719 reprint).

MARY OF CASTLE-CARY.

AIR, "BONNIE DUNDEE."   ARRANGED BY J. T. SURENNE.

♩ = 104

ANDANTINO
CON
ESPRESSIONE.

Saw ye my wee thing? Saw ye mine ain thing! Saw ye my true love down on yon lea?

Cross'd she the meadow yes-treen at the gloamin'? Sought she the burn-ie whar flow'rs the haw-tree?

Her hair it is lint-white; her skin it is milk-white; Dark is the blue o' her saft roll - ing e'e;   Red, red her ripe lips, and   sweet - er than ros - es:

poco rall.

Whar could my wee thing wan - der frae me!

colla voce.

I saw na your wee thing, I saw na your ain thing,
  Nor saw I your true love down on yon lea;
But I met my bonnie thing late in the gloamin',
  Down by the burnie whar flow'rs the haw-tree.
Her hair it was lint-white; her skin it was milk-
  white;
Dark was the blue o' her saft rolling e'e;
Red were her ripe lips, and sweeter than roses:
Sweet were the kisses that she ga'e to me.

It was na my wee thing, it was na my ain thing,
  It was na my true love ye met by the tree;
Proud is her leal heart! and modest her nature!
  She never lo'ed onie till anee she lo'ed me.
Her name it is Mary; she's frae Castle-Cary:
  Aft has she sat, when a bairn, on my knee :—
Fair as your face is, wer't fifty times fairer,
  Young braggart, she ne'er would gi'e kisses to thee.

It was then your Mary; she's frae Castle-Cary;
  It was then your true love I met by the tree;
Proud as her heart is, and modest her nature,
  Sweet were the kisses that she ga'e to me.
Sair gloom'd his dark brow, blood-red his cheek grew,
  Wild flash'd the fire frae his red rolling e'e !—
Ye's rue sair this morning your boasts and your scorn-
  ing;
Defend ye, fause traitor ! fu' loudly ye lie.

Awa' wi' beguiling, cried the youth, smiling :—
  Aff went the bonnet ; the lint-white locks flee ;
The belted plaid fa'ing, her white bosom shawing,
  Fair stood the loved maid wi' the dark rolling e'e!
Is it my wee thing ! is it my ain thing !
  Is it my true love here that I see !
O Jamie, forgi'e me; your heart's constant to me;
  I'll never mair wander, my true love, frae thee !

  "MARY OF CASTLE-CARY." Mr. Stenhouse says,—"This charming ballad, beginning, ' Saw ye my wee thing ?
saw ye my ain thing?' was written by Hector Macneil, Esq., author of the celebrated poem of 'Will and Jean,' and
several other esteemed works. It first appeared in a periodical publication, entitled 'The Bee,' printed at Edinburgh in May 1791. Mr. Macneil informed the writer of this article, that the tune to which his song is adapted in
the Museum is the genuine melody that he intended for the words." See Museum Illustrations, vol. v. p. 393. The
melody given in the Museum, No. 443, is entitled, "The wee thing, or Mary of Castle-Cary;" it is now quite
unknown, having been supplanted in the public favour by the beautiful and well-known air, "Bonnie Dundee;"
in a future number, however, we shall revive this forgotten melody, which ought not to be altogether lost sight of.
"Bonnie Dundee" is nearly the same air as that which we have just before given from the Skene MS. with words
by Lord Neaves, under the title of "Adieu, Dundee!" The latter is the more simple and touching of the two.

BUSK YE, BUSK YE.

AIR, "THE BRAES O' YARROW."   ARRANGED BY T. M. MUDIE.

$\stackrel{\frown}{} = 60$

ANDANTE
ESPRESSIVO.

Busk ye, busk ye, my bon-nie, bon-nie bride,

Busk ye, busk ye, my win-some marrow. Busk ye, busk ye, my bon-nie, bon-nie bride, And

let us to the braes o' Yarrow. Where gat ye that bon-nie, bon-nie bride!

Where gat ye that win-some mar-row? I gat her where I daur-na weel be seen,

Pu'-ing the birks on the braes o' Yar-row.

Melody for the first line of the third verse.

Lang maun she weep, lang, lang maun she weep.

Weep not, weep not, my bonnie, bonnie bride,
Weep not, weep not, my winsome marrow;
Nor let thy heart lament to leave
Pu'ing the birks on the braes o' Yarrow.
Why does she weep, thy bonnie, bonnie bride?
Why does she weep, thy winsome marrow?
And why daur ye nae mair weel be seen,
Pu'ing the birks on the braes o' Yarrow?

Lang maun she weep, lang, lang maun she weep,
Lang maun she weep wi' dule and sorrow,
And lang maun I nae mair weel be seen,
Pu'ing the birks on the braes o' Yarrow;

For she has tint her lover, lover dear,
Her lover dear, the cause o' sorrow;
And I hae slain the comeliest swain,
That e'er pu'ed birks on the braes o' Yarrow.

Fair was thy love, fair, fair indeed thy love!
In flowery bands thou didst him fetter;
Though he was fair, and well beloved again,
Than me he did not love thee better.
Busk ye then, busk, my bonnie, bonnie bride,
Busk ye, busk ye, my winsome marrow,
Busk ye, and lo'e me on the banks o' the Tweed,
And think nae mair o' the braes o' Yarrow.

"BUSK YE, BUSK YE." The melody was formerly called "The braes o' Yarrow." In a MS. book of tunes in tablature for the Lyra-viol, which belonged to the celebrated Dr. John Leyden, there is a tune called "The lady's goune," which seems to be an old and simple set of "The braes o' Yarrow." That MS. was sent to the editor of the present work, in 1844, with permission to translate and transcribe it. The transcript he made of it is intended for the Library of the Faculty of Advocates, Edinburgh. In the Orpheus Caledonius, 1725-33, there is a set of "Busk ye," which does not exhibit the wrong accentuation found in more modern versions, where the accent is painfully thrown upon the word "ye" in the first line. In the present edition that set has been restored, and the air now agrees in accent with the words. The verses here given are from a beautiful ballad written by William Hamilton of Bangour, who died in 1751, aged fifty. The ballad consists of thirty stanzas, and was first printed in Ramsay's Tea-Table Miscellany. Eight of these stanzas have been selected on this occasion. These contain the essential parts of the story. The first three lines belong to an ancient ballad, now lost.

THE BUSH ABOON TRAQUAIR.

ARRANGED BY A. LAWRIE.

Hear me, ye nymphs, and ev' - ry swain, I'll tell how Peg - gy

grieves me; Tho' thus I lan - guish and com - plain, A - las! she ne'er be -

lieves me. My vows and sighs, like si - lent air, Un - heed - ed, ne - ver *a piacere.*   *a tempo.*

move her: The bon - nie bush a - boon Traquair, Was where I first did

love her.

That day she smiled and made me glad,
No maid seem'd ever kinder;
I thought myself the luckiest lad,
So sweetly there to find her.
I tried to soothe my amorous flame,
In words that I thought tender;
If more there pass'd, I'm not to blame,
I meant not to offend her.

Yet now she scornful flies the plain,
The fields we then frequented;
If e'er we meet, she shows disdain,
And looks as ne'er acquainted.
The bonnie bush bloom'd fair in May,
Its sweets I'll aye remember;
But now her frowns make it decay,
It fades as in December.

Ye rural powers, who hear my strains,
Why thus should Peggy grieve me?
Oh! make her partner in my pains,
Then let her smiles relieve me.
If not, my love will turn despair,
My passion no more tender;
I'll leave the bush aboon Traquair,
To lonely wilds I'll wander.

"THE BUSH ABOON TRAQUAIR." Mr. Stenhouse says:—"This charming pastoral melody is ancient. It was formerly called 'The bonnie bush aboon Traquhair.' It appears in the Orpheus Caledonius, 1725, adapted to the same beautiful stanzas that are inserted in the Museum, beginning 'Hear me, ye nymphs, and every swain,' written by William Crawford, Esq., author of Tweedside, &c.; but the old song, it is believed, is lost." (See Museum Illustrations, vol. i., pp. 84-5.) Mr. D. Laing, however, (ibid. pp. 113-115,) points out the error of Mr. Stenhouse and other editors who ascribe the song to William Crawfurd (of Auchinames), while it, "Tweedside," &c., were written by Robert Crawford, a cadet of the family of Drumsoy. It appears that this gentleman was drowned in returning from France in 1732. The bush, or clump of trees, that gave name to the tune, is said to have stood on a hill above the lawn of the Earl of Traquair's house in Peeblesshire. We think that the tune was probably written down at first for some musical instrument; as its compass is too great for ordinary voices. This is the case with many old Scottish melodies. It may also be remarked, that the *accentuation* of the words, as applied to the tune, is often faulty; but this seems to have been little heeded by our older singers, and writers of verses to music. We must now take these old things as we find them; and be thankful that they are not altogether lost.

LORD RONALD.

ARRANGED BY T. M. MUDIE.

O where ha'e ye been, Lord Ron - ald, my

son! O where ha'e ye . been, Lord Ron - ald, my

son! I ha'e been wi' my sweet - heart, mother, make my bed

soon, For I'm wea-ry wi' the hunt-ing, and fain wad lie

down.

rall.

What got ye frae your sweetheart, Lord Ronald, my son?
What got ye frae your sweetheart, Lord Ronald, my son?
I ha'e got deadly poison, mother, make my bed soon,
For life is a burden that soon I'll lay down.

"LORD RONALD, MY SON." These two stanzas of the ancient ballad, with their simple and pathetic melody, were recovered by Burns in Ayrshire, and sent by him to Johnson's Museum. Sir Walter Scott, in his "Minstrelsy of the Scottish Border," gives six stanzas of the ballad as sung in the Ettrick Forest, under the title of "Lord Randal." The legend on which it is founded is very widely spread; for besides its several Scottish forms, it has been discovered in Suffolk, in Germany, and more recently in Italy. In regard to the melody, Burns (*Reliques*) observes, "This air, a very favourite one in Ayrshire, is evidently the original of Lochaber. In this manner most of the finest of our more modern airs have had their origin. Some early minstrel or musical shepherd composed the simple original air, which being picked up by the more learned musician, took the improved form it bears." We demur to Burns's theory of musical shepherds, and improved form by more learned musicians; but we have no reason to doubt Burns's opinion that the air of "Lord Ronald" was the original of "Lochaber." The former, however, as happens with most of our oldest Scottish melodies, consists of one strain, while the latter consists of two, thus throwing back the greater probability of antiquity upon "Lord Ronald."—(G. F. G.) It must not be forgotten, however, that this Scottish tradition respecting the air is confronted by an Irish one, given by Edward Bunting in his account of Irish Harpers (Collection 1840), where he says that the air was composed by Miles Reilly, a harper of Cavan, born 1635. The earliest documentary evidence, however, for the air with two strains is the Scottish MS. of 1692. which belonged to Dr. John Leyden (see Introduction); it is there called "King James's March to Ireland." The next evidence for the air is Playford's Dancing Master, 1701, where it is named "Reeve's Maggot." A few years later—how many is not now ascertainable— Allan Ramsay wrote for it his celebrated song, "Farewell to Lochaber." We thus find that the air was generally known in all the three kingdoms about the end of the seventeenth century: a popularity which may fairly be attributed to its use as a regimental march-tune not only *to* Ireland and *in* Ireland, but wherever our troops were sent. The belief that this air was sung in 1675 to "Since Celia's my foe" has recently been proved by Mr. Chappell to be an error. He shows that though Durfet's words were sung to "Lochaber" about 1730, yet that they originally had an Irish air of their own, which he has discovered and printed (Roxburghe Ballads, Part VIII.). With regard to the term Irish often applied to the air, we need, perhaps, to be reminded that nearly up to the present century, all that we now term Gaelic was in Scotland itself called Irish; further, what Bunting in his Second Collection (1809) gives as the true Irish tune, is a version of the air much more Scottish in style than any other now known.— See Grove's Dictionary.

FAREWELL TO LOCHABER.

ARRANGED BY T. M. MUDIE

Fare - well to Loch - a - ber, fare - well to my Jean, Where heart - some wi' her I ha'e mo - ny day been; For Loch - a - ber no more, Loch - a - ber no more, We'll may - be re - turn to Loch - a - ber no more. These tears that I shed they are

colla voce.

all for my dear, And no for the dan-gers at-tend-ing on weir; Tho'

horne on rough seas to a far dis-tant shore, May-be to re-turn to Loch-

a-her no more.

Though hurricanes rise, though rise every wind,
No tempest can equal the storm in my mind;
Though loudest of thunders on louder waves roar,
There's naething like leavin' my love on the shore.
To leave thee behind me my heart is sair pain'd;
But by case that's inglorious no fame can be gain'd;
And beauty and love's the reward of the brave;
And I maun deserve it before I can crave.

Then glory, my Jeanie, maun plead my excuse;
Since honour commands me, how can I refuse?
Without it, I ne'er can have merit for thee;
And losing thy favour I'd better not be.
I gae then, my lass, to win honour and fame;
And if I should chance to come glorious hame,
I'll bring a heart to thee with love running o'er,
And then I'll leave thee and Lochaber no more.

"LOCHABER NO MORE." In the preceding Note upon "Lord Ronald," we have discussed the derivation of "Lochaber" from that tune, or from "King James' March to Irland," as in the Leyden MS. The received air of "Lochaber" is evidently of modern construction, because in it the fourth and the major seventh of the tonic (or key-note) are freely employed. The verses here given are to the air of "Lochaber" were written by Allan Ramsay. A lady still living, in whose father's house at Edinburgh Robert Burns was a frequent and honoured guest, one evening played the tune of "Lochaber," on the harpsichord, to Burns. He listened to it attentively, and then exclaimed, with tears in his eyes, "Oh, that's a fine tune for a broken heart!" The lady in question stood so high in Burns' estimation, that he offered to write to her a journal of his intended tour in the Highlands of Scotland. A trifling circumstance prevented him from completing his offer of so valuable a communication.

D

GALA WATER.

ARRANGED BY J. T. SURENNE.

Braw, braw lads on Yar - row braes, Ye wan - der through the bloom - ing hea - ther; But Yar - row braes, nor Et - trick shaws, Can match the lads o' Ga - la wa - ter.

a piacere.

Braw, braw lads. *Piu lento.*

mf *p* *pp*

But there is ane, a secret ane,
  Aboon them a' I lo'e him better;
An' I'll be his, an' he'll be mine,
  The bonnie lad o' Gala water.

Altho' his daddie was nae laird,
  An' tho' I hae nae meikle tocher;
Yet, rich in kindest, truest love,
  We'll tent our flocks by Gala water.

It ne'er was wealth, it ne'er was wealth,
  That coft[1] contentment, peace, or pleasure;
The bands and bliss o' mutual love,
  O that's the chiefest warld's treasure!

[1] Bought.

"GALA WATER." One of the most beautiful of our old Scottish melodies. It is somewhat singular, however, that it is not to be found in any of our earlier collections. Neil Stewart gives it under the name of "Coming thro' the broom," in his "Thirty Scots songs for a voice and harpsichord," a work probably published between 1780, 1790, the copy we have seen bears a manuscript date of 1783. Mr. Stenhouse says, "This tune was greatly admired by the celebrated Dr. Haydn, who harmonized it for Mr. William Whyte's Collection of Scottish Songs. On the MS. of the music, which I have seen, the Doctor expressed his opinion of the melody, in the best English he was master of, in the following short but emphatic sentence:—'This one Dr. Haydn favourite song.'" In January 1793, Burns wrote the verses here published to this air. The Gala river rises in Mid-Lothian, and after uniting with the Heriot, runs south, and falls into the Tweed about four miles above Melrose, and a short distance below Abbotsford. See Museum Illustrations, vol. ii. pp. 120-122. The last detached measure, to the words "Braw, braw lads," does not belong to the original melody, but is inserted because the air is generally so sung at the present day. The singer may adopt or reject that additional measure.

The following is a portion of what Mr. Robert Chambers gives as *probably* the original song of "Gala Water :"

"Out owre yon moss, out owre yon muir,
  Out owre yon bonnie bush o' heather,
O a' ye lads whae'er ye be,
  Show me the way to Gala water.
   *   *   *   *   *

"Lords and lairds cam here to woo,
  An' gentlemen wi' sword an' dagger,
But the black-ee'd lass o' Galashiels
  Wad hae nane but the gree o' Gala water.
   *   *   *   *   *

James Oswald, in the 8th Book of his Flute Collection, gives a set of the air, which, being pentatonic, is probably more ancient than any other now known. It has several unvocal intervals, which have been altered in the modern version.—See "Scottish Music" in Grove's *Dictionary of Music.*

Dr. Joyce, in his Ancient Music of Ireland (1873), gives an Irish version of this air, and adds, "I have known it, and heard it sung, as long as I can remember." This may possibly mean fifty years, but it should not be forgotten that many of our Scottish airs were printed in Dublin as sixpenny half-sheet songs considerably before the end of last century; not to mention that Irish reapers have been cutting our crops in Teviotdale and Tweeddale for a century and a half, and might very readily carry home so simple and charming a melody.

THE BONNIE HOUSE O' AIRLY.

ARRANGED BY J. T. SURENNE.

♩ = 66

ANDANTINO.

mf   *dim.*

It fell on a day, And a bon-nie summer day, When the corn grew green and

p

yel-low, That there fell out a great dis-pute Be-tween Ar-gyle and Air-ly.

The Duke o' Montrose has written to Argyle To come in the morn-ing

mf

ear - ly, An' lead in his men, by the back o' Dunkeld, To plun-der the bonnie house o'

Air - ly.

The lady look'd o'er her window sae hie,
And, oh! but she look'd weary.
And there she espied the great Argyle
Come to plunder the bonnie house o' Airly.

"Come down, come down, Lady Margaret," he says,
"Come down and kiss me fairly,
Or before the morning clear day-light,
I'll no leave a standing stane in Airly."

"I wadna kiss thee, great Argyle,
I wadna kiss thee fairly,
I wadna kiss thee, great Argyle,
Gin you shouldna leave a standing stane in Airly."

He has ta'en her by the middle sae sma',
Says, "Lady, where is your drury[1]?"
"It's up and down the bonnie burn side,
Amang the planting of Airly."

They sought it up, they sought it down,
They sought it late and early,
And found it in the bonnie balm-tree,
That shines on the bowling-green o' Airly.

He has ta'en her by the left shoulder,
And, oh! but she grat sairly,
And led her down to yon green bank
Till he plunder'd the bonnie house o' Airly.

"O! its I ha'e seven braw sons," she says,
"And the youngest ne'er saw his daddie,
And although I had as mony mae,
I wad gi'e them a' to Charlie.

"But gin my good lord had been at hame,
As this night he is wi' Charlie,
There durst na a Campbell in a' the west
Ha'e plunder'd the bonnie house o' Airly."

· Treasure.

"THE BONNIE HOUSE O' AIRLY." When Montrose was driven out of Perth by Argyle in September 1644, he marched into Angus-shire, where he was joined by the old Earl of Airly and two of his sons, who never forsook him in success or disaster. During Montrose's retreat from the Castle of Fyvie, in Aberdeenshire, we learn from Sir Walter Scott, (History of Scotland,) that "on the road he was deserted by many Lowland gentlemen who had joined him, and who saw his victories were followed with no better results than toilsome marches among wilds, where it was nearly impossible to provide subsistence for man or horse, and which the approach of winter was about to render still more desolate. They left his army, therefore, promising to return in summer; and of all his Lowland adherents, the old Earl of Airly and his sons alone remained. They had paid dearly for their attachment to the Royal cause, Argyle having (1640) plundered their estates, and burnt their principal mansion, the 'Bonnie house o' Airly,' situated on the river Isla, the memory of which conflagration is still preserved in Scottish song." We give the ballad as it is published in Messrs. Blackie's Book of Scottish Song, according to John Finlay's version.

MARCH, MARCH, ETTRICK AND TEVIOTDALE.

AIR, "O DEAR MOTHER."

ARRANGED BY T. M. MUDIE.

♩· = 80

ALLEGRO
SPIRITOSO.

f

March, march, Et-trick and Teviotdale, Why, my lads, dinna ye march forward in or - der?

March, march, Eskdale and Liddesdale, All the blue bonnets are o - ver the Bor - der.

8va alta ad lib.

Ma - ny a ban - ner spread, flut - ters a - bove your head, Ma - ny a crest that is *fam - ous in sto - ry, Mount and make ready then, sons of the moun - tain glen,*

Sva alta.

Fight for your Queen and the old Scottish glo - ry.

Come from the hills where your hirsels are grazing,
Come from the glen of the buck and the roe :
Come to the crag where the beacon is blazing:
Come with the buckler, the lance, and the bow.

Trumpets are sounding, war-steeds are bounding;
Stand to your arms, and march in good order;
England shall many a day tell of the bloody fray,
When the blue bonnets came over the Border.

"MARCH, MARCH, ETTRICK AND TEVIOTDALE." These verses appeared for the first time in Sir Walter Scott's novel, "The Monastery," published in 1820. They were evidently modelled upon an old Cavalier song, beginning, "March! march! pinks of election," which we find in the first volume of James Hogg's "Jacobite Relics of Scotland," pp. 5–7. The air given by Hogg to these old verses is a bad set of "Lesley's March," not at all corresponding with the air in Oswald's Second Collection, p. 33, although Hogg erroneously says that it "is copied from Mr. Oswald's ancient Scottish music." In Niel Gow's Second Collection of Reels, p. 5, we find an altered version of "Lesley's March," under the name of "Duplin House;" but the modern tune seems rather to have been taken from "O dear mother, what shall I do?" which will be found both in Macgibbon's and Oswald's Collections; indeed a jig variation in the latter differs but little from the present air. R. A. Smith calls the air "Blue Bonnets," but it differs entirely from the air of that name, in common time, given by Oswald in his Second Collection, p. 5. We subjoin "Lesley's March" according to Oswald.

Brisk.

ORAN AN AOIG; OR, THE SONG OF DEATH.

ARRANGED BY G. F. GRAHAM

$\text{♩} = 84$

LENTO ASSAI.

pp cres.

Fare -

well, thou fair day, thou green earth, and ye skies, Now gay with the broad setting sun: Fare -

well, loves and friendships, ye dear ten - der ties! Our rao · of ex - is - tence is run!

Thou grim king of ter - rors, thou life's gloomy foe, Go fright - en the coward and

* Wherever this passage occurs, the high notes may be sung if the voice cannot reach the lower notes of the melody

slave ! Go teach them to tremble, fell ty - rant! but know No terrors hast thou for the

brave !

Thou strik'st the dull peasant, he sinks in the dark,
Nor saves e'en the wreck of a name :
Thou strik'st the young hero, a glorious mark !
He falls in the blaze of his fame.

In the field of proud honour, our swords in our hands,
Our king and our country to save ;
While victory shines on life's last ebbing sands,
Oh, who would not die with the brave !

"ORAN AN AOIG ; OR, THE SONG OF DEATH." In a letter addressed to Mrs. Dunlop, dated Ellisland, 17th December 1791, Burns says, "I have just finished the following song, which, to a lady, the descendant of many heroes of his truly illustrious line, and herself the mother of several soldiers, needs neither preface nor apology. Scene—a field of battle. Time of the day—evening. The wounded and the dying of the victorious army are supposed to join in the following Song of Death—'Farewell, thou fair day,' &c. The circumstance that gave rise to the foregoing verses, was looking over, with a musical friend, Macdonald's Collection of Highland Airs. I was struck with one, an Isle of Skye tune, entitled *Oran an Aoig; or, The Song of Death*, to the measure of which I have adapted my stanzas." In a recent work, entitled "The Romance of War, or the Highlanders in France and Belgium," by James Grant, Esq., late 62d Regiment, we find two very remarkable passages, one of which relates to the air *Oran an Aoig*. We quote from both. Speaking of the Gordon Highlanders, Mr. Grant, in his Preface, says, "Few, few indeed of the old corps will remember, yet with equal pride and sorrow,

> ' How, upon bloody Quatre Bras,
> Brave Cameron heard the wild hurra
> Of conquest as he fell ;'

and, lest any reader may suppose that in these volumes the national enthusiasm of the Highlanders has been over-drawn, I shall state one striking incident which occurred at Waterloo. On the advance of a heavy column of French infantry to attack La Haye Sainte, a number of the Highlanders sang the stirring verses of 'Bruce's Address to his army,' which, at such a time, had a most powerful effect on their comrades ; and long may such sentiments animate their representatives, as are the best incentives to heroism, and to honest emulation." The following passage from the same work, relates to Colonel Cameron abovementioned, and to the air *Oran an Aoig*. Colonel Cameron of Fassifern, mortally wounded, is carried by some of his men and the surgeon to a house in the village of Waterloo, to die. P. 163, *et seq.* Cameron addresses the piper : "'Come near me, Macvurich ; I would hear the blast of the pipe once more ere I die. Play the ancient Death-Song of the Skye-men ; my fore-fathers have often heard it without shrinking.' '*Oran an Aoig?*' said the piper, raising his drones. The Colonel moved his hand, and Macvurich began to screw the pipes and sound a prelude on the reeds, whose notes, even in this harsh and discordant way, caused the eyes of the Highlander to flash and glare, as it roused the fierce northern spirit in his bosom. 'He ordered that strange old tune to be played from the first moment I declared his wound to be mortal,' said the surgeon in a low voice. 'It is one of the saddest and wildest I ever heard'" And thus died the brave Cameron at Waterloo, the last earthly sounds he heard being those of the air *Oran an Aoig*

MY HEART'S IN THE HIGHLANDS.

AIR, " CRO CHALLIN. "

ARRANGED BY J. T. SURENNE.

$\bullet = 66$

ANDANTE CANTABILE.

My heart's in the High - lands, my heart is not here; My

heart's in the Highlands, a - chas - ing the deer. A - chas - ing the

wild deer, and follow - ing the roe, My heart's in the Highlands where -

Farewell to the Highlands, farewell to the north,
The birth-place of valour, the country of worth;
Wherever I wander, wherever I rove,
The hills of the Highlands for ever I love.

Farewell to the mountains high cover'd with snow,
Farewell to the straths and green vallies below;
Farewell to the forests and wild-hanging woods;
Farewell to the torrents and loud-pouring floods.

"MY HEART'S IN THE HIGHLANDS." The first half stanza of this song is old, the rest was written by Burns for Johnson's Museum. Instead of the air "Failte na moisg," to which it is adapted in that work, we have adopted a much finer Gaelic air, which in some books is called "Crodh Challin," while in others that name is given to an entirely different tune.

In George Thomson's Collection the following song, translated by Mrs. Grant of Laggan, is adapted to this melody. It is preceded by a long Note sent by the translator, a portion of which is subjoined.

"The verses of 'Cro Chalhin' have lived from the days when agriculture was in its infancy, and continue still to soothe every fold and lull every cradle in these wild regions. . . . Anciently the hunter was admired as a person of manly courage, who, in the pursuit of a livelihood, exerted the virtues of patience and fortitude, and followed Nature into her most sublime retirements. Herdsmen were then accounted the sons of little men; sordid, inferior beings, who preferred ease and safety to noble daring and boundless variety, and were considered to be as much below the hunter as the cattle they tended were inferior in grace and agility to the deer the others pursued. Interest, however, reversed such opinions; in process of time the maidens boasted of the numerous herds of their lovers, and viewed the huntsman as a poor wandering adventurer. About this time the song here translated seems to have been composed. The enamoured nymph, willing to think Colin as rich as others, talks in an obscure manner of the cattle of Colin, and pursues the metaphor through many playful allusions to the deer, in a style too minute for translation. In the end, however, it appears that the boasted cattle of Colin were no other than those wild commoners of nature, and his sole profession that of hunting. I have endeavoured to preserve the tender simplicity of the original, and to render almost literally the fond repetition of endearing epithets."

My Colin, loved Colin, my Colin, my dear!
Who wont the wild mountains to trace without fear,
O where are thy flocks that so swiftly rebound
And fly o'er the heath without touching the ground?

So dappled, so varied, so beauteous their hue,
So agile, so graceful, so charming to view;
O'er all the wide forest there's nought can compeer
With the light-bounding flocks of my Colin, my dear.

My Colin, dear Colin, my love!
O where are thy herds that so loftily move,
With branches so stately their proud heads are crown'd,
With their motion so rapid the woods all resound?

Where the birch-trees hang weeping o'er fountains so clear,
At noon-day they're sleeping round Colin, my dear;
O Colin, sweet Colin, my joy!
Must those flocks and those herds all thy moments employ?

O Colin, my darling, my pleasure, my pride!
While the flocks of rich shepherds are grazing so wide,
Regardless I view them, unheeded the swains
Whose herds scattered round me adorn the green plains.

Their offers I hear, and their plenty I see,
But what are their wealth and their offers to me,
While the light-bounding roes, and the wild mountain deer
Are the cattle of Colin, my hunter, my dear?

HIGHLAND MARY.

AIR, "KATHERINE OGIE." *

ARRANGED BY T. M. MUDIE

$\quad$ = 72

ANDANTE MESTO.

Ye banks, and braes, and streams a - round The cas - tle o' Mont -

go - mo - ry, Green be your woods, and fair your flow'rs, Your wa - ters ne - ver

drum - lie! There sim - mer first un - fauld her robes, And

* Ogie, in the Celtic, means little or young.

there the lang - est tar - ry! For there I took the last fare - weel O'

my sweet High - land Ma - ry.

How sweetly bloom'd the gay green birk,
How rich the hawthorn's blossom,
As underneath their fragrant shade,
I clasp'd her to my bosom !
The golden hours, on angel wings,
Flew o'er me and my dearie ;
For dear to me as light and life
Was my sweet Highland Mary.

Wi' monie a vow, and lock'd embrace,
Our parting was fu' tender ;
And pledging aft to meet again,
We tore ourselves asunder :

But oh ! fell death's untimely frost,
That nipp'd my flower sae early !
Now green 's the sod, and cauld 's the clay,
That wraps my Highland Mary !

O pale, pale now those rosy lips
I aft ha'e kiss'd sae fondly !
And closed for aye the sparkling glance
That dwelt on me sae kindly ;
And mouldering now in silent dust,
That heart that lo'ed me dearly !
But still within my bosom's core
Shall live my Highland Mary.

"HIGHLAND MARY." There has been considerable debate as to whether this air belongs to England or to Scotland. It is first found in a supplement (1688) to Playford's Dancing Master of 1686, where it is called "Lady Katherine Ogle, a new Dance." This, however, must not be held to mean that it was then a new tune. Playford's book was published to teach the figures of the dances, and the music was given simply as an accessory, without which dancing could not go on. This is proven by a tune being occasionally inserted more than once in the work, each time with a different name, thus serving to distinguish the figure that was meant to be danced. It would appear either that the dance called "Lady Katherine Ogle" had no success, or that some unpleasant associations prevented it from appearing in any subsequent edition of the Dancing Master. It did a_ _ear, however, without a name, but as a "Scotch tune," in Playford's Apollo's Banquet, 1690, and the air is to be found in almost every Scottish MS. of these times that has come down to us. The versions vary somewhat ; that of 1690 adheres to the old tonality, going down in the first bar to the minor seventh instead of up to the second of the scale, as it does in the version of 1686, and in that of our own times. This shows that the air belongs to an earlier age than that of James II. I have no doubt that it was a vocal melody, and that it had an earlier name, but the later loose songs written to it by some of D'Urfey's imitators, caused both old name and words to be forgotten, in the same way as Burns' Highland Mary has now superseded Katherine Ogie. It is changes such as these that have made it so difficult to trace our airs back to ancient times. We have old songs, and probably also the airs to which they were sung, without being able to establish the connection, from the tune having come down to us under a later name.

I believe the air to be Scottish chiefly from internal evidence, but partly from the facts mentioned above. In connection with this I have to acknowledge the extreme kindness of Mr. Wm. Chappell, F.S.A., in giving me the use of some of the rarest editions of Playford's Dancing Master and Apollo's Banquet, as well as other works of the times of Charles II. and the later Stuarts, many of which are unique.—(J. M. W.)

THE LAND O' THE LEAL.

AIR. "HEY, TUTTIE TAITIE."

ARRANGED BY J. T. SURENNE.

I'm wear - in' a - wa', John, Like snaw-wreaths in thaw,* John ; I'm

wear - in' a - wa' To the land o' the leal. There's nae sor - row

there, John, There's nei - ther cauld nor care, John, The day is aye fair In the

* In some editions, "Like snaw in a thaw."

land o' the leal.

poco rall.

Our bonnie bairn 's there, John,
She was baith gude and fair, John,
And oh! we grudged her sair
To the land o' the leal.
But sorrow's sel' wears past, John,
And joy is comin' fast, John,
The joy that 's aye to last
In the land o' the leal.

Oh! dry your glist'ning e'e, John,
My soul langs to be free, John,
And angels beckon me
To the land o' the leal.
Now, fare ye weel, my ain John,
This warld's cares are vain, John,
We 'll meet and we 'll be fain
In the land o' the leal.

"THE LAND O' THE LEAL." The air has long been commonly called "Hey, tuttie taitie," apparently from a passage in the last stanza of an anonymous song, supposed to have been written about the beginning of last century, and sung to the air here given. The passage alluded to is—
"When you hear the pipe sound
Tuttie taitie, to the drum," &c.
Burns speaks of the air as follows :—"I am delighted with many little melodies which the learned musician despises as silly and insipid. I do not know whether the old air, ' Hey, tuttie taitie,' may rank among this number ; but well I know that with Frazer's hautboy, it has often filled my eyes with tears. There is a tradition, which I have met with in many places of Scotland, that it was Robert Bruce's march at the battle of Bannockburn."
In Sibbald's Chronicle of Scottish Poetry, published at Edinburgh in 1802, there is a set of "Hey, tuttie taitie " given under the name of "Hey, now the day dawis." It differs from Johnson's set, (No. 170 of Museum,) not only in several notes, but in the relative position of the two strains into which the air is divided : in Johnson, the second strain being placed before the first. Mr. Stenhouse (Museum, vol. ii. pp. 162, 163) says, "The more ancient title of this tune was ' Hey, now the day dawis,' the first line of a song which had been a very great favourite in Scotland several centuries ago. It is quoted by Gawin Douglas, Bishop of Dunkeld, in the prologue to the thirteenth book of his admirable translation of Virgil into Scottish verse, which was finished in 1513. It is likewise mentioned by his contemporary, the poet Dunbar, and many others. This song was long supposed to be lost ; but it is preserved in an ancient manuscript collection of poems belonging to the library of the College of Edinburgh." We think it very doubtful that the air of "Hey, tuttie taitie," and the air of "Hey, now the day dawis," were the same. In the Straloch MS. Lute-Book—already noticed in this work—we find an air called "The day dawis," which differs totally from the air "Hey, tuttie taitie." The former has no Scottish characteristics, and may have been composed by some English, or French, or Italian musician attending the Scottish Court. That there were many foreign musicians, as well as Scottish, English, and Irish ones, employed at the Court of Scotland, appears from documents preserved in the General Register House at Edinburgh ; and from the curious passages from these in the "Extracts from the Accounts of the Lords High Treasurers of Scotland, relative to music," from A.D. 1474 to 1550, given in No. III. of Appendix to the late Mr. William Dauney's valuable work, "Ancient Scottish melodies," &c., 1838.—(G. F. G.)
The excellent verses here given were published anonymously about the end of last century. The words were originally "I'm wearin' awa', John," but were altered, seemingly with the intention of making the song appear to be the parting address of Burns to his wife. In 1821 a somewhat different version appeared in the Scottish Minstrel (vol. iii. 54), with the initials B. B. attached, as the signature of Mrs. Bogan of Bogan, a name assumed by the authoress to conceal her identity not only from the public, but even from the publisher. It was not until after her death in 1845 that Caroline Oliphant, Lady Nairne, was discovered to be the writer not only of this, but of many other excellent songs. A stanza beginning, "Sae dear's that joy was bought," (added in 1821,) has not been generally accepted as an improvement, and has been here omitted.

SCOTS, WHA HAE WI' WALLACE BLED.

AIR, "HEY, TUTTIE TATTIE."

ARRANGED BY J. T. SURENNE.

Scots, wha hae wi' Wal - lace bled! Scots, wham Bruce has af - ten led!

Wel - come to your go - ry bed, Or to vic - to - rie! Now's the day, an'

now's the hour: See the front of bat - tle lour: See approach proud Edward's power;

Chains and sla - ver - ie!

Wha will be a traitor knave?
Wha can fill a coward's grave?
Wha sae base as be a slave?
Let him turn an' flee!
Wha, for Scotland's king an' law,
Freedom's sword will strongly draw,
Freeman stand, or freeman fa',
Let him follow me!

By oppression's woes an' pains,
By our sons in servile chains,
We will drain our dearest veins,
But they shall be free.
Lay the proud usurpers low!
Tyrants fall in every foe!
Liberty's in every blow!
Let us do or die!

"SCOTS, WHA HAE WI' WALLACE BLED." We have already spoken of the air "Hey, now the day dawis," in the preceding Note. We have now to speak of the admirable words written for that air by Burns on 1st August 1793. It appears, that on 30th July 1793, Burns and his friend, Mr. John Syme, set out on horseback from the house of Mr. Gordon of Kenmure, for Gatehouse, a village in the Stewartry of Kirkcudbright. "I took him (says Mr. Syme) by the moor-road, where savage and desolate regions extended wide around. The sky was sympathetic with the wretchedness of the soil; it became lowering and dark. The hollow winds sighed; the lightnings gleamed; the thunder rolled. The poet enjoyed the awful scene—he spoke not a word, but seemed wrapt in meditation. What do you think he was about? He was charging the English army along with Bruce at Bannockburn. He was engaged in the same manner on our ride home from St. Mary's Isle, and I did not disturb him. Next day, (2d August 1793,) he produced me the following Address of Bruce to his troops, and gave me a copy for Dalzell."

Mr. Lockhart, in his "Life of Burns," gives a very interesting passage regarding Burns' visit to Bannockburn in August 1787, from some fragments of his journal that had come into Mr. Lockhart's hands. "Here (says Burns) no Scot can pass uninterested. I fancy to myself I see my gallant countrymen coming over the hill, and down upon the plunderers of their country, the murderers of their fathers, noble revenge and just hate glowing in every vein, striding more and more eagerly as they approach the oppressive, insulting, bloodthirsty foe. I see them meet in glorious triumphant congratulation on the victorious field, exulting in their heroic royal leader, and rescued liberty and independence." Mr. Lockhart adds, "Here we have the germ of Burns' famous Ode on the Battle of Bannockburn." Burns' original words to the air that he chose himself, are much superior to his altered ones, adapted to a very paltry air in Johnson's Museum, (No. 577,) or to "Lewie Gordon," in Mr G. Thomson's Collection. We here give Burns' original words, with the air for which he composed them.

The oldest known song to this air, and that from which it has received the name it is usually known by, "Hey tutti taitie," seems to have been written after the Scottish rising of 1715, and before the death of Charles XII. of Sweden, 1718. That the air had an older name need not be doubted, but the popularity of the Jacobite song has long since extinguished all knowledge of it.

Here's to the King, sir,
Ye ken wha I mean, sir,
And to every honest man
  That will do 't again.
Chorus.—Fill, fill your bumpers high,
  We'll drain a' your barrels dry,
  Out upon them, fy! fy!
  That winna do 't again.

Here's to the chieftains
O' the gallant Highland clans,
They ha'e dune it mair nor ance,
  And will do 't again.—Fill, fill, etc.

When you hear the trumpet sound
" Tutti taiti " to the drum,
Up sword, and doun gun,
  And to the loons again.—Fill, fill, etc.
Here's to the King o' Swede,
Fresh laurels croun his head!
Shame fa' every sneaking blade
  That winna do 't again.—Fill, fill, etc.

But to mak' things right now,
He that drinks maun fecht too,
To show his heart's upricht too,
  And that he'll do 't again.—Fill, fill, etc.

E

UP IN THE MORNING EARLY.

ARRANGED BY J. T. SURENNE.

Cauld blaws the wind frae north to south, The drift is drift - ing sair - ly; The sheep are cow'r - ing in the heugh,¹ O, Sirs! its wint - er fair - ly. Now up in the morn - ing's no for me,

Up in the morn-ing ear-ly; I'd ra-ther gae supper-less to my bed, Than rise in the morn-ing ear-ly.

Loud roars the blast amang the woods,
And tirls the branches barely;
On hill and house hear how it thuds![1]
The frost is nipping sairly.
Now up in the morning's no for me,
Up in the morning early;
To sit a' nicht wad better agree
Than rise in the morning early.

The sun peeps owre yon southland hills,
Like ony timorous carlie,[3]
Just blinks a wee, then sinks again;
And that we find severely.
Now up in the morning's no for me,
Up in the morning early;
When snaw blaws in at the chimley cheek,
Wha'd rise in the morning early?

Nae linties lilt on hedge or bush:
Poor things, they suffer sairly;
In cauldrife quarters a' the nicht;
A' day they feed but sparely.
Now up in the morning's no for me,
Up in the morning early;
A pennyless purse I wad rather dree[4]
Than rise in the morning early.

A cosie[5] house and canty wife,
Aye keep a body cheerly;
And pantries stow'd wi' meat and drink,
They answer unco rarely.
But up in the morning—na, na, na!
Up in the morning early!
The gowans maun glent[6] on bank and brae,
When I rise in the morning early.

[1] A dell; a ravine. [2] To beat; to strike. [3] A little man. [4] Endure.
[5] Comfortable; snug. [6] Peep out, or shine.

"UP IN THE MORNING EARLY." Mr. Stenhouse, the annotator of Johnson's Museum, believes that the English borrowed this air from us, and sang to it some of their old songs. It would rather seem that we borrowed the air from them, and that we never had an old Scottish song adapted to it; at least neither Allan Ramsay nor David Herd knew of such a thing. Our earliest song to the tune was written by Burns about 1788; that given above, which is now usually sung to the air, is by John Hamilton, music-seller in Edinburgh, who died so recently as 1814.

The idea of the air being Scottish appears to have arisen from the fact that Queen Mary II., on a noted occasion when Purcell was present, and had been playing on the harpsichord to her, asked one of her attendants to sing the "old Scottish ballad, 'Cold and raw the north did blow.'" Now "Cold and raw" had then been only recently written by Tom d'Urfey, and was therefore neither old nor Scottish. At that time the music of our country was in fashion in England, and it was customary to call every simple air Scottish, whether it possessed any other claim to the title or not.

The music-books of the period literally swarm with such tunes, frequently giving the name of the composer; so that there was no idea of nationality necessarily attached to them, any more than there is to the "Schottisch" of our own times.

Mr. Chappell gives the successive names of the air in England as "Stingo, or, The oyle of barley," during the Commonwealth; "The country lass," under Charles II., and "Cold and raw," under James II. See Popular Music of the Olden Time.

MUIRLAND WILLIE.

ARRANGED BY J. T. SURENNE.

[O] heark'n, and I will tell you how Young Muir-land Wil-lie cam' here to woo, Tho' he could nei-ther say nor do; The truth I tell to you. But aye he cries, Whate'er be-tide, Mag-gy I'se ha'e to be my bride, With a fal da ra, fal

lal da ra, la fal lal da ra, lal da ra la.

On his gray yade, as he did ride,
Wi' dirk and pistol by his side,
He prick'd her on wi' meikle pride,
　Wi' meikle mirth and glee,
Out o'er yon moss, out o'er yon muir,
Till he came to her daddie's door,
　With a fal da ra, &c.

Gudeman, quoth he, be ye within?
I'm come your dochter's love to win,
I carena for making meikle din;
　What answer gi'e ye me?
Now, wooer, quoth he, would ye light down,
I'll gi'e ye my dochter's love to win,
　With a fal da ra, &c.

Now, wooer, sin' ye are lighted down,
Where do ye won,[1] or in what town?
I think my dochter winna gloom,
　On sic a lad as ye.
The wooer he stepp'd up the house,
And wow but he was wond'rous crouse,[2]
　With a fal da ra, &c.

The maid put on her kirtle[3] brown,
She was the brawest in a' the town;
I wat on him she didna gloom,
　But blinkit bonnilie.
The lover he stended up in haste,
And gript her hard about the waist,
　With a fal da ra, &c.

The maiden blush'd and bing'd[4] fu' law,
She hadna will to say him na,
But to her daddie she left it a',
　As they twa could agree.
The lover gi'ed her the tither kiss,
Syne[5] ran to her daddie, and tell'd him this,
　With a fal da ra, &c.

The bridal day it came to pass,
Wi' mony a blythsome lad and lass;
But siccan[6] a day there never was,
　Sic mirth was never seen.
This winsome couple straked hands,
Mess John ty'd up the marriage bands,
　With a fal da ra, &c.

1 Dwell.　　2 Brisk; lively.　　3 An upper garment.　　4 Curtsied.　　5 Afterwards.　　6 Such.

"MUIRLAND WILLIE." As this air has been known in England since 1667 under the name of "The Northern Lass," we are scarcely entitled to assume it to be undeniably Scottish, however much it may appear to ourselves to be so. A song, "Betty Maddocks, the fair Maid of Doncaster," has been traced back to that year by Mr. Chappell, and the air itself to 1669. Our claim rests on the fact that Allan Ramsay (born 1686), mentions the song specially in the preface to his Tea-Table Miscellany as known "time out of mind," and marks it in the body of the work with a Z, to indicate its being an ancient song. It may also be remarked that the measure of the Scottish verses seems better fitted to the air than the double rhymes on the second and fourth lines of the English song. The tune having been known in both countries for upwards of two centuries, it may be considered as the common property of the northern counties of the one, and the southern counties of the other kingdom.

THERE WAS A LAD WAS BORN IN KYLE.

AIR, "O GIN YE WERE DEAD, GUDEMAN."   ARRANGED BY T. M. MUDIE.

There was a lad was born in Kyle, But what - na day, o' what - na style, I doubt its hard - ly worth the while To be sae nice wi' Ro - bin.

For Ro - bin was a rov - in' boy, A rant - in', rov - in',

ran - tin', rov - in', Ro - bin was a rov - in' boy; O ran - tin', rov - in'

Ro - bin.

Our monarch's hindmost year but ane
Was five-and-twenty days begun,
'Twas then a blast o' Janwar' win'
Blew hansel in on Robin.
     For Robin was a rovin' boy, &c.

The gossip keekit [1] in his loof, [2]
Quo' scho, wha lives will see the proof,
This waly [3] boy will be nae coof, [4]
I think we'll ca' him Robin.
     For Robin was a rovin' boy, &c.

He'll ha'e misfortunes great and sma',
But ay a heart aboon them a';
He'll be a credit till us a',
We'll a' be proud o' Robin.
     For Robin was a rovin' boy, &c.

But sure as three times three mak' nine,
I see by ilka score and line,
This chap will dearly like our kin',
So leeze me on thee, Robin.
     For Robin was a rovin' boy, &c.

[1] Looked.   [2] Palm of the hand.   [3] Large, thriving.   [4] Fool.

" THERE WAS A LAD WAS BORN IN KYLE." This song was written by Burns; but the sixth stanza is omitted for obvious reasons. The old air of " O gin ye were dead, gudeman," consisted of one strain only. The second strain was taken from one of Oswald's variations of the original air, published in the fourth volume of his Caledonian Pocket Companion. The air is thought to be of an older date than 1549, as the Reformers are said to have sung it then to one of their spiritual hymns.

O MY LOVE IS LIKE A RED RED ROSE.

AIR, "LOW DOUN IN THE BROOM." ARRANGED BY T. M. MUDIE

* Some editions have "sung."

a' the seas gang dry, my dear, Till   a' the seas gang dry, And   I will love thee still, my dear, Till

a' the seas gang dry.

_p_

Till a' the seas gang dry, my dear,
And the rocks melt wi' the sun;
[O] I will love thee still my dear,
While the sands o' life shall run.
And fare thee weel, my only love,
And fare thee weel a while!

And I will come again, my love,
Though it were ten thousand mile!
Though it were ten thousand mile, my love!
Though it were ten thousand mile!
And I will come again, my love,
Though it were ten thousand mile!

"O MY LOVE IS LIKE A RED RED ROSE." In the Note on "Mary Morison" we have alluded to this being an old song, which Burns revised and extended for Johnson's Museum. The subject must at one time have been a favourite with our minstrels, for no less than three versions of it are given in the second volume of Burns' works edited by Hogg and Motherwell. The first was furnished by Mr. Peter Buchan, who says,—"The song which supplied Burns with such exquisite ideas, was written by Lieutenant Hinches as a farewell to his sweetheart." No farther information is given as to this gentleman; not even when or where he lived. This is unfortunate, for authorities are desirable in old songs as well as in graver matters. The next version is from a common stall ballad, picked up by Mr. Motherwell, entitled, "The turtle-dove, or True love's farewell." The third is taken from a small Garland, without date, but supposed to be printed about 1770, entitled, "The Horn fair Garland, containing six excellent new songs." This tract is believed to have been in the possession of Burns, as his name, in a boyish hand, is scrawled on the margin of the last page. The present song seems to owe some of its lines to Song VI., "The loyal lover's farewell to his sweetheart on going a long journey;" and Mr. Motherwell observes, "this song shows how tenaciously his (Burns') memory retained every idea which a rude ditty suggested to his creative mind." We are in possession of further information on the subject, but this we shall reserve for the Appendix, merely remarking here, that the first six lines do not appear in any of these old versions.
In Johnson's Museum the song was set to two different airs, one a strathspey, called by Gow, "Major Graham," and the other a fine old melody of one strain, called, "Queen Mary's Lament." Neither of these has retained possession of the song, which is now invariably sung to a modern version of "Low down in the broom," the air to which it is adapted in this work. Sibbald, in his Chronicle of Scottish Poetry, vol. iii. p. 274, states it as his opinion, that to this tune was written, "My love murnis for me, for me," one of Wedderburne's "Psalms and Ballands of Godlie purposes." These spiritual songs were undoubtedly sung to the popular tunes of the day; but every attempt to identify the latter with any air now known, must, with perhaps a few exceptions, rest purely on conjecture. Wedderburne's "Gude and Godlie Ballates," are supposed to be alluded to in a Canon of the Provincial Council, 1549, which denounces severe punishments against those who kept in their possession "aliquos libros rythmorum seu cantilenarum vulgarum, scandalosa ecclesiasticorum, aut quamcunque hacresim in se continentia." See Sibbald, vol. iii. p. 238.

MY AIN FIRESIDE.

AIR, "TODLEN HAME."

ARRANGED BY J. T. SURENNE.

♩ = 108

ANDANTINO
ANIMATO.

O
I ha'e seen great anes, and sat in great ha's, 'Mang
At feasts made for prin - ces, wi' prin - ces I've been, Where the

lords and 'mang la - dies a' cov - er'd wi' braws; But a sight sae de - light - ful, I
great shine o' splendour has daz - zled my e'en;

trow I ne'er spied, As the bon - nie blythe blink o' my ain fire - side.

My ain fire - side, my ain fire - side, O cheering's the blink o' my

ain fire - side.

As the succeeding stanzas are each two lines longer than the first, it is necessary in singing them to repeat the second as well as the first strain of the melody. Another, and a very objectionable, mode is, however, more generally adopted; this is, to omit a portion of each stanza, and thus accommodate it to the music.

Ance mair, gude be praised, round my ain heartsome ingle,
Wi' the friends o' my youth I cordially mingle;
Nae forms to compel me to seem wae or glad,
I may laugh when I'm merry, and sigh when I'm sad.
Nae falsehood to dread, and nae malice to fear,
But truth to delight me, and friendship to cheer;
Of a' roads to happiness ever were tried,
There's nane half so sure as ane's ain fireside.
My ain fireside, my ain fireside,
O there's nought to compare wi' ane's ain fireside.

When I draw in my stool on my cosey hearth-stane,
My heart loups sae light I scarce ken't for my ain;
Care's down on the wind, it is clean out o' sight,
Past troubles they seem but as dreams of the night.
I hear but kend voices, kend faces I see,
And mark saft affection glent fond frae ilk e'e;
Nae fleechings o' flattery, nae boastings o' pride,
'Tis heart speaks to heart at ane's ain fireside.
My ain fireside, my ain fireside,
O there's nought to compare wi' ane's ain fireside.

"MY AIN FIRESIDE." In Cromek's "Remains of Nithsdale and Galloway Song," these verses are ascribed to Mrs. Elizabeth Hamilton, the authoress of "The Cottagers of Glenburnie," and various other prose works, chiefly relative to education. She was the sister of Captain Charles Hamilton, in the service of the East India Company, who was also an author. She died about 1817. The air is that given in Johnson's Museum under the title of "Todlen hame." This ancient air has been wrought into a variety of modern tunes, under different names; such as, "Armstrong's Farewell," "Robidh donna gorrach," "The days o' Langsyne," "Lude's Lament," "The death of the chief," &c. See Museum Illustrations, vol. iii. p. 258

WHEN THE KING COMES OWRE THE WATER.

ARRANGED BY A. C. MACKENZIE.

1. I may sit in my wee croo-house, At the rock and the reel to toil fu' drear - y; I may think on the day that's gane, And sigh and sab till I grow wear - y.

2. O gin I live to see the day That I ha'e begg'd, and begg'd frae heav - en; I'll fling my rock and my reel a - way, And dance and sing frae morn till ev - en.

mf   cres. *f*   *p*

I ne'er could brook, I ne'er could brook A for - eign loon to own or flatter, But
For there is ane I win - na name That comes the bein - gin byke to scatter, And

mf   *ff*   *a little slower.*

I will sing a rant - in' sang The day our king comes owre the water.
I'll put on my brid - al goun The day our king comes owre the water.

Concluding symphony.   *ritard.*

I ha'e seen the gude auld day,
The day o' pride and chieftain's glory,
When royal Stuarts bore the sway,
And ne'er heard tell o' Whig nor Tory.
Though lyart be my locks and grey,
And eild has crook'd me doun—what matter!
I 'll dance and sing ae other day,
That day the king comes owre the water.

A curse on dull and drawling Whig,
The whining, rantin', low deceiver,
Wi' heart sae black, and look sae big,
And cantin' tongue o' chishmaclaver!
My father was a gude lord's son,
My mother was an earl's daughter,
And I 'll be Lady Keith again
The day our king comes owre the water.

"WHEN THE KING COMES OWRE THE WATER." This is said to be a genuine old Jacobite song, though it is not known to have appeared earlier than in Hogg's Jacobite Relics (1819). He says in a note, "It seems to have been composed by the Lady Marischall, or by some kindred bard in her name. Her maiden name was Lady Mary Drummond, daughter of the Earl of Perth. She was a Roman Catholic, and so strongly attached to the exiled family, that on the return of her two sons to Scotland, she would not suffer them to enjoy any rest till they engaged actively in the cause of the Stuarts." George, the elder of her sons, was attainted in 1716, and died abroad in 1778. James, the younger, was the celebrated Field-Marshal Keith, who, after attaining the highest military rank in the Russian service, entered that of Frederick the Second of Prussia, by whom he was held in great esteem. He was killed at the battle of Hochkirchen in 1758, and was buried with military honours by Marshal Daun, his Austrian opponent. Frederick, however, afterwards transferred his body to Berlin, and there erected a superb monument to his memory.
The air has been discovered in William Graham's MS. Flute Book (1694), under the name "Playing amang the rashes ;" Oswald has it in his Caledonian Pocket Companion, and calls it "The rashes," thus showing that we had an earlier song to the tune than the "The Boyne Water." It will be found in Ramsay's Tea-Table Miscellany (I. 60), and is marked Z as an old song. It begins, "My Jockey blyth."

THE SOLDIER'S RETURN.

AIR, "THE MILL, MILL, O."

ARRANGED BY T. M. MUDIE.

When wild war's dead - ly blast was blawn, And gen - tle peace re -

turn - ing, Wi' mo - ny a sweet babe fa - ther - less, And mo - ny a wi - dow

mourn - ing: I left the lines and tent - ed field, Where

lang I'd been a lodg - er; My hum - ble knap - sack a' my wealth; A

poor and hon - est sodg - er.

A leal light heart beat in my breast,
  My hands unstain'd wi' plunder ;
And for fair Scotia, hame again,
  I cheery on did wander.
I thought upon the banks o' Coil,
  I thought upon my Nancy ;
I thought upon the witchin' smile,
  That caught my youthful fancy.
At length I reach'd the bonnie glen,
  Where early life I sported ;
I pass'd the mill and trystin' thorn,
  Where Nancy oft I courted.
Wha spied I but my ain dear maid,
  Down by her mother's dwelling !
And turn'd me round to hide the flood
  That in my e'e was swelling.
Wi' alter'd voice, quoth I, Sweet lass,
  Sweet as yon hawthorn's blossom,
O ! happy, happy may he be,
  That's dearest to thy bosom !
My purse is light, I've far to gang,
  And fain wad be thy lodger,
I've served my king and country lang :
  Tak' pity on a sodger.
Sae wistfully she gazed on me,
  And lovelier was than ever ;
Quoth she, A sodger ance I loved
  Forget him will I never !

Our humble cot and hamely fare,
  Ye freely shall partake it ;
That gallant badge, the dear cockade,
  Ye're welcome for the sake o't !
She gazed—she redden'd like a rose—
  Syne pale as ony lily ;
She sank within my arms, and cried,
  Art thou my ain dear Willie ?
By Him who made yon sun and sky,
  By whom true love's regarded,
I am the man ! and thus may still
  True lovers be rewarded.
The wars are o'er, and I'm come hame,
  And fiud thee still true-hearted ;
Though poor in gear, we're rich in love,
  And mair we'se ne'er be parted.
Quoth she, My grandsire left me gowd,
  A mailin' plenish'd fairly ;
Then come, my faithfu' sodger lad,
  Thou'rt welcome to it dearly.
For gold the merchant ploughs the main,
  The farmer ploughs the manor ;
But glory is the sodger's prize,
  The sodger's wealth is honour.
The brave poor sodger ne'er despise,
  Nor count him as a stranger :
Remember he's his country's stay,
  In day and hour of danger.

"WHEN WILD WAR'S DEADLY BLAST WAS BLAWN." This song was written by Burns, in the spring of 1793, to take place of unseemly old verses that used to be sung to the same air. Captain Charles Gray, R.M., in his "Cursory Remarks on Scottish Song," No. 15, thinks that the song was probably suggested by a casual meeting with "a poor fellow of a sodger," in a little country inn ; which Burns mentions in a letter to John Ballantine, Esq. The air is probably much older than the date of Mrs. Crockat's MS., 1709, beyond which Mr. Stenhouse does not trace its antiquity. Gay chose the air for one of his songs in "Polly," printed in 1729.

BARBARA ALLAN.

ARRANGED BY J. T. SURENNE.

It was in and a-bout the Mart'-mas time, When the green leaves were a - fall - in', That

Sir John Græme, in the west coun-try, Fell in love wi' Bar - b'ra Al - lan. He

sent his man down thro' the town, To the place where she was dwall - in': O, haste and come to my mas - ter dear, Gin   ye   be Bar - b'ra   Al - lan.

O, hooly,[1] hooly, rase she up
 To the place where he was lyin',
And when she drew the curtain by—
 Young man, I think ye're dyin'.

It's oh, I'm sick, I'm very very sick,
 And it's a' for Barbara Allan.
O, the better for me ye'se never be,
 Though your heart's blude were a-spillin'.

Oh, dinna ye mind, young man, she said,
 When the red wine ye were fillin',
That ye made the healths gae round and round,
 And slichtit Barbara Allan?

He turn'd his face unto the wa',
 And death was with him dealin':
Adieu, adieu, my dear friends a',
 And be kind to Barbara Allan.

And slowly, slowly rase she up,
 And slowly, slowly left him,
And sighin', said, she could not stay,
 Since death of life had reft him.

She hadna gane a mile but twa,
 When she heard the deid-bell knellin',
And every jow[2] that the deid-bell gi'ed,
 It cried, Woe to Barbara Allan

Oh, mother, mother, mak' my bed,
 And mak' it saft and narrow,
Since my love died for me to-day,
 I'll die for him to-morrow.

[1] Slowly.   [2] Peal.

"BARBARA ALLAN." "This ballad is ancient. Bishop Percy had an old printed copy in his possession, which was entitled, 'Barbara Allan's Cruelty, or the Young Man's Tragedy,' reprinted in the third volume of his Ancient Songs and Ballads, at London in 1767. It is evidently an embellished edition of the old Scottish ballad in the Museum, which is taken *verbatim* from that preserved in Ramsay's Miscellany in 1724. The learned prelate's copy makes the heroine's residence at *Scarlet Town*, (the city of Carlisle, perhaps,) and calls the hero *Jemmye Grove*. In other respects the story is nearly the same in both ballads, and may possibly have had its origin from circumstances that really occurred. Be that as it may, it has been a favourite ballad at every country fire-side in Scotland, time out of memory. The strains of the ancient minstrel who composed this song may, indeed, appear harsh and unpolished when compared with modern refinements; nevertheless he has depicted the incidents of his story with such a bold, glowing, and masterly pencil as would do credit to any age. A learned correspondent informs me, that he remembers having heard the ballad frequently sung in Dumfries-shire, where it was said the catastrophe took place—that there were people of the name of Allan who resided in the town of Annan—and that, in some papers which he had seen, mention is made of a Barbara of that family; but he is of opinion she may have been baptized from the ballad." See Museum Illustrations, vol. iii. pp. 213, 214. In the Add. Illust., p. 300*, C. K. Sharpe, Esq., writes as follows, regarding the preceding Note:—"In this Note Mr. Stenhouse alludes to me. Unluckily I lost the paper I found at Hoddam Castle, in which Barbara Allan was mentioned. I remember that the peasantry of Annandale sang many more verses of this ballad than have appeared in print, but they were of no merit—containing numerous magnificent offers from the lover to his mistress—and, among others, some ships in sight, which may strengthen the belief that this song was composed near the shores of the Solway. I need scarcely add, that the name of Grahame, which the luckless lover generally bears, is still quite common in and about Annan."

Allan Cunningham remarks of this ballad :—"Never was a tale of love-sorrow so simply and so soon told ; yet we learn all that we wish to know, and any further incidents would only cumber the narrative, and impair the effect. I have often admired the ease and simplicity of the first verse, and the dramatic beauty of the second."

The melody bears marks of antiquity, from the nature of the tonality employed. Its author is unknown. We find in Mr. W. Chappell's "National English Airs," a melody of the same name, which is, however, quite different from the Scottish melody, besides being in a major key, and in three crotchet time

F

LORD GREGORY.

ARRANGED BY F. M. MUDIE.

O mirk, mirk is this mid - night hour, An' loud the tem - pest's

roar;   A wae - fu' wan - d'rer seeks thy tow'r, Lord Gre - gory,

ope thy door!   An ex - ile frae her fa - ther's ha', An'

* This note is B in other editions: it has been altered, as C is more characteristic of Scottish melody.—T. M. M.

a' for lov - ing thee; At least some pi - ty on me

shaw, If love it may na be.

Lord Gregory, mind'st thou not the grove
  By bonnie Irwin-side,
Where first I own'd that virgin-love
  I lang, lang had denied?
How often didst thou pledge and vow
  Thou wad for aye be mine;
An' my fond heart, itsel' sae true,
  It ne'er mistrusted thine.

Hard is thy heart, Lord Gregory,
  An' flinty is thy breast—
Thou dart of heaven that flashest by,
  O wilt thou give me rest!
Ye mustering thunders from above,
  Your willing victim see!
But spare an' pardon my fause love,
  His wrangs to heaven an' me!

"LORD GREGORY." "This is a very ancient Gallowegian melody." The air is No. 5 of Museum, and is the first in P. Urbani's Collection; but does not appear in any older collections. It is defective in rhythmical structure, four measures alternating with three, in both strains. In the present edition, this defect is supplied by additional measures in the pianoforte arrangement, while the air is left intact.

Burns remarks, "It is somewhat singular, that in Lanark, Renfrew, Ayr, Wigton, Kirkcudbright, and Dumfries-shires, there is scarcely an old song or tune, which, from the title, &c., can be guessed to belong to, or to be the production of these counties. This, I conjecture, is one of these very few, as the ballad, which is a long one, is called, both by tradition and in printed collections, 'The Lass o' Lochroyan,' which I take to be Lochroyan, in Galloway." *Reliques*, p. 196. The words adopted in this collection, were written by Burns in 1793 for Mr. George Thomson's work. The song is founded upon the ballad above mentioned, "The Lass o' Lochroyan," which was first published in a perfect state by Sir Walter Scott in his Minstrelsy of the Border, vol. ii. p. 41? We subjoin a fragment of the original.—

"O open the door, Lord Gregory,
  O open, an' let me in;
For the wind blaws thro' my yellow hair
  An' the rain draps o'er my chin."
"Awa, awa, ye ill woman
  Ye're no come here for good;
Ye're but some witch or wil-warlock,
  Or mermaid o' the flood."

"O dinna ye mind, Lord Gregory,
  As we sat at the wine,
We changed the rings frae our fingers.
  An' I can shew thee thine?
O your's was gude, an' gude enough,
  But ay the best was mine;
For your's was o' the gude red gowd,
  But mine o' the diamond fine."

HERE AWA', THERE AWA'.

ARRANGED BY T. M. MUDD.

Here a - wa', there a - wa', wan - der - ing

Wil - lie! Here a - wa', there a - wa', Haud a - wa' hame!

Come to my bo - som, my ain on - ly dear - ie; Tell me thou

bring'st me my Wil - lie the same. :S: *Concluding symphony.*

Winter winds blew loud and cauld at our partin ;
Fears for my Willie brought tears in my e'e :
Welcome now, summer, and welcome, my Willie;
The summer to nature, my Willie to me.

Rest, ye wild storms, in the caves of your slumbers !
How your dread howling a lover alarms !
Wauken, ye breezes ! row gently, ye billows !
And waft my dear laddie ance mair to my arms.

But, oh, if he's faithless, and minds na his Nannie,
Flow still between us, thou wide roarin' main !
May I never see it, may I never trow it,
But, dying, believe that my Willie's my ain !

" HERE AWA', THERE AWA'." This simple and charming little melody was first published by James Oswald,
in his Caledonian Pocket Companion, Book vii. Its melodic structure is remarkable. The commencement indicates the major key of F, while the close is in D minor. We have seen such modulation in modern classical
music, but only in the first strain of an Andante ; the second strain reverting to the key first indicated, and
concluding in it. In this Scottish melody there is, therefore, a curious peculiarity of modulation, which is not
only free from harshness, but is pathetically pleasing and effective. It is a common error to believe that a
melody *must* begin and end in one and the same key. There is no *reason* for that, save custom and arbitrary
rules. If the modulation is smoothly and artistically managed, a melody may begin in one key and end in
another *relative* key, without any real impropriety ; nay, often with good effect, as is shown in this very air.
Technical and scholastic rules for the structure of music and poetry are continually liable to exceptions, which
it is the province of genius to discover. The date of the composition of this air, or its author, cannot now be
ascertained.

Burns' first version of his song, " Here awa', there awa'," was written in March 1793, and sent to Mr. George
Thomson. Some alterations were proposed by the Honourable Andrew Erskine and Mr. George Thomson, in
which Burns at first acquiesced. But, as Doctor Currie remarks in his edition of Burns' Works, " our poet,
with his usual judgment, adopted some of these alterations, and rejected others. The last edition is as follows."
This last edition given by Dr. Currie, is the one here published. In his letter to Mr. George Thomson, April
1793, regarding " Here awa', there awa'," and some other songs, Burns thus expresses his opinion of what is
essential to a song or a ballad—simplicity ! " Give me leave to criticise your taste in the only thing in which it
is in my opinion reprehensible. You know I ought to know something of my own trade. Of pathos, sentiment,
and point, you are a complete judge ; but there is a quality more necessary than either in a song, and which is
the very essence of a ballad,—I mean simplicity ; now, if I mistake not, this last feature you are a little apt to
sacrifice to the foregoing."

A custom has recently crept in of repeating the first part of the air to the 3d and 4th lines of the song ; the
5th and 6th lines are then sung to the second part of the air, and the stanza is completed by again singing the
first part, substituting, however, the fifteenth for the seventh bar, as that makes a finer close.

SAW YE JOHNNIE COMIN'?

ARRANGED BY T. M. MUDIE.

$\text{♩} = 60$

MODERATO
A PIACERE.

Saw ye Johnny comin'? quo' she,

Saw ye John - nie com - in'? Saw ye John - nie com - in'? quo' she, Saw ye John - nie

com - in'? Wi' his blue bon - net on his head, And his dog - gie rin - nin'; Wi'

his blue bon - net on his head, And his dog - gie rin - nin'? quo' she,

And his dog-gie rin - nin'!

Fee him, father, fee him, quo' she,
  Fee him, father, fee him ;
Fee him, father, fee him, quo' she,
  Fee him, father, fee him ;
For he is a gallant lad,
  And a weel-doin' ;
And a' the wark about the house,
  Gaes wi' me when I see him, quo' she,
  Wi' me when I see him.

What will I do wi' him, quo' he,
  What will I do wi' him ?
He's ne'er a sark upon his back—
  And I ha'e nane to gi'e him.
I ha'e twa sarks into my kist,
  And ane o' them I'll gi'e him
And for a merk o' mair fee
  Dinna stand wi' him, quo' she,
  Dinna stand wi' him.

For weel do I lo'e him, quo' she,
  Weel do I lo'e him ;
For weel do I lo'e him, quo' she,
  Weel do I lo'e him.
O fee him, father, fee him, quo' she,
  Fee him, father, fee him ;
He'll haud the plough, thrash in the barn,
  And crack wi' me at e'en, quo' she,
  And crack wi' me at e'en.

"SAW YE JOHNNIE COMIN'?" "This song, for genuine humour, and lively originality in the air, is unparalleled.
I take it to be very old."—*Burns's Reliques.* This observation has been hastily made; for the air, either when
played or sung slowly, as it ought to be, is exceedingly pathetic, not lively. Burns afterwards became sensible
of this; for, in one of his letters to Thomson, inserted in Currie's edition of his works, he says, "I inclose you
Fraser's set of this tune; when he plays it slow, in fact he makes it the language of despair. Were it possible,
in singing, to give it half the pathos which Fraser gives it in playing, it would make an admirable pathetic song.
I shall here give you two stanzas in that style, merely to try if it will be any improvement." These stanzas begin
"Thou hast left me ever, Jamie," &c. "Mr. Thomas Fraser, to whom Burns alludes, was an intimate acquaintance
of the poet, and an excellent musician. He still lives, and is at present (1820) the principal oboe concerto player
in Edinburgh, of which city he is a native. His style of playing the melodies of Scotland is peculiarly chaste and
masterly." See Museum Illustrations, vol. i. pp. 5, 6. The Editor of the present work can speak of the abilities
of Thomas Fraser as an excellent oboe player. For him, expressly, were written several solo passages in Orches-
tral Symphonies by the Editor, which were performed at the public Edinburgh "Fund Concerts," &c. Fraser
died in 1825.
The following are the two stanzas written by Burns for this air, and sent to Mr. Thomson in September 1793 :—

Thou hast left me ever, Jamie,
  Thou hast left me ever ;
Thou hast left me ever, Jamie,
  Thou hast left me ever.
Aften hast thou vow'd that death
  Only should us sever ;
Now thou's left thy lass for aye—
  I maun see thee never, Jamie,
  I'll see thee never.

Thou hast me forsaken, Jamie,
  Thou hast me forsaken ;
Thou hast me forsaken, Jamie,
  Thou hast me forsaken.
Thou canst love anither jo,
  While my heart is breaking :
Soon my weary e'en I'll close,
  Never mair to waken, Jamie,
  Ne'er mair to waken

TAM GLEN.

ARRANGED BY A. C. MACKENZIE.

1. My heart is a - breakin', dear tittie, Some coun - sel un - to me come lend; To an - ger them a' is a pit - y, But what will I do wi' Tam Glen? I'm think - in' wi' sic a braw fallow, In puirtith I might mak a fen'; What

2. There's Low - rie, the laird o' Drum - meller, "Gude day to ye," cuif! he comes ben; He brags and he blaws o' his siller, But when will he dance like Tam Glen? My min - nie does constant - ly deave me, And bids me be - ware o' young men; They

cres.

(My daddie says gin I 'll forsake him,
　He 'll gi'e me guid hunder merks ten ;
But if it 's ordain'd I maun tak him,
　O wha will I get but Tam Glen ?)
Yestreen at the valentines' dealin',
My heart to my mou' gied a sten',
For thrice I drew ane without failin',
And thrice it was written Tam Glen.

(The last Hallowe'en I was waukin'
　My droukit sark sleeve, as ye ken,
His likeness cam' up the house staulkin',
　And the very grey breeks o' Tam Glen.)
Come counsel, dear tittie, don't tarry,
I 'll gi'e you my bonnie black hen,
Gin ye will advise me to marry
The lad I lo'e dearly, Tam Glen.

"TAM GLEN." The air to which Burns's words are now usually sung is of some antiquity; it was formerly known as "The mucking of Geordie's byre." Wm. Thomson gave it a place in the fifty airs which formed the first edition of the Orpheus Caledonius, 1725, and adapted to it the words, "My daddie's a delver of dykes." This, however, is not the tune which Burns sent to Johnson, and to which he wrote his song. Where or how he acquired that air will never be known ; but it seems not a little strange that a forgotten English air should be found wandering about in Ayrshire. It is as old as the Commonwealth, and was then sung in derision of "Old Hewson the Cobbler" and regicide, whose name it bears. The air is pretty, but being short—eight bars only—the ear tires of the repetition in a long song, hence the cause of its having been superseded by "Geordie's byre." We subjoin the original air for those who may wish to sing it to Burns's words.

MY NAME IS OLD HEWSON THE COBBLER.

Mr. Wm. Chappell, in his excellent work, "Popular Music of the Olden Time," gives a version of the air differing but little from the above, together with an account of the works in which he has found it. Dean Christie also has it in his Traditional Ballad Airs, vol. ii., and in his note states that it was sent to his father in 1812 by an aged farmer in Buchan, who had known it under the name of "I winna ha'e tailor or sutor." Like almost all the airs collected in Aberdeenshire by the Dean, it has a second part ; this, while showing the fertility of invention of our northern ballad singers, rather disturbs our ideas of the antiquity of their versions.

· AULD ROB MORRIS.

ARRANGED BY J. T. SURENNE.

♩ = 80

MODERATO.

There's auld Rob Mor - ris, that wons[1] in yon glen, He's the king o' guid[2] fel - lows, and wale[3] o' auld men; He has gowd[4] in his cof - fers, he has ow - sen⁵ and kine, And ae bon - nie las - sie, his

dar - ling and mine.

dim.

mf

p

She's fresh as the morning, the fairest in May;
She's sweet as the ev'ning amang the new hay;
As blythe and as artless as the lamb on the lea,
And dear to my heart as the light to the e'e.

But O! she's an heiress—auld Robin's a laird,
And my daddie⁶ has nocht but a cot-house and yard;
A wooer like me maunna⁷ hope to come speed;
The wounds I must hide that will soon be my dead.⁸

The day comes to me, but delight brings me nane;
The night comes to me, but my rest it is gane;
I wander my lane⁹ like a night-troubled ghaist,¹⁰
And I sigh as my heart it wad¹¹ burst in my breast.

O had she but been of a lower degree,
I then might ha'e hoped she wad smiled upon me;
O, how past descriving¹² had then been my bliss,
As now my distraction no words can express.

| ¹ Dwells. | ² Good. | ³ Choice. | ⁴ Gold. | ⁵ Oxen. | ⁶ Father. |
| ⁷ Must not. | ⁸ Death. | ⁹ Lone. | ¹⁰ Ghost. | ¹¹ Would. | ¹² Describing. |

"AULD ROB MORRIS." This air appears in tablature in the Leyden MS. Lyra-Viol Book, mentioned in the Introduction to this work. It differs a little from the sets given by Johnson and others. The set adopted by the arranger for this work is nearly the one given in Watts' Musical Miscellany, 1730. The neglect of the ordinary compass of voices, alluded to in a previous Note, again occurs here. The air was published in the Orpheus Caledonius, in 1725, and in Watts' Musical Miscellany, 1730, vol. iii. p. 174, and in Craig's Select Scottish Tunes, printed in the same year. Mr. D. Laing notices the air as occurring in Mr. Blaikie's M.S., dated 1692, under the name of "Jock the Laird's Brother." In November 1792, Burns wrote for the air the words here given. The first two lines only belong to the old ballad given in Allan Ramsay's Tea-Table Miscellany.

O SWEET ARE THY BANKS, BONNIE TWEED!

AIR. "TWEEDSIDE."

ARRANGED BY J. T. SURENNE.

O sweet are thy banks, bonnie Tweed, An' sweet-er the mays* wha there

hide; But sweet-est of a' is the lass Wha hauds fast my

heart on Tweed - side! She's brown as the ba - zel nut ripe; She's

* Maids

grace - fu' as young bir - ken tree; Her smile's like the glint o' spring

dawn, 'Boon a' she is dear - est to me!

I woo'd her when puirtith's cauld hand
  Lay sair on hersel' an' her kin ;
But though I had plenty o' gear,
  She ay said, " My tocher's to win !"

O sweet are thy banks, bonnie Tweed !
  And sweeter the mays wha there bide ;
But sweetest of a' is the lass
  Wha hauds fast my heart on Tweedside !

"TWEEDSIDE." The composer of this old and beautiful Scottish melody is unknown. Some persons, upon no foundation of evidence, have given to David Rizzio the credit of its composition. In the last century, James Oswald, a very unscrupulous man, ascribed several of our Scottish melodies to Rizzio, for the purpose of enhancing the value of his collections of Scottish airs in the eyes of the public. That Oswald frequently passed off his own tunes in private as the compositions of Rizzio, we learn from the following lines of a poem printed in the Scots Magazine, 1741 :—

    " When wilt thou teach our soft Æidian [Edinian ?] fair
    To languish at a false Sicilian air ;
    Or when some tender tune compose again,
    And cheat the town wi' David Rizo's name ?"

In some of his publications, however, Oswald did not scruple to claim these airs as his own. In consequence of this double mystification, old airs with the name of Rizzio attached to them came also to be considered as compositions of Oswald ; and we are even told by his deceived relatives, (Museum Introduction, p. li.) that "The airs in this volume (second Collection) with the name of David Rizo affixed, are all Oswald's ; I state this on the authority of Mrs. Alexander Cumming and my mother—his daughter and sister." Signed, "H. O. Weatherly." That most of these airs were in existence before Oswald was born, can be proved from MSS. and printed works. Besides, Oswald's own compositions want the simplicity of the old airs, and do not rise above mediocrity. Consequently, not even one of them has taken its place among the popular melodies of Scotland.

In Dr. Leyden's MS. Lyra-Viol Book, referred to in the Introduction to this work, we find (No. 75) a set of "Twide Syde," differing in some respects from the more modern sets, especially in the close. That close, which seems to us more truly Scottish in character, we have given in the present edition ; while those who prefer a different close, may adopt either of those given in the symphony and ritornel. These are likewise old, and are much better than the ordinary minuet closes adopted during last century, and which are still allowed to disfigure all modern versions of the air. A set of "Tweedside," differing little from the modern sets of the air, appears in a work of the famous Florentine violinist, F. M. Veracini, pp. 67-69, with variations. This is the first instance we have seen of a Scottish air introduced in the violin solos of any old Italian violinist. The air is not *named* in Veracini's work, but is merely indicated as "Scozzese," i. e. Scottish. This work of Veracini, which is now very rare, is entitled "Sonate Accademiche a violino solo e basso," &c., and is dedicated to the King of Poland. The verses here given were written for this work by a friend of the publishers.

O THE EWE-BUGHTING'S BONNIE.

AIR.—" THE YELLOW-HAIR'D LADDIE."   ARRANGED BY T. M. MUDIE.

O the ewe - bught - ing's bon - nie, both e'e - ning and morn, When our blithe shepherds play on the bog - reed and horn ; While we're milk - ing they're lilt - ing sae jo - cund and clear ; But my heart's like to break when I think on my

dear !

O the shepherds take pleasure to blow on the horn,
To raise up their flocks i' the fresh simmer morn :
On the steep ferny banks they feed pleasant and free—
But alas ! my dear heart, all my sighing's for thee !

O the sheep-herding's lightsome amang the green braes,
Where Cayle wimples clear 'neath the white-blossomed slaes,
Where the wild-thyme and meadow-queen scent the saft gale,
And the cushat croods leesomely down in the dale.

There the lintwhite and mavis sing sweet frae the thorn,
And blithe lilts the laverock abune the green corn.
And a' things rejoice in the simmer's glad prime—
But my heart's wi' my love in the far foreign clime.

"THE YELLOW-HAIR'D LADDIE." Mr. G. Farquhar Graham, a very competent judge, says the present form of the air is "probably not older than about the end of the seventeenth century." The florid and somewhat refined style of the melody sufficiently show this. But it appears to be more than probable that there existed an earlier, simpler, and more Scottish version. That our airs lost much of their simple pathos between the reigns of Charles I. and George I. we know, by examples found in the Skene and other MSS., such as the old "Flowers of the Forest," "Sae merrie as we ha'e been," and others. Mr. Wm. Chappell, in his excellent notes to the Ballad Society's edition of the Roxburgh Ballads (Rox. Coll. ii. 76, Ballad Soc. rep. ix. 1880), points out that "The countryman's care in choosing a wife" is to be sung to the tune of "I'll have one I love," or, "The yellow-hair'd laddie," and that as Brooksby, who printed the broadside, dates from 1672 to 1695, we have here a proof of the air having been popularly known in England long before it was claimed for Scotland. This is so far undeniable ; we have no copy either of the air or of the song quite so early ; but in Allan Ramsay's Tea-Table Miscellany (1724), besides several contemporary songs to the tune, we have "The auld yellow-hair'd laddie," which begins,

"The yellow-hair'd laddie sat down on yon brae,
Cries, milk the ewes, lassie, let nane of them gae."

This is evidently the song that gave its name to the air, and must therefore have existed with its tune before Brooksby printed his ballad ; indeed probably nearer to the times of James VI. than of James VII. The first eight lines of the song are by Lady Grizel Baillie (before 1692), and might almost be cited as a proof of her familiarity with the air ; for though it cannot be said with any certainty that they were written expressly for it, yet both in measure and in sentiment they suit it exactly, even the subject being the same as that of the old song. In modern days the measure is not uncommon, but I know only one other pastoral air of Lady Grizel's time that would suit it, namely, "My apron, dearie." Her fragment was completed by Thomas Pringle, a poet of Roxburghshire (1789-1834). He added many more stanzas, but the additional eight lines are quite sufficient for singing.

WHAT AILS THIS HEART O' MINE?

AIR, "MY DEARIE, AN' THOU DEE."   ARRANGED BY T. M. MUDIE.

poco rall. What ails this heart o' mine? What ails this wa - t'ry e'e? What

gars[1] me a' turn cauld as death When I take leave o' thee? When thou art far a - wa' Thou'lt

dear - er grow to me; But change o' place an' change o' folk May gar thy fan - cy jee.[2]

When I gae out at e'en,
    Or walk at morning air,
Ilk[2] rustling bush will seem to say
    I used to meet thee there.
Then I'll sit down and cry,
    And live aneath the tree,
And when a leaf fa's in my lap
    I'll ca't a word frae thee.

I'll hie me to the bower
    That thou wi' roses tied
And where wi' mony a blushing bud
    I strove mysel' to hide.

I'll doat on ilka spot
    Where I ha'e been wi' thee,
And ca' to mind some kindly word
    By ilka burn and tree!

Wi' sic thoughts i' my mind,
    Time through the world may gae,
And find my heart in twenty years
    The same as 'tis to-day.
'Tis thoughts that bind the soul,
    And keep friends i' the e'e;
And gin I think I see thee aye.
    What can part thee and me!

¹ Make; cause.   ² Move; change.   ³ Each.

"WHAT AILS THIS HEART O' MINE?" The words are by Miss Susanna Blamire. The melody is old, and was formerly called, "My dearie, an' thou dee:" it appears in its simpler form in the Leyden MS. Mr. Patrick Maxwell, in his edition of Miss Blamire's poems, 1842, informs us, that she was born at Cardew Hall, Cumberland, on 12th January 1747; that she passed a good deal of her time in Scotland—her eldest sister, Sarah, having married Colonel Graham of Duchray in 1767; and that she died at Carlisle on 5th April 1794. Mr. Maxwell says of her:—"She had a graceful form, somewhat above the middle size, and a countenance, though slightly marked with the small-pox, beaming with good nature; her dark eyes sparkled with animation, and won every heart at the first introduction. She was called by her affectionate countrymen, 'a bonnie and varra lish young lass,'—which may be interpreted as meaning a beautiful and very lively young girl. Her affability and total freedom from affectation put to flight that reserve which her presence was apt to create in the minds of her humbler associates; for they quickly perceived that she really wished them happiness, and aided in promoting it by every effort in her power. She freely mingled in their social parties, called *merry neets*, in Cumberland; and by her graceful figure, elegant dancing, and kind-hearted gaiety, gave a zest to the entertainments, which, without her presence, would have been wanting."

In an earlier note we had occasion to animadvert on the share that James Oswald had taken in the promulgation of a belief that Rizzio was the composer of some of our old Scottish melodies. Since writers, who ought to have acquired better information, have not only re-echoed Oswald's mis-statement, but have, besides, asserted that Rizzio was the originator of the Scottish style of melody, we consider it our duty to examine the question thoroughly, with the view of bringing it to a true conclusion. This will require more space than can be afforded to any single Note; we shall therefore present our materials in such paragraphs as they may naturally fall into. How or when such a belief originated, may be difficult to determine; but certainly there are no traces of it for a century and a-half after Rizzio's death. During all that time there is no historical hint that Rizzio ever composed anything in any style of music; and not a vestige of any music, sacred or secular, is ascribed to him. Tassoni, his countryman, (born in 1565, the year of Rizzio's murder,) speaking of music, says, that James, King of Scotland, invented a new and plaintive style of melody. Whether this assertion be correct or not, is of no consequence to our present inquiry. In either case Tassoni's assertion is sufficient to show, not only that no claim had till then been set up in favour of Rizzio, but also, that an earlier origin was then assigned to Scottish melody. We here exclude from consideration James VI., as he was King of England long before Tassoni died, (1635); and we consider it probable that James I. was meant—he at least being known to have included music among his accomplishments, and being said to have been an excellent performer on the lute, the harp, and other instruments.

G

THOU ART GANE AWA'.

ARRANGED BY T. M. MUDIE.

Thou art gane a - wa', thou'rt gane a - wa', Thou art gane a - wa' frae me, Ma - ry! Nor friends nor I could make thee stay; Thou hast cheat - ed them an' me, Ma - ry! Un - til this hour I ne - ver thought That ought could al - ter

Whate'er he said or might pretend,
    That stole that heart o' thine, Mary,
True love, I'm sure, was ne'er his end,
    Or nae sic love as mine, Mary.
I spoke sincere, nor flatter'd much,
    Nae selfish thought's in me, Mary,
Ambition, wealth, nor naething such;
    No, I loved only thee, Mary!

Though you've been false, yet while I live,
    I'll lo'e nae maid but thee, Mary;
Let friends forget, as I forgive,
    Thy wrongs to them and me, Mary;
So then, farewell! o' this be sure,
    Since you've been false to me, Mary:
For a' the world I'd not endure
    Half what I've done for thee, Mary

"THOU ART GANE AWA'." This melody is evidently derived from the old Scottish air "Haud awa' frae me, Donald," which was published in Playford's "Dancing Master," under the title of "Welcome home, old Rowley," not, however, in 1657, as asserted by Stenhouse, but in the ninth edition of that work, published in 1690. It affords an example of the remodelling of old airs, to which we shall have frequent occasion to advert in future Notes.

The melody, as here given, is nearly the same as that published by Pietro Urbani at Edinburgh, in his Collection of Scottish Airs, etc., about the close of the last century. Some of his redundant embellishments have been omitted. Urbani, a good singer and a good musician, had the merit of being the first person who attempted, at great cost, to get up some of Handel's Oratorios in Edinburgh and Glasgow in 1802; but the meritorious attempt was not encouraged, and Urbani was ruined. He afterwards went to reside in Dublin, and died there in 1816. The author of the verses is not known. They were printed anonymously in Urbani's Collection and in Johnson's Museum.

As the transformation which the old air has undergone is curious, we subjoin it in the same key as the new air to facilitate comparison.

OH! THOU ART ALL SO TENDER.

AIR. " MY LOVE HAS FORSAKEN ME."   ARRANGED BY T. M. MUDIE.

Oh! thou art all so ten - der, so love - ly, and mild, The

heart can ne - ver wan - der, which thou hast be - guiled.

Pure as the calm e - mo - tion of half re - mem - ber'd

Though long and deep my sorrow, all lonely thus may be,
Oh! still my heart shall borrow a ray of joy from thee;
To thee the charms seem given of earth that never sprung,
The melting hymns of heaven are round thy spirit sung.

Then let thy form be near me, that I that form may see,
I've tried to live, but eerie, I cannot live from thee;
Nor grudge deep kindness either, to sooth me when I sigh,
I know thou'lt give it rather than thou would'st see me die.

Though mine thou may'st be never, and ceaseless woes betide,
Still nought on earth shall ever my love from thee divide;
My mind may cease to cherish the hope of bliss to be,
But of the hopes that perish the last shall breathe of thee.

"OH! THOU ART ALL SO TENDER." This song was written by the Rev. Henry Scott Riddell, and is here repub-lished by his express permission. The air is that given in Johnson's Museum, vol. ii., under the name of "My love has forsaken me," and which is stated, by Mr. Stenhouse, to have been furnished for the Museum by Doctor Blacklock, about the close of 1787. It has somewhat of a Gaelic cast, and from the simplicity of its style, and the tonality on which it is composed, we would pronounce it to be considerably older than Dr. Blacklock's time.

As a preliminary to the consideration of Rizzio's alleged authorship of many Scottish melodies, we subjoin a few particulars of his life. We are told by Chalmers that David Rizzio* was born at Turin, of poor parents; and that he came to Scotland in the suite of the Piedmontese Ambassador, towards the end of the year 1561. Soon afterwards he entered the service of Queen Mary, for we find that on the 8th January 1561-2, he received £50 Scots, as "virlet of the Queen's chalmer;" and again, three months later, £15, as "chalmer-chield," (page or usher.) The account given of his entrance into the Queen's household, is, that a fourth singer was occasionally wanted to take a part in the performance of madrigals and other concerted vocal music, and that he, having a good voice and being skilled in music, was engaged to fill the situation. In this position he seems to have remained for several years, for in 1564 we find that four payments were made to him at the rate of £80 a-year, still as "virlet." In 1565, the Queen's French Secretary having been dismissed, Rizzio was appointed to succeed him, but did not long enjoy his new office, as he was murdered about the close of the same year, (9th March); having thus been little more than four years in the country.

* Or rather Riccio; for thus Queen Mary spells the name in writing an account of the murder to the Archbishop of Glasgow, then her Ambassador at the Court of France.

ON ETTRICK BANKS.

ARRANGED BY J. T. SURENNE.

On Et - trick banks ae sim - mer nicht, At gloam - in' when the

sheep gaed hame, I met my las - sie braw and ticht, While wand'ring through the

mist her lane.¹ My heart grew licht. I want - ed lang To

tell my las - sie a' my mind, And ne - ver till this hap - py hour, A

can - nie⁵ meet - ing could I find.

Said I, My lassie, will ye gae
  To the Highland hills and be my bride?
I'll bigg³ thy bower beneath the brae,
  By sweet Loch Garry's silver tide.
And aft as o'er the moorlands wide,
  Kind gloamin' comes our faulds to steek,⁴
I'll hasten down the green hill side,
  Where curls our cozy cottage reek.

All day when we ha'e wrought eneuch,
  When winter frosts and snaws begin,
Sune as the sun gaes west the loch,
  At nicht when ye sit down to spin,
I'll screw my pipes, and play a spring,
  And thus the weary nicht we'll end,
Till the tender kid and lamb-time bring
  Our pleasant simmer back again.

Syne when the trees are in their bloom,
  And gowans glent⁵ o'er ilka field,
I'll meet my lass among the broom,
  And lead her to my simmer shield;
There, far frae a' their scornfu' din,
  That make the kindly hearts their sport,
We'll laugh, and kiss, and dance, and sing,
  And gar the langest day seem short!

¹ Alone.   ² Quiet; favourable.   ³ Build.   ⁴ Close; shut up.   ⁵ Peep out; or shine.

"ON ETTRICK BANKS." Mr. Stenhouse's Note upon this song and air is as follows :—"This is another of those delightful old pastoral melodies which has been a favourite during many generations. It is inserted in the Orpheus Caledonius in 1725, with the same elegant stanzas that appear in the Museum, beginning, 'On Ettrick banks, ae summer's night.' Ramsay has left no key to discover the author of the song: it does not appear, however, to be his; and indeed it is not claimed by his biographer as his composition. In the Museum, the fourth line of stanza first, in place of 'Came wading barefoot a' her lane,' was changed into 'While wand'ring through the mist her lane;' but I do not consider it any improvement on the elegant simplicity of the original. . . . The Ettrick, of such poetical celebrity, is a river in Selkirkshire; it rises in the parish of the same name, and after a winding course of thirty miles in a north-east direction, during which it receives the Yarrow near Philiphaugh, falls into the Tweed three miles above Melrose." See Museum Illustrations, vol. i. pp. 85, 86. The first stanza has here been slightly, and the second entirely altered, in order to suit modern requirements.

THE GLOOMY NIGHT IS GATH'RING FAST.

AIR, "HUGHIE GRAHAM."

ARRANGED BY J. T. SURENNE.

The gloom - y night is ga - th'ring fast, Loud roars the

wild in - con - stant blast, Yon mur - ky cloud is

foul with rain, I see it driv - ing o'er the

The hunter now has left the moor,
The scatter'd coveys meet secure,
While here I wander, press'd with care,
Along the lonely banks of Ayr.

The autumn mourns her ripening corn
By early winter's ravage torn;
Across her placid azure sky
She sees the scowling tempest fly:

Chill rins my blood to hear it rave—
I think upon the stormy wave,
Where many a danger I must dare,
Far from the bonnie banks of Ayr.

'Tis not the surging billows' roar,
'Tis not that fatal, deadly shore;
Though death in every shape appear,
The wretched have no more to fear:

But round my heart the ties are bound,
That heart transpierced with many a wound;
These bleed afresh, those ties I tear,
To leave the bonnie banks of Ayr.

Farewell, old Coila's hills and dales,
Her heathy moors and winding vales;
The scene where wretched fancy roves,
Pursuing past, unhappy loves!

Farewell, my friends, farewell, my foes,
My peace with these, my love with those;
The bursting tears my heart declare;
Farewell, the bonnie banks of Ayr.

"THE GLOOMY NIGHT IS GATH'RING FAST." "I composed this song," says Burns, "as I convoyed my chest so far on the road to Greenock, where I was to embark in a few days for Jamaica. I meant it as my farewell dirge to my native land."—*Reliques.* This was in 1786. It appears that this song was set to music by his friend Mr. Allan Masterton, a Writing-master in Edinburgh. Masterton's air is mediocre enough, and is singularly unvocal and ill-suited to the words in the first part of the second strain. At that period, and long before, as well as long after, most of the amateur musicians in Great Britain were men who could merely play a little on some musical instrument, or sing a little, without any farther knowledge of music, or cultivation of their own musical capabilities, whatever these might be. Hence so many very indifferent Scottish melodies that infest our printed musical collections; mere imitations, and mostly affected and bad ones, of the better and more ancient Scottish airs; combining want of knowledge of musical composition with want of feeling and judgment.

The air to which Burns' words are given in this work, is found in Oswald's Caledonian Pocket Companion, under the name of "Drimon Duff;" in the Museum, vol. iv., it is set to the Border ballad, "Hughie Graham." We believe it to be an old Highland air, and that its original title was "Drumion dubh," or "The black cow." Whatever its origin or its antiquity, it is undoubtedly Scottish, and is a very good and characteristic melody. For the old ballad of "Hughie Graham," see Minstrelsy of the Scottish Border, vol. iii. edit. 1833.

We now return to Rizzio. From what we have already stated, and from what follows, we are inclined to believe that Rizzio's name was first connected with Scottish melody by his countrymen who were in England about the beginning of last century. We know that Italian music was then fashionable in London, and that Scottish song divided the public taste with it. Whether the flowing style of melody peculiar to the Lowland pastoral airs induced the belief that an Italian only could have written them, we do not pretend to say, but it is certain that Rizzio was first heard of as a composer in 1725, when Thomson published his Orpheus Caledonius. In this there are seven airs ascribed to Rizzio; "An thou wert mine ain thing," "Bessie Bell," "Auld Rob Morris," "The boatman," "The bush aboon Traquair," "The lass o' Patie's mill," and "Down the burn Davie;" of these at least three certainly had not existed much above half a century, and the last was probably a very recent composition. Such is the earliest evidence in favour of Rizzio, and slight as it is, its authority is considerably lessened by the fact, that in the second edition of the Orpheus Caledonius, (1733,) Thomson, perhaps taking shame to himself for having been an accessory to the imposture, suppressed Rizzio's name entirely.

THE LASS OF PATIE'S MILL.

ARRANGED BY G. F. GRAHAM.

The lass of Pa - tie's mill, So bon - nie, blythe, and gay, In spite of all my skill, She stole my heart a - way. When ted - ding of the hay, Bare -

head - ed on the green, Love 'midst her locks did play, And

wan - ton'd in her een.

Without the help of art,
  Like flow'rs which grace the wild,
She did her sweets impart,
  Whene'er she spoke or smiled.
Her looks they were so mild,
  Free from affected pride,
She me to love beguiled ;
  I wish'd her for my bride.

O ! had I all that wealth
  Hopetoun's high mountains[1] fill,
Insured long life and health,
  And pleasure at my will ;
I'd promise and fulfil
  That none but bonnie she,
The lass of Patie's mill,
  Should share the same with me.

[1] The Lead-hills, belonging to the Earl of Hopetoun.

"THE LASS OF PATIE'S MILL." Mr. Stenhouse, in his Note upon No. 20 of the Museum, gives a romantic account of the heroine of this song, from the Statistical Account of Scotland, which the reader may consult, if curious in matters so uncertain as old family traditions of the sixteenth century. From that account we learn that she was the only daughter of John Anderson, Esq., of Patie's Mill, in the parish of Keith-hall, and county of Aberdeen. That she was very beautiful and accomplished, and a rich heiress in prospect. That a Mr. Sangster, the Laird of Boddom, tried to carry off Miss Anderson, clandestinely, about the year 1550, and was disappointed, and soundly drubbed by her father. That she afterwards married a Mr. Anderson, who "composed a song in her praise, the air of which only is now preserved." All this may be true, or not ; but Mr. Stenhouse's assertion, that "the air as has been shown, is at least as old as the middle of the sixteenth century," cannot be received without written or printed evidence in musical notation ; of which there is not a shadow. The air, No. 20 of Johnson's Museum, is very unlike a Scottish air of "the middle of the sixteenth century." So is the set given in the first volume of John Watts' "Musical Miscellany," London, 1729, page 97 ; while that set differs materially from Johnson's. All the sets of the air that we have seen, bear internal evidence—from certain passages and cadences—of modern structure, not earlier than the commencement of the eighteenth century. It is surprising that Mr. Stenhouse did not perceive this. Mr. Stenhouse adds, in his Note on this song and air, "Allan Ramsay adapted his modern words to the old melody, and transferred the heroine of his muse to the parish of Galston, in the county of Ayr, where a mill with a similar name was existing. Burns gives us the following account of this translocation, upon the authority of Sir William Cunningham of Robertland, Baronet, to whom the anecdote was communicated by the late John, Earl of Loudon :—'The then Earl of Loudon, father of Earl John before-mentioned, had Ramsay at Loudon, and one day walking by the banks of Irvine water, near New-Mills, at a place yet called Patie's Mill, they were struck with the appearance of a beautiful country girl. His Lordship observed that she would be a fine theme for a song. Allan lagged behind in returning to Loudon Castle, and at dinner produced this identical song.' "—Burns's Reliques.

In this work the second stanza of Ramsay's song is omitted, for very obvious reasons.

LOGIE O' BUCHAN.

ARRANGED BY J. M MUDIE.

O Lo - gie o' Buch - an, O Lo - gie the laird, They ha'e ta'en a - wa' Ja - mie, that delved in the yard, Wha play'd on the pipe, an' the vi - ol sae sma'; They hae ta'en a - wa' Ja - mie, the flow'r o' them a'. He said, Think na lang,[1] lass-ie, tho' I gang a - wa'; For I'll come an'

see thee in spite o' them a'.

Though Sandie has owsen, has gear, and has kye,
A house, an' a hadden,[2] an' siller forbye,
Yet I'd tak' my ain lad, wi' his staff in his hand,
Before I'd ha'e him, wi' his houses an' land.
But simmer is comin', cauld winter's awa',
An' he'll come an' see me in spite o' them a'.

My daddie looks sulky, my minnie looks sour.
They gloom upon Jamie because he is puir :
Though I lo'e them as weel as a daughter should do,
They are no half so dear to me, Jamie, as you.
He said, Think na lang, lassie, tho' I gang awa',
For I'll come an' see thee in spite o' them a'

I sit on my creepie,[3] an' spin at my wheel,
An' think on the laddie that lo'es me sae weel;
He had but ae saxpence, he brak it in twa,
An' he ga'e me the half o't when he gaed awa'.
But the simmer is comin', cauld winter's awa',
Then haste ye back, Jamie, an' bide na awa'

[1] Do not weary.   [2] The stocking of a farm : furniture of a house.   [3] A low foot-stool.

"LOGIE O' BUCHAN." The date of the verses may be among the earlier years of the last century. Mr. Peter Buchan, formerly of Peterhead, now of Glasgow, states, in his "Gleanings of scarce old Ballads," Peterhead, 1825, that it was written by George Halket, a schoolmaster at Rathen, in Aberdeenshire, who died in 1756. Halket was a great Jacobite, and wrote various pieces in support of his party : one of the best known of these is the song called "Whirry, Whigs, awa', man." Another, now lost, called "A Dialogue between the Devil and George II.," having fallen into the hands of the Duke of Cumberland, when on his way to Culloden, a reward of £100 was offered for the author, either dead or alive. The Logie mentioned in the song is situated in Crimond, a parish adjoining the one where Halket resided, and the hero of the piece was a James Robertson, gardener at the place (mansion-house) of Logie.—(G. F. G.)

The date of the air is not known ; but an old version of it is found in Atkinson's MS. (1694), under the name of "Tak tent to the ripells,[1] Gudeman ;" the Macfarlane MS. (1740) calls it "The ripells, Gudeman," and Oswald, "Beware of the ripells ;" it is probable, therefore, that this was a line of a song now lost. In Johnson's Museum a bad set of the air is given to rather ridiculous words, "The taylor fell through the bed, thimble and a';" Urbani's version of the air is not much better. Napier (1792) is the first who has given the melody in its present simple form. George Thomson somewhat hurt its simplicity by inserting a florid passage in the sixteenth bar, and in this has been followed in too many subsequent collections. The air is also known as "The March of the Corporation of Tailors," and was usually played at the annual meeting for choosing the deacons of the body.

[1] Jamieson explains "ripells" as palns in the back.

O WHA IS SHE THAT LO'ES ME.

AIR, "MORAG."   ARRANGED BY FINLAY DUN.

$\bullet = 100$

ADAGIO.

wha   is   she   that   lo'es   me,   An'   has   my   heart   in   keep - ing!   O

sweet   is   she   that   lo'es   me,   As   dews   o'   sim - mer   weep - ing,   In

tears   the   rose - buds   steep - ing!   O   that's the   las - sie   o'   my   heart,   My las - sie e - ver dear - er; O that's the queen o' wo - man - kind, An'

ne'er a ane to peer her.

If thou shalt meet a lassie
In grace and beauty charming,
That e'en thy chosen lassie,
Erewhile thy breast sae warming,
Had ne'er sic powers alarming.
O that's the lassie o' my heart. &c.

If thou hadst heard her talking,
An' thy attentions plighted,
That ilka body talking
But her by thee is slighted,
An' thou art all delighted.
O that's the lassie o' my heart, &c.

If thou hast met this fair one;
When frae her thou hast parted,
If every other fair one,
But her, thou hast deserted,
An' thou art broken-hearted:
O that's the lassie o' my heart, &c.

"O WHA IS SHE THAT LO'ES ME." This song was written by Burns for the Gaelic air called "Morag," which is the Highland name for Marion. Burns was so fond of the air, that, in 1787, he wrote two other songs for it. One beginning "Loud blaw the frosty breezes," and the other, "Streams that glide in orient plains." The latter is less of a *song* than of stanzas in praise of Castle-Gordon, and in vituperation of Oriental despotism. "In Fraser's Gaelic airs, lately published, is another set of 'Morag,' in which the sharp seventh is twice introduced, in place of the perfect fifth, along with a variety of notes, graces, and a *ritardando*, not to be found in any of the older sets of this air, and which indeed are equally superfluous, as well as foreign to the genuine spirit of ancient Gaelic melodies." See Museum Illustrations, vol. ii. pp. 134-136. We may remark that in Fraser's set of "Morag," No. 119, p. 57, the members of the air do not occur in the same order as in Johnson's set. They are transposed. Also, that the sharp seventh occurs twice in the notes of *embellishment*, as well as twice in the principal notes of the air. Allan Cunningham, in his edition of Burns' works, makes the following remarks upon the song "O wha is she that lo'es me," and its air "Morag:" "Of the air of 'Morag' Burns was passionately fond; yet it cannot be said that he was more than commonly successful in wedding it to words. The measure which the tune requires is cramp and difficult, and the sentiment is interrupted before it has well begun to flow. This song was found among the papers of Burns; the exact period of its composition is not known, nor has the heroine been named."

O TRUE LOVE IS A BONNIE FLOWER.

AIR, "TWINE WEEL THE PLAIDEN."   ARRANGED BY T. M. MUDIE.

$\flat = 69$

ANDANTE CON
ESPRESSIONE.

true love is a bon - nie flow'r, That buds in ma-ny a bo-som; But pride's cauld blast will

nip its bloom, And wi - ther il - ka blossom. A - las! I've lost my luck-less heart, And

rall.   a tempo.

o' this life I'm wea - ry; Wi' a' on earth I'd eith - ly part, But

colla voce.

no   wi'   thee, my   dea - rie.

When first I saw thy bonnie face,
Love's pawkie glances won me;
Now could neglect, and studied scorn,
Have fatally undone me!
Alas! I've lost, &c.

Were our fond vows but empty air,
And made but to be broken?
That ringlet of thy raven hair,
Was't but a faithless token?
Alas! I've lost, &c.

In vain I've tried each artfu' wile,
That's practised by the lover,
But nought, alas, when once it's lost,
Affection can recover.
Then break, my poor deluded heart,
That never can be cheerie;
But while life's current there shall flow,
Sae lang I'll lo'e my dearie!

"O TRUE LOVE IS A BONNIE FLOWER." Air, "Twine weel the plaiden." Speaking of the verses to this air in Johnson's Museum, beginning, "O! I have lost my silken snood," Mr. Stenhouse says, "I remember an old lady who sang these verses to a very plaintive and simple air, in slow treble time, a copy of which, but corrupted with embellishments, appears in Oswald's Collection, No. 12, under the title of 'The lassie lost her silken snood.' Napier, who first published the song, being unacquainted, perhaps, with the original melody, adapted the verses to the same air which is inserted in Johnson's Museum. This song, though undoubtedly of considerable antiquity, is neither to be found in the Orpheus Caledonius, nor in Ramsay's Tea-Table Miscellany." See Museum Illustrations, vol. i. p. 29.* The excellent verses now given in this collection were written by Captain Charles Gray, R.M.—a well known veteran in poetry, as well as in warfare; and one of the ablest of modern Scottish poets. This gentleman has of late done much to rectify mistakes regarding the songs of Robert Burns, as well as the character of that extraordinary and unfortunate man. Captain Gray's verses were written at the request of a Fifeshire lady,† with whom this air was a favourite, but who did not choose to sing the old words given in the Collections of Johnson and others, as she considered them objectionable. We have been informed that this air was a great favourite with P. Urbani, who used frequently to sing it at his benefit concerts.

* Napier's Selection of Scottish Songs, first volume, was published in 1790. The airs were harmonized by Dr. Samuel Arnold, William Shield, F. H. Barthelemon, and Thomas Carter. His second volume of Scottish Songs was published in 1792; the airs harmonized by Joseph Haydn alone. In the first volume, page 26, is "Twine weel the plaiden," harmonized by Barthelemon, who was a singular character, and a Swedenborgian.

† The publishers have to acknowledge the kindness of Captain Gray in permitting them to grace their work with these verses, which are now for the first time printed in connexion with the air to which they are so admirably suited.

H

MY NANNIE, O.

ARRANGED BY T. M. MUDIE.

Be - hind yon hills where Lugar flows, 'Mang muirs and moss - es ma - ny, O, The win - try sun the day has closed, And I'll a - wa' to Nan - nie, O. The westlin wind blaws loud and shrill, The night's baith mirk and rain - y, O; But I'll get my plaid, and out I'll steal, And o'er the hills to

Nan - nie, O.

My Nannie's charming, sweet, and young;
Nae artfu' wiles to win ye, O:
May ill befa' the flattering tongue
That wad beguile my Nannie, O!
Her face is fair, her heart is true,
As spotless as she's bonnie, O;
The opening gowan wat wi' dew
Nae purer is than Nannie, O.

A country lad is my degree,
And few there be that ken me, O:
But what care I how few they be?
I'm welcome aye to Nannie, O.
My riches a's my penny fee,
And I maun guide it cannie, O:
But warld's gear ne'er troubles me,
My thoughts are a' my Nannie, O.

Our auld gudeman delights to view
His sheep and kye thrive bonnie, O;
But I'm as blythe that hauds his plough,
And has nae care but Nannie, O.
Come weel, come wae, I carena by,
I'll tak' what heaven will send me, O;
Nae ither care in life hae I,
But live and love my Nannie, O.

"MY NANNIE, O." Mr. Stenhouse characterizes the melody as a "fine old air," and Mr. G. Farquhar Graham adds, "it is indeed one of the best of our Scottish melodies." Mr. Chappell, on the other hand, believes it to be English, and points out that in the Roxburghe Collection there is a Northumbrian ballad, "Willy and Nanny: to a pleasant new tune, or Nanny, O." This merely proves, however, that "Nanny, O" was then a well-known air in Northumberland, but without showing on which side of the border it originated. We should remember that there was once a Debateable Land, and we should not forget that the melodies sung, both to the north and south of it, may often be equally debateable. The people had the same origin and much the same tastes; they were equally ready to meet each other with sword and spear in the morning, and over the wine-cup and with song at night.

The verses here given were written by Burns in 1783; and it has generally been said on Agnes Fleming, a farmer's daughter in Tarbolton parish. Mrs. Begg, however, Burns's youngest sister, alledges that this is a mistake, and that Peggy Thomson was the real heroine of the song. See Captain Charles Gray on the heroines of Burns's songs.

In deference to modern prejudices the major seventh is used in the seventh and fifteenth bars of the air, but the B flat of the old tonality is really much finer, and is more in keeping with the antique style of the tune.

LOGAN WATER.

ARRANGED BY T. M. MUDIE.

By Logan's streams, that rin sae deep, Fu' aft wi' glee I've herd - ed sheep; Herd - ed sheep, or ga - ther'd slaes, Wi' my dear lad on Lo - gan braes. But waes my heart! thae days are gane, And, fu' o' grief, I herd my lane, While my dear lad maun face his faes, Far, far frae me and

Lo - gan braes.

Nae mair, at Logan kirk, will he,
Atween the preachings, meet wi' me—
Meet wi' me, or, when it's mirk,
Convoy me hame frae Logan kirk.
I weel may sing, thae days are gane;
Frae kirk and fair I come alane,
While my dear lad maun face his faes,
Far, far frae me and Logan braes.

At e'en, when hope amaist is gane,
I daunder dowie an' forlane,[1]
Or sit beneath the trystin'-tree,
Where first he spak' o' love to me.
O! could I see thae days again,
My lover skaithless,[2] an' my ain;
Rever'd by friends, an' far frae faes,
We'd live in bliss on Logan braes!

[1] I wander melancholy and alone.

[2] Unharmed.

"LOGAN WATER." The melody is of considerable antiquity; pathetic, and very Scottish in its character. In the second strain of some printed sets, we find F♯ twice introduced instead of F♮. The F♯ is very clearly a modern interpolation; especially in the second measure of the second strain, where it occurs in the difficult and unvocal form of a leap from F♮ to the augmented octave above, F♯. In William Napier's Collection, 1790, we find (p. 17) the same air harmonized by F. H. Barthelemon, the celebrated French violinist. It is there in A minor, and G, the seventh of the scale, is, throughout, G♮. In some other sets, (M'Gibbon's and Oswald's,) the seventh of the scale is also minor throughout. We give the melody as it appears in older sets, and as it agrees with the true old Scottish tonalities.

The excellent song here published to the air of "Logan Water," was written by John Mayne, a native of Dumfries, who, in his earlier years, served an apprenticeship as a compositor to the Messrs. Foulis, the celebrated Glasgow printers. He afterwards went to London, and there was connected for many years with the "Star" newspaper. He was born in 1759, and died on the 14th March 1836. In the Preface to the edition of Mayne's poem, "The Siller Gun," London, 1836, dedicated to King William IV., we find a kind critical letter from the late talented Lord Woodhouselee, one of the Scottish Lords of Session, to John Mayne, dated 6th October 1808; and Mayne's interesting answer to that letter, of date, London, 19th December 1808. From this we quote what Mayne himself says regarding some of his poems, and his ballad of "Logan Water:"—"You wish to know, my Lord, the names of such other pieces as I have written besides the poems of 'Glasgow,' and the 'Siller Gun.' There are but few of these in Scottish verse, and fewer still, I fear, that are worthy of your Lordship's notice. They consist generally of a single thought, suggested by the feeling and clothed in the language of the moment. The ballad of 'Logan Water' is of this description: it was written and circulated in Glasgow about the year 1781; inserted in the 'Star' newspaper, on Saturday the 23d of May 1789; thence copied and sung at Vauxhall, and published soon afterwards by a Music-dealer in the Strand."

Logan water, so famed in Scottish song, has its source among the hills which separate the parishes of Lesmahago and Muirkirk, in the south-west of Scotland; runs eastward for eight miles, and unites with the river Nethan.

KIND ROBIN LO'ES ME.

ARRANGED BY T. M. MUDIE.

Ro - bin is my on - ly joe, For Ro - bin has the art to lo'e, So

to his suit I mean to bow, Be - cause I ken he lo'es me.

Hap - py, hap - py, was the show'r That led me to his

bir - ken bow'r, Where first o' love I fand the pow'r, And

kend that Ro . bin lo'ed me.

The verses within brackets may be omitted.

[They speak of napkins, speak of rings,
Speak of gloves and kissing strings,
And name a thousand bonny things,
  And ca' them signs he lo'es me.
But I'd prefer a smack of Rob,
Sporting on the velvet fog,
To gifts as lang's a plaiden wab,
  Because I ken he lo'es me.]

He's tall and soncy, frank and free,
Lo'ed by a', and dear to me;
Wi' him I'd live, wi' him I'd dee,
  Because my Robin lo'es me!
My sister Mary, said to me,
Our courtship but a joke wad be,
And I, or lang, be made to see,
  That Robin did na lo'e me

But little kens she what has been
Me and my honest Rob between,
And in his wooing, O so keen
  Kind Robin is that lo'es me.
Then fly ye lazy hours away,
And hasten on the happy day,
When, "Join your hands," Mess John shall say,
  And mak' him mine that lo'es me.

[Till then let every chance unite,
To weigh our love, and fix delight,
And I'll look down on such wi' spite,
  Wha doubt that Robin lo'es me.
O hey, Robin, quo' she,
O hey, Robin, quo' she,
O hey, Robin, quo' she,
  Kind Robin lo'es me.]

"KIND ROBIN LO'ES ME." The words of this song, beginning "Robin is my only joo," were printed in David Herd's Ancient and Modern Songs, 1776. The tune bears marks of antiquity. Its composer is unknown. See Museum Illustrations, vol. v. p 421. The last four lines seem to be a fragment of an older song to the same air. They will not sing to the modern version of the air, and therefore it has been thought that the genuine old air also was lost. But we have met with an old version of the air, which proves that the only difference between it and the modern one consisted in the occasional dividing of one note into two, in order to suit the greater number of syllables in each line of the modern song. If the first, third, and fifth bars (measures) are each made to consist of two minims, and the first two crotchets of the seventh bar be changed into one minim, the air will then be found to suit the last four lines of the song. This version of the air was discovered in the Macfarlane MS., a Collection made for the Laird of Macfarlane about 1740-43, and now in the possession of the Society of Antiquaries of Scotland. It consisted of three folio volumes, the first of which has unfortunately been lost, and the second mutilated by the date upon it being torn away

JOCK O' HAZELDEAN.

ARRANGED BY J. T. SURENNE.

♩ = 100

MODERATO.

mf   *p*

"Why

weep ye by the tide, la-dye? Why weep ye by the tide? I'll wed ye to my

youngest son, And ye sall be his bride; And ye sall be his bride, ladye, Sae

poco rall.

come-ly to be seen;"— But aye she loot the tears down fa', For Jock o' Ha-zel-

p   *p*

colla voce.

"Now let this wilful grief be done,
And dry that check so pale:
Young Frank is chief of Errington,
And lord of Langley dale;
His step is first in peaceful ha',
His sword in battle keen:"—
But aye she loot the tears down fa',
For Jock o' Hazeldean.

"A chain o' gold ye sall not lack,
Nor braid to bind your hair,
Nor mettled hound, nor managed hawk,
Nor palfrey fresh and fair;
And you, the foremost o' them a',
Shall ride our forest queen:"—
But aye she loot the tears down fa',
For Jock o' Hazeldean.

The kirk was deck'd at morning-tide,
The tapers glimmer'd fair;
The priest and bridegroom wait the bride,
And dame and knight were there;
They sought her baith by bower and ha';
The ladye was not seen!—
She's o'er the Border and awa'
Wi' Jock o' Hazeldean!

"JOCK O' HAZELDEAN." There is mention made by some writers of an old ballad called "Jock o' Hazelgreen," but without documentary authority. It appears that Mr. Thomas Pringle gave, in Constable's Magazine, the first stanza of the present song, as that of an old ballad which he had heard his mother sing; and that Sir Walter Scott, upon inquiry, adopted that stanza as old, and added to it those that now make up his very popular song of "Jock o' Hazeldean," which he wrote for the first volume of Mr. Alexander Campbell's work, named "Albyn's Anthology." The melody, in an older and more Scottish form, occurs in the Leyden MS., No. 50, under the name of "The bony brow;" but we give the version of the air now more generally current.[1] The melody published in Book Second of Jo. Playford's "Choice Ayres," London, 1679, appears to have been that now an imitation of a Scottish song by Thomas D'Urfey, in his comedy of "The Fond Husband, or the Plotting Sisters," acted in 1676; and closely resembles the air given in the Leyden MS. In the older Scottish collections the tune is called "The bonny brow," "The glancing of her apron," and "In January last," all three being lines of the same song, that already mentioned written by D'Urfey in his collection, 1709.

Thomas Moore, in the Preface to the fifth volume of his Works collected by himself, London, 1841, remarks—that, "with the signal exception of Milton, there is not to be found, among all the eminent poets of England, a single musician."—p. v. In the same Preface he touches, gently, upon Sir Walter Scott's deficiency of musical ear. The Editor of this work was personally acquainted with Sir Walter Scott, and had his own good-humoured confession that he was totally destitute of an ear for music. Sir Walter himself, in his "Autobiography," after speaking of his ineffectual attempts at sketching or drawing landscapes, says :—"With music it was even worse than with painting. My mother was anxious we should at least learn psalmody; but the incurable defects of my voice and ear soon drove my teacher to despair.[2] It is only by long practice that I have acquired the power of selecting or distinguishing melodies; and although now few things delight or affect me more than a simple tune sung with feeling, yet I am sensible that even this pitch of musical taste has only been gained by attention and habit, and as it were by my feeling of the words being associated with the tune; although my friend Dr. Clarke, and other musical composers, have sometimes been able to make a happy union between their music and my poetry." See Lockhart's Life of Scott, vol. i. pp. 73, 74.

[1] A copy of that Leyden MS. was deposited by the Editor in the Library of the Faculty of Advocates on 26th November 1847.
[2] That teacher may have been ignorant and unskilful as too many were in Scott's early days. They required to go to school themselves.—ED.

O PUIRTITH CAULD.

AIR, "I HAD A HORSE." ARRANGED BY T. M. MUDIE.

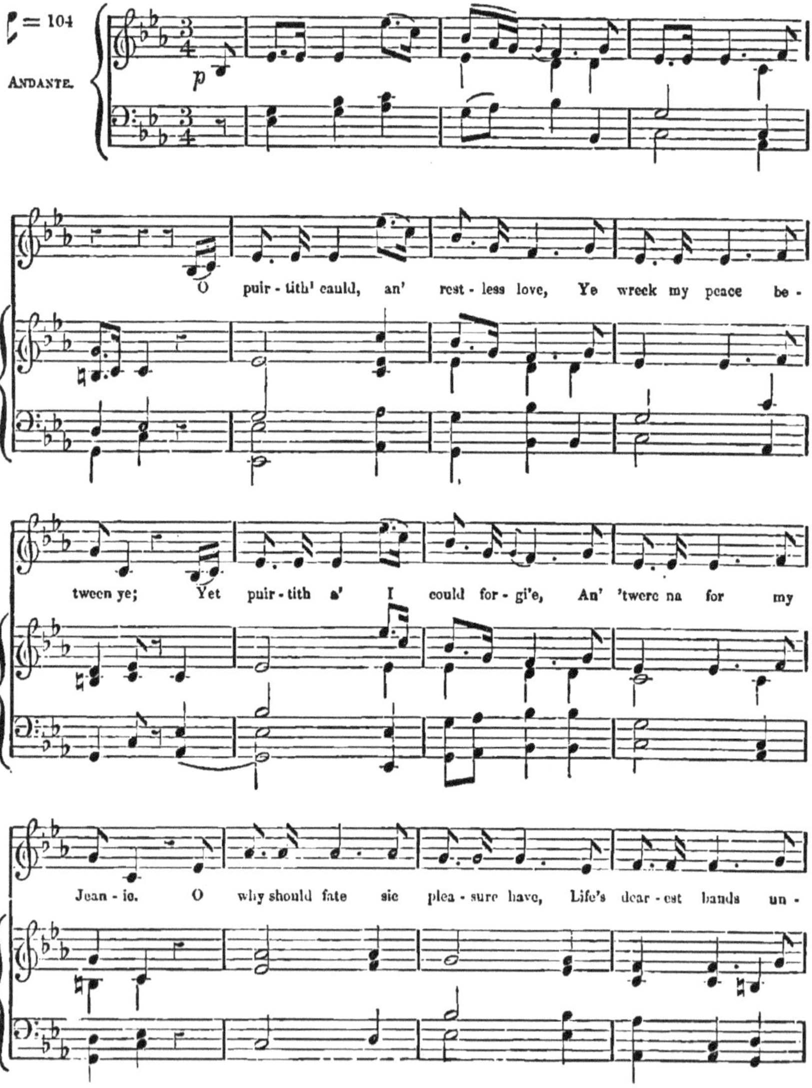

This world's wealth when I think on,
  Its pride, an' a' the lave[2] o't;
Fie, fie on silly coward man,
  That he should be the slave o't.
    O, why should fate, &c.

Her een, sae bonnieblue, betray
  How she repays my passion;
But prudence is her owerword[3] aye,
  She talks of rank an' fashion.
    O, why should fate, &c.

O, wha can prudence think upon,
  An' sic a lassie by him?
O, wha can prudence think upon,
  An' sae in love as I am?
    O, why should fate, &c.

How blest the humble cottar's fate!
  He woos his simple dearie;
The silly bogles,[4] wealth an' state,
  Can never make them eerie.[5]
    O, why should fate, &c.

[1] Poverty.   [2] Rest, remainder.   [3] Any word frequently repeated in conversation or otherwise.   [4] Scarecrow, bugbear.
[5] Affrighted; affected with fear from whatever cause; but generally applied to the feeling inspired by the dread of ghosts or spirits.

"O PUIRTITH CAULD." This song was written by Burns in January 1793, and slightly altered a few months later. It was inspired by Jean Lorimer of Kemmishall, a fair-haired, blue-eyed maiden, whom, for the next two years, he "made use of as a kind of lay figure," and celebrated in his verses under the name of Chloris. The words were intended for the air "Cauld kail in Aberdeen;" but George Thomson having objected that they were not well suited for so lively a tune, they were laid aside, no other melody being ever suggested for them by the poet. In 1798, after Burns's death, they appeared in the second portion of Thomson's first volume set to the air, "I had a horse." It would seem therefore that in this instance we owe the adaptation to the publisher rather than the poet; and this ought to be borne in mind by those who speak of Thomson's "perversity" in setting Burns's words to unsuitable airs. The melody is plaintive, and appears to be of considerable antiquity. Like several other old Scottish airs, it begins in a major key, and ends in the nearest relative minor.

Mr. Robert Chambers, in his Scottish Songs (1829), says, "I have been informed that Burns wrote this song in consequence of hearing a gentleman (now a respectable citizen of Edinburgh) sing the old homely ditty which gives name to the tune, with an effect which made him regret that such pathetic music should be united to such unsentimental poetry. The meeting, I have been further informed, where this circumstance took place, was held in *Johnnie Dowie's*, in the Lawnmarket, Edinburgh; and there, at a subsequent meeting, the new song was also sung, for the first time, by the same individual."

We give this story for what it is worth, though it evidently rests on no very solid basis. Burns may indeed have regretted to hear so fine an air used as the vehicle for a humorous song, but as he visited Edinburgh for the last time in 1791, *he* evidently could not have been present at the singing of the new words.

BLYTHE, BLYTHE, AND MERRY ARE WE.

AIR, "ANDRO AND HIS CUTTY GUN."

ARRANGED BY T. M. MUDIE.

Blythe, blythe, and mer - ry are we,

Blythe are we, ane and a'; Can - ty days we've af - ten seen, A nicht like this we

ne - ver saw! The gloamin' saw us a' sit down, And mei - kle mirth has

been our fa'; Then let the toast and sang gae round Till chan - ti - cleer be - gins to crawl

Blythe, blythe, and mer - ry are we, Pick and wale[1] o' mer - ry men; What care we tho' the

cock may craw, We're masters o' the tap - pit - hen![2]

The succeeding verses begin at the sign :𝕊:

The auld kirk bell has chappit twal—
  Wha cares though she had chappit twa!
We're licht o' heart and winna part,
  Though time and tide may rin awa!
Blythe, blythe, and merry are we—
  Hearts that care can never ding;[3]
Then let Time pass—we'll steal his glass,
  And pu' a feather frae his wing!

Now is the witchin' time o nicht,
  When ghaists, they say, are to be seen;
And fays dance to the glow-worm's licht
  Wi' fairies in their gowns o' green.
Blythe, blythe, and merry are we—
  Ghaists may tak' their midnicht stroll;
Witches ride on brooms astride,
  While we sit by the witchin' bowl!

Tut! never speir[4] how wears the morn—
  The moon's still blinkin i' the sky,
And, gif like her we fill our horn,
  I dinna doubt we'll drink it dry!
Blythe, blythe, and merry are we—
  Blythe out-owre the barley bree;
And let me tell, the moon hersel'
  Aft dips her toom[5] horn i' the sea!

Then fill us up a social cup,
  And never mind the dapple dawn;
Just sit awhile, the sun may smile,
  And syne[6] we'll see the gait[7] we're gaun!
Blythe, blythe, and merry are we;—
  See! the sun is keekin'[8] ben;
Gi'e Time his glass—for months may pass
  Ere sic a nicht we see again!

[1] Choice. [2] A measure containing a Scottish pint, that is, two English quarts. [3] Crush, depress.
[4] Ask, inquire. [5] Empty. [6] Then. [7] Road, way. [8] Peeping.

"BLYTHE, BLYTHE, AND MERRY ARE WE." The air is supposed to be old, and sounds very like a bag-pipe tune. It is now impossible to trace the authorship of our older Scottish airs; but the editor is disposed to believe that some of them may have been composed in the fifteenth and sixteenth centuries.
The song is by Captain Charles Gray, R.M. Two stanzas of it were written for the first anniversary of the Musomanik Society of Anstruther, 1814. It appeared in the third volume of the "Harp of Caledonia," Glasgow, 1819, and subsequently in Mr. G. Thomson's "Melodies of Scotland," adapted to a Jacobite air. Its merit having obtained for it a place in these and many other collections, no apology is necessary for uniting it here to the lively melody in the very spirit of which it is conceived and written. Captain Gray's "jolly song," (as Mrs. Joanna Baillie called it,)—differing in some slight degree from that printed in his "Lays and Lyrics"—having received his final corrections, is here published by his express permission.

THE BIRKS OF ABERFELDIE.

AIR, "THE BIRKS OF ABERGELDIE."   ARRANGED BY T. M. MUDIE.

Bon - nie las - sie, will ye go, Will ye go, will ye go,

Bon - nie las - sie, will ye go To the birks of A - ber - fel - die? Now simmer blinks on flow'ry braes, And

o'er the crystal streamlet plays; Come let us spend the lightsome days In the birks of A - ber - fel - die.

Bon - nie las-sie, will ye go, Will ye go, will ye go, Bon - nie las - sie, will ye go To the

birks of A - ber - fel - die? *Concluding Symphony.*

Scherzando.

The following verses begin at the sign :S:

While o'er their head the hazels hing,
The little burdies blythely sing,
Or lightly flit on wanton wing,
In the birks of Aberfeldie.
Bonnie lassie, &c.

The braes ascend like lofty wa's,
The foamin' stream deep-roaring fa's,
O'erhung wi' fragrant spreadin' shaws,
The birks of Aberfeldie.
Bonnie lassie, &c.

The hoary cliffs are crown'd wi' flow'rs,
White o'er the linn the burnie pours,
And, risin', weets wi' misty show'rs
The birks of Aberfeldie.
Bonnie lassie, &c.

Let fortune's gifts at random flee,
They ne'er shall draw a wish frae me,
Supremely bless'd wi' love and thee,
In the birks of Aberfeldie.
Bonnie lassie, &c.

"THE BIRKS OF ABERFELDIE." "This old sprightly air," says Mr. Stenhouse, "appears in Playford's 'Dancing-master,' first printed in 1657, under the title of 'A Scotch Ayre.'" The words here given, except the chorus, which is old, were written by Burns for Johnson's Musical Museum, in September 1787, while standing under the Falls of Moness, near Aberfeldie, in Perthshire. Burns, at that time, was travelling in the Highlands of Scotland with his intimate friend William Nicol, one of the masters of the Edinburgh High-School. Mr. Lockhart, in his Life of Robert Burns, chap. vi., records a remarkable trait of the pride and passion of William Nicol when Burns and he were together at Fochabers; and of Burns' kind self-denial and breach of etiquette with a Duke, in order to soothe his irritated friend. "Burns, who had been much noticed by this noble family when in Edinburgh, happened to present himself at Gordon Castle, just at the dinner hour, and being invited to take a place at the table, did so, without for a moment adverting to the circumstance that his travelling companion had been left alone at the inn in the adjacent village. On remembering this soon after dinner, he begged to be allowed to rejoin his friend; and the Duke of Gordon, who now for the first time learned that he was not journeying alone, immediately proposed to send an invitation to Mr. Nicol to come to the Castle. His Grace's messenger found the haughty schoolmaster striding up and down before the inn-door, in a state of high wrath and indignation, at what he considered Burns' neglect; and no apologies could soften his mood. He had already ordered horses; and the poet finding that he must choose between the ducal circle and his irritable associate, at once left Gordon Castle and repaired to the inn; whence Nicol and he, in silence and mutual displeasure, pursued their journey along the coast of the Moray Frith."—Lockhart's Life of Burns. Regarding the air, we have to observe, that in the earlier copies the melody seems to have been disfigured by a misprint of the sixth note of the first measure, where three D's occur consecutively, instead of D, E, D. In the present edition that wrong note has been altered.

Playford's Dancing Master was first printed in 1651, but this air does not appear in any edition of it till after 1703. It is impossible that Mr. Stenhouse can ever have seen an early edition of the work, else he would not have quoted from it so recklessly and erroneously. His own copy must have been as late as 1718 or 1721, both of which contain all the tunes he mentions.

THE LAIRD O' COCKPEN.

AIR, " WHEN SHE CAM' BEN, SHE BOBBED."

ARRANGED BY H. E. DIBDIN.

The laird o' Cock-pen, be's proud and he's great; His mind is ta'en up wi' the things o' the state; He want-ed a wife his braw house to keep; But fa-vour wi' woo-in' was

fash - ous to seek.

Doun by the dyke-side a lady did dwell,
At his table-head he thought she'd look well;
M'Cleish's ae daughter o' Claverse-ha' Lee,
A pennyless lass wi' a lang pedigree.

His wig was weel pouther'd, an' as gude as new,
His waistcoat was white, his coat it was blue;
He put on a ring, a sword, an' cock'd hat,
An' wha could refuse the Laird wi' a' that?

He took the gray mare, an' rade cannilie,
An' rapp'd at the yett o' Claverse-ha' Lee;
"Gae tell mistress Jean to come speedily ben,
She's wanted to speak wi' the Laird o' Cockpen."

Mistress Jean she was makin' the elder-flower wine
"An' what brings the Laird at sic a like time?"
She put aff her apron, an' on her silk goun,
Her mutch wi' red ribbons, an' gaed awa' doun.

An' when she cam' ben, he bowed fu' low;
An' what was his errand, he soon let her know.
Amazed was the Laird when the lady said, Na!
An' wi' a laigh curtsie, she turn'd awa'.

Dumfounder'd was he, but nae sigh did he gi'e;
He mounted his mare, and he rade cannilie;
An' aften he thought, as he gaed through the glen,
She's daft to refuse the Laird o' Cockpen.

"THE LAIRD O' COCKPEN." Mr. Stenhouse says, "The musical reader will scarcely require to be informed that this spirited air, ["When she cam' ben, she bobbed,"] of one simple strain, is among the oldest of our Scottish melodies. It is preserved in the first book of Oswald's Caledonian Pocket Companion, with some of his own variations upon the air. It also appears in Mrs. Crockat's Manuscript Book of Tunes, dated 1709." See Museum Illustrations, vol. iv. pp. 326, 327. In Oswald's First Collection, dedicated to Frederick Prince of Wales, (p. 43,) we find "When she came ben, she bobed," in three-fourth time, and differing in some other respects from the set No. 353 of Museum. In Dr. John Leyden's MS. Lyra-Viol Book—referred to ante, p. 25—there is a tune, No. 77, entitled, "When she came ben," in a major key, and yet evidently the prototype of the two sets last mentioned, in minor keys. In most sets of the melody, the sharp seventh is given in the fourth measure. This, we think, is erroneous, and have therefore made the seventh natural in the present work; especially as we find our alteration supported by a set of the air published in James Oswald's "Curious Collection of Scots Tunes, &c.," 1740, dedicated to the Duke of Perth.

The clever and humourous stanzas given to the air, "When she came ben," in this work, are modern. They are now generally ascribed to Lady Nairne, yet if really by her, it is somewhat strange that in the third volume of the Scottish Minstrel they appear without the usual B. B., the initials of her pseudonym, Mrs. Bogan of Bogan; while in the same volume those initials are appended to "I'm wearin' awa'," as well as to other two songs known to have been written by her. Lady Nairne was the principal member of the coterie of ladies who superintended the literary portion of that work, and yet the writer of "The Laird of Cockpen" is in the Index marked "unknown."

Two additional stanzas have appeared by another hand: as they are occasionally sung, we subjoin them:—

An' now that the Laird his exit had made,
Mistress Jean she reflecked on what she had said;
"Oh! for ane I'll get better, its waur I'll get ten—
I was daft to refuse the Laird o' Cockpen!"

Neist time that the Laird and the Lady were seen,
They were gaun arm an' arm to the kirk on the green;
Now she sits in the ha' like a weel-tappit hen;
But as yet there's nae chickens appear'd at Cockpen.

I

MY TOCHER'S THE JEWEL.

ARRANGED BY H. E. DIBDIN.

O mei - kle thinks my love o' my beau - ty, And mei - kle thinks my love

o' my kin; But lit - tle thinks my love I ken brawlie, My tocher's the jew - el has

charms for him. Its a' for the ap - ple he'll nourish the tree, Its a' for the hinney he'll ober - ish the bee, My lad - die's sae mei - kle in love wi' the sil - ler, He

can - na hae love to spare for me.

Your proffer o' love's an arle-penny,
My tocher's the bargain ye wad buy;
But an ye be crafty, I am cunnin',
Sae ye wi' anither your fortune maun try.

Ye're like to the timmer o' yon rotten wood,
Ye're like to the bark o' yon rotten tree,
Ye'll slip frae me like a knotless thread,
And ye'll crack your credit wi' mae nor me.

"MY TOCHER'S THE JEWEL." Mr. Stenhouse says, "The words of this song, 'O meikle thinks my love o' my beauty,' were written by Burns, in 1790, for the Museum. They are adapted to a jig in Oswald's Caledonian Pocket Companion, book iii. p. 28, composed by him from the subject of an old air, in slow common time, called 'The highway to Edinburgh.' . . . Burns was mistaken in asserting, in the Reliques, that Gow, or any of his family, claimed this melody as their own composition; or even that it had been notoriously taken from 'The mucking o' Geordie's byre,' for it is nothing more than the subject of the old air of 'The highway to Edinburgh,' thrown into treble time." See Museum Illustrations, vol. iv. p. 304. There are three errors in this statement. 1st. Burns did not write the whole words of this song, but only a few of them, the others being old. This is given on the authority of Burns' sister, Mrs. Begg, who communicated the fact to Captain Charles Gray, R. M. 2d. Mr. Stenhouse is inconceivably wrong in stating that the tune is taken from the subject of an old air called "The highway to Edinburgh." 3d. Mr. Stenhouse is equally wrong when he says, that Burns was mistaken in asserting that the tune "My tocher's," &c., had been notoriously taken from "The mucking o' Geordie's byre." Burns was quite right, for the chief melodic forms of these two airs are almost identical; though the rhythm has been changed by additional measures interpolated in the former tune. The older tune is in three-four, and the derivative one in six-eight time, the former easily convertible into the latter.

In regard to "The highway to Edinburgh," it is evidently the same in all essentials as a tune called "The black eagle, by *David Rizo*," given in Oswald's second collection, and in M'Gibbon's as "The bonny black eagle." An older and better version than either is found in tablature in the MS. Lyra Viol-Book of the celebrated Dr. John Leyden, under the name of "Women's work will never be done." This curious Leyden MS., which was supposed to be lost, when Mr. William Dauncy published the Skene MS. in December 1838, was, in 1843, sent to Mr. G. F. Graham, with permission to copy and translate the whole. He made a copy of the MS., which he deposited in the Advocates' Library for preservation.

MAGGIE LAUDER.

ARRANGED BY J. T. SURENNE.

Wha wad-na be in love Wi' bon - nie Maggie Lau - der! A

pip - er met her gaun to Fife, And speir'd what was't they ca'd her, Right scornful-ly she answer'd him; "Be-

gone ye hal-lan-sha-ker![1] Jog on your gate, ye bladderskate,[2] My name is Mag - gie Lau - der."

¹ A beggarly knave.   ² An indiscreet talker.

For the first four verses. For the last verse.

Maggie, quo' he, and by my hags,
  I'm fidgin' fain to see thee;
Sit down by me, my bonnie bird,
  In troth I winna steer thee:
For I'm a piper to my trade,
  My name is Rob the Ranter;
The lasses loup as they were daft,
  When I blaw up my chanter.

Piper, quo' Meg, ha'e ye your bags?
  Or is your drone in order?
If ye be Rob, I've heard of you,
  Live you upon the border?
The lasses a', baith far and near,
  Have heard o' Rob the Ranter;
I'll shake my foot wi' right gude will,
  Gif you'll blaw up your chanter.

Then to his bags he flew wi' speed,
  About the drone he twisted;
Meg up and wallop'd o'er the green,
  For brawly could she frisk it.
Weel done! quo' he—play up! quo' she;
  Weel bobb'd! quo' Rob the Ranter;
'Tis worth my while to play indeed,
  When I ha'e sic a dancer.

Weel ha'e you play'd your part, quo' Meg,
  Your cheeks are like the crimson;
There's nane in Scotland plays sae weel,
  Since we lost Habbie Simson.*
I've lived in Fife, baith maid and wife,
  These ten years and a quarter;
Gin ye should come to Anster fair,
  Speir ye for Maggie Lauder.

We subjoin the spirited verses written by Captain Charles Gray, R.M., to the same tune, and published in his "Lays and Lyrics," 1841.

Tho' Boreas bauld, that carle auld,
  Should sough a surly chorus;
And Winter snell walk out himsel'
  And throw his mantle o'er us;—
Tho' winds blaw drift adown the lift,
  And drive hailstanes afore 'em;
While you and I sit snug and dry—
  Come push about the jorum!

Tho' no a bird can now be heard
  Upon the leafless timmer;
Whate'er betide, the ingle side
  Can mak' the winter—simmer!
Tho' cauldrife souls hate reekin' bowls,
  And loath what's set before 'em;
How sweet to tout the glasses out—
  O leeze me on a jorum!

The bie hill taps, like baxter's baps,
  Wi' snaw are white and floury;
Skyte doun the lum the hailstanes come,
  In Winter's wildest fury!
Sharp Johnnie Frost, wi' barkynt boast,
  Mak's travellers tramp the quicker;
Should he come here to spoil our cheer,
  We'll drown him in the bicker!

Bess, beet the fire—come, big it higher,
  Lest cauld should mak' us canker'd;—
This is our hame, my dainty dame,
  Sae fill the tither tankard.
Wi' guid ait cakes, or butter bakes,
  And routh o' whisky toddy,
Wha daur complain, or mak' a mane,
  That man's a saul-less body?

"MAGGIE LAUDER." There is a surmise, for it is scarcely more, that this is an English air. It rests upon the fact that in a ballad opera called "The Beggar's Wedding" (1729), the tune is styled "Moggy Lauther on a day." This is supposed to be the first line of an Anglo-Scottish song, of which, however, nothing more is known. It is not to be found, either with or without music, in any of the numerous collections of songs published about that time, neither does this first line ever appear again. The evidence in favour of its English origin is thus somewhat slender; especially as the air is found in Adam Craig's "Collection of the choicest Scots Tunes," Edinburgh, 1730. The words, first printed by Herd in 1769, are ascribed to Francis Semple of Beltrees, who is said to have written them in 1642. One would be glad to think, that in the midst of straitened means, Francis Semple had been able to write so merry a song as Maggie Lauder, but there is no contemporary copy, nor contemporary evidence of any kind, to show that it existed even in his time. The claim is founded on the belief of grandchildren who died a century after him (1789 and later). Their testimony cannot be esteemed as of much value, seeing they also believed he wrote "She rose and let me in," a song now known to have been written by Tom d'Urfey. Although Maggie Lauder cannot thus be traced back to Francis Semple, it proves itself by internal evidence to be much older than Herd's time by its loose and haphazard rhymes, *see thee, steer thee,—ranter, dancer,—*and, above all, *Lauder* rhyming with *shaker* and *quarter.*

* See "The Life and Death of the Piper of Kilbarchan, Habbie Simpson," in Watson's Collection of Scots Poems, Edinburgh, 1706.

IT WAS UPON A LAMMAS NIGHT.

AIR, "CORN RIGS."

ARRANGED BY A. LAWRIE.

It was up-on a Lam-mas night, When corn rigs are bon-nie, O, Be-

neath the moon's un-cloud-ed light, I held a-wa' to An-nie, O: The time flew by wi'

tent-less heed, Till 'tween the late and ear-ly, O, Wi' sma' per-sua-sion she a-greed To see me thro' the bar - ley, O.   Corn   rigs, and   bar - ley rigs,   Corn   rigs   are

a piacere   *a tempo.*

bon - nie, O : I'll ne'er for - get that hap - py night, A - mang the rigs wi' An - nie, O.

f   *colla voce.*

The sky was blue, the wind was still,
The moon was shining clearly, O :
I set her down wi' right good will,
Amang the rigs o' barley, O :
I ken't her heart was a' my ain ;
I loved her most sincerely, O ;
I kiss'd her ower and ower again,
Amang the rigs o' barley, O.
    Corn rigs, &c.

I lock'd her in my fond embrace !
Her heart was beating rarely, O :
My blessings on that happy place,
Amang the rigs o' barley, O !

But by the moon and stars so bright,
That shone that hour so clearly, O!
She aye shall bless that happy night,
Amang the rigs o' barley, O !
    Corn rigs, &c.

I hae been blithe wi' comrades dear,
I hae been merry drinkin', O ;
I hae been joyfu' gath'rin' gear ;
I hae been happy thinkin', O :
But a' the pleasures e'er I saw,
Tho' three times doubled fairly, O,
That happy night was worth them a',
Amang the rigs o' barley, O.
    Corn rigs, &c.

"THE RIGS OF BARLEY." The above verses were written by Burns in his earlier years.   Mr. Scott Douglas says that Anne Rankine, daughter of a farmer at Adamhill, two miles west of Lochlie, boasted to her dying day that she was the Annie of "The rigs of barley."

The air has been known in Scotland since about the beginning of the eighteenth century under the name of Corn Rigs ; nevertheless there can be no doubt that the air is really English, and was originally composed in 1680—says Mr. Chappell—to D'Urfey's words, "Sawney was tall." But setting aside all historical evidence, of which there is plenty, whoever will look at the air without prejudice, must see that it has no Scottish characteristics whatever, and that its flowing English style is apparent from the first bar to the last. We cannot too soon recognise that the statements regarding English music made by Stenhouse, and in which he has been unfortunately followed by others, who ought to have examined the subject for themselves, are unsupported by evidence, and frequently at variance with fact.

O THIS IS NO MY AIN LASSIE.

AIR, "THIS IS NO MY AIN HOUSE."   ARRANGED BY J. T. SURENNE.

O this is no my ain las - sie, Fair tho' the las - sie be; O

weel ken I my ain las - sie, Kind love is in her e'e. I see a form, I

see a face, Ye weel may wi' the fair - est place; It wants to me the witch - in' grace, The

Da Capo al Segno.

kind love that's in her e'e.

p

The succeeding verses begin with the Second Part of the Air, and end with the First Part.

She's bonnie, bloomin', straight, an' tall,
An' lang has had my heart in thrall;
An' aye it charms my very saul,
The kind love that's in her e'e.
O this is no my ain lassie, &c.

A thief sae pawkie[1] is my Jean;
She'll steal a blink by a' unseen;
But gleg[2] as light are lover's een,
When kind love is in the e'e.
O this is no my ain lassie, &c.

It may escape the courtly sparks,
It may escape the learned clerks;
But weel the watchin' lover marks
The kind love that's in her e'e.
O this is no my ain lassie, &c.

[1] Cunning, sly.

[2] Sharp, ready.

"O THIS IS NO MY AIN LASSIE." In the summer of 1795, Burns wrote these stanzas for Mr. George Thomson's Collection. James Hogg, in his Jacobite Relics, vol. i. pp. 57, 58, gives the old words, and says, p. 224, "The air to which I have set this song is not the original one; but it is the most popular, being always sung both to this song and 'This is no my ain lassie,' by Burns. For my part, I like the old original one much better." Hogg prints the original air on the same page; and his is a better set than the one given in Johnson's Museum, No. 216, where, at the end of the first and second strains, the introduction of the sharp 7th of the tonic spoils the whole character of the air. In the Museum Illustrations, vol. iii. p. 210, Mr. Stenhouse gives what he says is "the original air" of "This is no my ain house," from Mrs. Crockat's book, written in 1709. This is the air, with some modifications found in later copies, which has been adopted in the present work. As a vocal air, it is much preferable to that given by Johnson. We have retained the leap of the 5th in the fourth measure of the first strain, according to the Crockat MS. cited by Mr. Stenhouse.

In a previous note, allusion was made to the unfortunate career of Burns. The following passages from the pen of his talented countryman, Thomas Carlyle, ("Heroes, and Hero-worship,") are given as flowers laid reverently on the tomb of the poet :—"The tragedy of Burns's life is known to all. Surely we may say, if discrepancy between place held and place merited constitute perverseness of lot for a man, no lot could be more perverse than Burns's. Among those second-hand acting figures, *mimes* for the most part, of the eighteenth century, once rose a giant Original Man; one of those men who reach down into the perennial deeps, who take rank with the heroic among men, and he was born in an Ayrshire hut. The largest soul in all the British lands came among us in the shape of a hard-handed Scottish peasant." (P. 296.) "Burns appeared under every disadvantage : uninstructed, poor, born only to hard manual toil; and writing, when it came to that, in a rustic special dialect, known only to a small province of the country he lived in. Had he written even what he did write in the general language of England, I doubt not he had already become universally recognized as being, or capable to be, one of our greatest men. That he should have tempted so many to penetrate through the rough husk of that dialect of his, is proof that there lay something far from common within it. He has gained a certain recognition, and is continuing to do so over all quarters of our wide Saxon world; wheresoever a Saxon dialect is spoken, it begins to be understood, by personal inspection of this and the other, that one of the most considerable Saxon men of the eighteenth century was an Ayrshire peasant, named Robert Burns." (P. 298, third edition, 1846.)

ROY'S WIFE OF ALDIVALLOCH.

ARRANGED BY G. F. GRAHAM.

Roy's wife of Al - di - val - loch,

Roy's wife of Al - di - valloch, Wat ye how she cheated me, As I cam' o'er the braes o' Balloch?

She vow'd, she swore she wad be mine; She said she lo'ed me best of onie; But

O the fickle, faithless quean, She's ta'en the carle¹ an' left her Johnnie! Roy's wife of Al - di - valloch,

The 2d and 3d stanzas begin at this mark :S:

O, she was a cantie² quean,
Weel could she dance the Highland walloch;
How happy I, had she been mine,
Or I been Roy of Aldivalloch.
Roy's wife, &c.

Her hair sae fair, her een sae clear,
Her wee bit mou' sae sweet and bonnie;
To me she ever will be dear,
Though she's for ever left her Johnnie.
Roy's wife, &c.

¹ An old man. ² Merry.

"Roy's Wife of Aldivalloch." This song was written by Mrs. Grant of Carron, afterwards Mrs. Dr. Murray of Bath, and is said to be founded on fact. We are told that in 1727 John Roy, son of Thomas Roy of Aldivalloch, was married to Isabel, daughter of Allister Stewart, sometime resident in the Cabrach, a highland district of Aberdeenshire. It would appear that the marriage was not a happy one, for she made an attempt to escape, but was brought back by her husband. Such an occurrence in a quiet locality is sure to be the occasion of a ballad more or less rude, and this did not fail in the present instance. Out of this rude beginning Mrs. Grant is said to have produced her song. (See Chambers's Songs of Scotland before Burns.) Burns also wrote verses for the same air, beginning, "Canst thou leave me thus, my Katy?"—but the lady's verses have always held their ground to this day. David Laing, Esq., in his Additional Illustrations to Johnson's Museum, (vol. iv. pp. 368, 369,) says:—"Through the obliging inquiries of John P. Grant, Esq., (son of the late Mrs. Grant of Laggan,) I have since learned the following particulars respecting this lady. Her maiden name was Grant; and she was born near Aberlour, on the banks of the river Spey, about the year 1745. She was twice married, first to her cousin, Mr. Grant of Carron, near Elchies, on the river Spey, about the year 1763; and, secondly, to a physician in Bath, whose name is stated to have been Brown, not Murray. She died at Bath sometime about 1814, and is not known to have written any other song than 'Roy's Wife.'" Mr. Laing is satisfied, from the authority of Mr. George Thomson and Mr. Cromek, that the lady's second husband was Dr. Murray of Bath. The tune is old, and was long known in the Lowlands as "The Ruffian's Rant." In several passages, modern improvers of our old melodies have, as usual, introduced flourishes that are incompatible with the simple character of this air. We have rejected these flourishes, as we shall always do, whenever we find them disfiguring our national Scottish airs. From the earlier part of the last century, the process of altering and pretended improving of these airs seems to have gone on, up to a certain point, when it was found necessary to stop short in disguising them. The rage for embellishment as applied to these simple melodies may be traced to the time when they became so fashionable in England, and got into the hands of public singers in London. Italian fioriture, of a particular kind, were not less liberally applied in those days to every melody than they have been of late years, with a change of form. National airs could not escape the contagion. In the Macfarland MS. (1740) and in Angus Cumming's Collection (1780) the tune is called "Cog na scalau;" the last a word very difficult to interpret. After much inquiry we learn from two of the highest Gaelic authorities that in one district it means a wicker basket for oat-cakes, and in another a baking-board or dough-trough. The name seems therefore to allude to some domestic squabble or dispute about the baking of oat-cakes. As to whether this may have been the origin of the quarrel between Roy and his wife tradition is silent.

CA' THE YOWES TO THE KNOWES.

ARRANGED BY T. M. MUDIE.

Ca' the yowes to the knowes, Ca' them where the hea-ther grows,

Ca' them where the bur-nie rows, My bon-nie dear-ie. Hark, the ma-vis'

eve-ning sang, Sound-ing Clu-den's woods a-mang; Then a-fauld-ing let us gang,

My bon - nie dear - io.

We'll gang doun by Cluden side,
Through the hazels spreading wide
O'er the waves that sweetly glide,
    To the moon sae clearly.

Yonder Cluden's silent towers,
Where, at moonshine midnight hours,
O'er the dewy bending flowers
    The fairies dance sae cheerie.

Ghaist nor bogle shalt thou fear:
Thou'rt to love and heaven sae dear,
Nocht of ill may come thee near,
    My bonnie dearie.

Fair and lovely as thou art,
Thou hast stoun my very heart;
I can die—but canna part,
    My bonnie dearie.

"CA' THE YOWES TO THE KNOWES." In a letter to Mr. G. Thomson, September 1794, Burns says, "I am flattered at your adopting 'Ca' the yowes to the knowes,' as it was owing to me that it saw the light. About seven years ago, I was well acquainted with a worthy little fellow of a clergyman, a Mr. Clunie, who sung it charmingly; and, at my request, Mr. Clarke took it down from his singing. When I gave it to Johnson, I added some stanzas to the song, and mended others, but still it will not do for you. In a solitary stroll which I took to-day, I tried my hand on a few pastoral lines, following up the idea of the chorus, which I would preserve. Here it is, with all its crudities and imperfections on its head." This is the song which we have given with the wild and pretty air which Burns thus rescued from oblivion. He saved many other good melodies from being lost; and, for this alone, Scotland owes him another debt of gratitude. This fact is not generally known, and is not alluded to by his biographers. Captain Charles Gray, R.M., in his "Cursory remarks on Scottish Song," was the first to point out our obligations to Burns in this respect.

The Cluden, or Clouden, is a river in Dumfries-shire, which rises near the feet of the Criffel hills, and falls into the Nith, nearly opposite to Lincluden College.

Following up what we have quoted above from Burns, it may not be out of place here to state in his own words his ideas of music and song, and his mode of composing verses to airs that pleased him, or that were sent to him for verses. The passages are from his letters to Mr. George Thomson. "November 8, 1792. There is a peculiar rhythmus in many of our airs, and a necessity of adapting syllables to the emphasis, or what I would call the feature notes, of the tune, that cramp the poet, and lay him under almost insuperable difficulties." "September, 1793. Until I am complete master of a tune in my own singing, (such as it is,) I never can compose for it. My way is: I consider the poetic sentiment correspondent to my idea of the musical expression; then choose my theme; begin one stanza; when that is composed, which is generally the most difficult part of the business, I walk out, sit down now and then, look out for objects in nature around me, that are in unison or harmony with the cogitations of my fancy, and workings of my bosom; humming every now and then the air with the verses I have framed. When I feel my muse beginning to jade, I retire to the solitary fireside of my study, and there commit my effusions to paper, swinging at intervals on the hind legs of my elbow-chair, by way of calling forth my own critical strictures, as my pen goes on. Seriously, this at home, is almost invariably my way."

That Burns had a fine feeling for the simple melodies of his country, the following extracts will show:—"April, 1793. I have still several MS. Scots airs by me which I have picked up, mostly from the singing of country lasses. They please me vastly; but your learned lugs would perhaps be displeased with the very feature for which I like them. I call them simple; you would pronounce them silly." "September, 1793. You know that my pretensions to musical taste are merely a few of nature's instincts, untaught and untutored by art. For this reason, many musical compositions, particularly where much of the merit lies in counterpoint, however they may transport and ravish the ears of you connoisseurs, affect my simple lug no otherwise than merely as melodious din. On the other hand, by way of amends, I am delighted with many little melodies, which the learned musician despises as silly and insipid." "September, 1794. Not to compare small things with great, my taste in music is like the mighty Frederick of Prussia's taste in painting: we are told that he frequently admired what the connoisseurs decried, and always without any hypocrisy confessed his admiration," &c.

HOW LANG AND DREARY IS THE NICHT.

AIR, "CAULD KAIL IN ABERDEEN."

ARRANGED BY FINLAY DUN.

lang and drear - y is the nicht, When I am frae my dear - ie; I restless lie frae

e'en till morn, Tho' I were ne'er so wear - y. For, oh! her lane - ly nichts are lang; And,

oh! her dreams are ee - rie; And, oh! her wi - dow'd heart is sair, That's ab - sent frae her dear - ie!

When I think on the lightsome days
　I spent wi' thee, my dearie;
And now, what seas between us roar—
　How can I be but ceric.
For, oh! her lanely nights are lang;
　And, oh! her dreams are ecrie;
And, oh! her widow'd heart is sair,
　That's absent frae her dearie!

How slow ye move, ye heavy hours—
　The joyless day, how dreary!
It was na sae ye glinted by
　When I was wi' my dearie.
For, oh! her lanely nights are lang;
　And, oh! her dreams are ceric;
And, oh! her widow'd heart is sair
　That's absent frae her dearie!

"CAULD KAIL IN ABERDEEN." "This beautiful air does not appear in any of our old Collections by Thomson, Craig, M'Gibbon, or Oswald. It seems to have been modelled from the ancient tune in triple time, called, *The sleepy body*, like that of another from the same source, called, *The Ploughman*. See No. 165. For upwards of half a century, however, few if any of our tunes have been greater favourites with the poets than that of 'Cauld kail in Aberdeen.' Although this air, particularly when played slow, is rather of a tender and plaintive cast, yet most of the songs that have been adapted to it are of a very opposite description." See Museum Illustrations, vol. ii. p. 150. The song beginning, "How lang and dreary is the night," of three stanzas of six lines each, was written by Burns to a Highland air. Long afterwards, in October 1794, he altered that song to suit the air of "Cauld kail in Aberdeen," for Mr. George Thomson's work. This is the version here given. Most of the humorous songs written for this air are objectionably coarse, not excepting the one written by Burns' noble friend, the Duke of Gordon. We give the following merry lines written for the air by the late Mr. William Reid, bookseller, Glasgow, not only because they are unobjectionable, but because they are good of their kind. He was a personal friend and great admirer of Burns, and published several pieces of poetry of considerable merit. David Laing, Esq., in his Additional Illustrations of Johnson's Museum, vol. ii. pages *212, 213, says :—" Having been favoured by Mr. James Brash of Glasgow, (through the kind application of Mr. P. A. Ramsay,) with some particulars of Mr. Reid's history, I take this opportunity of inserting them, as a tribute of respect to his memory. He was remarkable for a fund of social humour, and was possessed of no inconsiderable poetical powers, with some of the eccentricities occasionally allied to genius. Mr. Reid was born at Glasgow on the 10th of April 1764. His parents were Robert Reid, baker in Glasgow, and Christian Wood, daughter of a farmer at Gartmore, in Perthshire. Having received a good education in his native city, he was originally employed in the type-foundery of Mr. Andrew Wilson, and afterwards served an apprenticeship with Messrs. Dunlop & Wilson, booksellers in Glasgow. He remained in their employment till the year 1790, when he commenced business as a bookseller, in partnership with the late Mr. James Brash; and, for a period of twenty-seven years, they carried on a most respectable business, under the well-known firm of 'Brash & Reid.' In a small publication which they issued in numbers, at one penny each, under the title of 'Poetry, Original and Selected,' between the years 1795 and 1798, and which forms four volumes, there are several contributions of Mr. Reid. Most of his compositions were of an ephemeral kind, and it is to be regretted that no selection of them has ever appeared. He died at Glasgow, 29th of November 1831 leaving a widow, Elizabeth, daughter of Mr. James Henderson, linen-printer, Newhall, and two sons and five daughters."

There's cauld kail in Aberdeen,
　And bannocks in Strathbogie—
But naething drives awa' the spleen
　Sae weel's a social cogie.

That mortal's life nae pleasure shares,
　Wha broods o'er a' that's fogie:
Whane'er I'm fasht wi' worldly cares,
　I drown them in a cogie.

Thus merrily my time I pass,
　With spirits brisk and vogie,
Blest wi' my buiks and my sweet lass,
　My cronies and my cogie.

Then haste and gi'e's an auld Scots sang,
　Siclike as Kath'rine Ogie;
A gude auld sang comes never wrang
　When o'er a social cogie.

THERE WAS A LASS, AND SHE WAS FAIR.

AIR, "WILLIE WAS A WANTON WAG."

ARRANGED BY FINLAY DUN.

There was a lass, and she was fair, At kirk and market to be seen, When a' the fair - est maids were met, The fair - est maid was bon - nie Jean. And aye she wrought her mam - mie's wark, And

aye she sang sae mer - ri - lie: The blith - est bird up - on the bush Had
ne'er a light - er heart than she.

But hawks will rob the tender joys
   That bless the little lintwhite's nest:
And frost will blight the fairest flowers,
   And love will break the soundest rest.
Young Robie was the brawest lad,
   The flower and pride of a' the glen ;
And he had owsen, sheep, and kye,
   And wanton naigies[1] nine or ten.

He gaed wi' Jeanie to the tryste,
   He danc'd wi Jeanie on the down;
And lang ere witless Jeanie wist,
   Her heart was tint,[2] her peace was stown.
As in the bosom o' the stream
   The moon-beam dwells at dewy e'en;
So trembling, pure, was tender love,
   Within the breast o' bonnie Jean.

And now she works her mammie's wark,
   And aye she sighs wi' care and pain;
Yet wist'na what her ail might be,
   Or what wad mak' her weel again.

But did na Jeanie's heart loup[3] light,
   And did na joy blink in her e'e,
As Robie tauld a tale o' love,
   Ae e'enin' on the lily lea?

The sun was sinking in the west,
   The birds sang sweet in ilka grove,
His cheek to her's he fondly prest,
   And whisper'd thus his tale o' love:
O Jeanie fair, I lo'e thee dear;
   O canst thou think to fancy me!
Or wilt thou leave thy mammie's cot,
   And learn to tent[4] the farms wi' me?

At barn or byre thou shalt na drudge,
   Or naething else to trouble thee;
But stray amang the heather-bells,
   And tent the waving corn wi' me.
Now what could artless Jeanie do?
   She had nae will to say him na :
At length she blush'd a sweet consent,
   And love was aye between them twa

[1] Young horses.   [2] Lost.   [3] Leap.   [4] To take charge of ; to watch.

"THERE WAS A LASS, AND SHE WAS FAIR." Burns wrote this song to the tune of "Bonnie Jean" for Mr. G. Thomson's Collection. Mr. T., however, adapted it to the tune of "Willie was a wanton wag," and we have here given it to the same air. The "Jeanie" thus celebrated by Burns, was Miss Jean Macmurdo, (afterwards Mrs. Crawford,) eldest daughter of John Macmurdo, Esq. of Drumlanrig. "I have not painted her," says Burns, "in the rank which she holds in life, but in the dress and character of a cottager." Burns himself considered this song as "in his best style ;" and so it certainly is. About the beginning of last century, Mr. Walkingshaw of that ilk, near Paisley, wrote a very humorous song beginning, "Willie was a wanton wag;" which was published in the Orpheus Caledonius in 1783, along with the air which now bears that name.
The earliest version of the air we have seen appears under the name of "Lady Strathallan's Tune," in a MS. apparently of the end of the seventeenth century, and now in the Advocates' Library.

K

SHE'S FAIR AND FAUSE.

ARRANGED BY J. T. SURENNE.

She's fair and fause that caus - es my smart, I lo'ed her meikle and lang; She's bro - ken her vow, she's bro - ken my heart, And I may e'en gae hang. A coof[1] cam' in wi' routh[2] o' gear,[3] And

I ha'e tint⁴ my dear - est dear; But wo - man is but warld's gear, Sae

let the bonnie lass gang.

Whae'er ye be that woman love,	O woman lovely! woman fair!
To this be never blind,	An angel form's fa'n to thy share,
Nae ferlie⁵ 'tis tho' fickle she prove,	'Twad been o'er meikle to [ha'e] gi'en thee mair—
A woman has't by kind.	I mean an angel mind.

¹ Fool ² Plenty. ³ Riches; goods. ⁴ Lost. ⁵ Wonder.

"SHE'S FAIR AND FAUSE." Mr. Stenhouse informs us, that "Burns picked up this charming old melody in the country, and wrote the verses to which it is so happily adapted in the Museum." See Museum Illustrations, vol. iv. p. 359. We have no doubt that this was the case, for Burns, as we have already had occasion to remark, was very successful in recovering old melodies that were but little known, and at once giving them a more extended circulation, by writing songs for them. In this instance, however, Oswald had already rescued the air from oblivion, by printing it in his Caledonian Pocket Companion, book iv., where it appears under the title of "The lads of Leith." In the first stanza of the song, the repetition of the word "gear" in rhyme, is rather a blemish.

In his "Cursory Remarks on Scottish Song," No. 3, Captain C. Gray, R.M., quotes Burns regarding "A Collection of Songs:"—"That volume was my vade mecum. I pored over them during my work, or walking to my labour, song by song, verse by verse—carefully noticing the true tender or sublime, from affectation or fustian; and I am convinced, that I owe to this practice most of my critic-craft, such as it is." Captain Gray thinks that this Collection of Songs, so much studied by Burns, was most probably the first or second edition of the "Scots Nightingale;" the second edition, "with one hundred modern songs," having been printed in 1779. Captain Gray gives reasons for his opinion by quotations; and, among others, quotes from the "Scots Nightingale," "The Address;" the last four lines of which seem to have suggested to Burns a striking idea in his song, "She's fair and fause."

The four last lines of the "Address" are :—

"To bless is Heaven's peculiar grace,
Let me a blessing find :
And since you wear an angel's face,
Oh show an angel's mind !"

Burns, doubtless, borrowed the idea; but he improved it, as his verses show. Chaucer, Shakespeare, Milton, and other great poets, were great borrowers—improving upon the ideas they adopted from others. The first poet who borrowed nothing from any one is yet unknown. In No. 4 of his Remarks, Captain Gray mentions another book, —"The Lark, being a Collection of the most celebrated and newest Songs, Scots and English, 1765,"—which also contains "The Address" above quoted; and thence infers, that "The Lark" may, still more probably, have been the Collection referred to by Burns.

AFTON WATER.

ARRANGED BY G. F. GRAHAM.

Flow gent - ly, sweet Af - ton, a - mong thy green

braes, Flow gent - ly, I'll sing thee a song in thy praise;

My Ma - ry's a - sleep by thy mur - mur - ing

stream; Flow gent - ly, sweet Af - ton, dis - turb not her

dream.

Thou stock-dove, whose echo resounds through the glen,
Ye wild whistling blackbirds, in yon flow'ry den,
Thou green-crested lap-wing, thy screaming forbear,
I charge you, disturb not my slumbering fair.

How lofty, sweet Afton, thy neighbouring hills,
Far mark'd with the courses of clear-winding rills;
There daily I wander, as morn rises high,
My flocks and my Mary's sweet cot in my eye.

How pleasant thy banks and green valleys below,
Where wild in the woodlands the primroses blow:

There oft, as mild evening creeps o'er the lea,
The sweet-scented birk shades my Mary and me.

Thy crystal stream, Afton, how lovely it glides,
And winds by the cot where my Mary resides!
How wanton thy waters her snowy feet lave,
As, gath'ring sweet flow'rets, she stems thy clear wave!

Flow gently, sweet Afton, among thy green braes;
Flow gently, sweet river, the theme of my lays:
My Mary's asleep by thy murmuring stream;
Flow gently, sweet Afton, disturb not her dream.

"AFTON WATER." "This song was written by Burns, and presented by him, as a tribute of gratitude and respect, to Mrs. Stewart of Afton Lodge, for the notice she had taken of the bard, being the first he ever received from any person in her rank of life. He afterwards transmitted the verses, along with the beautiful melody to which they are adapted, to Johnson, the publisher of the Museum. Afton is a small river in Ayrshire, a tributary stream of the Nith. Mrs. Stewart inherited the property of Afton Lodge, which is situated upon its banks, in right of her father." See Museum Illustrations, vol. iv. p. 355. It does not appear whence Burns obtained the air, of which the author is unknown.

After the publication of the Orpheus Caledonius (Thomson), we hear no more of Rizzio till the appearance of Oswald's Second Collection of Scottish Airs in 1742. There we find four of those airs, formerly ascribed to Rizzio by Thomson, passed over without any such ascription, while six others have the name of "Rizo" attached to them; these are, "The cock laird," "The last time I cam' o'er the muir," "Peggy, I must love thee," "The black eagle," "The lowlands of Holland," and "William's ghost;" the last of these airs being a composition of the day, perhaps even by Oswald himself. We thus see clearly enough that no dependence can be placed on these men—their pretended knowledge is mere assumption, which, however it might have imposed on the credulous and the uninformed, will not bear the test of sober criticism. It is to be remarked, that both these works, the Orpheus Caledonius, and Oswald's Second Collection, appeared in London; and that the contemporaneous Edinburgh Collections, Allan Ramsay's, circa 1726, Adam Craig's, 1730, and William Macgibbon's, 1742, while they contain most, if not all the airs already named, do not make any mention whatever of Rizzio. On the contrary, Craig, in dedicating his work to the "Musical Society of Mary's Chappell," states, that the airs are "the native and genuine product of the country;" words which he would not have used without alluding in some way to Rizzio, had there been any tradition then current in Scotland, connecting him with Scottish melody.

MARY MORISON.

ARRANGED BY FINLAY DUN.

Ma - ry, at thy win - dow be; It is the wish'd, the tryst - ed hour: Those

smiles and glan - ces let me see, That make the mi - ser's trea - sure poor.

How blythe - ly wad I bide the stoure, A wea - ry slave frae sun to sun, Could I the rich re - ward secure, The love - ly Ma - ry

Mo - ri-son.

Yestreen, when to the stented[2] string
The dance gaed through the lichtit ha',
To thee my fancy took its wing—
I sat, but neither heard nor saw.
Though this was fair, and that was braw,
And yon the toast o' a' the town,
I sigh'd, and said amang them a',
Ye are na Mary Morison.

O, Mary, canst thou wreck his peace,
Wha for thy sake wad gladly dee?
Or canst thou break that heart of his,
Whase only faut is loving thee?
If love for love thou wilt na gi'e,
At least be pity to me shown,
A thocht ungentle canna be
The thocht of Mary Morison.

[1] Appointed; agreed upon.
[2] Dust; metaphorically—labour, hardship.
[3] Tightened.—In some editions "trembling" is substituted for "stented."

"MARY MORISON." In Johnson's Museum the air is called "The Miller;" and is there given with verses written by Sir John Clerk of Pennycuik, Bart., one of the Barons of the Court of Exchequer in Scotland, and a man of remarkable learning and accomplishments in his day. One of his younger sons was John Clerk of Eldin, Esq., distinguished for his work on "Naval Tactics," and the father of the late Lord Eldin, an eminent Scottish lawyer. See Museum Illustrations, vol. ii. pp. 120-203. The humorous verses by Sir John Clerk do not appear to us to be very suitable to the air, which is in a minor key, and of a tender and rather pathetic character. We have therefore substituted for them the words by Burns, which begin, "O, Mary, at thy window be," and which were, as he says, "one of his juvenile works." He had written them to the air of "Bide ye yet;" and we think his having done so exhibits one of the very rare instances in which Burns did not perceive that the air was not well suited to the words that he wrote for it. The air of "The Miller," on the contrary, is well adapted to the song of "Mary Morison."

The author of the air is not known. Its date seems to belong to a period not earlier than the commencement of the last century. Captain Charles Gray, R.M., in his "Cursory Remarks on Scottish Song," introduces "Mary Morison" as follows:—"The late William Hazlitt, who wrote many works on the belles lettres, pays a high compliment to the genius of Burns, in his 'Lectures on the British Poets.' The passage has often been quoted, but as the memories of all the admirers of our Bard may not be so good as our own, we may be pardoned if we quote it again. 'Of all the productions of Burns, the pathetic and serious love-songs which he has left behind him, in the manner of the old ballads, are perhaps those which take the deepest and most lasting hold of the mind. Such as the lines on 'Mary Morison,' those entitled, 'Jessie,' and the song beginning, 'Oh, my love is like a red, red rose.'' Now, it so happens that 'My love, &c.,' is an old ballad, which proves the discernment of Hazlitt as a critic."

HUNTINGTOWER.

ARRANGED BY T. M. MUDIE.

(JEANIE.)

= 104

MODERATO.

1. When ye gang a-
2. That's nae gift, a-
3. Be my gude-man your

wa', Jam - ie,   Far a - cross the sea, lad - die;   When ye gang to
va' Jam - ie,   That's nae gift a - va', lad - die; There's ne'er a gown in
sel', Jam - ie, Be my gudeman your - sel', lad - die: And tak me ower to

(JAMIE.)

Ger - man - ie, What will ye send to me, lad - die? I'll send ye a braw new
a' the land I'd like when ye're a - wa', lad - die. When I come back a-
Ger - man - ie, Wi' you at hame to dwell, lad - die. I dinna ken how that wad

gown, Jean - ie, I'll send ye a braw new gown, lass - ie; And it shall be o'
gain, Jean - ie, When I come back a - gain, lass - ie; I'll bring wi' me a
do, Jean - ie, I dinna see how that can do, lass - ie; For I've a wife and

cress. . . . .   *f*

silk and gowd, Wi' Val - enciennes set round, lass - ie.
gallant gay, To be your ane gude - man, lass - ie.
bairnies three, And I'm no sure how ye'd 'gree,[1] lass - ie.

p   *f*   *riten* . . . .

JEANIE.

4. Ye shou'd ha'e telt me that in time, Jamie,
    Ye shou'd ha'e telt me that lang syne, laddie ;
    For had I kent o' your fause heart,
    You ne'er had gotten mine, laddie.

5. Gae back to your wife and hame, Jamie,
    Gae back to your bairnies three, laddie ;
    And I will pray they ne'er may thole[2]
    A broken heart like me, laddie !

6. Think weel, for fear ye rue, Jamie,
    Think weel, for fear ye rue, laddie ;
    For I have neither gowd nor lands,
    To be a match for you, laddie.

[1] Agree.

JAMIE.

4. Your e'en were like a spell, Jeanie,
    Your e'en were like a spell, lassie ;
    That ilka day bewitch'd me sae,
    I could na help mysel', lassie.

5. Dry that tearfu' e'e, Jeanie,
    Dry that tearfu' e'e, lassie ;
    I've neither wife nor bairnies three,
    And I'll wed nane but thee, lassie.

6. Blair in Athol's mine, Jeanie,
    Fair Dunkeld is mine, lassie,
    Saint Johnstoun's bow'r, and Huntingtow'r,
    And a' that's mine is thine, lassie.

[2] Suffer.

"HUNTINGTOWER." This ballad is traditional in Perthshire, and is believed to be ancient. It is not known to have been published, however, before 1827, when Kinloch gave, in his Ancient Scotch Ballads, a version of it, taken down from the recitation of an idiot boy in Wishaw. Since that time various versions have appeared, but whether they were taken down from recitation, or are merely specimens of modern work, is uncertain. One of them was written by Lady Nairne, with the express intention of making the ballad agree rather better with modern notions.

The air has all the simplicity of the olden time, and may be coeval with the ballad ; but it is not known to have been written down till within the last half century. There is, however, a tune in Durfey's Pills, v. 42 (Repr. 1719), which bears so strong a resemblance to it, as to suggest the idea that it may have been the form of the melody at that time. The song there adapted to it is an Anglo-Scottish version of "Hey, Jenny, come doun to Jock," and is styled the Scotch Wedding.

THE LOWLANDS O' HOLLAND.

ARRANGED BY J. T. SURENNE.

The love that I had cho - sen, Was to ny heart's con - tent, The

saut sea sall be fro - zen Be - fore that I re - pent; Re - pent it will I ne - ver, Un -

til the day I dee, Tho' the Low - lands o' Hol - land Ha'e

twinned my love and me. _dim._

_mf_   _p_

The stanzas within brackets may be omitted in singing.

My love lies in the saut sea,
  And I am on the side,
Enough to break a young thing's heart
  Wha lately was a bride;
Wha lately was a bonnie bride,
  And pleasure in her e'e;
But the Lowlands o' Holland
  Ha'e twinned my love and me.

[My love he built a bonnie ship,
  And sent her to the sea,
Wi' seven score brave mariners
  To bear her companie;
Threescore gaed to the bottom,
  And threescore died at sea,
And the Lowlands o' Holland
  Ha'e twinned my love and me.]

[My love he built anither ship,
  And sent her to the main,
He had but twenty mariners,
  And a' to bring her hame;
But the weary wind began to rise,
  And the sea began to rout,
And my love, and his bonnie ship,
  Turn'd widdershins[1] about!]

There sall nae coif[2] come on my head,
  Nae kame come in my hair,
There sall neither coal nor candle licht,
  Come in my bower mair;
Nor sall I ha'e anither love,
  Until the day I dee,
I never loved a love but ane,
  And he's drown'd in the sea.

[O, haud your tongue, my daughter dear,
  Be still, and be content,
There are mair lads in Galloway,
  Ye needna sair lament.
O! there is nane in Galloway,
  There's nane at a' for me;
For I never lo'ed a lad but ane,
  And he's drown'd in the sea.]

[1] In a direction contrary to the sun.   [2] Cap, head-dress.

"THE LOWLANDS O' HOLLAND." This ballad is said to have been composed about the beginning of last century by a young widow in Galloway, whose husband was drowned on a voyage to Holland. "The third verse in the Museum, (says Mr. Stenhouse,) is spurious nonsense, and Johnson has omitted the last stanza altogether." In Oswald's second Collection there is a tune called "The Lowlands of Holland," but it is quite different from the excellent air given by Johnson, and by Pietro Urbani, and is evidently modelled upon the air in the Skene MS., "My love she winns not here away." The late Mr. William Marshall, butler to the Duke of Gordon, borrowed his highly popular tune, "Miss Admiral Gordon's Strathspey," from "The Lowlands of Holland," as given by Johnson and Urbani. To Marshall's altered air, Burns wrote his charming song, "Of a' the airts the wind can blaw." Mr. Stenhouse says, "The Editor of the late Collection of Gaelic Airs in 1816, puts in a claim for 'The Lowlands of Holland' being a Highland air, and that it is called, 'Thuile toabh a sheidas goagh.' By writing a few Gaelic verses to each Lowland song, every Scottish melody might easily be transferred to the Highlands. This is rather claiming too much." See Museum Illustrations, vol. ii. p. 115. To this we have to add, that with admirable coolness, and without offering any evidence, the Editor of that Collection gives a "List of Highland Melodies already incorporated with Scottish song;" and among these we find "Wilt thou be my dearie?" "Coming through the rye;" "My love's in Germany;" "Green grow the rashes;" "Wat ye wha's in yon town?" "Gloomy winter's now awa';" "Wat ye wha I met yestreen?" &c., in all twenty-five airs, which he claims as Highland! We had intended to make some farther remarks upon this most untenable claim; but perhaps the above may suffice for the present.

O LAY THY LOOF IN MINE, LASS.

ARRANGED BY T. M. MUDIE.

O lay thy loof[1] in mine, lass, In mine, lass, in mine, lass; And swear on thy white hand, lass, That thou wilt be my ain. A slave to Love's unbound-ed sway, He aft has wrought me mei-kle wae; But now he is my dead-lie fae, Un-less thou'lt be my ain.

O lay thy loof in mine, lass, In mine, lass, in mine, lass; And swear on thy white hand, lass, That

thou wilt be my ain.

The next verse begins at the sign :𝄪:

There's mony a lass has broke my rest,
That for a blink[2] I ha'e lo'ed best;
But thou art queen within my breast
For ever to remain!
O lay thy loof in mine, lass,
In mine, lass, in mine lass,
And swear on thy white hand, lass,
That thou wilt be my ain.

[1] Palm of the hand.   [2] A short time.

"O LAY THY LOOF IN MINE, LASS." "This song was written by Burns for the Museum. It is adapted to the favourite old tune, called *The Cordwainer's March*, which, in former times, was usually played before that ancient and useful fraternity at their annual procession on St. Crispin's day. The tune is also preserved in Aird's first volume of Select Airs, and other Collections." See Museum Illustrations, vol. vi. pp. 491, 492. This air of "The Cordwainer's March" suggests to us a Russian air that resembles it in some leading passages, and is found in a MS. Collection of Russian airs, made in 1817-18, by Dr. William Howison of Edinburgh, when he was in Russia. We here quote the air, No. 29 of Dr. Howison's Collection, and obligingly sent to us by him at our request. The Russian title of the song for the air is translated "I did not know for what."

Andante Molto.

This is an air of one strain, modulating half between A minor and E minor, on which last key it ends. In general, Russian airs in a minor key, if they consist of *two* strains, modulate from the minor to its next relative major; for example, from A to C—and in the second strain modulate back from the relative major to the original minor.

THE WEARY PUND O' TOW.

ARRANGED BY G. F. GRAHAM.

wea - ry pund, the weary pund, The wea - ry pund o' tow; I think my wife will

end her life, Be - fore she spin her tow. I bought my wife a

stane o' lint, As gude as e'er did grow; And a' that she has made o' that Is ac poor pund o' tow. The wea-ry pund, the wea-ry pund, The

wea-ry pund o' tow; I think my wife will end her life, Be-fore she spin her

tow.

Dal Segno

There sat[1] a bottle in a bole,[2]
Beyont the ingle[3] low ;[4]
And ay she took the tither souk,
To drouk[5] the stourie[6] tow.
The weary pund, &c.

Quoth I, For shame, ye dirty dame,
Gae spin your tap o' tow !
She took the rock, and wi' a knock,
She brak it o'er my pow.[7]
The weary pund, &c.

At last her feet, I sang to see't,
Gaed[8] foremost o'er the knowe ;[9]
And or I wad[10] anither jad,
I'll wallop in a tow ![11]
The weary pund, &c.

[1] In Ayrshire, *sit* is generally used instead of *stand.* [2] A recess. Fire. [4] Flame. [5] To moisten [6] Dusty. [7] Head. [8] Went. [9] Hillock. [10] E'er I wed. [11] Dangle in a rope.

"THE WEARY PUND O' TOW." The tune and the title of this song are from Oswald's Caledonian Pocket Companion, Book viii. The verses were written by Burns for Johnson's Museum. There is no trace of the author of the air, which is one of our best modern Scottish airs. Its structure shows it to be *modern ;* that is to say, that it is not older than the earlier part of the eighteenth century. (See Appendix.) From the skilful way in which Burns composed verses to Scottish airs, we have long been of opinion that he must not only have had a musical ear, but must have had some practical knowledge of music. On mentioning our opinion to a friend, he confirmed it by facts which we are not at liberty to state, but which we hope he will soon give to the public.

ROSLIN CASTLE.

ARRANGED BY FINLAY DUN

$\text{♩} = 104$

LARGHETTO.

'Twas in the sea . son of the year, When all things gay and

sweet appear, That Co - lin, with the morn - ing ray, A - rose and sung his

ru - ral lay. Of Nan - ny's charms the shep - herd sung, The hills and dales with

Nan - ny rung; And Ros - lin Cas - tle heard the swain, And

e - cho'd back the cheer - ful strain.

Awake, sweet muse! the breathing spring
With rapture warms; awake, and sing!
Awake, and join the vocal throng
Who hail the morning with a song:
To Nanny raise the cheerful lay,
O bid her haste and come away;
In sweetest smiles herself adorn,
And add new graces to the morn.

O hark, my love, on every spray
Each feather'd warbler tunes his lay
'Tis beauty fires the ravish'd throng:
And love inspires the melting song.
Then let my raptur'd notes arise,
For beauty darts from Nanny's eyes,
And love my rising bosom warms,
And fills my soul with sweet alarms.

O come, my love! thy Colin's lay
With rapture calls, O come away!
Come, while the muse this wreath shall twine
Around that modest brow of thine;
O hither haste, and with thee bring
That beauty blooming like the spring,
Those graces that divinely shine,
And charm this ravish'd breast of mine.

"ROSLIN CASTLE." The composer of this melody is not known; it is comparatively modern however, and from its style seems to belong to the early part of the eighteenth century. It has been wrongly ascribed to James Oswald, who never laid any claim to it. In his collection it is not marked as one of his own tunes; and indeed it was published in a prior Collection, M'Gibbon's, under the name of the "House of Glams." Oswald practised several unpardonable deceptions upon the public, by passing off tunes of his own as compositions of David Rizzio. His tricks of that kind are pointedly alluded to in a poetical epistle to him, printed in the Scots Magazine for October 1741. The verses here given, which Burns called "beautiful," were written by Richard Hewitt, a native of Cumberland, who died in 1764. When a boy, he was engaged to lead blind Dr. Blacklock; who, pleased with his intelligence, educated him, and employed him as his amanuensis. See Museum Illustrations, vol. i., pp. 5 and 108, and vol. iv., pp. 406-7.

L

THE MURMUR OF THE MERRY BROOK.

AIR, ' THE BONNIE BRIER BUSH."

ARRANGED BY T. M. MUDIE.

The mur-mur of the mer-ry brook, As, gush-ing-ly and free, It
wim-ples, with its sun-bright look, Far down yon shel-ter'd lea, And hums to ev'-ry
drow-sy flow'r A low quaint lul-la-by, Speaks to my spi-rit, at this hour, Of

The music of the gay green wood,
  When every leaf and tree
Is coax'd by winds, of gentlest mood,
  To utter harmony;
And the small birds, that answer make
To the winds' fitful glee,
In me most blissful visions wake,
  Of love and thee.

The rose perks up its blushing cheek,
  So soon as it can see,
Along the eastern hills, one streak
  Of the sun's majesty:
Laden with dewy gems, it gleams
A precious freight to me,
For each pure drop thereon me seems
  A type of thee.

[And when abroad in summer morn,
  I hear the blythe bold bee
Winding aloft his tiny horn,
  (An errant knight perdy.)

That winged hunter of rare sweets,
  O'er many a far country,
To me a lay of love repeats,
  Its subject—thee.]

And when, in midnight hour, I note
  The stars so pensively,
In their mild beauty, onward float
  Through heaven's own silent sea:
My heart is in their voyaging
To realms where spirits be,
But its mate, in such wandering,
  Is ever thee.

[But, oh, the murmur of the brook,
  The music of the tree;
The rose with its sweet shamefaced look,
  The booming of the bee;
The course of each bright voyager,
In heaven's unmeasured sea,
Would not one heart pulse of me stir,
  Loved I not thee!]

The stanzas within brackets may be omitted.

"THE MURMUR OF THE MERRY BROOK." This song was written by William Motherwell, and was published in his Poems, Glasgow, 1832. We have adapted it here to the melody "The brier bush," as the words usually sung to that air are but indifferent. We subjoin them, however, in case they should be preferred to those we have given above. They are an improved version of the original song sent to Johnson's Museum by Burns. For an account of the air, see the next Note.

There grows a bonnie brier bush in our kail-yard;
And white are the blossoms o't in our kail-yard:
Like wee bit white cockauds for our loyal Hieland lads;
And the lassies lo'e the bonnie bush in our kail-yard.

But were they a' true that were far awa'?
Oh! were they a' true that were far awa'?
They drew up wi' glaiket[1] Englishers at Carlisle ha',
And forgot auld frien's when far awa'.

Ye'll come nae mair, Jamie, where aft you've been;
Ye'll come nae mair, Jamie, to Athole's Green;
Ye lo'ed ower weel the dancin' at Carlisle ha',
And forgot the Hieland hills that were far awa'.

He's comin' frae the North that's to fancy me,
He's comin' frae the North that's to fancy me;
A feather in his bonnet, a ribbon at his knee;
He's a bonnie Hieland laddie, and you be na he.

[1] Giddy; thoughtless

WE'LL MEET BESIDE THE DUSKY GLEN.

AIR, "YON BURN SIDE."

ARRANGED BY T. M. MUDIE.

We'll meet be - side the dus - ky glen, on yon burn - side, Where the bush - es form a co - zie den, on yon burn - side; Tho' the broom - y knowes be green, Yet there we may be seen; But we'll meet, we'll meet at e'en, down by

colla voce.

yon burn - side.

I'll lead thee to the birken bow'r, on yon burn-side,
Sae sweetly wove wi' woodbine flow'r, on yon burn-side;
There the mavis we will hear,
And the blackbird singin' clear,
As on my arm ye lean, down by yon burn-side.

Awa', ye rude unfeeling crew, frae yon burnside;
Those fairy scenes are no for you, by yon burn-side;
There fancy smooths her theme,
By the sweetly murmuring stream,
And the rock-lodged echoes skim, down by yon burn-side.

Now the plantin' taps are tinged wi' gowd, on yon burn-side.
And gloamin'[3] draws her foggy shroud o'er yon burn-side;
Far frae the noisy scene,
I'll through the fields alane;
There we'll meet, my ain dear Jean! down by yon burn-side.

1 Warm, snug, well sheltered.　　2 Hillocks.　　3 Twilight.

"YON BURN SIDE." This air is the second part of "For lack of gold" modified, and seems to have been recovered by R. A. Smith. It was published by him in connexion with Tannahill's song, early in the present century. As the poet and the musician were intimately acquainted, the following extracts from a letter of R. A. Smith, (published in "The Harp of Renfrewshire,") may be interesting to the admirers of Tannahill's genius :—

"My first introduction to Tannahill was in consequence of hearing his song, 'Blythe was the time,' sung while it was yet in manuscript. I was so much struck with the beauty and natural simplicity of the language, that I found means shortly afterwards of being introduced to its author. The acquaintance thus formed, gradually ripened into a warm and steady friendship, that was never interrupted in a single instance till his lamented death." "It was only from his compositions that a stranger could form any estimate of his talents—his appearance indicated no marks of genius—his manner was rather distant, and it was but in company with a few with whom he was very intimate, that his conversation became animated: in a large assembly he appeared to great disadvantage; was quite uneasy, and seldom spoke, except to the person nearest him, if he happened to be an acquaintance."

The older version of "The brier bush," which we have already given, was first published in the fifth volume of Johnson's Museum, about 1798. Mr. Stenhouse's Note upon the air and song, as given in the Museum, is as follows :—"This song, with the exception of a few lines, which are old, was written by Burns for the Museum. It is accordingly marked with the letter Z, to denote its being an old song with additions. Burns likewise communicated the air to which the words are adapted. It is apparently the progenitor of the improved tune, called 'For the lake of gold she's left me,' to which Dr. Austin's words are adapted, and which the reader will find inserted in the second volume of the Museum." See Museum Illustrations, vol. v. p. 432. Whatever part of these verses was written by Burns, is by no means worthy of his pen. Instead of the air communicated by Burns being "the progenitor" of the air called "For the lack of gold," &c., the reverse seems much more probable; since the melody of an old song, "For the lak of gold I lost her, O," is given by Oswald in his "Pocket Companion." The air communicated by Burns seems but an altered fragment of the other; and was, perhaps, picked up by him from the singing of some country girl.

WHERE HA'E YE BEEN A' THE DAY?

AIR, "BONNIE LADDIE, HIGHLAND LADDIE."   ARRANGED BY T. M. MUDIE.

Where ha'e ye been a' the day, Bon - nie lad - die, Highland lad - die! Saw ye him that's far a - way, Bonnie laddie, Highland laddie! On his head a bon - net blue, Bon - nie lad - die, Highland lad - die; Tar - tan plaid and

When he drew his gude braid sword,
 Bonnie laddie, Highland laddie,
Then he gave his royal word,
 Bonnie laddie, Highland laddie,
That frae the field he ne'er would flee,
 Bonnie laddie, Highland laddie,
But wi' his friend would live or dee,
 Bonnie laddie, Highland laddie.

Weary fa' the Lawland loon
 Bonnie laddie, Highland laddie,
Wha took frae him the British crown.
 Bonnie laddie, Highland laddie;
But blessings on the kilted clans,
 Bonnie laddie, Highland laddie,
That fought for him at Prestonpans.
 Bonnie laddie, Highland laddie.

"WHERE HA'E YE BEEN A' THE DAY?" In James Hogg's Jacobite Relics, second series, No. 105, p. 202, occurs a song beginning, "Geordie sits in Charlie's chair," to be sung to the air which is given to No. 63 of the same volume, called "The Highland Laddie." Hogg's version of the air differs from the one we have adopted. The song, No. 105, is horribly ludicrous, but we cannot give it entire, on account of the extreme coarseness of some of the stanzas. A modification of it is published in Mr. George Thomson's Collection, with two introductory stanzas not in Hogg's edition. The stanza beginning, "Weary fa' the Lawland loon," is the second in Hogg's copy. As an additional song, we give below the first and fourth stanzas (the best, and long enough for singing) of a humorous song published anonymously in Blackie's Book of Scottish Song, p. 262. Mr. Stenhouse, in his note on "The Highland Laddie," (No. 468 of Johnson's Museum,) quotes two songs from a "Collection of loyal songs, poems, &c., 1750," and says,—"The air to which the foregoing songs are adapted is very spirited. It appears without a name in Oswald's Caledonian Pocket Companion, Book i. p. 36, under a slow air called 'The Highland Laddie.' But the old appellation of the air was 'Cockle Shells,' and (it) was known in England during the usurpation of Cromwell, for it is printed in Playford's 'Dancing Master,' first edition, in 1657." Mr. Stenhouse here confounds both dates and airs. The first edition of Playford is dated 1651, and "Cockle Shells" appears for the first time in the eleventh edition, 1701. "Cockle Shells" is evidently the old version of the air which we have given above to the words beginning, "Where ha'e ye been a' (the) day?" but has nothing in common with the tune in Oswald to which Mr. Stenhouse refers. The air of "Cockle Shells" has a starting-note, and concludes on the *sixth* of the key; while the modern versions of the same air, under the name of "The Highland Laddie," or "Highland Laddie," omit the starting-note, and close upon the *fifth* of the key; thus destroying characteristic features of the melody. The tune called "The Lass of Livingston," is another version of "Cockle Shells."

To ha'e a wife and rule a wife,
 Taks a wise man, taks a wise man;
But to get a wife to rule a man,
 O that ye can, O that ye can.
So the wife's that's wise we aye maun prize,
 For they're few ye ken, they're scarce ye ken;
O Solomon says ye'll no fin' ane
 In hundreds ten, in hundreds ten.

Sae he that gets a guid, guid wife,
 Gets gear aneugh, gets gear aneugh;
An' he that gets an ill, ill wife,
 Gets cares aneugh, gets fears aneugh.
A man may spen', an ha'e to the en',
 If his wife be ought, if his wife be ought;
But a man may spare, an aye be bare,
 If his wife be nought, if his wife be nought.

THE CAMPBELLS ARE COMIN'.

ARRANGED BY FINLAY DUN.

ALLEGRO MARCATO.

mf   *cres.*   *f*   *p*

The Campbells are comin', O - ho, O - ho! The Campbells are comin', O - ho, O - ho! The

Campbells are comin' to bon - nie Lochle - ven; The Campbells are comin', O - ho, O - ho!

Up - on the Lomonds I lay, I lay, Up - on the Lomonds I

lay, I lay; I look - ed down to bonnie Loch - le - ven, And saw three bon - nie

perches play.

Great Argyle, he goes before,
He makes the cannons and guns to roar,
Wi' sound o' trumpet, pipe, and drum,
The Campbells are comin', O-ho, O-ho!
The Campbells are comin', &c.

The Campbells they are a' in arms,
Their loyal faith and truth to show;
Wi' banners rattling in the wind,
The Campbells are comin', O-ho, O-ho!
The Campbells are comin', &c.

"THE CAMPBELLS ARE COMIN', O-HO, O-HO!" Mr. Stenhouse's note on this (No. 299 of Museum) is as follows :— "In the index to the third volume of the Museum, this song is said to have been composed on the imprisonment of the unfortunate Mary Queen of Scots, in the Castle of Lochleven, in 1567. The Earl of Argyle was on the Queen's party at the battle of Langside, in 1568, and, perhaps, the tune may have been the Campbells' quick-march for two centuries past; but, nevertheless, the words of the song contain intrinsic evidence that it is not much above a century old. In all probability it was written about the year 1715, on the breaking out of the rebellion in the reign of George I., when John Campbell, the great Duke of Argyle, was made commander-in-chief of his Majesty's forces in North Britain, and was the principal means of its total suppression. I have seen the *tune*, however, in several old collections." See Museum Illustrations, vol. iii. pp. 291, 292. See also the song "The Clans are coming," in Hogg's second series of Jacobite Relics, and his note upon it, p. 289. We subjoin one from the first volume of James Aird's Selection of Airs, published at Glasgow about 1784. Another, slightly different, is found in Part I. of Gow & Sons Complete Repository.

O KENMURE'S ON AND AWA', WILLIE.

ARRANGED BY T. M. MUDIE.

Kenmure's on, and a - wa', Willie, O Kenmure's on, and a - wa': And

Kenmure's lord's the brav - est lord That ev - er Gal - loway saw.

Suc - cess to Kenmure's band, Willie, Suc - cess to Kenmure's band! There's *no a heart that fears a Whig, That rides in Kenmure's band.*

Ritornel for the first two verses.   To conclude.

Here's Kenmure's health in wine, Willie,
  Here's Kenmure's health in wine;
There ne'er was a coward o' Kenmure's blude,
  Nor yet o' Gordon's line.
O Kenmure's lads are men, Willie,
  O Kenmure's lads are men;
Their hearts and swords are metal true,
  And that their foes shall ken.

They'll live or die wi' fame, Willie,
  They'll live or die wi' fame;
But soon, wi' sounding victorie,
  May Kenmure's lord come hame.
Here's him that's far awa', Willie,
  Here's him that's far awa';
And here's the flower that I lo'e best,
  The rose that's like the snaw.

"O KENMURE'S ON AND AWA'." "The hero of this ballad," says Mr. Stenhouse, "was the Right Honourable William Gordon, Viscount Kenmure, commander-in-chief of the Chevalier's forces in the south-west of Scotland in 1715. Having left Kenmure at the head of about two hundred horsemen, and formed a junction with the troops under the command of General Forster, he marched as far as Preston in Lancashire. Here, however, his lordship surrendered himself a prisoner at discretion, and was appointed to be conducted, with many of his unfortunate followers, to London, in 1715. Arriving at Highgate, each of the prisoners was placed on horseback, with his arms firmly pinioned, and a foot-soldier holding the reins of his bridle. On the 9th of that month, General Tatton, who commanded the detachment, left Highgate with the prisoners, and proceeded to London, drums beating a victorious march, and the mob strengthening the chorus with the horrid din of marrow-bones, cleavers, and warming-pans. In this disgraceful triumph were the unhappy captives led through the streets of the city, amidst the hootings and insults of a barbarous rabble, and conducted to the several prisons assigned to receive them. Lord Kenmure and several other noblemen were committed to the Tower. He was afterwards tried, and (very unjustly, as some thought) beheaded on Tower-hill, 24th February 1716. Burns transmitted the ballad, in his own handwriting, with the melody to which it is adapted, to Mr. Johnson. Cromek, in his 'Remains of Nithsdale and Galloway Song,' printed in 1810, has inserted three additional stanzas, which he pretends are of equal merit and antiquity with those in Ritson's Scottish Songs (copied from the Museum), but they are evidently spurious and modern. They are here annexed, however, for the reader's inspection.

'There's a rose in Kenmure's cap, Willie,
  There's a rose in Kenmure's cap;
He'll steep it red in ruddie heart's blede
  Afore the battle drap.

'He kiss'd his ladie's hand, Willie,
  He kiss'd his ladie's hand;
But gane's his ladie-courtesie,
  When he draws his bludie brand.

'His ladie's cheek was red, Willie,
  His ladie's cheek was red;
When she saw his steely jupes put on,
  Which smell'd o' deadly feud.'

It might rather have been supposed that the lady's cheeks would have assumed a pale in place of a red colour, situated as she was; and as to the expressions, *ruddie heart's blede* and *ladie courtesie*, they seem inexplicable." See Museum Illustrations, vol. iv. pp. 338, 339.

THE WEE WEE GERMAN LAIRDIE.

ARRANGED BY A. C. MACKENZIE.

1. Wha the deil ha'e we got - ten for a king, But a wee wee Ger - man laird - ie, And when we gaed to bring him hame, He was delv - ing in his kail yaird - ie. He was sheughing kail and lay - ing leeks With - out the hose, and but the breeks, And up his beg - gar

2. And he's clap - pit down in our gudeman's chair, The wee wee Ger - man laird - ie, And he's brought fouth o' for - eign trash, And dibbled them in his yaird - ie. He's pu'd the rose o' Eng-lish loons, And brok-en the harp o' Ir - ish clowns, But our Scots thistle will

Come up amang our Highland hills,
  Thou wee wee German lairdie,
And see how the Stuarts' lang kail thrive,
  They dibbled in our yairdie:
And if a stock thou daur to pu',
  Or haud the yokin' o' a plough,
We'll break your sceptre owre your mou',
  Thou wee bit German lairdie!

Auld Scotland thou 'rt owre cauld a hole
  For nursin' siccan vermin;
But the very dogs o' England's court
  They bark and howl in German.
Then keep thy dibble in thy ain hand,
  Thy spade but and thy yairdie,
For wha the deil now claims your land
  But a wee wee German lairdie!

"THE WEE WEE GERMAN LAIRDIE." This song was first printed in Cromek's Nithsdale and Galloway Relics, 1810. What part of it is old is uncertain; the rest being by Allan Cunningham, who could rarely resist an opportunity of adding a verse or two to any song that passed through his hands. One stanza has been omitted for an obvious reason. The air is merely a slightly altered version of "Blythe, blythe and merry was she," with the position of the parts reversed. The Ettrick Shepherd, in his Jacobite Relics, sets the song to an original air of his own, but also gives that which we have adopted. His outspoken vanity is always very amusing; he says of the air, "I have, however, added the best original one that I could find, which, though scarcely so good a tune as my own, is more in character. It is a capital song sung to either of these airs." We give the Shepherd's tune below as it is occasionally sung to the words.

THE PIPER OF DUNDEE.

ARRANGED BY T. M. MUDIE.

ALLEGRETTO.

The Pip - er came to our town, To our town, to our town, The Pip - er came to our town, And he play'd bon - nie - lie.

1. He play'd a spring the Laird to please, A spring brent new frae yont the seas; And then he gae his
2. He play'd the "Welcome o'er the main," And "Ye'se be fou, and I'se be fain," And "Auld Stuarts

bags a heeze, And play'd an-ith-er key. And was-na he a ro - guy, A ro - guy, a
back a-gain," Wi' meik-le mirth and glee.

ro - guy, And was-na he a ro - guy, The Pip-er o' Dun-dee.

1st and 2d times.

riten, . .   *Last time.*

He play'd " The Kirk," he play'd " The Queir,"
" The Mullin dhu " and " Chevalier,"
And " Lang away, but welcome here,"
Sae sweet, sae bonnielie.
And wasna he a roguy,
A roguy, a roguy,
And wasna he a roguy,
The Piper o' Dundee.

The Piper of Dundee.—The air to which this song is set is a Reel, called "The Drummer." The piper is said to have been Carnegie of Finhaven, who changed sides during the contest in 1715. He was a great coward, if we may believe the Jacobite writers; he certainly ran away at Sheriffmuir, but so many on both sides did the same, that this should not count for much against him. The tunes played by the piper are the airs of Jacobite songs, no doubt well known at the time; though some of them have not come down to us, notwithstanding the endeavours of Hogg and Dr. Charles Mackay to rescue from oblivion everything of the kind. See Hogg's Jacobite Relics, II. 260.

MY AIN KIND DEARIE, O.

ARRANGED BY T. M. MUDIE.

When o'er the hill the east - ern star Tells bught - in - time is

near, my jo; And ow - sen frae the fur - row'd field Re - turn sae dowf 'and wea - ry, O;

Down by the burn, where scent - ed birks Wi' dew are hang - ing clear, my jo; I'll meet thee on the lea - rig, My ain kind dear - ie, O.

poco riten.

In mirkest[3] glen, at midnight hour,
  I'd rove, and ne'er be eerie,[4] O;
If thro' that glen I gaed to thee,
  My ain kind dearie, O!
Although the night were ne'er sae wild,
  And I were ne'er sae weary, O,
I'd meet thee on the lea-rig,
  My ain kind dearie, O!

The hunter lo'es the morning sun,
  To rouse the mountain deer, my jo;
At noon the fisher seeks the glen,
  Along the burn to steer, my jo;
Gi'e me the hour o' gloamin' gray,
  It mak's my heart sae cheerie, O,
To meet thee on the lea-rig,
  My ain kind dearie, O.

[1] The hour when the ewes are driven into the pen to be milked.   [2] Dull : exhausted.   [3] Darkest.   [4] Frightened.

"MY AIN KIND DEARIE, O." James Oswald published the old melody in his Caledonian Pocket Companion, vol. viii. Its author is not known. It was more anciently called "The lea-rig," from a song beginning,

> "I'll rowe thee o'er the lea-rig,
>   My ain kind dearie, O;
> I'll rowe thee o'er the lea-rig,
>   My ain kind dearie, O.
> Although the night were ne'er sae wat,
>   And I were ne'er sae weary, O,
> I'll rowe thee o'er the lea-rig,
>   My ain kind dearie, O."

The words here given to the air were written by Burns in October 1792. It will be seen that he availed himself of the fifth and sixth lines of the old song in his second stanza. In his letter to Mr. Thomson, sending two stanzas of the new song, he says, "Let me tell you, that you are too fastidious in your ideas of songs and ballads. I own that your criticisms are just; the songs you specify in your list have, all but one, the faults you remark in them; but who shall mend the matter? Who shall rise up and say—Go to, I will make a better? For instance, on reading over 'The lea-rig,' I immediately set about trying my hand on it, and, after all, I could make nothing more of it than the following, which, heaven knows, is poor enough."

The following stanzas were written for this air by William Reid, Bookseller, Glasgow. Ferguson's song, of which they were intended to be a continuation, is scarcely fit for insertion here.—

At gloamin', if my lane I be,
  Oh, but I'm wondrous eerie, O :
And mony a heavy sigh I gi'e,
  When absent frae my dearie, O;
But seated 'neath the milk-white thorn,
  In ev'ning fair and clearie, O,
Enraptured, a' my cares I scorn,
  When wi' my kind dearie, O.

Whare through the birks the burnie rows,
  Aft ha'e I sat fu' cheerie, O,
Upon the bonnie greensward bowes,
  Wi' thee, my kind dearie, O.
I've courted till I've heard the craw
  Of honest chanticleerie, O,
Yet never miss'd my sleep ava,
  Whan wi' my kind dearie, O.

For though the night were ne'er sae dark,
  And I were ne'er sae weary, O,
I'd meet thee on the lea rig,
  My ain kind dearie, O.
While in this weary warld of wae,
  This wilderness sae drearie, O,
What makes me blythe, and keeps me sae ?
  'Tis thee, my kind dearie, O!

M

BEHOLD, MY LOVE, HOW GREEN THE GROVES.

AIR, "DOUN THE BURN, DAVIE.   ARRANGED BY T. M. MUDIE

Be - hold, my love, how green the groves, The prim - rose banks, how

fair ; The balm - y gales a - wake the flow'rs, And wave thy flax - en hair.

The lave - rock shuns the pal - ace gay, And o'er the cot - tage

Let skilful minstrels sweep the string
In lordly lighted ha',
The shepherd stops his simple reed
Blythe in the birken shaw.[1]
The princely revel may survey
Our rustic dance wi' scorn;
But are their hearts as light as ours
Beneath the milk-white thorn?

The shepherd in the flow'ry glen,
In hamely phrase will woo;
The courtier tells a finer tale—
But is his heart as true?
These wild-wood flowers I've pu'd to deck
That spotless breast o' thine;
The courtier's gems may witness love—
But 'tis na love like mine.

[1] A piece of flat ground at the bottom of a hill covered with short scraggy birches.

"BEHOLD, MY LOVE, HOW GREEN THE GROVES." "Burns says :—'I have been informed that the tune of *Doun the burn, Davie,* was the composition of David Maigh, keeper of the blood sleuth-hounds belonging to the Laird of Riddell, in Tweeddale.'—RELIQUES. But he was probably misinformed; for the tune occurs, note for note, in the Orpheus Caledonius, printed in 1725." See Museum Illustrations, vol. i. p. 78. In making this statement, Mr. Stenhouse must have quoted from memory without verification. Had he turned up the Orpheus Caledonius of 1725, he would have seen that the version there given differs so much from that of Johnson, as scarcely to be recognisable. Between the dates of the two editions of the Orpheus, 1725 and 1733, many changes were made, and this air was in a measure re-written, probably by William Thomson, the editor of the work, so that it can scarcely be said to be older than 1733. The tradition, if there really is such a thing, that the original song alludes to Queen Mary and Rizzio, is too absurd to require any refutation. Both words and tune are a century and a half later than *their* time. Instead of Crawfurd's very objectionable words, given in the Museum to the air of *Doun the burn, Davie,* we give those written by Burns for the same air. It seems as if Burns had had in view the following song, though in a different measure, written by James Thomson, author of "The Seasons."

THE HAPPY SHEPHERD.

If those who live in shepherd's bow'rs
Press not the rich and stately bed,
The new-mown hay and breathing flow'rs
A softer couch beneath them spread.

If those who sit at shepherd's board
Soothe not their taste by wanton art,
They take what Nature's gifts afford,
And take it with a cheerful heart.

If those who drain the shepherd's bowl
No high and sparkling wines can boast,
With wholesome cups they cheer the soul,
And crown them with the village toast.

If those who join in shepherd's sport,
Gay dancing on the daisied ground,
Have not the splendour of a court,
Yet love adorns the merry round.

ARGYLE IS MY NAME.

AIR. "BANNOCKS O' BARLEY-MEAL."   ARRANGED BY J. T. SURENNE.

Allegretto con Spirito.

Ar - gyle is my name, and you may think it strange, To live at a Court, yet never to change: To faction, or ty - ran - ny, e - qually foe; The good of the land's the sole mo - tive I know. The foes of my country and King I have faced; In ci - ty or battle I ne'er was disgraced: I've done what I could for my country's weal; Now I'll

feast upon bannocks o' barley-meal.

Ye riots and revels of London, adieu!
And Folly, ye foplings, I leave her to you!
For Scotland I mingled in bustle and strife—
For myself I seek peace and an innocent life:
I'll haste to the Highlands, and visit each scene
With Maggie, my love, in her rocklay[1] o' green;
On the banks o' Glenaray what pleasure I'll feel,
While she shares my bannock o' barley-meal!

And if it chance Maggie should bring me a son,
He shall fight for his King as his father has done;
I'll hang up my sword with an old soldier's pride—
Oh, may he be worthy to wear't on his side!
I pant for the breeze of my loved native place,
I long for the smile of each welcoming face—
I'll aff to the Highlands as fast's I can reel,
And feast upon bannocks o' barley-meal.

[1] A short cloak.

"ARGYLE IS MY NAME." The words given in the present work were written by the late Sir Alexander Boswell of Auchinleck, but are only a modification of the older words. In his Note on No. 560 of the Museum, Mr. Stenhouse says:—"This ballad is universally attributed to John Campbell, the renowned Duke of Argyle and Greenwich, whose uncorrupted patriotism and military talents justly entitled him to be ranked among the greatest benefactors of his country. He died on the 4th of October 1743, in the sixty-third year of his age. The tune is of Gaelic origin." The present Editor would rather say that the tune is very probably of Irish origin. Certainly it has never been claimed by Ireland, nor ever appeared in any collection of Irish melodies. It may therefore be a Scottish imitation of the Irish style. Charles Kirkpatrick Sharpe, Esq., writes the following Note on the ballad, p. 523, vol. i. of Museum:—"This song is older than the period here assigned to it; and if the name of Maggie is to be trusted, can only apply to the first Marquis of Argyle, whose wife was Lady Margaret Douglas, daughter of the Earl of Morton. He was so very notorious a coward, that this song could have been made by nobody but himself, unless to turn him into ridicule." Pope, in the Epilogue to his Satires, Dialogue ii., verses 86, 87, speaks thus in praise of the Duke of Argyle and Greenwich:—

"Argyll, the State's whole thunder born to wield,
And shake alike the senate and the field."

One of his biographers says of him—"In private life the Duke's conduct was highly exemplary. He was an affectionate husband and an indulgent master. He seldom parted with his servants till age had rendered them incapable of their employments; and then he made provision for their subsistence. He was liberal to the poor, and particularly to persons of merit in distress: but though he was ready to patronize deserving persons, he was extremely cautious not to deceive any by lavish promises, or leading them to form vain expectations."

O LOVE WILL VENTURE IN.

ARRANGED BY T. M. MUDIE.

♩ = 104
ANDANTE ESPRESSIVO.

p

O love will ven - ture in where it daur - na weel be seen; O

poco riten.

love will ven - ture in where wis - dom ance has been; But I will doun yon

poco riten.

ri - ver rove, a - mang the woods sae green, And a' to pu' a po - sie to my

colla voce.

ain   dear   May.

The primrose I will pu', the firstlin' o' the year;
And I will pu' the pink, the emblem o' my dear;
For she's the pink o' womankind, and blooms without a peer:
    And a' to be a posie to my ain dear May.

I'll pu' the buddin' rose, when Phœbus peeps in view,
For it's like a baumy kiss o' her sweet bonnie mou;
The hyacinth's for constancy, wi' its unchangin' blue :—
    And a' to be a posie to my ain dear May.

The lily it is pure, and the lily it is fair,
And in her lovely bosom I'll place the lily there;
The daisy's for simplicity, of unaffected air :—
    And a' to be a posie to my ain dear May.

The hawthorn I will pu', wi' it's locks o' siller grey,
Where, like an aged man, it stands at break o' day;
But the songster's nest within the bush I winna take away :—
    And a' to be a posie to my ain dear May.

The woodbine I will pu' when the e'enin' star is near,
And the diamond-draps o' dew shall be her een sae clear;
The violet's for modesty, which weel she fa's to wear :—
    And a' to be a posie to my ain dear May.

I'll tie the posie round wi' the silken band o' love,
And I'll place it in her breast, and I'll swear by a' above,
That to my latest breath o' life the band shall ne'er remove :—
    And this will be a posie to my ain dear May.

────────────────────

"O LOVE WILL VENTURE IN," &c., was written by Burns for Johnson's Museum. In a letter to Mr. George Thomson, 19th October 1794, Burns says, "The Posie, in the Museum, is my composition; the air was taken down from Mrs. Burns' voice. It is well known in the west country; but the old words are trash." He remarked how closely it resembled, in some passages, the air named "Roslin Castle," which he wrongly imagined that James Oswald had composed. See Note on "Roslin Castle," in an earlier page. In Cromek's Reliques, Burns gives a specimen of the old song. The following is the first stanza :—
        "There was a pretty May,[1] and a milkin' she went,
        Wi' her red rosy cheeks, and her coal-black hair;
        And she has met a young man comin' o'er the bent,[2]
        With a double and adieu to thee, fair May."
Professor Wilson, comparing "Heliodora's Garland," by Meleager, with "The Posie," by Burns, says, "The Scot surpasses the Greek in poetry as well as passion, his tenderness is more heartfelt, his expression is even more exquisite; for the most consummate art, even when guided by genius, cannot refine and burnish, by repeated polishing, the best selected words, up to the breathing beauty, that, warm from the fount of inspiration, sometimes colours the pure language of nature." See Allan Cunningham's Works of Burns, vol. iv. p. 236.

    [1] Maid.   [2] The open field.

THE LASS O' BALLOCHMYLE.

AIR, "JOHNNIE'S GREY BREEKS."   ARRANGED BY J. T. SURENNE.

'Twas ev'n, the dew - y fields were green, On ev' - ry blade the pearls hung; The

zeph - yrs wan - ton'd round the bean, And bore its fra - grant sweets a - lang:

In ev - 'ry glen the mav - is sang, All na - ture list - 'ning seem'd the while, Ex - cept where greenwood e - choes rang, A - mang the braes o'

Bal - loch - myle.

p   *f*   *dim.*   *p*

With careless step I onward stray'd,
   My heart rejoic'd in nature's joy,
When, musing in a lonely glade,
   A maiden fair I chanced to spy.
Her look was like the morning's eye,
   Her air like nature's vernal smile—
Perfection whisper'd, passing by,
   Behold the lass o' Ballochmyle!

Fair is the morn in flowery May,
   And sweet is night in autumn mild,
When roving through the garden gay,
   Or wandering in the lonely wild;
But Woman, Nature's darling child!
   There all her charms she does compile;
Ev'n there her other works are foil'd
   By the bonnie lass o' Ballochmyle.

O, had she been a country maid,
   And I the happy country swain,
Though shelter'd in the lowest shed
   That ever rose in Scotland's plain,
Through weary winter's wind and rain,
   With joy, with rapture, I would toil;
And nightly to my bosom strain
   The bonnie lass o' Ballochmyle.

Then pride might climb the slippery steep
   Where fame and honours lofty shine;
And thirst of gold might tempt the deep,
   Or downward seek the Indian mine:
Give me the cot below the pine,
   To tend the flocks or till the soil,
And every day have joys divine
   With the bonnie lass o' Ballochmyle.

"THE LASS O' BALLOCHMYLE." In the second volume of the beautiful edition of Burns' works published by Messrs. Blackie and Son, we find, p. 13, the following passage in a long Note regarding this song :—"The braes of Ballochmyle extend along the right or north bank of the Ayr, between the village of Catrine and Howford bridge, and are situate at the distance of about two miles from Burns' farm of Mossgiel. They form the most important part of the pleasure-grounds connected with Ballochmyle House, the seat of Claud Alexander, Esq. of Ballochmyle, whose sister, Miss Wilhelmina Alexander, was the subject of the poem. Bending in a concave form, a mixture of steep bank and precipice, clothed with the most luxuriant natural wood, while a fine river sweeps round beneath them, they form a scene of bewildering beauty, exactly such as a poet would love to dream in during a July eve." It appears that Burns composed the song in the spring of 1786, when he had wandered forth one evening on the banks of Ayr, as he says, "to view Nature in all the gaiety of the vernal year." He sent the song in a letter to Miss Alexander, dated 18th November 1786, which she did not answer, although she was proud of both, and preserved them most carefully.

Oswald, in his Caledonian Pocket Companion, usually gives a variation or two *after* each air, but in some cases, where the original is a quick tune, he reverses the process, giving a slow variation the place of honour, while he reserves the true air for the end, as if it were a mere variation. Probably no deception was intended, but this mode of printing has led to considerable misconception in regard to the original form of certain airs, the present being one of them.

WILT THOU BE MY DEARIE?

ARRANGED BY G. F. GRAHAM.

$\bullet = 80$

ANDANTINO
AFFETTUOSO.

Wilt thou be my dear - ie? When

sor - row wrings thy gen - tle heart, O wilt thou let me cheer thee?

By the trea - sures of my soul, That's the love I bear thee! I swear and vow that

on - ly thou Shall e - ver be my dear - ie. On - ly thou, I swear and vow, Shall a - ver be my dear - ie.

Lassie, say thou lo'es me ;
Or, if thou wilt not be my ain,
Say na thou'lt refuse me :
If it winna, canna be,
Thou, for thine, may choose me;
Let me, lassie, quickly dee,
Trusting that thou lo'es me.
Lassie, let me quickly dee,
Trusting that thou lo'es me.

"WILT THOU BE MY DEARIE?" Mr. Stenhouse says, "This charming little song was written by Burns for the
Museum. It is adapted to the first strain of an old strathspey, called 'The Souter's Daughter.' Burns, in a
Note annexed to the words, says, 'Tune, *The Souter's Daughter.* N. B.—It is only the first part of the tune to
which the song is to be set.' The 'Souter's Daughter' is printed in Bremner's Collection of Reels, in 1764. It
also appears in Neil Gow and Son's Collection, and in several others." See Museum Illustrations, vol. v. p. 415.

We cannot refrain from pointing out here the utter falseness and absurdity of an opinion which has met with its
ignorant abettors, and which arose from an old misinterpretation of a passage in Tassoni's "Pensieri Diversi,"
(Venice, 1646.) The passage is as follows:—"Noi ancora possiamo connumerar tra nostri Jacopo Rè di Scozia,
che non pur cose sacre compose in canto, ma trovò da se stesso una nuova musica lamentevole, e mesta,
differente da tutte l'altre. Nel che poi è stato imitato da Carlo Gesualdo, principe di Venosa, che in questa nostra
età ha illustrato anch'egli la musica con nuove e mirabili invenzioni." Lib. x. c. xxiii. This passage has been
erroneously interpreted as signifying that King James I. of Scotland composed our old Scottish melodies, and that
he was imitated in the same style of composition by the Prince of Venosa. No documents exist to show the style
of the sacred music that James is said by Tassoni to have composed, nor to show the style of that new plaintive
and mournful music, different from all other music, which he is said to have invented. Tassoni's words plainly
mean, not that the Prince of Venosa imitated the style of James' new music, but that he imitated the example of
James in inventing a new plaintive and mournful music, different from all other music; and that this is the true
meaning, is evident from the concluding words of the passage, where it is said that "in our age he also has illustrated music by new and wonderful inventions." We add only a few words to set the matter at rest. Carlo
Gesualdo, Prince of Venosa in the Neapolitan States, was a remarkable composer of music in the latter part of
the sixteenth century. Alessandro Tassoni, a Modenese, was born in 1565, and died in 1635. James I. was
assassinated in 1437, in the forty-fourth year of his age. Fortunately, the compositions of the Prince of Venosa
have been printed, and are therefore open to examination, and to comparison with Scottish melodies. They are
very curious compositions—madrigals ; but contain no *melodies* of any kind, but merely dry and crude harmonic
combinations and modulations, some of which are very strange and original. Not one of the voice parts that we
have examined contains anything in the least resembling any known Scottish melody, or anything else now named
melody. Some of the best of the Prince of Venosa's compositions are given in the works of Padre Martini, Choron,
&c.; and to these the Editor of this work refers the reader. It is high time that the received nonsense written
about the imitation of Scottish melodies by the Prince of Venosa should be for ever set aside. That remarkable
amateur, like several others of his countrymen about the same period, was striving to emancipate himself from
the fetters of the old ecclesiastical tonalities and harmonies, which, till then, had confined the musical genius of
all Europe to an inexpressive order of forms, with a few popular exceptions. The production of the modern
tonalities—a major and a minor scale—and a revolution in musical melody and harmony—were due to the genius
of Claudio Monteverde. an eminent Italian musician, at the close of the sixteenth, and the commencement of the
seventeenth centuries.

THE BRAES O' BALQUHIDDER.

ARRANGED BY J. T. SURENNE.

♩ = 96

ANIMATO
E BEN
MARCATO

Will ye go, las-sie, go, To the braes o' Balquhidder? Where the

blae - ber - ries grow, 'Mang the bon - nie bloomin' heather; Where the deer and the

rae, Lightly bound - ing to - ge - ther, Sport the lang summer day 'Mang the braes o' Bal-

I will twine thee a bower
  By the clear siller fountain,
An' I'll cover it o'er
  Wi' the flowers o' the mountain :
I will range through the wilds,
  An' the deep glens sae dreary,
An' return wi' their spoils
  To the bower o' my deary.
      Will ye go, &c.

When the rude wintry win'
  Idly raves round our dwellin',
An' the roar o' the linn
  On the night-breeze is swellin',—

Sae merrily we'll sing,
  As the storm rattles o'er us,
Till the dear sheeling[1] ring
  Wi' the light liltin' chorus.
      Will ye go, &c.

Now the summer is in prime,
  Wi' the flowers richly bloomin',
An' the wild mountain thyme
  A' the moorlands perfumin',—
To our dear native scenes
  Let us journey together,
Where glad innocence reigns
  'Mang the braes o' Balquhidder
      Will ye go, &c.

[1] A shepherd's cottage ; a hut.

"THE BRAES O' BALQUHIDDER." This song was written by Robert Tannahill, a Paisley weaver, born in that town 3d June 1774. His death occurred on 17th May 1810, by suicide. His biographers assure us that this lamentable act arose from no pressure of poverty : "his means were always above his wants." His constitution was delicate; his temperament shy and morbidly sensitive; his sedentary occupation, and various griefs and disappointments, seem to have produced that mental alienation which clouded the latter days of his brief career. None but those who have well considered the insidious progress of mental alienation, and who truly feel how "fearfully and wonderfully we are made," can bestow a just tribute of pity and sorrow upon the solemn fate of poor Tannahill. Who shall dare to say in his pride, "I am secured from this terrible visitation!" A very celebrated modern poet, in prosperous circumstances, but suffering under great mental depression, declared to a friend that he was determined to drown himself. Fortunately the poet's mind recovered its tone, and he died quietly in his bed. But he *might* have committed suicide, while labouring under that mental depression which seems so frequently to attend the temperament of genius.

In Captain S. Fraser's Collection of Melodies of the Highlands and Islands of Scotland, 1816, we find, No. 77, Bochuiddar—Balquhidder—which is the air applied to Tannahill's song, with some slight differences, as found in vol. i. p. 49, of R. A. Smith's "Scottish Minstrel."

WHISTLE O'ER THE LAVE O'T.

ARRANGED BY J. T. SURENNE.

First when Mag-gie was my care, Heaven I thought was in her air;

Now we're married, speir' nae mair, But whistle o'er the lave² o't. Meg was meek and

Meg was mild, Sweet and harm-less as a child; Wis-er men than me's beguiled; Sae whistle o'er the lave o't.

How we live, my Meg and me,
How we love, and how we gree,[2]
I care-na-by[4] how few may see;
Sae, whistle o'er the lave o't.
Wha I wish were maggots' meat,
Dish'd up in her winding sheet,
I could write—but Meg maun see't;
Sae, whistle o'er the lave o't.

¹ Ask. ² Rest: remainder. ³ Agree. ⁴ A Scottish idiom meaning "I am totally indifferent.

" WHISTLE O'ER THE LAVE O'T." "This fine air was formerly adapted to some witty, but indelicate verses, a fragment of which is preserved in Herd's Collection. The humorous song in the Museum, beginning, 'First when Maggie was my care,' was written by Burns in 1789, as a substitute for the old verses. The air was composed about the year 1720, by John Bruce, a musician of the town of Dumfries; and Oswald afterwards published it with variations in the last volume of his Caledonian Pocket Companion." See Museum Illustrations, vol. iii. p. 286. John Bruce's title to be considered the composer of this air is at best very doubtful. We learn from John Mayne, who mentions him among his worthies in the " Siller Gun," 1836, that Bruce was born at Braemar—was engaged in the rebellion of 1745—was taken prisoner, and confined for some time in Edinburgh Castle—and afterwards settled in Dumfries, where he spent the remainder of his life. Mayne adds—" He is supposed by Burns to have been the composer of the favourite Scots air of 'Whistle o'er the lave o't.' This opinion is altogether erroneous; for, although John Bruce was an admirable performer, he never was known as a composer of music. The air in question was composed long before he existed."

In order to render the melody of the seventh bar (measure) more vocal, a slight alteration has been made upon it; but the original passage is given in the first bar of the ritornel.

This air affords examples of what has been called the " Scottish catch," or "snap," a characteristic of the strath-spey, which, though not confined entirely to that species of dance music, is yet only occasionally met with in our old slow vocal airs. This peculiarity was seized upon during last century by the English imitators of Scottish music, and was used most unsparingly in their productions. Of this the Anglo-Scottish airs contained in the first volume of Johnson's Museum afford abundant proof; among these we may particularise " The banks of Tweed," " My dear Jockey," " Kate of Aberdeen," and " Sweet Annie frae the sea-beach came." The use or abuse of this " catch" was not confined, however, to imitations of Scottish airs, but was even introduced into the Italian Operatic music of the day. Writing of the London Opera in 1748, Dr. Burney, (History of Music, vol. iv. p. 457,) says,— ' There was at this time too much of Scots catch, or cutting short the first of two notes in a melody, thus:—

Again, at p. 466, note (d), writing about Tito Manlio, an opera brought out by Abos, a composer of the Neapolitan school, in 1756, he says,—" The first air, however, is pleasing, 'Se che più amor,' but has too much repetition and Scots snap of the first two notes." And again, same page, note (c), giving some account of the airs in the pasticcio " Olimpiade," brought out in 1755, he says,—"' Grandi è ver,' by Pergolesi, not in his best manner, nor without Scoticisms." As we have not seen the music here alluded to, we suppose that he refers to the " snap" or " catch" that he mentions elsewhere as being so prevalent. At p. 472, speaking of the Neapolitan school, he says,—" The Scots snap seems to have been contagious in that school at this time, (1759,) for all the three masters concerned in this opera, (Vologeso,) are lavish of it." The masters alluded to are Perez, Cocchi, and Jomelli.

JENNY DANG THE WEAVER.

ARRANGED BY J. T. SURENNE.

Willie's wedding on the green, The lassies, bonnie witch - es, Were a' dress'd out in aprons clean, And braw white Sunday mutches :[1] Auld Maggie bade the lads tak' tent,[2] But Jock would not believe her ; But soon the fool his fol - ly kent, For Jen - ny dang the weaver. And Jen - ny dang, Jen - ny dang,

Jen-ny dang the weav-er; But soon the fool his fol-ly kent, For Jen-ny dang the weav-er.

ff   *ritenuto.*   *fz*

At ilka country dance or reel,
  Wi' her he would be bobbin';
When she sat down—he sat down,
  And to her would be gabbin';
Where'er she gaed, baith butt and ben,[2]
  The coof[4] would never leave her;
Aye kecklin' like a clockin' hen,
  But Jenny dang the weaver.
And Jenny dang, Jenny dang,
  Jenny dang the weaver;
Aye kecklin' like a clockin' hen,
  But Jenny dang the weaver.

Quo' he, My lass, to speak my mind,
  In troth I needna swither;
You've bonnie een, and if you're kind,
  I'll never seek anither;
He humm'd and haw'd, the lass cried, Peugh!
  And bade the coof no deave her;
Syne snapt her fingers, lap and leugh,
  And dang the silly weaver.
And Jenny dang, Jenny dang,
  Jenny dang the weaver;
Syne snapt her fingers, lap and leugh,
  And dang the silly weaver.

[1] Head-dresses for females.   [2] To be on one's guard.   [3] Outer and inner apartments of a house.   [4] Simpleton.

"JENNY DANG THE WEAVER." This humorous song was written by the late Sir Alexander Boswell, Bart., of Auchinleck, mentioned before, p. 181 of this volume, and regarding whom we shall state some further particulars in the Appendix. As to the air, Mr. Stenhouse and others make no mention of its origin; but we quote the following very amusing Note from pp. 308, 309, of Mr. Hugh Paton's "Contemporaries of Burns," &c., Edinburgh, 1840 :—"The origin of the air of 'Jenny dang the weaver,' is somewhat curious. The Rev. Mr. Gardner, minister of the parish of Birse in Aberdeenshire, well known for his musical talent and for his wit, was, one Saturday evening, arranging his ideas for the service of the following day, in his little study, which looked into the court-yard of the manse, where Mrs. Gardner, *secunda*—for he had been twice married—was engaged in the homely task of 'beetling' the potatoes for supper. To unbend his mind a little, he took up his Cremona, and began to step over the notes of an air he had previously jotted down, when suddenly an altercation arose between Mrs. Gardner and Jock, the 'minister's-man'—an idle sort of weaver from the neighbouring village of Marywell, who had lately been engaged as man-of-all-work about the manse. 'Here, Jock,' cried the mistress, as he had newly come in from the labours of the field, 'gae wipe the minister's shoon.' 'Na,' said the lout, 'I'll do nae sic thing: I cam' here to be yir ploughman, but no yir flunky; and I'll be d——d gif I'll wipe the minister's shoon!' 'Deil confound yir impudence!' said the enraged Mrs. Gardner, as she sprung at him with a heavy culinary instrument in her hand, and giving him a hearty beating, compelled him to perform the menial duty required. The minister, highly diverted with the scene, gave the air he had just completed the title of 'Jenny dang the weaver.' This is supposed to have occurred about the year 1746." Se non è vero, è ben trovato! (1849.)

As might have been expected, the story, in as far as the air is concerned, is only "*ben trovato*," for the tune has recently been found under another name in the Gairdyn MS. written a quarter of a century earlier.

N

O, FOR ANE-AND-TWENTY, TAM!

AIR, "THE MOUDIEWART."

ARRANGED BY J. T SURENNE.

O, for ane - and - twen - ty, Tam! And hey, for ane - and - twen - ty, Tam! I'll

learn my kin a ratt - lin' sang, Gin I saw ane - and - twen - ty, Tam.

They snool[1] me sair, and haud me down, And gar me look like bluntie,[2] Tam; But three short years will soon wheel roun', And then comes ane-and-twen-ty, Tam.

for

The close for the first two verses. For the last verse.

A gleib o' lan', a claut o' gear,[3]
Were left me by my auntie, Tam
At kith and kin I needna speir,
Gin I saw ane-and-twenty, Tam.

They'll ha'e me wed a wealthy coof,[4]
Though I mysel' ha'e plenty, Tam;
But hear'st thou, laddie?—there's my loof[5]—
I'm thine at ane-and-twenty, Tam!

[1] To subjugate by tyrannical means.   [2] Stupid.   [3] A sum of money.   [4] Fool.   [5] Hand.

"AND O, FOR ANE-AND-TWENTY, TAM!" Mr. Stenhouse gives the following Note upon this song and air :—"This comic song, the manuscript of which is before me, was written by Burns on purpose for the Museum. The subject of the song had a real origin. A young girl having been left some property by a near relation, and at her own disposal on her attaining majority, was pressed by her relations to marry an old rich booby. Her affections, however, had previously been engaged by a young man, to whom she had pledged her troth when she should become of age, and she of course obstinately rejected the solicitations of her friends to any other match. Burns represents the lady addressing her youthful lover in the language of constancy and affection. The verses are adapted to an old tune, called, *The Moudiewart*. In the 'Reliques,' Burns says, 'this song is mine.'" See Museum Illustrations, vol. iv. p. 327.

In the course of this work we have occasionally noticed the remarkable popularity of Burns' songs, and their influence upon his countrymen. One of the most striking instances on record is that given in the Note on the air Oran an Aoig, where we quote from James Grant, Esq., an incident during the battle of Waterloo. The following humble individual instance of Burns' influence is interesting, and was communicated to us by a respected literary friend, who, when a boy, for amusement, took part in the harvest operations which he mentions. Our friend says :—"It may not be uninteresting to you to know how strongly, if not extensively, the prose and poetical writings of Burns had taken possession of the minds of his countrymen; and many more instances than the one I give might be adduced as illustrative of this. The educated were not more enthusiastic concerning the Bard than were the peasantry, as the following short narrative will abundantly prove. It might be about the year 1811, that the harvest came suddenly upon us, and being resident with an uncle whose farm was situate in a landward district, many miles remote from any town, all hands were called on to assist. The ploughman was to be builder of the ricks, and your humble servant was to fork to him. He was an uncouth-looking man, with a very slender education, but possessed of great natural powers, and an extraordinary relish for wit and humour; so you may easily conceive how pleasantly the time flew by us. Bob (Robert Stevenson by name) delighted me with his scraps from Burns. We had plenty of leisure, and were not overwrought, luckily for my young arms; and I shall never forget how aptly he introduced his quotations, both grave and gay, (for Bob appreciated both,) and with what a *gusto* the more notable and pithy parts of the Bard were uttered by my pleasant fellow-labourer. This took place in Dumfries-shire, about thirty miles from the town of Dumfries, and you will see by the date, not many years after the lamented death of the Bard. I have said *prose* as well as *poetry*; the latter is nothing wonderful, but the former was, and remains with me a matter of greater astonishment, since Currie's edition was the only one at that time extant, and which could have been but seldom within his reach to peruse with any thing like leisure."

TULLOCHGORUM.

ARRANGED BY G. F. GRAHAM.

♩ = 104

NON TROPPO PRESTO,
MA SPIRITOSO.

Come

gio's a sang, Montgomery*cried, And lay your disputes a' a-side, What sig-ni-fies't for folks to chide, For

Staccato sempre.

what was done be-fore them.   Let Whig and To-ry a' a-gree, Whig and To-ry, Whig and To-ry,

Whig and To-ry a' a-gree, To drop their Whigmigmorum; Let Whig and To-ry a' a-gree To

* This is generally sung, "Come gic's a sang, the lady cried."

spend the night in mirth and glee, And cheer - fu' sing a - lang wi' me, The   reel o' Tul - loch - go - rum.

f

Rall. a piacere.

dim.

O, Tullochgorum's my delight,
It gars us a' in ane unite,
And ony sumph that keeps up spite,
  In conscience, I abhor him ;
For blythe and merry we'll be a',
Blythe and merry, blythe and merry,
Blythe and merry we'll be a',
  And make a happy quorum.
For blythe and merry we'll be a',
As lang as we hae breath to draw,
And dance till we be like to fa',
  The reel o' Tullochgorum.

What needs there be sae great a fraise,
Wi' dringing dull Italian lays,
I wadna gie our ain strathspeys
  For half a hunder score o' them.
They're dowf and dowie at the best,
Dowf and dowie, dowf and dowie,
Dowf and dowie at the best,
  Wi' a' their variorum.
They're dowf and dowie at the best,
Their *allegros*, and a' the rest.
They canna please a Highland taste,
  Compared wi' Tullochgorum.

Let warldly worms their minds oppress
Wi' fears o' want and double cess,
And sullen sots themselves distress
  Wi' keeping up decorum.
Shall we sae sour and sulky sit?
  Sour and sulky, sour and sulky,

Sour and sulky shall we sit,
  Like auld Philosophorum?
Shall we sae sour and sulky sit,
Wi' neither sense, nor mirth, nor wit,
Nor ever rise to shake a fit
  To the reel o' Tullochgorum?

May choicest blessings aye attend
Each honest open-hearted friend,
And calm and quiet be his end,
  And a' that's gude watch o'er him.
May peace and plenty be his lot,
Peace and plenty, peace and plenty,
And dainties a great store o' them.
May peace and plenty be his lot,
Unstain'd by any vicious spot,
And may he never want a groat,
  That's fond o' Tullochgorum !

But for the silly fawning fool,
Who loves to be oppression's tool,
May envy gnaw his rotten soul,
  And discontent devour him !
May dool and sorrow be his chance,
Dool and sorrow, dool and sorrow,
Dool and sorrow be his chance,
  And none say, Wae's me, for him.
May dool and sorrow be his chance,
And a' the ills that come frae France,
Whae'er be that winna dance
  The reel o' Tullochgorum.

" TULLOCHGORUM." The composer of the tune, a reel, is not known. Mr. Stenhouse says it is derived from an old Scottish song-tune, printed in Craig's Collection in 1730. The words were written by the Rev. John Skinner, pastor of the Episcopal Chapel at Langside, near Peterhead, Aberdeenshire. They were first printed in the Scots Weekly Magazine for April 1776, and were enthusiastically termed by Burns, the " first of songs !" The copy here given is that with the reverend author's last corrections, as printed in Museum Illustrations, vol. iii. pp. 283, 284. Mr. Skinner died in 1807, aged 86. See Museum Illustrations, vol. iii. pp. 281-284. We have heard Tullochgorum sung with much spirit, many years ago, by the late eminent printer, Mr. James Ballantyne. Every good musician will at once perceive the difficulty of applying anything like regular modern harmony to such a tune.

THE EWIE WI' THE CROOKIT HORN!

ARRANGED BY J. T. SURENNE.

O were I a - ble to rehearse My ew - ie's praise in

pro - per verse, I'd sound it out as loud and fierce As ev - er piper's drone could blaw.

The ew - ie wi' the crook - it horn! Wha bad kent her might ha'e sworn, Sic a ewe was nev-er born, Here-a-bout, nor far a-wa'.

I never needed tar nor keil,
To mark her upo' hip or heel;
Her crookit hornie did as weel,
    To ken her by amang them a'.

She never threaten'd scab nor rot,
But keepit ay her ain jog-trot;
Baith to the fauld and to the cot,
    Was never sweirt to lead nor ca'.

Cauld nor hunger never dang[1] her,
Wind nor weet could never wrang her;
Ance she lay an ouk[2] and langer
    Furth aneath a wreath o' snaw.

Whan ither ewies lap the dyke,
And ate the kail for a' the tyke,
My ewie never play'd the like,
    But tyc'd[3] about the barn wa'.

A better, or a thriftier beast,
Nae honest man could weel ha'e wist;
For, silly thing, she never mist
    To ha'e, ilk year, a lamb or twa.

The first she had I ga'e to Jock,
To be to him a kind o' stock:
And now the laddie has a flock
    O' mair nor thirty head ava.

I lookit aye at even for her,
Lest mischanter shou'd come o'er her,
Or the foumart[4] might devour her,
    Gin the beastie hade awa'.

My ewie wi' the crookit horn,
Weel deserved baith gerse and corn:
Sic a ewe was never born,
    Hereabout, or far awa.

Yet, last ouk, for a' my keeping,
(Wha can speak it without greeting?)
A villain cam', when I was sleeping,
    Sta' my ewie, horn and a'.

I sought her sair upo' the morn;
And down aneath a buss o' thorn,
I got my ewie's crookit horn,
    But my ewie was awa'.

O! gin I had the loon that did it,
Sworn I have, as weel as said it,
Though a' the warld should forbid it;
    I wad gi'e his neck a thra'.

I never met wi' sic a turn
As this, sin' ever I was born;
My ewie wi' the crookit horn,
    Silly ewie, stown awa'.

O! had she deid o' crook or cauld,
As ewies do when they are auld,
It wadna been, by mony fauld,
    Sae sair a heart to nane o's a'.

For a' the claith that we ha'e worn,
Frae her and her's sae aften shorn;
The loss o' her we cou'd ha'e borne,
    Had fair strae-death ta'en her awa'.

But thus, puir thing, to lose her life,
Aneath a bluidy villain's knife;
I'm really fiey't that our gudewife
    Will never win aboon't ava.

O! a' ye bards benorth Kinghorn,
Call your muses up and mourn
Our ewie wi' the crookit horn,
    Stown frac's, an' fell't an' a'!

[1] Overcame.   [2] A week.   [3] Nibbled.   [4] A polecat.

"THE EWIE WI' THE CROOKIT HORN." Mr. Stenhouse says:—"This excellent song, beginning, 'O were I able to rehearse,' is another production of the Rev. Mr. John Skinner. The verses are adapted to a fine lively Highland reel, of considerable antiquity, which received its name from a 'Ewie' of a very different breed; namely, the whisky-still, with its *crooked*, or rather spiral apparatus." Museum Illustrations, vol. iii., p. 287. Mr. Stenhouse gives the song, "with the author's last corrections," some of which we have adopted.

O'ER THE MUIR AMANG THE HEATHER.

ARRANGED BY A. LAWRIE.

$\textbf{♩} = 72$

MODERATO.

Com-in' thro' the craigs o' Kyle,¹ A - mang the bon - nie bloomin' heather, There I met a bon - nie las - sie, Keep-ing a' her yowes the - gither. O'er the muir a - mang the heather, O'er the muir a - mang the heather, There I met a bon - nie las - sie,

Keeping a' her yowes the-gither.

Says I, My dear, whare is thy hame?
In muir or dale, pray tell me whether?
She says, I tent these fleecy flocks
That feed amang the bloomin' heather.
O'er the muir amang the heather,
O'er the muir amang the heather;
She says, I tent these fleecy flocks
That feed amang the bloomin' heather.

We laid us down upon a bank,
Sae warm and sunny was the weather;
She left her flocks at large to rove
Amang the bonnie bloomin' heather.
O'er the muir amang the heather,
O'er the muir amang the heather;
She left her flocks at large to rove
Amang the bonnie bloomin' heather.

While thus we lay she sang a sang,
Till echo rang a mile and farther;
And aye the burden o' the sang
Was, O'er the muir amang the heather.
O'er the muir amang the heather,
O'er the muir amang the heather;
And aye the burden o' the sang
Was, O'er the muir amang the heather.

She charm'd my heart, and aye sinsyne
I couldna think on ony ither:
By sea and sky! she shall be mine,
The bonnie lass amang the heather.
O'er the muir amang the heather,
O'er the muir amang the heather;
By sea and sky! she shall be mine,
The bonnie lass amang the heather.

1 " The Craigs o' Kyle are a range of small hills about a mile south of the village of Coilton, in the parish of that name."—*Paton.*

"O'ER THE MUIR AMANG THE HEATHER." In that curious and entertaining work, "The Contemporaries of Burns, and the more recent Poets of Ayrshire," published at Edinburgh in 1840, by Mr. Hugh Paton, Carver and Gilder to Her Majesty, &c., and which we have occasionally quoted in the Notes to this Collection, we find some information regarding the authoress of this song. We quote part of it, and refer the reader to the work itself, pp. 34-37. "Burns communicated this song to 'Johnson's Scots Musical Museum;' and in his 'Remarks on Scottish Songs and Ballads,' he states, in language somewhat rude, 'that it is the composition of a Jean Glover, a girl who . . . . . . has visited most of the correction-houses in the West. She was born I believe in Kilmarnock. I took the song down from her singing, as she was strolling with a sleight-of-hand blackguard through the country.' Notwithstanding this positive testimony, there is another claimant for the authorship, Stuart Lewis, who alleges that Jean merely altered a song previously written by him, and which will be found in Dr. Rogers' Modern Scottish Minstrel, vol. iii. p. 31. When we come to inquire still further into the matter, we find that there must have been an earlier song than either, and on a similar subject, for the name of the air in the Macfarlan MS. (1740) is, "An I had thee 'mang the beather." We resume the quotation. "When at Muirkirk, we were fortunate enough to learn some particulars relative to Jeanie Glover. A niece of hers still resides there; and one or two old people distinctly remember to have seen her. She was born at the Townhead of Kilmarnock, on the 31st October 1758, of parents respectable in their sphere. That her education was superior, the circumstances of her birth will not permit us to believe; but she was brought up in the principles of rectitude, and had the advantage of that early instruction which few Scottish families are without. She was remarkable for beauty—both of face and figure—properties which, joined to a romantic and poetic fancy, had no doubt their influence in shaping her future unfortunate career. She was also an excellent singer. Until within these few years Kilmarnock had no theatre, or at least any building so called; but strolling parties of players were in the habit of frequenting the town at fairs, and on other public occasions, sometimes performing in booths, or in the 'Croft Lodge,' long known as a place of amusement. Having been a witness to some of these exhibitions, Jeanie unhappily became enamoured of the stage; and in an evil hour eloped with one of the heroes of the sock and buskin. Her subsequent life, as may be guessed, was one of adventure, checkered, if Burns is to be credited, with the extremes of folly, vice, and misfortune." Jean Glover died in 1801, in the town of Letterkenny, in Ireland. In order to lessen the compass of the air, alternative notes have been inserted in the first and second bars.

THERE CAM' A YOUNG MAN TO MY DADDIE'S DOOR.

AIR, "THE BRISK YOUNG LAD."

ARRANGED BY A. LAWRIE.

There cam' a young man to my dad - die's door, My dad - die's door, my

dad - die's door; There cam' a young man to my dad - die's door, Cam'

seek - ing me to woo. And wow! but he was a bon - nie young lad, A brisk young lad, an' a braw young lad; An' wow! but he was a

bon - nie young lad, Cam' seek - ing me to woo.

But I was bakin' when he cam',
When he cam', when he cam';
I took him in and gied him a scone,[1]
　To thowe his frozen mou'.
　　And wow! but he was, &c.

I set him in aside the bink;[2]
I gied him bread and ale to drink,
But ne'er a blythe styme[3] wad he blink
　Till he was warm an' fu'.
　　And wow! but he was, &c.

Gae, get you gone, you cauldrife wooer;
Ye sour-looking, cauldrife wooer!
I straightway show'd him to the door,
　Saying, Come nae mair to woo.
　　And wow! but he was, &c.

There lay a deuk-dub before the door,
Before the door, before the door;
There lay a deuk-dub before the door,
　An' there fell he, I trow!
　　And wow! but he was, &c.

Out cam' the gudeman, an' heigh he shouted;
Out cam' the gudewife, an' laigh she louted;
An' a' the toun-neebours were gather'd about it;
　An' there lay he, I trow!
　　And wow! but he was, &c.

Then out cam' I, an' sneer'd an' smiled.
Ye cam' to woo, but ye're a' beguiled;
Ye've fa'en i' the dirt, an' ye're a' befyled;
　We'll ha'e nae mair o' you!
　　And wow! but he was, &c.

[1] A thin cake of wheat or barley meal.
[2] Bench; long seat beside the fire in a country house; seat of honour.
　"Want o' wyse men make fules to sit on binks."—JAMIESON.
[3] A particle; a whit; a transitory glance.

"THERE CAM A YOUNG MAN TO MY DADDIE'S DOOR." This song, which contains a good deal of vulgar humour, was published in Herd's Collection, in 1769. The author of the words is not known, and the date of the air is uncertain. The last line of the third stanza is one substituted by Allan Cunningham for the coarser line in the original.

THE BRAES ABOON BONAW.

ARRANGED BY J. T. SURENNE.

Wilt thou go, my bon-nie las-sie, Wilt thou go, my braw las-sie,

Wilt thou go, say ay or no, To the braes aboon Bo-naw, lassie? Tho' Donald has nae

mickle fraise,[1] Wi' Law-land speeches fine, lassie, What he'll impart comes frae the heart, Sae *poco rall.*   *a tempo.*

let it be frae thine, lassie.   Wilt thou go, my bonnie lassie, Wilt thou go, my braw lassie,

Wilt thou go, say ay or no, To the braes aboon Bo - naw, lassie?

When simmer days cleed n' the braes
Wi' blossom'd broom sae fine, lassie,
At milking sheel,[2] we'll join the reel,
My flocks shall a' be thine, lassie.
    Wilt thou go, &c.

I'll hunt the roe, the hart, the doe,
The ptarmigan sae shy, lassie,
For duck and drake, I'll beat the brake,
Nae want shall come thee nigh, lassie.
    Wilt thou go, &c.

For trout and par, wi' canny care,
I'll wiley skim the flee, lassie;
Wi' sic-like cheer I'll please my dear,
Then come awa' wi' me, lassie.
    "Yes, I'll go, my bonnie laddie,
    Yes, I'll go, my braw laddie,
    Ilk joy and care wi' thee I'll share,
    'Mang the braes aboon Bonaw, laddie."

1 Cajoling discourse.   2 An out house for cattle.

"THE BRAES ABOON BONAW." In the first volume of "The Scottish Minstrel," we find this song and air, but the editor of that work indicates that the author is *unknown.* Messrs. Blackie, in their "Book of Scottish Song," give the verses, with merely this Note:—"Written, and music arranged by W. Gilfillan." The air is obviously borrowed, in some measure, from the popular dance-tune of "Duncan Davidson," formerly called, "You'll aye be welcome back again." Mr. Stenhouse says of "Duncan Davidson," (Museum Illustrations):—"This lively tune was inserted, about a century ago, in John Welsh's *Caledonian Country Dances,* book ii. p. 45. It is also to be found in Oswald's Pocket Companion, and several other old collections." "The braes aboon Bonaw," with the air, was first printed as a single-sheet song.

The Editor has been favoured with the following reply to his letter to Robert Gilfillan, Esq.:—"Leith, 14th March, 1848. I regret I cannot give you any direct information regarding the author of 'The braes aboon Bonaw.' Twenty-one years ago, R. A. Smith wrote me, inquiring if I were the author of the song. In reply, I answered that the song was written before I was born, and that my father, then living, believed it to be the composition of a second cousin of his own, who, in early life, went abroad, and died shortly after. The few families of Gilfillan in Scotland almost all *count kin ;* the history of the clan being as follows :—Originally it belonged to the Isle of Mull; but, during the feudal wars, was overcome by a more powerful clan, and completely extirpated. Two of the widows, however, by a coincidence, bore each twin sons, from whom we have all sprung. . . . . My father wrote occasional verses on local subjects, but none of them were ever printed."

THE CAULD CAULD WINTER'S GANE, LUVE.

AIR. "MY WIFE HAS TA'EN THE GEE."   ARRANGED BY J. T. SURENNA.

= 104

MODERATO
CON
ESPRESSIONE.

cauld cauld winter's gane, luve, Sae bitter and sae snell;[1] And spring has come a - gain, luve, To

deck yon lee - some dell.   The   buds burst frae   the   tree, luve ; The

birds sing   by   the   shaw ;[2]   But   sad sad is   my dow - ie heart, For

I thoeht the time wad flee, luve,
　As in the days gane bye;
While I wad think on thee, luve,
　And a' my patience try;
But O! the weary hours, luve,
　They wadna flee ava,
And they ha'e borne me nocht but dule,[2]
　Sin'[4] ye ha'e been awa'.

Waes me! they're sair to bide, luve,
　The dirdums[5] ane maun dree,[6]
The feelings wunna hide, luve,
　Wi' saut tears in the e'e:
And yet the ills o' life, luve,
　Compared wi' joys are sma',—
Sae will it be when ye return
　Nae mair to gang awa'.

[1] Sharp; piercing.　　[2] A wood.　　[3] Grief.　　[4] Since.　　[5] Noisy vexations.　　[6] Endure.

"THE CAULD CAULD WINTER'S GANE, LUVE." With regard to the author of this song we have been favoured with the following information:—"The words are by Mr. William Train of Haddington, son of Mr. Joseph Train of Loch-Vale Cottage, Galloway—the friend and correspondent of Sir Walter Scott. Mr. W. Train was born at Newton Stewart, in Galloway, on 9th August 1816. He studied for the Law; but, in 1838, became Cashier of the Southern Bank of Scotland in Dumfries—an establishment since merged in the Edinburgh and Glasgow Bank. He was, thereafter, for several years, an Inspector of an English Bank, and now holds the office of Government Surveyor of Stamps and Taxes for East-Lothian. Mr. Train compiled a Memoir of his father, which is prefixed to Mr. Train, senior's, History of the Isle of Man, and several of his poetical pieces have appeared in different works. The above verses were published in 'The Book of Scottish Song,' by Messrs. Blackie of Glasgow."

About the middle of last century a clever and humorous song, beginning, "A friend o' mine came here yes-treen," was composed to the air, "My wife has ta'en the gee," and appears in Herd's Collection, 1769, without any author's name. It appears again in Johnson's Museum, vol. v. p. 422, with the air communicated by Burns, and called "My wife has ta'en the gee," and which is evidently borrowed from an older air called "The Miller," already given in previous pages of this work, to Burns's words, "Mary Morison." In Gow's Fifth Collection of Reels and Strathspeys, p. 32, we find an air called, "My wife has ta'en the gee," communicated to Gow by the late Alexander Gibson Hunter of Blackness, Writer to the Signet, Edinburgh. It is there said to be old, and may have been the air to which the words in Herd were originally sung. It does not resemble "The Miller," or the air sent by Burns to Johnson for the old words. The latter air is the one we have adopted in this work.

OLD AIR, "MY WIFE HAS TA'EN THE GEE."

THE MAID THAT TENDS THE GOATS.

ARRANGED BY A. C. MACKENZIE.

MODERATELY
SLOW, WITH
FEELING.

1. Up a - mang yon clif - fy rocks   Sweetly rings the ris - ing echo,
2. San - dy herds a flock o' sheep,   Aft - en does he blaw the whistle,

To the maid that tends the goats,   Lilting o'er her na - tive notes. Hark ! she sings young
In a strain sae saft - ly sweet,   Lammies list'ning daur - na bleat.   He 's as fleet 's the

Sandy's kind,   An' he's promised ay to lo'e me ; Here's a brooch I ne'er shall tine,[1]
mountain roe,   Har - dy as the Highland heather,   Wad - ing through the wint - er snaw,

[1] Lose.

Till he's fair - ly married to me;
Keeping ay his flocks the - gither;

Drive a - way, ye drone time, An' bring about our
But¹ a plaid, wi' bare knees, He braves the bleakest

brid - al day.
nor - land blast.

Brawly he can dance and sing
Canty glee or Highland cronach ;²
Nane can ever match his fling
At a reel, or round a ring.
Wightly can he wield a rung,³
In a brawl he's ay the bangster ;
A' his praise can ne'er be sung
By the longest-winded sangster.
  Sangs that sing o' Sandy
  Seem short though they were o'er sae lang.

¹ Without.   ² Dirge.   ³ A heavy staff.

"THE MAID THAT TENDS THE GOATS." William Dudgeon, the writer of this song, was a farmer in Berwickshire ; but being a man of varied talent, he found time to cultivate besides the fine arts of poetry, painting, and music. At Berrywell, the residence of his uncle, Mr. Ainslie, he was introduced to Burns, who, with his usual rapid discrimination, thus writes of him in the Journal of his Border Tour :—" Mr. Dudgeon, a poet at times—a worthy remarkable character—natural penetration—a great deal of information, some genius, and extreme modesty." It is not known that any of his other songs ever appeared in print ; the present one was brought into notice from having been sung on the stage. Mr. Dudgeon was born in 1753, and died in 1813.

The air "Nian donn nan gabhar" is believed to be old, but first appeared in the Rev. Patrick Macdonald's Collection of Highland Airs (1781). It has since been included in most of the larger collections of Scottish songs, and it may be remarked as a singular circumstance in regard to a Gaelic air, that all the copies agree, having probably been drawn from the same source.

O

CRAIGIE-BURN-WOOD.

ARRANGED BY J. T. SURENNE.

Sweet fa's the eve on Craig - ie burn, And blythe a - wakes the mor - row; But a' the pride o' spring's re - turn Can yield me nocht but sor - row. I see the flowers and spread - ing trees, I hear the wild birds sing - ing; But what a wea - ry wight can please, And

care his bo - som wring - ing?

Fain, fain would I my griefs impart,
Yet dare na for your anger;
But secret love will break my heart,
If I conceal it langer.

If thou refuse to pity me,
If thou shalt love anither,
When yon green leaves fade frae the tree,
Around my grave they'll wither.

"CRAIGIE-BURN-WOOD." Burns wrote his first version of this song to aid the eloquence of a Mr. Gillespie, who was paying his addresses to Jean Lorimer, then residing at Craigie-burn-wood, near Moffat. Neither the poet's verse nor the lover's language could prevail: the lady married an officer of the name of Whelpdale—lived with him a few months—quitted him in consequence of great provocation—and afterwards took up her residence in Dumfries. The song was re-written in 179-, for Mr. George Thomson's Collection, and the chorus, part of an old ballad, was discarded. Mr. Stenhouse tells us,—"The air called 'Craigie-burn-wood,' taken down from a country girl's singing, was considered by the late Mr. Stephen Clarke, as one of our finest Scottish tunes. At the foot of the manuscript of the music of this song (written for Johnson's Museum) is the following note, in the hand-writing of Mr. Clarke:—*There is no need to mention the chorus. The man that would attempt to sing a chorus to this beautiful air, should have his throat cut to prevent him from doing it again!!*" "It is remarkable of this air," says Burns, "that it (its name) is the confine of that country where the greatest part of our lowland music, (so far as from the title, words, &c., we can localize it,) has been composed. From Craigie-burn, near Moffat, until one reaches the West Highlands, we have scarcely one slow air of any antiquity."—*Reliques.*

Dr. Currie informs us, that "Craigie-burn-wood is situated on the banks of the river Moffat, and about three miles distant from the village of that name, celebrated for its medicinal waters. The woods of Craigie-burn and of Dumcrieff were at one time favourite haunts of Burns. It was there he met the 'Lassie wi' the lint-white locks,' and that he conceived some of his beautiful lyrics.'" See Museum Illustrations, vol. iv. pp. 295, 296.

WHA'LL BE KING BUT CHARLIE?

ARRANGED BY H. E. DIBDIN.

The news frae Moidart cam' yestreen, Will soon gar¹ mo - ny fer - lie,² For ships o' war ha'e

just come in, And land - ed Roy al Char - lie! Come through the heather, A - round him gather, Ye're

a' the wel-com-er ear - ly, A - round him cling wi' a' your kin, For wha'll be king but

Char - lie! Come thro' the heather, A - round him gather, Come Ronald, come Donald, come a' thegither, And

crown him right - fu', law - fu' king, For wha'll be king but Char - lie?

The Highland clans wi' sword in hand,
Frac John o' Groats to Airly,
Ha'e to a man declared to stand
  Or fa' wi' Royal Charlie.
    Come through the heather, &c.

The Lowlands a', baith great an' sma',
Wi' mony a lord an' laird, ha'e
Declared for Scotia's king an' law,
An' speir² ye wha but Charlie?
    Come through the heather, &c.

There's ne'er a lass in a' the land,
But vows baith late an' early,
To man she'll ne'er gi'e heart or hand,
  Wha wadna fecht for Charlie.
    Come through the heather, &c.

Then here's a health to Charlie's cause,
An' be't complete an' early,
His very name our heart's blood warms—
  To arms for Royal Charlie!
    Come through the heather, &c.

¹ Make.   ² Wonder   ³ Ask, inquire.

"WHA'LL BE KING BUT CHARLIE?" This air was published by Captain Simon Fraser in his "Airs and Melodies peculiar to the Highlands of Scotland and the Isles; Edinburgh, 1816." It is No. 136 of that work, the editor of which gives the following singularly curious Note upon it:—

"No. 136. This is a melody common to Ireland, as well as to the Highlands of Scotland,—but, having been known in this country since the 1745, as one of the incentives of rebellion ; if originally Irish, some of the troops or partisans engaged for Charles from that country might have brought it over,—but the melody is simple and beautiful, assimilating itself very much to the stile of either."

The author of the words has not been discovered

We subjoin the following particulars of the memorable landing of Prince Charles Edward:—"On the 19th July 1745, Charles cast anchor in Lochnanuagh, a small arm of the sea, partly dividing the countries of Moidart and Arisaig.   Charles came on shore upon the 25th; when the Doutelle, having landed her stores, again set sail for France. He was accompanied by only seven men,—the Marquis of Tullibardine; Sir Thomas Sheridan, an Irish gentleman who had been tutor to the Prince; Sir John Macdonald, an officer in the Spanish service; Francis Strickland, an English gentleman ; Kelly, an English clergyman ; Æneas Macdonald, a banker in Paris, brother to Kinlochmoidart; and one Buchanan, a messenger. He first set foot on Scottish ground at Borodale, a farm belonging to Clanranald, close by the south shore of Lochnanuagh. Borodale is a wild piece of country, forming a kind of mountainous tongue of land betwixt two bays. It was a place suitable, above all others, for the circumstances and designs of the Prince, being remote and inaccessible, and, moreover, the very centre of that country where Charles's secret friends resided. It belongs to a tract of stern mountain land, prodigiously serrated by testuaries, which lies immediately to the north of the débouché of the great Glen of Albyn, now occupied by the Caledonian Canal."—CHAMBERS' History of the Rebellion of 1745.

JOHNNIE COPE.

WORDS BY ADAM SKIRVING.　　　　　　　ARRANGED BY FINLAY DUN.

♩ = 126
CON SPIRITO
MA NON
TROPPO PRESTO.

mf

1. Cope sent a chal - lenge frae Dunbar, (Saying) Char - lie, meet me
2. When Char - lie look'd the letter up - on, He drew his sword the

an ye daur, And I 'll learn you the art o' war, If you 'll meet me in the
scab - bard from, Come, fol - low me, my mer - ry men, And we 'll meet Johnnie Cope i' the

mor - ning. Hey! John - nie Cope, are ye wauk - in' yet? Or
mor - ning. Hey! John - nie Cope, are ye wauk - in' yet? Or

are your drums a - beat - in' yet? If ye are wauk - in'
are your drums a - beat - in' yet? If ye are wauk - in'

I would wait To gaug to the coals i' the mor - ning.
I would wait To gang to the coals i' the mor - ning.

The close for the first four verses. For the last verse.

p *dim.*

Now, Johnnie, be as good as your word,
Come, let us try baith fire and sword,
And dinna flee like a frighted bird
That's chased frae its nest i' the morning.—*Hey! etc.*

When Johnnie Cope he heard of this,
He thought it wadna be amiss
To ha'e a horse in readiness,
To flee awa' in the morning.—*Hey! etc.*

Fye now, Johnnie, get up an' rin,
The Highland bagpipes mak' a din;
It's best to sleep in a hale skin,
For 'twill be a bluidie morning.—*Hey! etc.*

When Johnnie Cope to Dunbar came,
They speir'd at him where's a' your men?
The deil coufound me gin' I ken,
For I left them a' in the morning.—*Hey! etc.*

Now, Johnnie, troth ye were na blate,
To come wi' the news o' your ain defeat,
And leave your men in sic a strait,
So early in the morning.—*Hey! etc.*

In faith, quo' Johnnie, I got sic flegs
Wi' their claymores and filabegs,
If I face them, deil break my legs,
So I wish you a' good morning.—*Hey! etc.*

"JOHNNIE COPE." This song was written in 1745, soon after the battle of Prestonpans, and is usually ascribed to Adam Skirving, a farmer who resided at Garleton, in the immediate neighbourhood of the field. He was the father of Archibald Skirving, the somewhat celebrated painter, and is said to have been a very handsome man, with a ready wit and a good deal of humour. "Johnnie Cope" has been a general favourite in Scotland, and no song probably has so many variations. As the original given in Stenhouse's Illustrations to Johnson's Musuem has quite as much poetic merit as the amended versions, it has been chosen for this work. The air, in its early form, had only one strain of eight bars, the second being merely a florid variation in the octave above. Its age is not known, but it appears to have been sung to a silly song, "Fye! to the coals in the morning," a phrase which has been retained in its successor, and may be supposed to allude to the extensive coal-fields of the district where the battle was fought.

WHA WADNA FIGHT FOR CHARLIE?

ARRANGED BY H. E. DIBDIN.

Wha wad - na fight for Charlie! Wha wad - na draw the sword? Wha wad - na up and ral - ly

At the roy - al Prince's word? Think on Sco - tia's an - cient he - roes, Think on fo - reign

foes re - pell'd, Think on glo - rious Bruce and Wallace, Who the proud u - surpers quell'd.

Rouse, rouse, ye kilted warriors!
Rouse, ye heroes of the north!
Rouse, and join your chieftains' banners —
'Tis your Prince that leads you forth!
Shall we basely crouch to tyrants?
Shall we own a foreign sway?
Shall a royal Stuart be banish'd,
    While a stranger rules the day?
        Wha wadna fight, &c.

See the northern clans advancing!
See Glengarry and Lochiel!
See the brandish'd broadswords glancing!—
Highland hearts are true as steel!
Now our Prince has raised his banner,
Now triumphant is our cause,
Now the Scottish lion rallies—
    Let us strike for Prince and laws.
        Wha wadna fight, &c.

"WHA WADNA FIGHT FOR CHARLIE?" James Hogg gives this song and air in the second series of his "Jacobite Relics of Scotland," pp. 100, 101; Edinburgh, William Blackwood; London, Cadell and Davies. 1821. Hogg's Note upon it, *ibid.*, p. 305, is as follows:—"Song LIV. 'Wha wadna fight for Charlie?' is likewise a Buchan song, sent me by Mr. John Wallace. The air has the same name; but in the south is called, ' *Will ye go and marry, Katie?*'" The air is evidently a strathspey. It is printed in Johnson's Museum, vol. v., with the words, "Will ye go and marry, Katie?" which appear to have been recovered and sent to the publisher of that work by Burns. In Gow's Second Collection of Strathspeys and Reels, it is called, "Marry Ketty."

Hogg does not say whether this lyric was sent to him as a real Jacobite war-song, written to rouse the clans to follow their Prince into the field, or whether it is merely a modern imitation. Internal evidence would lead us to the belief that its composition dates much nearer to 1845 than to 1745. To be an old song, it is too correct in rhymes, too refined in language, and it wants that characteristic of the Jacobite muse—unsparing abuse of the House of Hanover.

A HIGHLAND LAD MY LOVE WAS BORN.

AIR, "THE WHITE COCKADE."   ARRANGED BY J. T. SURENNE.

A High - land lad my love was born, The Law - land laws he

held in scorn; But he still was faith - fu' to his clan, My gal - lant, braw John

High - land - man ! Sing hey, my braw John High - land - man ! Sing ho, my braw John High-land-man! There's no a lad in a' the lan' Was

match for my John High-land-man!

Wi' his philabeg an' tartan plaid,	They banish'd him beyond the sea;
An' gude claymore down by his side,	But, ere the bud was on the tree,
The ladies' hearts he did trepan,	Adown my cheeks the pearls ran,
My gallant, braw John Highlandman.	Embracing my John Highlandman.
Sing hey, &c	Sing hey, &c.

But, oh! they catch'd him at the last,
An' bound him in a dungeon fast;
My curse upon them every one,
They've hang'd my braw John Highlandman,
Sing hey, &c.

"A HIGHLAND LAD MY LOVE WAS BORN." This song, by Burns, occurs in his Cantata, "The Jolly Beggars," after the following "Recitative:"

"Then neist outspak a raucle carlin,	Her dove had been a Highland laddie,
Wha kent fu' weel to cleek the sterling,	But weary fa' the waefu' wuddic!
For mony a pursie she had hookit,	Wi' sighs and sobs she thus began
And had in mony a well been dookit.	To wail her braw John Highlandman."

The song in "The Jolly Beggars" is to the tune "O an' ye were dead, gudeman," an old air, which probably suggested the more modern air of "The White Cockade," given to the song in the present publication. In the Museum Illustrations, vol. v. p. 366, Mr. Stenhouse gives what he says is a correct set of the original melody of "I wish that ye were dead, gudeman," "from a very old manuscript in his possession." He does not inform us of the date of that "very old" MS., nor does he say whence it came, or to whom it belonged before it came into his hands. He adds, "This tune must have been quite common in Scotland long before 1540; for it is one of the airs to which the Reformers sung one of their spiritual hymns." Mr. Stenhouse quotes the first stanza of this "spiritual hymn," which we decline to repeat, on account of its profane absurdity. Coarse, vulgar, "hand and glove" familiarity with the most sacred subjects, prevailed to a shocking extent in those days of the sixteenth century. This old air is now sung to the words "There was a lad was born in Kyle," and will be found in an earlier page. The more modern air is found in Aird's Collection, 1784, under the name of "The ranting High-landman." It was introduced by O'Keefe in his opera, The Highland Reel, 1788. The Jacobite song to the air begins, "My love was born in Aberdeen," but Herd, who printed it in 1776, was still too near the '45, and omits all allusion to "The White Cockade."

O CHARLIE IS MY DARLING.

ARRANGED BY G. F. GRAHAM.

Charlie is my dar-ling, My dar-ling, my dar-ling; O Charlie is my dar-ling, The

young Che - va - lier!
1. 'Twas on a Mon - day mor - ning, Right
2. As he cam' march-ing up the street, The

ear - ly in the year, When Char - lie cam' to our toun, The
pipes play'd loud and clear, And a' the folk cam' run - ning out To

young Che - va - lier,
meet the Che - va - lier,   O   Charlie is my dar - ling,   My   dar - ling,   my   dar - ling;   O

Charlie is my dar - ling,   The young Che - va - lier!

The succeeding verses begin at the sign :S:

Wi' Hieland bonnets on their heads,
And bright claymores and clear,
They cam' to fight for Scotland's right
And the young Chevalier.
O Charlie is my darling, etc.

They 've left their bonnie Hieland hills,
Their wives and bairnies dear,
To draw the sword for Scotland's lord,
The young Chevalier.
O Charlie is my darling, etc.

Oh! there was mony a beating heart,
And mony a hope and fear ;
And mony were the prayers put up
For the young Chevalier.
O Charlie is my darling, etc.

"O CHARLIE IS MY DARLING." It has been the fate of this air to undergo several odd transformations. James Hogg, in the second volume of his Jacobite Relics, p. 92, gives what he says is the original air. It is very different from that in Johnson's Museum (No. 428), "modernized" by Mr. Stephen Clarke, a friend of Burns, and father of the late William Clarke, who succeeded him as organist of the Episcopal Chapel, Canongate, Edinburgh. Stephen Clarke was an Englishman, and seems to have been a worthy man, though but a mediocre musician.

In their present form, both the air and the words of this enthusiastic Jacobite song are very modern, dating from the early part of the present century only. James Hogg, as mentioned above, gives the old air—quaint and pretty, though less vigorous than the modern one—together with two sets of words, one written by himself, and the original, which speaks more of love than of war. It ends with a stanza said to have been frequently quoted by Sir Walter Scott, while travelling abroad in failing health, and thinking probably of the gray hills of his native land,—

"It 's up yon heathery mountain, and doun yon scroggy glen,
We daurna gang a-milking for Charlie and his men."

The song adopted in the present volume appeared anonymously in the Scottish Minstrel (1821). It was probably written by one, or perhaps more, of the coterie of ladies who edited the literary portion of that work, and has much of the style of Lady Nairne, for whom it has been claimed by Dr. Charles Rogers. Still, as it neither has the initials B. B., under which she usually wrote, nor yet S. M., which seems to have been the signature used when the verses were the work of more than one hand, there appears to be a little uncertainty on the subject. One thing generally admitted is, that the song is the most popular hitherto written for the air.

I WISH I WERE WHERE GOWDIE RINS.

ARRANGED BY T. M. MUDIE.

MODERATO.

wish I were where Gowdie rins, Where Gowdie rins, where Gowdie rins, I wish I were where

Gowdie rins, At the back o' Ben - na - chie.

1. Ance mair to hear the wild bird's sang, To
2. Oh mony a day in blithe spring time, Oh

wander birks and braes a - mang, Midst friends and fav'rites left sae lang At the back o' Ben-na-
mony a day in summer's prime, I've wandering wiled a - wa' the time At the back o' Ben-na-

chie.
chie.

I wish I were where Gowdie rins, Where Gowdie rins, where Gow - die rins, I

wish I were where Gowdie rins, At the back o' Ben - na - chie.

Oh there wi' Jean, on ilka night,
When baith our hearts were young and light,
We 've wandered, by the cool moonlight,
At the back o' Bennachie.
I wish I were where Gowdie rins,
Where Gowdie rins, where Gowdie rins,
I wish I were where Gowdie rins,
At the back o' Bennachie.

Oh Fortune's flow'rs wi' thorns are rife,
And wealth is won wi' toil and strife,
Ae day gie me o' youthfu' life
At the back o' Bennachie.
Ance mair, ance mair where Gowdie rins,
Where Gowdie rins, where Gowdie rins,
Oh let me die where Gowdie rins,
At the back o' Bennachie.

"I WISH I WERE WHERE GOWDIE* RINS." The Air is not Scottish, but seems to have become a favourite in the north about the middle of last century. It is given in a volume of slow airs and dances, published in 1820 by William Christie, where it is called, "O if I were where Gadie runs," or "The Hessian's March." On making application to Dean Christie, Fochabers, he has kindly sent the following information :—"I have a copy of the air, sent to my father in 1815, by a gentleman farmer in Buchan. This farmer's father heard it played in the Duke of Cumberland's army as he passed from Aberdeen to Culloden. The air shows that it was composed for horns (bugle), and is a grand one for soldiers on the march."

Several songs have been written to it, all beginning in nearly similar words. That given in the present volume is said to be by a clergyman who desired to remain unknown. Another, also good, by John Imlah —(b. 1799, D. 1846)—will be found in that excellent collection, Blackie's Book of Scottish Song, p. 183.

* The Gadie, Gaudie, or Gowdie, takes its rise in the parish of Clatt, and running through Leslie and Premnay, falls into the Urie, in the parish of Oyne. Bennachie or Bennochce—a hill in the neighbourhood.

THE BOATIE ROWS.

WORDS BY JOHN EWEN (1741-1821).

ARRANGED BY J. T. SURENNE.

= 108

MODERATO.

mf

p

animato.

mf

1. O   weel   may the   boat - ie   row,   And   bet - ter   may she   speed;   And
2. When Jamie vow'd he   would be   mine, And   wan   frae me   my   heart,   O
3. When Sawnie, Jock, and Jan - e - tie,   Are   up   and   got - ten   lear,[1]   They 'll

weel   may the   boat - ie   row,   That wins the bairns' bread.   The   boat - ie rows, the
muckle light - er grew my   creel! He   swore we'd never   part.   The   boat - ie rows, the
help to gar the   boat - ie   row,   And light - en a' our   care.   The   boat - ie rows, the

boat - ie rows, The   boat - ie rows in - deed;   And   happy be   the   lot of a' That
boat - ie rows, The   boat - ie rows fu' weel;   And   muckle light - er is the lade When
boat - ie rows, The   boat - ie rows fu' weel;   And   lightsome be her heart that bears The

[1] Education.

wish the boat - ie speed.
love bears up the creel.
mur - lain and the creel!

I cuist my line in Lar - go bay, And fish - es I caught
My curtch[1] I put up - on my head, And dress'd mysel' fu'
And when wi' age we are worn down, And hir - plin' round the

nine, There's three to boil, and three to fry, And three to bait the line.
braw; I trow my heart was dowf[2] and wae, When Jam - ie gaed a - wa':
door, They'll row to keep us dry and warm As we did them be - fore:

animato.

The boat - ie rows, the boat - ie rows, The boat - ie rows in - deed;
But weel may the boat - ie row, And luck - y be her part;
Then, weel may the boat - ie row, That wins the bairns' bread;

And hap - py be the
And lightsome be the
And hap - py be the

lot of a' That wish the boat - ie speed.
lass - ie's care That yields au hon - est heart.
lot of a' That wish the boat - ie speed!

mf

[1] A linen cap, tying under the chin.   [2] Melancholy.

BIDE YE YET.

ARRANGED BY H. E. DIBDIN.

Gin I had a wee house, and a can-ty wee fire, A
bon-nie wee wi-fie to praise and admire, A bon-nie wee yardie be-side a wee burn; Fareweel to the bodies that yammer and mourn. Sae bide ye yet, and bide ye yet, Ye lit-tle ken what may be-

tide me yet, Some bon - nie we bod - ie may fa to my lot, And I'll aye be can - ty wi'

thinkin' o't, wi' thinkin' o't, wi' thinkin' o't, I'll aye be canty wi' thinkin' o't.

When I gang afield, and come hame at e'en,
I'll get my wee wifie fu' neat and fu' clean,
And a bonnie wee bairnie upon her knee,
That will cry papa or daddy to me.
    Sae bide ye yet, &c.

An' if there should happen ever to be
A difference atween my wee wifie an' me,
In hearty good humour, although she be teas'd,
I'll kiss her and clap her until she be pleas'd.
    Sae bide ye yet, &c.

"BIDE YE YET." The song first appeared in Herd's Collection (1776), and with its tune in Johnson's Museum (1787). Recently (1877), under the name of March Tune, the air has been included in Hoffmann's Selection from Dr. Petrie's Irish Airs. As there are no explanatory notes to that volume, it is not known either when or where Dr. Petrie obtained it. He was so scrupulously exact, however, that we may be sure he had what he believed to be satisfactory reasons for considering it to be an Irish tune; but as we have had not only this song, but an earlier one (1769), sung to it for more than a century, the evidence is very strong in favour of the Scottish claim. The name given to it by Dr. Petrie—March Tune—seems to suggest that it may have been introduced into Ireland by the band of a marching regiment.

The earlier song, "The Wayward Wife," which begins, "Alas, my son, you little know," was written by Miss Jenny Graham, daughter of William Graham, Esq. of Shaw, in Annandale. That which we give here with the music takes a happier view of wedlock, and was probably meant to be an answer to it. The author is not known.

LAST MAY A BRAW WOOER.

AIR, "THE LOTHIAN LASSIE."   ARRANGED BY T. M. MUDIE.

ALLEGRETTO.

Last May a braw woo - er cam' down the lang glen, And sair wi' his love he did deave me; I said there was naething I hated like men; The deuce gae wi' him to be - lieve me, be - lieve me, The deuce gae wi' him to be - lieve me !

He spak' o' the darts o' my bonnie black c'en,
And vow'd for my love he was decin'.
I said he micht dee when he liked for Jean;
The guid forgi'e me for lecin', for lecin',
The guid forgi'e me for lecin' !

A weel-stockit mailin',[1] himsel' o't the laird,
And marriage aff-hand, was his proffer.
I never loot on that I kenn'd it or cared;
But thocht I micht ha'e a waur[2] offer, waur offer,
But thocht I micht ha'e a waur offer.

But what do ye think, in a fortnicht or less—
The diel's in his taste to gang near her !—
He up the Gateslack to my black cousin Bess—
Guess ye how, the jaud ! I could bear her, could
bear her,
Guess ye how, the jaud ! I could bear her !

But a' the next week, as I fretted wi' care,
I gaed to the tryst o' Dalgarnock;
And wha but my braw fickle wooer was there !
Wha glower'd[3] as if he'd seen a warlock, a war-
lock,
Wha glower'd as if he'd seen a warlock.

Out ower my left shouther I gi'ed him a blink,[4]
Lest neebors micht say I was saucy;
My wooer he caper'd as he'd been in drink,
And vow'd that I was his dear lassie, dear lassie,
And vow'd that I was his dear lassie.

I speir'd for my cousin, fu' couthie[5] and sweet,
Gin she had recovered her hearin'?
And how my auld shoon fitted her shauchled[6] feet ?
Gude sauf us ! how he fell a-swearin', a-swearin',
Gude sauf us ! how he fell a-swearin'.

He begged for gudesake ! I wad be his wife,
Or else I wad kill him wi' sorrow;
Sae, e'en to preserve the puir body in life,
I think I maun wed him to-morrow, to-morrow,
I think I maun wed him to-morrow.

<table>
<tr><td>[1] A well-stocked farm.</td><td>[2] Worse.</td><td>[3] Who stared.</td><td>[4] Smiling look.</td><td>[5] Kindly.</td><td>[6] Distorted.</td></tr>
</table>

"LAST MAY A BRAW WOOER." Mr. Stenhouse says—"This humorous song was written by Burns in 1787, for the second volume of the Museum; but Johnson, the publisher, who was a religious and well-meaning man, appeared fastidious about its insertion, as one or two expressions in it seemed somewhat irreverent. Burns after-wards made several alterations upon the song, and sent it to Mr. George Thomson for his Collection, who readily admitted it into his second volume, and the song soon became very popular. Johnson, however, did not consider it at all improved by the later alterations of our bard. It soon appeared to him to have lost much of its pristine humour and simplicity; and the phrases which he had objected to were changed greatly for the worse. He there-fore published the song as originally written by Burns for his work." (Museum, vi.) We have for the most part adopted the earlier version of the song, as it is the better of the two. Mr. George Thomson, in his Collection, gives a reading of one line in the penultimate stanza which we do not follow—" And how *her new shoon* fit her auld shauchled feet." Johnson's reading is much better—" And how *my auld shoon* fitted her shauchled feet"— the phrase "auld shoon" being a sarcastic expression when applied to a discarded lover who pays his addresses to another fair one. Of the second edition of the song Mr. Stenhouse says, justly—"These alterations, in general, are certainly far from being in the happiest style of Burns. Indeed he appears to have been in bad health and spirits when he made them; for, in the letter inclosing the song, he says—'I am at present quite occupied with the charming sensations of the toothach, so have not a word to spare.' " Mr. Stenhouse adds—"It only remains to be observed that this song is adapted to the tune called, *The Queen of the Lothians*, the name of a curious old ballad, which is produced in the sixth volume of the Museum, and inserted after the modern words by Burns." See Museum Illustrations, vol. vi. pp. 460-463.

DUNCAN GRAY.

ARRANGED BY J. T. SURENNE.

Dun - can Gray cam' here to woo, Ha, ha, the

woo - ing o't; On blythe Yule night, when we were fu',[1] Ha, ha, the

woo - ing o't. Mag - gie coost[2] her head fu'[3] heigh,[4] Looked a - sklent[5] and un - co⁶ skeigh,⁷ Gart⁸ poor Dun - can stand a - beigh,⁹ Ha, ha, the

woo - ing o't.

Duncan fleech'd,¹⁰ and Duncan pray'd,
  Ha, ha, the wooing o't,
Meg was deaf as Ailsa Craig,¹¹
  Ha, ha, the wooing o't.
Duncan sigh'd baith out and in,
Grat¹³ his een baith bleer'd¹⁴ and blin',¹⁹
Spak' o' lowpin'¹⁵ o'er a linn,¹⁶
  Ha, ha, the wooing o't.

Time and chance are but a tide,
  Ha, ha, the wooing o't,
Slighted love is sair¹⁷ to bide,¹⁸
  Ha, ha, the wooing o't.
Shall I, like a fool, quo' he,
For a haughty hizzie¹⁹ die?
She may gae to—France for me!
  Ha, ha, the wooing o't.

How it comes, let doctors tell,
  Ha, ha, the wooing o't,
Meg grew sick as he grew well,
  Ha, ha, the wooing o't.
Something in her bosom wrings,
For relief a sigh she brings;
And O, her een, they spak' sic things!
  Ha, ha, the wooing o't.

Duncan was a lad o' grace,
  Ha, ha, the wooing o't,
Maggie's was a piteous case,
  Ha, ha, the wooing o't.
Duncan couldna be her death,
Swelling pity smoor'd²⁰ his wrath;
Now they're crouse²¹ and canty²² baith,
  Ha, ha, the wooing o't.

¹ Tipsy.   ² Cast.   ³ Full.   ⁴ High.   ⁵ Askance.   ⁶ Very.
⁷ Proud; saucy.   ⁸ Made; forced.   ⁹ At a shy distance.   ¹⁰ Supplicated flatteringly.
¹¹ A remarkably large and lofty rock, rising in the Firth of Clyde, between the coasts of Ayrshire and Kintyre.   ¹² Wept.
¹³ Bleared.   ¹⁴ Blind.   ¹⁵ Leaping.   ¹⁶ A waterfall; a precipice.   ¹⁷ Sore; painful.
¹⁸ Bear; endure.   ¹⁹ A young girl.   ²⁰ Smothered.   ²¹ Cheerful.   ²² Merry.

"DUNCAN GRAY." "It is generally reported, (says Mr. Stenhouse,) that this lively air was composed by
Duncan Gray, a carter or carman in Glasgow, about the beginning of last century, and that the tune was taken
down from his whistling it two or three times to a musician in that city. It is inserted both in Macgibbon and
Oswald's Collections." Their versions, however, differ considerably,—indeed in modern times every editor seems
to adopt a version of his own, so there is really no present standard. The words given in this work are those
written by Burns in December 1792 for George Thomson.

LASSIE WI' THE LINT-WHITE LOCKS.

AIR, "ROTHIEMURCHUS' RANT."   ARRANGED BY J. T. SURENNE.

Las - sie wi' the lint-white locks, Bon - nie las - sie, art - less lassie; Wilt thou wi' me tent the flocks?

Wilt thou be my dear - ie, O? Now na - ture cleads the flow' - ry lea, And a' is young and

sweet like thee; . O wilt thou share its joys wi' me? And say thou'lt be my dear - ie, O!

Las - sie wi' the lint-white locks; Bou - nie las - sie, art - less lassie; Wilt thou wi' me tent the flocks?

Wilt thou be my dear - ie, O ?

marcato.

The succeeding verses begin at the sign :S:

And when the welcome simmer-shower
Has cheer'd ilk drooping little flower,
We'll to the breathing woodbine bower
   At sultry noon, my dearie, O.
    Lassie wi' the lint-white locks, &c.

When Cynthia lights, wi' silver ray,
The weary shearer's homeward way;
Thro' yellow waving fields we'll stray,
   And talk o' love, my dearie, O.
    Lassie wi' the lint-white locks, &c.

And when the howling wintry blast
Disturbs my lassie's midnight rest;
Enclasped to my faithfu' breast,
   I'll comfort thee, my dearie, O.
    Lassie wi' the lint-white locks, &c.

"LASSIE WI' THE LINT-WHITE LOCKS." Burns, in a letter to George Thomson, September 1794, makes the following observations :—"I am sensible that my taste in music must be inelegant and vulgar, because people of undisputed and cultivated taste can find no merit in my favourite tunes. Still, because I am cheaply pleased, is that any reason why I should deny myself that pleasure? Many of our strathspeys, ancient and modern, give me most exquisite enjoyment, where you and other judges would probably be showing disgust. For instance, I am just now making verses for 'Rothemurche's Rant,' an air which puts me in raptures; and, in fact, unless I be pleased with the tune, I never can make verses to it. Here I have Clarke on my side, [Stephen Clarke, an Englishman,] who is a judge that I will pit against any of you. 'Rothemurche,'* he says, 'is an air both original and beautiful;' and on his recommendation, I have taken the first part of the tune for a chorus, and the fourth, or last part, for the song. I am but two stanzas deep in the work, and possibly you may think, and justly, that the poetry is as little worth your attention as the music." The song that Burns here alluded to was "Lassie wi' the lint-white locks," which he sent to Mr. Thomson in November 1794.

* Rothiemurchus

THE LASS O' GOWRIE.

AIR, "LOCH-EROCH SIDE."   ARRANGED BY J. T. SURENNE.

'Twas on a simmer's af - ternoon, A wee before the sun gaed down, My

las - sie, wi' a braw new gown, Cam' o'er the hills to Gow - rie.

The rose - bud tinged wi' morning show'r, Blooms fresh with - in the

I praised her beauty loud an' lang,
Then round her waist my arms I flang,
And said, My dearie, will ye gang
  To see the Carse o' Gowrie?
I'll tak' ye to my father's ha',
In yon green field beside the shaw;
I'll mak' you lady o' them a',
  The brawest wife in Gowrie.

Saft kisses on her lips I laid,
The blush upon her cheeks soon spread,
She whisper'd modestly, and said,
  I'll gang wi' ye to Gowrie!
The auld folks soon ga'e their consent,
Syne for Mess John they quickly sent,
Wha tyed them to their heart's content,
  And now she's Lady Gowrie.

"THE LASS O' GOWRIE." The air is that more commonly called "Loch-Eroch Side," a favourite modern Strath-spey, taken from the air of an old Scottish song and dancing tune, named, "I'm o'er young to marry yet." Loch Erocht, or Ericht, is a large lake in the north-west of Perthshire. The words here given to this air are from page 10 of a small pamphlet entitled, "One hundred and fifty Songs," printed by David Halliday, Dumfries, about 1839. Halliday's version consists of three stanzas only, while some later versions contain five. Two of the stanzas of these later versions seem to us not only superfluous but objectionable; and therefore we have adopted Halliday's version, which contains also what we think a better reading of the first line of the second stanza. The song that evidently appears to have suggested the later one was published by Brash and Reid of Glasgow, without date, in one of their penny numbers of a Collection entitled "Poetry, Original and Selected." These numbers were after-wards published in four volumes 18mo, and in the third volume we find, "The gowd o' Gowrie; a Scots song never before published: tune—Dainty Davie," and beginning :—

"When Katie was scarce out nineteen,
O but she had twa coal-black een—
A bonnier lass ye couldna seen
  In a' the Carse o' Gowrie."

It is believed that these words were written by Mr. William Reid, (of that firm of Brash and Reid,) the author of several popular Scottish songs. These words were afterwards published in Mr. Robert Chambers' edition of "The Scottish Songs collected and illustrated," vol. ii. pp. 512, 513. The tune indicated by Mr. Chambers is "Loch-Eroch Side."

OCH, HEY! JOHNNIE LAD.

ARRANGED BY J. T. SURENNE.

♩ = 72

MODERATO

mf

Och, hey! John-nie lad, Ye're no sae kind's ye should ha'e been; Och, hey! John-nie lad, Ye did-na keep your tryst yestreen. I wait-ed lang be-side the wood, Sae wae and wea-ry a' my lane; Och, hey! John-nie lad, Ye're no sae kind's ye should ha'e been.

Ye cam' na, Johnnie, to the fauld.
Ye cam' na to the trysting-tree ;
I trowed na love would turn sae cauld
And ye sae sune wad lightlie me.
I pu'd the rose, sae sweet and fine,
The fairest flower on a' the lea ;
Tho' fresh and fair, it wither'd syne,
E'en like the love ye promised me.

Ye said ye lo'ed but me alane,
Nor could ye keep your fancy free ;
An' gin that I would be your ain,
The chains o' love wad lightsome be.
O ! gin ye had sincerely loved,
They lightsome aye had been to me ;
But sin' that ye ha'e faithless proved,
I'll strive to keep my heart a wee.

"OH, HEY! JOHNNIE LAD!" The first stanza only is by Robert Tannahill ; as his second and third have ceased to be sung on account of their containing certain so-called "vulgarisms," other two, written by Robert Allan of Kilbarchan, have been substituted. They were published in the Scottish Minstrel, iii. 1821. The subject seems to have been a favourite with our poets ; in David Herd's Collection, 1776, we find a song, "Heigh, how! Johnnie lad ;" and in his Popular Ballads and Songs, 1806, Robert Jamieson gives another, written by himself, which begins in the same way. The air is said to be in Bremner's Collection of Reels, under the name of "The Lasses of the Ferry." It bears considerable resemblance to a number of tunes ; some of which we give below. See Notes to "Coming thro' the rye" and "Auld lang syne."

THE DUKE OF BUCCLEUGH'S TUNE. Apollo's Banquet, 1690.

THE MILLER'S WEDDING. From Cumming's Collection, 1780.

I'VE BEEN COURTING AT A LASS. Johnson, No. 306.

I FEE'D A LAD AT MICHAELMAS ; or, O CAN YOU LABOUR LEA? Johnson, No. 394.

COMIN' THRO' THE RYE.

ARRANGED BY T. M. MUDIE.

Gin a bo - dy meet a bo - dy com - in' thro' the rye,

Gin a bo - dy kiss* a bo - dy, Need a bo - dy cry? Ilk a' las - sie

has her lad - die, Nane, they say, ha'e I! Yet a' the lads they smile at me, When

*Often sung "greet."

a tempo.

com - in' thro' the rye.

Gin a body meet a body
Comin' frae the well,
Gin a body kiss a body,
Need a body tell?
Ilka lassie has her laddie,
Ne'er a ane ha'e I ; .
But a' the lads they smile on me
When comin' thro' the rye.

Gin a body meet a body
Comin' frae the town,
Gin a body greet a body,
Need a body gloom?
Ilka lassie has her laddie,
Nane they say ha'e I ;
But a' the lads they lo'e me weel,
And what the waur am I?

The following stanzas are very frequently sung to this air ; they were written by Mr. Dunlop, Collector of Customs, Port-Glasgow :—

Oh ! dinna ask me gin I lo'e thee ;
Troth, I daurna tell :
Dinna ask me gin I lo'e ye ;
Ask it o' yoursel'.
Oh ! dinna look sae sair at me,
For weel ye ken me true ;
And, gin ye look sae sair at me,
I daurna look at you.

When ye gang to yon braw, braw town,
And bonnier lasses see,
O, dinna, Jamie, look at them,
For fear ye mind na me.
For I could never bide the lass
That ye'd lo'e mair than me ;
And O, I'm sure, my heart would break,
Gin ye'd prove false to me.

¹ If.   ² Each ; every.

"COMIN' THROUGH THE RYE." There is a considerable number of Scottish tunes known under different names which have a strong family likeness. Perhaps the earliest of these is published in Playford's *Apollo's Banquet*, 1690, under the name of "The Duke of Buccleugh's Tune," which has a leading characteristic of all the later airs. The chief of these are, (1.) "I've been courting at a lass," No. 306. (2.) "Hey, how ! Johnnie, lad," No. 357. (3.) "I fee'd a lad at Michaelmas," No. 394 ; all in Johnson's *Museum*, iv., 1792. From the first we have got a modified "Comin' thro' the rye ;" the second continues to be known under its old name ; and the third, by the very slightest change, has become the modern "Auld lang syne." (See Notes upon these airs.) In the following volume of the *Museum* (Nos. 417, 418) there are two more versions of the present air, the second being that now always sung. Each of these has its own words ; that sent by Burns beginning, "Jenny's a' weet, puir body," has an old style about it, and is probably an old song " brushed up " for Johnson. Though not published till 1797, the year after the poet's death, the song must have been in Johnson's hands in 1794 ; for in February of that year Burns writes, "I have now sent you forty-one songs for your fifth volume, and Clarke has some more if he have not *cast them at the cocks*." It has been thought necessary to allude to this, for Mr. Wm. Chappell, whose knowledge of such matters is both extensive and accurate, has pointed out (*Popular Music of the Olden Time*, 795) that in a Christmas pantomime, produced 1795, there is a song, " If a body meet a body going to the fair," which he thinks may probably have been altered for the Museum into "Gin a body meet a body comin' thro' the rye." But in the only letters which Burns wrote to Johnson after that date, he alludes to his long silence, and to having neglected him and his work, without however sending either poetry or music.

Recently an opinion has been expressed that by " Rye " is meant a streamlet of that name in Ayrshire,— very plausible, but quite at variance with all known facts. The word was never either written or printed with a capital letter till about 1867, when there was a newspaper controversy over it ; and Mr. Scott Douglas has quoted a stanza written by Burns on a pane of glass at Mauchline, which ought to settle the question completely—

"Gin a body kiss a body comin' through the grain.
Need a body grudge a body what's a body's ain!"

AULD LANG SYNE.

ARRANGED BY J. T. SURENNE.

Should auld ac - quain - tance

be for - got, And ne - ver brought to mind! Should auld ac - quain - tance be for - got, And

days o' lang syne? For auld lang syne, my dear, For

We twa ha'e run about the braes,
And pu'd the gowans[1] fine,
But we've wander'd mony a weary foot,
Sin' auld lang syne.
For auld lang syne, &c.

We twa ha'e paidelt[2] in the burn,[3]
Frae morning sun till dine;
But seas between us braid ha'e roar'd,
Sin' auld lang syne.
For auld lang syne, &c.

And here's a hand my trusty fere,[4]
And gie's a hand o' thine;
And we'll take a richt-gude-willie waught,[5]
For auld lang syne.
For auld lang syne, &c.

And surely ye'll be your pint-stoup,
And surely I'll be mine;
And we'll tak' a cup o' kindness yet,
For auld lang syne.
For auld lang syne, &c.

[1] Daisies. [2] Walked backwards and forwards. [3] Brook.
[4] Companion.—In some editions the word is "friend." [5] A draught with right good will.

"AULD LANG SYNE." "Burns admitted to Johnson, that three of the stanzas of Lang-syne only were old; the other two being written by himself. These three stanzas relate to the *cup*, the *pint-stoup*, and a *gude-willie waught;* those two introduced by Burns have relation to the innocent amusements of youth, contrasted with the cares and troubles of maturer age." In introducing this song to Mrs. Dunlop of Dunlop, the daughter of Sir Thomas Wallace of Craigie, and a descendant of the race of Ellerslie, the poet says:—"Is not the Scotch phrase, 'auld lang syne,' exceedingly expressive? There is an old song and tune (of this name) which have often thrilled through my soul. . . . . Light be the turf on the breast of the heaven-inspired poet who composed this glorious fragment! There is more of the fire of native genius in it than in half-a-dozen of modern Bacchanalians!"

As Burns had mentioned that the old tune adapted to the song in Johnson's Museum was but *mediocre*, Mr. Thomson got the words arranged to the air, "I fee'd a lad at Michaelmas," to which they are now always sung. "Shield introduced it in his overture to the opera of Rosina, written by Mr. Brooks, and acted at Covent-Garden in 1783. It is the last movement of that overture, and in imitation of a Scottish bagpipe tune, in which the oboe is substituted for the *chanter*, and the *bassoon* for the *drone*." The air bears so strong a resemblance to "Comin' thro' the rye," "Oh! hey, Johnnie lad," "For the sake of somebody," as well as to several dance tunes known under various names, that it almost requires a native to tell the one from the other. See the Note to "Oh! hey, Johnnie lad," where portions of several of these tunes are placed side by side for comparison.

In Johnson's Museum the last stanza stands second; George Thomson removed it to the end, and in this has been followed by subsequent editors. The fourth stanza seems to make the best close; the fifth should immediately precede it.

O

THE WINTER IT IS PAST.

ARRANGED BY J. T. SURENNE.

The win-ter it is past, and the sum-mer comes at last, And the small birds sing on ev' - ry tree; Now ev' - ry thing is glad, while I am ve - ry sad; For my

The rose upon the brier, by the waters running clear,
   May have charms for the linnet or the bee;
Their little loves are blest, and their little hearts at rest,
   But my true love is parted from me.

My love is like the sun, that in the sky does run
   For ever so constant and true;
But his is like the moon, that wanders up and down,
   And every month it is new.

All you that are in love, and cannot it remove,
   I pity the pains you endure;
For experience makes me know, that your hearts are full of woe,
   A woe that no mortal can cure.

"THE WINTER IT IS PAST." Oswald printed this plaintive little air in his Caledonian Pocket Companion, Book vii., about 1765 (?). Until recently it was believed to be a Scottish tune, but it now seems rather doubtful whether it is not merely the Scottish form of an Irish air, of which Dr. Petrie has given the original in his "Ancient Music of Ireland" (1855). If so, our version is a good specimen of the transformation which usually takes place through traditional rendering. Both versions begin and end on the same note; but this, in the Irish form, is the fifth (dominant), in the Scottish, the first (key-note) of the scale; the phrases have a certain similarity, modified by the necessity of keeping within the usual compass of the voice while yet changing the key. In order to facilitate comparison, Dr. Petrie's air is given below. In Thompson's Country Dances, London,—date not now ascertainable, probably between 1765-85,—there is a form of the tune which differs considerably from those here given, it is named, "Red, and all red," and begins and ends on the key-note.

Another version, not differing greatly from that of Dr. Petrie, excepting that it has a second part, has been recovered by Dean Christie and inserted in his Traditional Ballad Airs, vol. i. The Dean has been so fortunate as also to recover a missing stanza of the original ballad, which seems to prove that it was written by the lady-love of a highwayman named Johnston, who rode (? robbed) on the Curragh of Kildare, and whose career was cut short by the strong arm of the law about the middle of last century. Dr. Petrie's copy of the song contains seven stanzas, Dean Christie's eight; the usual Scottish form, which we give in this work, has only four. It is nearly the same as that in Johnson's Museum, 1788, sent by Burns, who, as Mr. W. Scott Douglas believes, wrote the second stanza, and selected the other three from the common stall broadside.

VERSION FROM DR. PETRIE'S ANCIENT MUSIC OF IRELAND.

O WHISTLE, AN' I'LL COME TO YOU, MY LAD.

ARRANGED BY J. T. SURENNE.

O whistle, an' I'll come to you, my lad ; O whistle, an' I'll come to you, my lad; Tho' fa - ther, an' mo - ther, an' a' should gae mad, O whis - tle, an' I'll come to you, my lad. But wa - ri - ly tent when ye come to court me, And come na un - less the back-yett be a - jee; Syne up the back-stile, and let nae bo - dy see, And come as ye were na com - in' to me, And

come as ye were na com - in' to me.

O whistle, an' I'll come to you, my lad,
O whistle, an' I'll come to you, my lad ;
Tho' father, an' mother, an' a' should gae mad,
O whistle, an' I'll come to you, my lad.
At kirk or at market, where'er ye meet me,
Gang by me as tho' that ye cared na a flie ;
But steal me a blink o' your bonnie black e'e,
Yet look as ye were na lookin' at me,
Yet look as ye were na lookin' at me.

O whistle, an' I'll come to you, my lad,
O whistle, an' I'll come to you, my lad ;
Tho' father, an' mother, an' a' should gae mad,
O whistle, an' I'll come to you, my lad.
Ay vow an' protest that ye care na for me,
And whiles ye may lightlie my beauty a wee ;
But court nae anither, tho' jokin' ye be,
For fear that she wile your fancy frae me,
For fear that she wile your fancy frae me.

"O WHISTLE, AN' I'LL COME TO YOU." This air is very Irish in style, but Burns always contended that though he had sung it to many Irishmen, not one of them either claimed it or even knew it. Further, he alleged that John Bruce, an excellent fiddle-player in Dumfries, was generally believed to have composed it. In his Reliques he says, "Bruce, who was an honest man, though a red-wud Highlander, constantly claimed it." Mr. Mayne, on the other hand, in his Notes to "The Siller Gun," says, "Although Bruce was an admirable performer (on the violin), he was never known as a composer of music." O'Keefe introduced the air in his opera, "The Poor Soldier," in 1783, along with other popular melodies, the greater portion of which are Irish ; still, as there are also three Scottish airs in the opera, this is not very conclusive in regard to nationality. Bunting, in his latest collection of Irish music (1840), gives an air, as an example of the omission of the fourth and seventh of the scale, which seems to suggest "O whistle, and I'll come to you." Though not by any means identical with that air, yet it has sufficient similarity to warrant its insertion below. In 1787 Burns sent the refrain and one stanza of his song to Johnson for insertion in the Museum ; and in 1796 he added two stanzas, and altered the former one, for George Thomson's work.

GO DE SIN DEN TE SIN. (WHAT IS THAT TO HIM?)

AULD ROBIN GRAY.

AIR, " THE BRIDEGROOM GRAT."

ARRANGED BY T. M. MUDIE.

$\wp = 54$

Poco Adagio,
con Sentimento.

When the sheep are in the fauld, and the kye at hame, And a' the warld to sleep are gane; The waes o' my heart fa' in show'rs frae my e'e, When

Young Jamie lo'ed me weel, and he sought me for his bride;
But saving a crown, he had naething beside;
To make that crown a pound, my Jamie gaed to sea—
And the crown and the pound were baith for me.

He hadna been gane a week but only twa,
When my father brake his arm, and the cow was stown awa;
My mither she fell sick, and my Jamie at the sea,
And auld Robin Gray came a courting me.

My father couldna work, and my mither couldna spin;
I toil'd day and night, but their bread I couldna win.
Auld Rob maintain'd them baith, and wi' tears in his e'e,
Said, "Jeanie, for their sakes, O marry me."

My heart it said nay—I look'd for Jamie back;
But the wind it blew high, and the ship it was a wrack.
The ship it was a wrack, why didna Jeanie dee?
And why do I live to say, wae's me?

My father urged me sair, my mither didna speak,
But she look'd in my face till my heart was like to break.
So they gi'ed him my hand, though my heart was at the sea,
And auld Robin Gray is gudeman to me.

I hadna been a wife a week but only four,
When sitting sae mournfully [ae night] at the door,
I saw my Jamie's wraith, for I couldna think it he,
Till he said, I'm come back for to marry thee!

O sair did we greet, and meikle did we say,
We took but ae kiss, and we tore ourselves away;
I wish I were dead, but I'm no like to dee;
Oh! why do I live to say, wae's me?

I gang like a ghaist and I carena to spin,
I darena think o' Jamie, for that wad be a sin;
But I'll do my best a gude wife to be,
For auld Robin Gray is [a] kind [man] to me.

"AULD ROBIN GRAY." (Old air, "The bridegroom grat.") The air appears to be old, and is the same to which the accompanying verses were written by Lady Anne Lindsay. See following Note.

From its tonality it is probably of the seventeenth century, but must have come down traditionally, for it is not known to have appeared anywhere previously to the ballad. The old words are entirely lost.

AULD ROBIN GRAY.

ENGLISH AIR, COMPOSED BY REV. MR. LEEVES.

ARRANGED BY T. M. MUDIE.

Young Ja - mie lo'ed me weel, and sought me for bis bride; But

sav - ing a crown, he had naething else be - side. To make that crown a pound, my

Ja - mie gaed to sea, And the crown and the pound were baith for me. He had na been gane a week but on-ly twa, When my fa-ther brake his arm, and our cow was stown a-wa'; My mither she fell sick, and Ja-mie at the sea, And auld Ro-bin Gray came a court-ing me.

The rest of the verses are given with the old air.

"AULD ROBIN GRAY." The story of the song has been so often told, that it is unnecessary to do more than allude to a few facts connected with it.

An old air, called "The bridegroom grat," was a favourite with Lady Anne Lindsay of Balcarras, but, like many other old airs, it had words which were not fitted for good society. Lady Anne therefore determined to write a new song for it, the present excellent ballad being the result. This was in 1770 or 1771, the authoress being then only in her twentieth year. The old air was, however, not long without a rival, and a successful one. The Rev. William Leeves, rector of Wrington, Somersetshire, having obtained a copy of the new words, a few months apparently after they were written, at once set them to music. His air is now that known to every one as "Auld Robin Gray;" the Scottish tune already given,—a simple old thing of one strain,—being now almost unknown. If sung at all, it is so to the first stanza, and as an introduction to the song.

In 1824 Lady Anne Barnard (née Lindsay) communicated to Sir Walter Scott a revised copy of "Auld Robin Gray," with two continuations of the ballad. These Sir Walter published the following year in a thin quarto dedicated to the Bannatyne Club; but the alterations are not considered to be improvements, and the continuations are much inferior to the original ballad.

O NANCY, WILT THOU GO WITH ME?

ENGLISH AIR.

ARRANGED BY H. E. DIBDIN.

♩ = 96

ANDANTE
AMOROSO.

O Nan - cy, wilt thou go with me, Nor sigh to leave the flaunt - ing town? Can si - lent glens have charms for thee, The low - ly cot and rus - set gown? No long - er drest in silk - en sheen, No long - er deck'd with jew - els rare, Say, canst thou quit each court - ly scene, Where thou wert fair - est of the fair! Say, canst thou quit each court - ly scene, Where thou wert fair - est

of the fair? Where thou wert fairest, Where thou wert fairest, Where

thou wert fair - est of the fair.

O Nancy! when thou'rt far away,
  Wilt thou not cast a wish behind?
Say, canst thou face the scorching ray,
  Nor shrink before the wintry wind?
O can that soft and gentle mien
  Extremes of hardship learn to bear
Nor, sad, regret each courtly scene,
  Where thou wert fairest of the fair?

O Nancy! canst thou love so true,
  Through perils keen with me to go;
Or when thy swain mishap shall rue,
  To share with him the pang of woe?

Say, should disease or pain befal,
  Wilt thou assume the nurse's care;
Nor, wistful, those gay scenes recal,
  Where thou wert fairest of the fair?

And when at last thy love shall die,
  Wilt thou receive his parting breath;
Wilt thou repress each struggling sigh,
  And cheer with smiles the bed of death?
And wilt thou o'er his breathless clay
  Strew flowers, and drop the tender tear;
Nor then regret those scenes so gay,
  Where thou wert fairest of the fair?

"O NANCY, WILT THOU GO WITH ME?" These words, by Thomas Percy, Bishop of Dromore, were set to music by Thomas Carter, an Irish musician, and sung at Vauxhall by Mr. Vernon, in 1773. We have inserted this very popular song for the purpose of proclaiming that it belongs to England, though a slightly Scotified version of it has been repeatedly published as a Scottish song. Those who prefer singing the latter, can easily make the alterations for themselves.

WITHIN A MILE OF EDINBURGH.

ARRANGED BY FINLAY DUN.

'Twas with-in a mile of E-din-bu-rgh town, In the ro-sy time of the year; Sweet flow-ers bloom'd, and the grass was down, And each shepherd woo'd his dear.

Bon - nie Jockie, blythe and gay, Kiss'd young Jenny mak-ing hay; The

las - sie blush'd, and frowning cried, "Na, na, it winna do; I

canna, canna, winna, winna, maunna buckle to."

Young Jockie was a wag that never wad wed,
   Though lang he had followed the lass;
Contented she earn'd and eat her brown bread,
   And merrily turn'd up the grass.
      Bonnie Jockie, blythe and free,
      Won her heart right merrily :
   Yet still she blush'd, and frowning cried, "Na, na,
      it winna do;
   I canna, canna, winna, winna, maunna buckle to."

But when he vow'd he wad make her his bride,
   Though his flocks and herds were not few,
She gi'ed him her hand and a kiss beside,
   And vow'd she'd for ever be true.
      Bonnie Jockie, blythe and free,
      Won her heart right merrily :
   At kirk she no more frowning cried, "Na, na, it
      winna do;
   I canna, canna, winna, winna, maunna buckle to."

"WITHIN A MILE OF EDINBURGH." In Playford's first volume of "Wit and Mirth," 1698, there appears an old
Anglo-Scottish song, entitled, "'Twas within a furlong of Edinborough town," supposed to be by Thomas D'Urfey.
The air, in G minor, evidently English, also appears in the latter portion of the *original* volume of the Leyden MS.,
in ordinary notation, *not in tablature ;* and is there named, "Two furlongs from Edinburgh town." See D'Urfey's
Pills, i. 326, Reprint, 1719. The words here given are only a modern though improved version of the old verses,
adapted to an air composed by Mr. James Hook, a very popular and prolific composer of his day. He was born
at Norwich in 1746, and died about thirty years ago, leaving two sons, the Rev. Dr. Hook, prebendary of Winchester,
and Theodore Edward Hook, the latter a man of most versatile talents—an *improvisatore* in music and poetry
—a clever novelist and journalist. Theodore Hook died in 1841. aged 53.

WHERE ARE THE JOYS I HAVE MET IN THE MORNING?

AIR, "SAW YE MY FATHER?"   ARRANGED BY FINLAY DUN.

Where are the joys I have met in the morn - ing, That danced to the lark's ear - ly song? Where is the peace that a - wait - ed my wan - d'ring At eve - ning, the wild woods a -

mong !

mf   cres.   f

The last stanza may be omitted.

No more a-winding the course of yon river,
And marking sweet flow'rets so fair ;
No more I trace the light footstops of pleasure,
But sorrow and sad sighing care.

Is it that summer's forsaken our vallies,
And grim surly winter is near ?
No, no ; the bees humming round the gay roses,
Proclaim it the pride of the year.

Fain would I hide what I fear to discover,
Yet long, long too well have I known
All that has caused this wreck in my bosom,
Is Jenny, fair Jenny, alone.

[Time cannot aid me, my griefs are immortal,
Nor hope dare a comfort bestow ;
Come then, enamour'd, and fond of my anguish,
Enjoyment I'll seek in my woe.]

"WHERE ARE THE JOYS I HAVE MET IN THE MORNING ?" The air, "Saw ye my father ?" does not appear in any very early musical publication. The old words first appeared in Herd's Collection, 1769. In a letter written in September 1793, to Mr. George Thomson, Burns expresses himself thus :—"'Saw ye my father' is one of my greatest favourites. The evening before last, I wandered out, and began a tender song, in what I think is its native style. I must premise that the old way, and the way to give most effect, is to have no starting-note, as the fiddlers call it, but to burst at once into the pathos. Every country girl sings, 'Saw ye my father,'" &c.

We have adopted this song of Burns' in the present work, and subjoin the old verses for those who may prefer them.

Saw ye my father, or saw ye my mither,
Or saw ye my true love John ?
I saw nae your father, I saw nae your mither,
But I saw your true love John.

It's now ten at night, an' the stars gi'e nae light,
An' the bells they ring ding-dang,
He's met wi' some delay that causes him to stay,
But he will be here ere lang.

The surly auld carle did naething but snarl,
An' Johnny's face it grew red,
Yet tho' he often sigh'd, he ne'er a word replied,
Till a' were asleep in bed.

Then up Johnny rose, an' to the door he goes,
An' gently tirl'd at the pin,
The lassie takin' tent, unto the door she went,
An' she open'd an' lat him in.

An' are ye come at last ! an' do I hold you fast !
An' is my Johnny true !
I have nae time to tell, but sae lang's I like mysel,
Sae lang sall I like you.

Flee up, flee up, my bonnie grey cock,
An' craw when it is day ;
An' your neck shall be like the bonnie beaten gold,
An' your wings of the silver grey.

The cock proved false, an' untrue he was,
For he crew an hour owre soon :
The lassie thocht it day when she sent her love away,
An' it was but a blink o' the moon.

The air is altogether English in character, and even a part of the old words seems to have been altered from an English original.

I LO'E NA A LADDIE BUT ANE.

ARRANGED BY A. LAWRIE.

I lo'e na a lad - die but ane, He lo'es na a las - sie but me; He's will - in' to mak' me his ain, And his ain I am will - in' to be. He coft¹ me a roke - lay² o' blue,   And a   pair   o' mit - tens o'   green;   He   vow'd that he'd e - ver be

a piacere

true,   And I   plight - ed my troth yes - treen.

Let ithers brag weel o' their gear,[3]
Their land, and their lordly degree;
I carena for ought but my dear,
For he's ilka[4] thing lordly to me.
His words are sae sugar'd, sae sweet!
His sense drives ilk fear far awa'!
I listen, poor fool! and I greet;
Yet how sweet are the tears as they fa'!

"Dear lassie," he cries, wi' a jeer,
"Ne'er heed what the auld anes will say:
Though we've little to brag o'—ne'er fear;
What's gowd to a heart that is wae?
Our laird has baith honours and wealth,
Yet see how he's dwining[5] wi' care;
Now we, though we've naething but health,
Are cantie and leal evermair.

"O Menie! the heart that is true,
Has something mair costly than gear;
Ilk e'en it has naething to rue,
Ilk morn it has naething to fear.
Ye warldlings, gae hoard up your store,
And tremble for fear ought ye tyne,[6]
Guard your treasures wi' lock, bar, and door,
True love is the guardian o' mine."

He ends wi' a kiss and a smile—
Wae's me, can I tak' it amiss!
My laddie's unpractised in guile,
He's free aye to daut[7] and to kiss!
Ye lasses wha lo'e to torment
Your wooers wi' fause scorn and strife,
Play your pranks—I ha'e gi'en my consent,
And this night I am Jamie's for life.

¹ Bought.   ² A short cloak.   ³ Riches; goods.   ⁴ Every.   ⁵ Pining away.   ⁶ Lose.   ⁷ Caress.

"I LO'E NA A LADDIE BUT ANE." The first stanza of this song, as well as a second which is here omitted, are said, on the authority of Burns, to have been written by the Rev. Mr. Clunie of Borthwick. In Ritson's Collection the song is directed to be sung to the tune, "Happy Dick Dawson." The four supplementary stanzas beginning, "Let others brag weel o' their gear," were composed by Hector Macneill.

The air has been claimed alike by England, Scotland, and Ireland; the probability however seems to be, that it is an old English dance tune, and that the Scottish version, with the long note in the 2d and 6th bars, is an early form of it. (See Aird's Collection, Glasgow, 1784.) This is a peculiarity common to many of the old jigs. The received version of the air, known as "My lodging is on the cold ground," may be prettier, but it is more artificial and more modern in style. Was it perhaps altered into its present form when, as Mr. Chappell informs us, Giordani introduced it as a Larghetto in one of his harpsichord concertos (1776-82)? Moore admitted the air into his Irish Melodies, set to the words, "Believe me, if all those endearing young charms;" but Bunting, a higher authority on the subject, entirely disclaimed all knowledge of it as an Irish air, for it was not played either by the harpers who assembled at Belfast in 1792, or by any of those whom he afterwards sought out in various parts of the country.

I MET FOUR CHAPS YON BIRKS AMANG.

AIR, "JENNY'S DAWBEE."

ARRANGED BY J. T. SURENNE

met four chaps yon birks amang, Wi' hing - ing lugs[1] and fa - ces lang: I spier'd at nee - bour

Baul - dy Strang, Wha's they I see? Quo' he, Ilk cream-faced paw - ky chiel,[2] Thocht

he was cun - ning as the deil, And here they cam' a - wa' to steal

Jen-ny's baw-bee.[4]

The first, a Captain to his trade,
Wi' skull ill-lined, but back weel-clad,
March'd round the barn, and by the shed,
    And pappit[5] on his knee :
Quo' he, "My goddess, nymph, and queen,
Your beauty's dazzled baith my een!"
But deil a beauty he had seen
    But—Jenny's bawbee.

A Lawyer neist, wi' blatherin' gab,[6]
Wha speeches wove like ony wab,
In ilk ane's corn aye took a dab,
    And a' for a fee.
Accounts he owed through a' the toun,
And tradesmen's tongues nae mair could drown,
But now he thocht to clout his goun
    Wi' Jenny's bawbee.

A Norland Laird neist trotted up,
Wi' bawsand[7] naig and siller whup,
Cried, "There's my beast, lad, haud the grup,
    Or tie 't till a tree ·
What's gowd to me?—I've walth o' lan'!
Bestow on ane o' worth your han'!"—
He thocht to pay what he was awn
    Wi' Jenny's bawbee.

Drest up just like the knave o' clubs,
A THING came neist, (but life has rubs,)
Foul were the roads, and fu' the dubs,[8]
    And jaupit[9] a' was he.
He danced up, squinting through a glass,
And grinn'd, "I' faith, a bonnie lass!"
He thought to win, wi' front o' brass,
    Jenny's bawbee.

She bade the Laird gae kame his wig,
The Sodger no to strut sae big,
The Lawyer no to be a prig,
    The fool, he cried, "Tehee !
I kenn'd that I could never fail!"
But she preen'd[10] the dishclout to his tail,
And soused him wi' the water-pail,
    And kept her bawbee.

Then Johnnie cam', a lad o' sense,
Although he had na mony pence;
And took young Jenny to the spence,[11]
    Wi' her to crack[12] a wee.
Now Johnnie was a clever chiel,
And here his suit he press'd sae weel,
That Jenny's heart grew saft as jeel,
    And she birled[13] her bawbee.

¹ Earn.   ² Asked.   ³ Sly fellow.   ⁴ Fortune; *Scotice*—tocher: literally—a half-penny.   ⁵ Popped; dropped.
⁶ Babbling tongue.   ⁷ Having a white spot on its forehead.   ⁸ Puddles; pools.   ⁹ Despattered.
¹⁰ Pinned.   ¹¹ The inner apartment of a country house.   ¹² To chat.   ¹³ Consented to share; to birl, means also to toss up.

"JENNY'S BAWBEE." This air has long been a favourite dancing tune; but it appears also to have been early adapted to words. A fragment of the old song is given by Herd, in his Collection of 1776: its merits are not great; but even had they been greater, it must still have been supplanted by the humorous verses which we give above. These were written by the late Sir Alexander Boswell, Bart., and were published by him anonymously in 1803. He afterwards presented them to Mr. George Thomson for his Collection of Scottish Melodies. Allan Cunningham, in his Songs of Scotland, 1825, gives Sir Alexander's verses with an additional stanza, (the last,) which did not appear in the earlier copies; whether it was an after-thought of the author himself, or was added by another, is uncertain. Sir Alexander Boswell was the eldest son of Dr. Johnson's biographer, and was born in 1775; he died 27th March 1822. He was distinguished as an amiable and spirited country gentleman, and also as a literary antiquary of considerable erudition. Perhaps his taste in the latter capacity was greatly fostered by the possession of an excellent collection of old manuscripts and books, gathered together by his ancestors, and well known under the title of the "Auchinleck Library." From the stores of this collection, Sir Walter Scott published, in 1804, the romance of "Sir Tristrem," which is believed to be the earliest specimen extant of poetry by a Scotsman. Its author, Thomas of Erceldoune, called the Rhymer, flourished in the thirteenth century See Chambers' Dictionary of Eminent Scotsmen.

GET UP AND BAR THE DOOR.

ARRANGED BY T. M. MUDIE.

$\bullet = 76$

ALLEGRETTO
SCHERZOSO.

It

fell a-bout the Mart'-mas time, And a gay time it was then, O! When

our gude-wife had puddings to mak', And she boil'd them in the

pan, O!   The wind blew cauld frae

north to south, And blew in - to the floor, O! Quoth our gudeman to

our gudewife, "Get up and bar the door, O!"

"My hand is in my husswyfskip,
  Gudeman, as ye may see, O!
An it should na be barr'd this hundred year,
  It's no be barr'd for me, O!"

They made a paction 'tween them twa,
  They made it firm and sure, O!
Whaever spak the foremost word
  Should rise and bar the door, O!

Then by there came twa gentlemen,
  At twelve o'clock at night, O!
And they could neither see house nor ha',
  Nor coal nor candle light, O!

Now, whether is this a rich man's house,
  Or whether is it a poor, O?
But never a word wad ane o' them speak,
  For barring o' the door, O!

And first they ate the white puddings
  And then they ate the black, O!

          ¹ Household affairs; housewifeship.

Tho' muckle² thought the gudewife to hersel',
  Yet ne'er a word she spak', O!

Then said the ane unto the other—
  "Here, man, tak' ye my knife, O!
Do ye tak' aff the auld man's beard,
  And I'll kiss the gudewife, O!"

"But there's nae water in the house,
  And what shall we do then, O?"
"What ails ye at the puddin' broo³
  That boils into the pan, O?"

O up then started our gudeman,
  And an angry man was he, O!
"Will ye kiss my wife before my een,
  And scaud me wi' pudding bree, O?"

Then up and started our gudewife,
  Gied three skips on the floor, O!
"Gudeman, ye've spoken the foremost word
  Get up and bar the door, O!"

          ² Much.   ³ Juice or soup.

"GET UP AND BAR THE DOOR." "This exceedingly humorous Scottish ballad was recovered by old David Herd, and inserted in his Collection, vol. ii. p. 159, anno 1776. It appears to be an amplification of the fine old song called 'Johnie Blunt,' which will be found in the fourth volume of the Museum, p. 376, song 365. It is a curious circumstance that this ballad furnished Prince Hoare with the incidents of his principal scene in his musical entertainment of 'No Song no Supper,' acted at Drury-lane, London, 1790, (the music by Storace,) and since, at all the theatres of the United Kingdom, with great success. It still continues a favourite on the acting list. Mr. Hoare was also indebted to another old Scottish ballad for several other material incidents in the same piece, namely, 'The Freirs of Berwick,' written by Dunbar prior to the year 1568, as it is inserted in the Bannatyne Manuscript, in the Library of the Faculty of [Advocates] Edinburgh, of that date, and which Allan Ramsay afterwards modernized, in a poem called 'The Monk and the Miller's Wife.'" See Museum Illustrations, vol. iii. p. 292.

AND ARE YE SURE THE NEWS IS TRUE?

AIR, "THERE'S NAE LUCK ABOUT THE HOUSE."

ARRANGED BY J. T. SURENNE.

And are ye sure the news is true? And are ye sure he's weel? Is this a time to think o' wark? Ye jauds, fling bye your wheel. Is this a time to think o' wark, When Colin's at the door? Rax' me my cloak, I'll to the quay, And see him come a - shore.

For there's nae luck a - bout the house, There's nae luck at a'; There's lit - tle plea - sure in the house, When our gudeman's a - wa'.

And gi'e to me my bigonet,[2]
My bishops' satin gown,
For I maun tell the bailie's wife
That Colin's come to town.
My turkey slippers maun gae on,
My hose o' pearl blue;
'Tis a' to please my ain gudeman,
For he's baith leal and true.
    For there's nae luck, &c.

Rise up and mak' a clean fireside;
Put on the muckle pot;
Gi'e little Kate her button gown,
And Jock his Sunday coat:
And mak' their shoon as black as slaes,
Their hose as white as snaw;
Its a' to please my ain gudeman,
For he's been lang awa'.
    For there's nae luck, &c.

There's twa fat hens upon the bauk,
They've fed this month and mair;
Mak' haste and thraw their necks about,
That Colin weel may fare;
And spread the table neat and clean,
Gar[3] ilka thing look braw;
For wha can tell how Colin fared,
When he was far awa'.
    For there's nae luck, &c.

Sae true his heart, sae smooth his speech,
His breath like caller air;
His very foot has music in't,
As he comes up the stair.
And will I see his face again?
And will I hear him speak?
I'm downright dizzy wi' the thought—
In troth, I'm like to greet.[4]
    For there's nae luck, &c.

The cauld blasts o' the winter wind,
That thirled through my heart,
They're a' blawn by, I ha'e him safe,
Till death we'll never part:
But what puts parting in my head?
It may be far awa';
The present moment is our ain,
The neist we never saw.
    For there's nae luck, &c.

Since Colin's weel, I'm weel content,
I ha'e nae mair to crave;
Could I but live to mak' him blest,
I'm blest aboon the lave:[5]
And will I see his face again?
And will I hear him speak?
I'm downright dizzy wi' the thought—
In troth, I'm like to greet.
    For there's nae luck, &c.

1 Stretch.   2 A linen cap, or coif.   3 Make.   4 To shed tears.   5 Remainder.

"THERE'S NAE LUCK ABOUT THE HOUSE." The air is a modernised version of "Up, and waur them a',
Willie." In D'Urfey's Pills (vol. v. 58, 1719, Reprint) there is a tune which bears a striking resemblance
to the chorus part of the melody. There has been much disputation regarding the authorship of the song ;
opinions are divided between William Julius Mickle, a native of Langholm, well known as the translator of
the Lusiad, and Jean Adams, a teacher of a day-school at Crawford's-dyke, near Greenock.

LEEZIE LINDSAY.

ARRANGED BY J. T. SURENNE.

♩ = 84

ANDANTE
AMOROSO.

"Will ye gang to the Hie - lands, Lee - zie

Lind - say! Will ye gang to the Hie - lands wi' me! Will ye

gang to the Hie - lands, Lee - zie Lind - say! My bride and my dar - ling to be."

mf   *dim.*   *p*

"To gang to the Hielands wi' you, Sir,
Wad bring the saut tear to my e'e,
At leaving the green glens and woodlands,
And streams o' my ain countrie."

"Oh, I'll shew you the red-deer roaming,
On mountains where waves the tall pine;
And, far as the bound of the red-deer,
Ilk moorland and mountain is mine.

"A thousand claymores I can muster,
Ilk blade and its bearer the same;
And when round their Chieftain they rally,
The gallant Argyle is my name."

There's dancing and joy in the Hielands,
There's piping and gladness and glee,
For Argyle has brought hame Leezie Lindsay
His bride and his darling to be!

"LEEZIE LINDSAY." The old air, probably Highland, was sent by Burns to Johnson, together with the first four lines of the song. Burns intended to send more verses, but never did. The other verses here given were written by Mr. Robert Gilfillan. The greater part of the old ballad of "*Lizie Lindsay*" was sent by Professor Scott of Aberdeen to Robert Jamieson, Esq., who published the fragment in the second volume of his "Popular Ballads and Songs," 1806, pp. 149-153. Burns evidently had the first stanza of the old ballad in view, though he changed the fourth line—"And dine on fresh cruds and green whey?" Another version of the story, in thirty-five stanzas, is inserted in Chambers's Scottish Ballads, 1827. There the wooer does not at first disclose his rank, but carries his bride home to a miserable sheiling, and only declares himself after she has expressed her willingness to live with *him* anywhere. It is evidently compiled from several copies in different measures, which must therefore have been sung to different tunes.

In 1821 Robert Allan of Kilbarchan wrote a continuation of Burns's single stanza for his friend R. A. Smith; and as there are two versions of the tune, which differ very considerably, wrote a second song on the same subject. Both are in the Scottish Minstrel, ii. 100-1. The air which we have given in the text is the more popular in most parts of Scotland; but as the other, which is indeed the older of the two, is often sung, we subjoin it, with Robert Allan's second song.

Will ye gang to the Hielands, Leezie Lindsay? Will ye gang to the Hie-lands wi'
me? Will ye gang to the Hielands, Leezie Lindsay? My pride and my darling to be?

To gang to the Hielands wi' you, Sir,
I dinna ken how that may be,
For I ken na the road I am gaeing,
Nor ken I the lad I'm gaun wi'!

Oh Leezie, lass, ye maun ken little,
If sae be ye dinna ken me;
For I am Lord Ronald MacDonald,
A chieftain o' high degree.

(Oh, if ye're the laird of MacDonald,
A great ane I ken ye maun be;
But how can a chieftain sae mighty
Think o' a puir lassie like me?)

She has gotten a gown o' green satin,
She has kilted it up to the knee,
And she's aff wi' Lord Ronald MacDonald,
His bride and his darling to be.

MY LOVE'S IN GERMANY.

WORDS BY HECTOR MACNEILL.   ARRANGED BY T. M. MUDIE.

MODERATO.

My love's in Ger - ma - ny; Send him hame, send him hame, My love's in Ger - ma - ny, Send him hame. My love's in Ger - ma - ny, Fight-ing for roy - al - ty; He may ne'er his Jean - ie see; Send him hame, send him hame; He may ne'er his Jean-ie see; Send him hame.

He's brave as brave can be;
  Send him hame, send him hame;
He's brave as brave can be,
  Send him hame.
He's brave as brave can be,
He wad rather fa' than flee;
But his life is dear to me;
  Send him hame, send him hame;
Oh! his life is dear to me,
  Send him hame.

Our faes are ten to three;
  Send him hame, send him hame,
Our faes are ten to three,
  Send him hame.
Our faes are ten to three,
He maun either fa' or flee,
In the cause o' loyalty;
  Send him hame, send him hame:
In the cause o' loyalty,
  Send him hame.

Your love ne'er learnt to flee,
  Bonny dame, winsome dame;
Your love ne'er learnt to flee,
  Winsome dame.
Your love ne'er learnt to flee,
But he fell in Germanie,
Fighting brave for loyalty,
  Mournfu' dame, mournfu' dame;
Fighting brave for loyalty,
  Mournfu' dame.

He'll ne'er come o'er the sea;
  Willie's slain, Willie's slain;
He'll ne'er come o'er the sea,
  Willie's gane!
He'll ne'er come o'er the sea,
To his love and ain countrie;
This warld's nae mair for me,
  Willie's gane, Willie's gane;
This warld's nae mair for me,
  Willie's gane!

"MY LOVE'S IN GERMANY." The air is not to be found in any of our older collections, and probably came under the notice of the poet, Hector Macneill, in his early sea-faring days, when it was sung to a well-known ballad on the pirate Paul Jones. Three-quarters of a century before this we find an English sea song, written on Admiral Benbow, "Come all you sailors bold, lend an ear, lend an ear," the air of which bears sufficient resemblance to justify one in thinking that it gave rise to the present tune, probably through the unintentional variation of an untrained singer imperfectly catching up by ear what he supposed to be the correct melody. The rhythm of both these songs is peculiar, and is at least as old as the sixteenth century, for in the Complaynt of Scotland (1549) a song is mentioned as sung by the shepherds, "My love is lyand seik, send him joye, send him joye;" again, in the following century, the same peculiarity is found in a black letter ballad on the Restoration. (See Euing Collection, No. 309, Glasgow University.) It is called, "The loyal subject's joye," and begins, "Ye loyal subjects all, sing for joye, sing for joye." The name of the tune is "Sound a charge," which is possibly the refrain of a cavalier song of the previous reign. There is unfortunately no document extant that would serve to show any connection between these old songs and the present air, but the measure of all is the same, and they would sing exactly to what we now call "My love's in Germanie." We subjoin the English tune.

ADMIRAL BENBOW (Died 1703)—"COME ALL YE SAILORS BOLD."

COME UNDER MY PLAIDIE.

AIR, "JOHNNIE M'GILL."

ARRANGED BY T. M. MUDIE.

Come under my plaidie, the night's gaun to fa'; Come in frae the cauld blast, the drift, an' the snaw; Come un - der my plai - die, and sit down be - side me, There's room in't, dear las - sie, be - lieve me, for twa. Come un - der my plai - die, and

sit down be - side me, I'll hap ye frae ev' - ry cauld blast that can blaw; Come
un - der my plai - die, and sit down be - side me, There's room in't, dear las - sie, be -
lieve me, for twa.

Gae 'wa wi' your plaidie! auld Donald, gae 'wa;
I fear na the cauld blast, the drift, nor the snaw !
Gae 'wa wi' your plaidie! I'll no sit beside ye;
Ye micht be my gutcher ! [1] auld Donald, gae wa'.
I'm gaun to meet Johnnie—he's young, and he's bonnie.
He's been at Meg's bridal, fu' trig [2] and fu' braw !
Nane dances sae lichtly, sae gracefu', or tichtly,
His cheek's like the new rose, his brow's like the snaw !

Dear Marion, let that flee stick fast to the wa';
Your Jock's but a gowk, [3] and has naething ava;
The haill o' his pack he has now on his back ;
He's thretty, and I am but three score and twa.
Be frank now and kindly—I'll busk [4] ye aye finely
To kirk or to market there'll few gang sae braw;
A bien house to bide in, a chaise for to ride in,
And flunkies [5] to 'tend ye as aft as ye ca'.

| [1] Grandfather. | [2] Neat. | [3] Fool. | [4] Dress. | [5] Livery servants. |

"COME UNDER MY PLAIDIE." This is another production of Hector Macneill, the writer of "Mary of Castlecary," and many other songs, which have deservedly been very popular. The air, a dance tune, of which there are several versions, has been named after its supposed composer, John Macgill, a musician of Girvan in Ayrshire. It is, however, also claimed as belonging to Ireland ; and Moore has made use of it in his Irish Melodies in a rather extraordinary fashion. He has joined the first half of it as a second part to the first part of the old Shakespearian tune, "Green sleeves," calling the combination "The basket of oysters."
See Appendix for the rest of Macneill's song.

MY BOY, TAMMY.

ARRANGED BY J. T. SURENNE.

Whar' hae ye been a' day, My boy, Tam-my! An'

whar' hae ye been a' day, My boy, Tam-my! I've

been by burn and flow'-ry brae, Meadow green, and mountain grey, Courtin' o' this young thing,

Just come frae her mam - my.

An' whar' gat ye that young thing,
  My boy, Tammy?
I gat her down in yonder howe,
Smiling on a broomy knowe,
Herding ae wee lamb an' ewe,
  For her puir mammy.

What said ye to the bonnie bairn,
  My boy, Tammy?
I praised her een, sae lovely blue,
Her dimpled cheek an' cherry mou';—
An' prec'd it aft, as ye may trow!—
  She said, she'd tell her mammy.

I held her to my beatin' heart,
  My young, my smilin' lammie.
I ha'e a house, it cost me dear,
I've walth o' plenishin' an' gear;
Ye'se get it a', wer't ten times mair,
  Gin ye will leave your mammy.

The smile gaed aff her bonnie face—
  I maunna leave my mammy.
She's gi'en me meat, she's gi'en me claes,
She's been my comfort a' my days:—
My father's death brought monie waes!—
  I canna leave my mammy.

We'll tak' her hame, an' mak' her fain,
  My ain kind-hearted lammie.
We'll gi'e her meat, we'll gi'e her claes,
We'll be her comfort a' her days.
The wee thing gi'es her hand, an' says—
  There! gang an' ask my mammy.

Has she been to the kirk wi' thee,
  My boy, Tammy?
She has been to the kirk wi' me,
An' the tear was in her e'e;
For O! she's but a young thing,
  Just come frae her mammy.

"MY BOY, TAMMY." "This fine ballad, beginning, 'Whar' hae ye been a' day, my boy, Tammy?' was written by Hector Macneill, Esq. It first appeared in a Magazine, printed at Edinburgh in 1791, entitled 'The Bee,' which was conducted by his friend Dr. James Anderson. The melody to which the words are adapted is very ancient, and uncommonly pretty." See Museum Illustrations, vol. vi. p. 440. Mr. Stenhouse here says, that the melody is "very ancient." If so, the Editor may remark, that there is no evidence of its antiquity in its present form. It is rather surprising that Mr. Stenhouse, who bestowed so many years on the subject of Scottish melodies, should not have perceived that the air of "My boy, Tammy," is a modern transformation of the tune called "Muirland Willie," to which last, Mr. Stenhouse refers in a Note on No. 369 of Museum, as appearing in Thomson's Orpheus Caledonius, in 1725, and in Mrs. Crockat's MS. Collection, written in 1709, and in his possession. If any good musician will examine the melodic structure of "Muirland Willie," and compare it with that of "My boy, Tammy," he will be convinced that the latter is derived from the former, by a process of transformation not uncommon in popular melodies; i. e. by changing the time, and altering some of the notes, &c. There is besides an air in two-fourth time, (No. 501 of Museum,) which seems clearly to have been a dance-tune, also owing its origin to "Muirland Willie," at least in the first strain. In the second bar of Johnson's set of "Muirland Willie," the sixth of the scale is minor in ascending. The sixth of the scale is also minor throughout Napier's set of "My boy, Tammy," published in 1792, arranged by Haydn. It must be observed that the sets of "Muirland Willie" given by Craig, M'Gibbon, and Johnson, are not the same, note for note; but the principal melodic features are identical. Hector Macneill, being a singer as well as a poet, was no doubt well acquainted with "Muirland Willie," and possibly also with the air to which Burns wrote "My Peggy's face," in both of which he would find leading hints for the air to his excellent words. Although the present air does not appear in any collection until after Macneill's verses were written, something like it may have been sung to a silly old song, of which the following lines are a specimen :—

    "Is she fit to soop the house, my boy, Tammy?
    She's just as fit to soop the house, as the cat to catch a mouse.
    And yet she's but a young thing, new come frae her mammy."

O DINNA THINK, BONNIE LASSIE.

slower.

Far's the gate ye ha'e to gang, dark's the night an' ee - rie; Far's the gate ye ha'e to gang,

mf

dark's the night an' ee - rie; O'er the muir an' thro' the glen, ghaists mayhap will fear ye: O

p

stay at hame, it's late at night, an' dinna gang an' leave me.

mf

It's but a night an' half a day that I'll leave my dearie;
But a night an' half a day that I'll leave my dearie;
But a night an' half a day that I'll leave my dearie;
When the sun gaes west the loch I'll come again an' see you.

Waves are rising o'er the sea, winds blaw loud and fear me;
Waves are rising o'er the sea, winds blaw loud and fear me;
While the waves an' winds do roar, I am wae and dreary;
An' gin ye lo'e me as ye say, ye winna gang and leave me.

O dinna think, bonnie lassie, I'm gaun to leave you;
Dinna think, bonnie lassie, I'm gaun to leave you;
Dinna think, bonnie lassie, I'm gaun to leave you;
For let the warld gae as it will, I'll come again an' see you.

"O DINNA THINK, BONNIE LASSIE." This song was written by Hector Macneill, but was not included in his works; as he probably became aware that a song on a similar subject, by Miss Susannah Blamire, had previously appeared.

S

IN THE GARB OF OLD GAUL.

ARRANGED BY T. M. MUDIE.

In the garb of old Gaul, with the fire of old Rome, From the heath-covered mountains of

Sco - tia we come; Where the Ro - mans en - dea - vour'd our coun - try to gain, But our

an - ces - tors fought, and they fought not in vain. Such our love of li - ber - ty, our coun - try, and our laws, That like our an - cestors of old, we stand by freedom's cause ; We'll

f colla voce.

bravely fight, like heroes bright, for honour and applause, And de - fy the French, with all their arts, to

al - ter our laws.

No effeminate customs our sinews unbrace,
No luxurious tables enervate our race;
Our loud-sounding pipe bears the true martial strain,
So do we the old Scottish valour retain.
    Such our love, &c.

As a storm in the ocean when Boreas blows,
So are we enraged when we rush on our foes;
We sons of the mountains, tremendous as rocks,
Dash the force of our foes with our thundering strokes.
    Such our love, &c.

"IN THE GARB OF OLD GAUL." Mr. Stenhouse, in his note on No. 210 of Johnson's Museum, says that this song was composed by the late Sir Harry Erskine of Torry, Baronet, and that it was printed in Herd's Collection, 1769 and 1776. Mr. David Laing corrects this by stating that "the writer of this song was Lieutenant-General Sir Henry Erskine, Baronet, but not of Torry, as erroneously stated at p. 202. He was the second son of Sir John Erskine of Alva, and succeeded to the baronetcy on the death of his elder brother. He was Deputy-Quartermaster-General, and succeeded his uncle, the Hon. General St. Clair, in the command of the Royal Scots, in 1762. He was long a distinguished member of the House of Commons. He died at York, when on his way to London, 9th of August 1765," &c. Mr. Laing also states that the song was previously printed in "The Lark," 1765. See Museum Illustrations, vol. iii. p. 298. We give here the three most tolerable stanzas of this very trashy song, which are as much as any one will care to sing. The air was composed by General John Reid, who bequeathed upwards of £70,000 to establish a Chair of Music in the University of Edinburgh.

FOR THE SAKE O' SOMEBODY.

ARRANGED BY J. T. SURENNE.

heart is sair, I daur-na tell, My heart is sair for some - bo - dy ; I could wake a

win - ter night, For the sake o' some - bo - dy. Oh-hon, for some - bo - dy!

Oh hey, for some - bo - dy! I could range the world a - round,

Ye powers that smile on virtuous love,
O sweetly smile on somebody!
Frae ilka danger keep him free,
And send me safe my somebody
Oh-hon, for somebody!
Oh hey, for somebody!
I wad do—what wad I not?—
For the sake o' somebody.

"For the sake o' somebody." In this work we have not adopted the set of the air given by Johnson in his Museum, but the long-received and established popular set of the air. The superiority of the latter is sufficient to justify this. When and by whom this modern air was composed is not very clear. It first appeared in the fourth part of Urbani's Collection of Scottish Songs (1801?). It has too much of the national style to have been the composition of Urbani himself, but he has at least the merit of having recovered and adapted to Burns's words a much better tune than that given by Johnson. Urbani was, perhaps, a little too fond of grace notes and florid passages, yet one cannot peruse his volumes without feeling assured, as he states in his preface, that "Having been struck with the elegant simplicity of the original Scottish melodies, he applied himself for several years in attending to the manner of the best Scottish singers, . . . and had thus acquired the true national taste. His sets of the melodies were procured from ladies and gentlemen well acquainted with the musical taste of their country."

Having now shown that Rizzio's name as a composer was not heard of for 160 years after his death, we shall now notice a few instances in which high merit is claimed for him as a melodist. Geminiani, in his "Treatise on good taste in the art of Music," London, 1749, has the following strange passage :—"Two composers of music have appeared in the world, who, in their different kinds of melody, have raised my admiration; namely, David Rizzio, and Gio. Baptista Lulli: of these, which stands highest is none of my business to pronounce; but when I consider that Rizzio was foremost in point of time, that till then melody was entirely rude and barbarous, and that he found means to civilize and inspire it with all the gallantry of the Scottish nation, I am inclinable to give him the preference." It is unnecessary for us to answer what we have already shown to be a fiction of recent origin. We shall merely place in opposition an extract from Dr. Campbell's Philosophical Survey of the South of Ireland:— "That this music, or any one single Scottish air, was invented or composed by the unfortunate Rizzio, is only noticed here as an absurd fable, which having no support, merits no refutation." Geminiani's assertion, that "till the time of Rizzio melody was entirely rude and barbarous," is signally refuted by many ancient popular airs of France, Italy, and Germany. We may particularly refer to the airs, Nos. 14 and 16, of the Plates given in G. F Graham's "Essay on Musical Composition," Edinburgh, 1838. One of these, a most graceful French air of the 15th century, we give below; the other is a free and elegant German melody of 1425.

See No. 14 of Plates of Essay on Musical Composition.

FOR A' THAT, AN' A' THAT.

ARRANGED BY J. T. SURENNE.

Is there, for ho - nest po - ver - ty, That hangs his head, an'

a' that? The cow - ard-slave, we pass him by; We dare be puir, for a' that.

For a' that, an' a' that, Our toils ob - scure, an' a' that, The rank is but the gui - nea - stamp; The man's the gowd, for a' that.

The first line ought to be sung thus :—

Is there, for ho - nest po - ver - ty, &c.

What tho' on hamely fare we dine,
Wear hodden-grey,[1] an' a' that?
Gi'e fools their silks, an' knaves their wine;
A man's a man, for a' that;
For a' that, an' a' that,
Their tinsel show, an' a' that,
The honest man, tho' e'er sae puir,
Is king o' men, for a' that.

Ye see yon birkie,[2] ca'd a lord,
Wha struts, an' stares, an' a' that;
Tho' hundreds worship at his word,
He's but a cuif,[3] for a' that.
For a' that, an' a' that,
His ribbon, star, an' a' that,
The man of independent mind,
He looks an' laughs at a' that.

A king can mak' a belted knight,
A marquis, duke, an' a' that;
But an honest man's abune his might—
Gude faith, he maunna fa'[4] that!
For a' that, an' a' that,
Their dignities, an' a' that,
The pith o' sense, the pride o' worth,
Are higher ranks than a' that.

Then let us pray, that come it may,
As come it will, for a' that,
That sense an' worth o'er a' the earth,
May bear the gree,[5] an' a' that.
For a' that, an' a' that,
It's comin' yet, for a' that,
That man to man, the warld o'er,
Shall brothers be, for a' that.

1 Cloth used by the peasantry, which has the natural colour of the wool. 2 A young fellow. 3 A simpleton; a fool.
4 Try; attempt; venture. See Appendix. 5 Pre-eminence; superiority.

"For a' that, an' a' that." We have no information regarding the authorship of the air. Burns wrote two songs to it; one for the Museum, in 1789, beginning "Tho' women's minds, like winter winds;" and the other in 1794. The latter is the song we have adopted. Mr. Stenhouse speaks of this song as follows:—"In 1794, Burns wrote the following capital verses to the same air, which were handed about in manuscript a considerable time before they appeared in print. They unfortunately came out at a period when political disputes ran very high, and his enemies did not fail to interpret every sentence of them to his prejudice. That he was the zealous friend of rational and constitutional freedom, will not be denied; but that he entertained principles hostile to the safety of the State, no honest man that knew him will ever venture to maintain. In fact, what happened to Burns, has happened to most men of genius. During times of public commotion, there are always to be found vile and dastardly scoundrels, who, to render themselves favourites with those in power, and push their own selfish views of interest and ambition, are ever ready to calumniate the characters, and misrepresent the motives and actions of their neighbours, however good, innocent, or meritorious." See Museum Illustrations, vol. iii. pp. 284, 285. In other editions, the melody begins with two semiquavers; for these we have substituted a quaver, as more manly and decided, and therefore better suited to the character of the words; and as the accentuation of the first line of the song requires a slight alteration of the melody, we have given the proper notation for it at the end of the air.

THE BRAES O' GLENIFFER.

ARRANGED BY A. C. MACKENZIE.

SLOW,
WITH
MOURNFUL
EXPRESSION.

1. Keen blaws the wind o'er the braes o' Gleniffer, The
3. Then ilk thing around us was blythesome and cheerie, Then

auld castle turrets are cover'd wi' snaw; How changed frae the time when I met wi' my lov - er, A-
ilk thing around us was bonnie and braw; Now nae - thing is heard but the wind whistling drearie, And

mang the broom bushes by Stanley green shaw. 2. The
naething is seen but the wide-spreading snaw. 4. The

wild flow'rs o' sim - mer were spread a' sae bon - nie, The
trees are a' bare, and the birds mute and dow - ie, They

ma - vis sang sweet frae the
shake the cauld drift frae their

green birk - en tree; But far, far a - wa' they ha'e ta'en my dear John - nie, And
wings as they flee; And chirp out their plaints, seeming wae for my John - nie; 'Tis

now it is winter wi' nature and me.
wint-er wi' them and 'tis winter wi' me.

Yon cauld sleety cloud skiffs alang the bleak mountain,
And shakes the dark firs on the stey rocky brae,
While down the deep glen brawls the snaw-flooded fountain,
That murmur'd sae sweet to my laddie and me.

It's no its loud roar, on the wintry winds swellin',
It's no the cauld blast brings the tears in my e'e,
For, oh! gin I saw but my bonnie Scots callan',
The dark days o' winter were simmer to me!

"THE BRAES O' GLENIFFER." In the "Harp of Renfrewshire" (1819), R. A. Smith makes the following remarks:—"Songs possessing great poetical beauty do not always become favourites with the public. 'Keen blaws the wind o'er the braes o' Gleniffer' is, perhaps, Tannahill's best lyrical effusion, yet it does not appear to be much known, at least it is but seldom sung. It was written for the old Scottish melody 'Bonnie Dundee,' but Burns had occupied the same ground before him. The language of the song appears to me beautiful and natural."

The song incidentally mentioned above, "True-hearted was he, the sad swain of the Yarrow," which Burns wrote for George Thomson's great work, has not retained its hold of "Bonnie Dundee," that air being now sung to Macneil's "Mary of Castle-Cary;" while the air to which Macneil really wrote his song was set aside, and has remained unknown for nearly a century. It is simple and pretty, and is here adapted to Tannahill's words, for which it seems to be peculiarly well fitted. Where Macneil got it has never been ascertained; fortunately it was included in Johnson's Museum, and so has come down to us.

I'M O'ER YOUNG TO MARRY YET!

ARRANGED BY J. T. SURENNE.

o'er young, I'm o'er young, I'm o'er young to marry yet, I'm o'er young, 'twad be a sin To

tak' me frae my Mammie yet. I am my Mammie's ae bairn, Nor

of my hame am weary yet; And I would have ye learn, lads, That ye for me must tarry yet.

I'm o'er young, I'm o'er young,
I'm o'er young to marry yet,
I'm o'er young, 'twad be a sin
To tak' me frae my Mammie yet.
For I've aye had my ain will,
Nane dared to contradict me yet.
And now to say I wad obey,
In truth I darna venture yet.
For I'm o'er young, &c.

"I'M O'ER YOUNG TO MARRY YET." The rude old version of this song was altered, but not much amended, by Burns for Johnson's Museum; it is not known who gave to it its present form; but about 1836-38 it was brought into notice, and made very popular, by the arch manner in which it was sung by Miss Coveney, a youthful vocalist of great promise, whose career was soon after cut short by death. The air to which it was then set is a slightly altered version of "The Braes of Balquither," as given in Johnson's Museum (ii. 201) to Burns's song, "I'll kiss thee yet, my bonnie Peggy Alison." In R. Bremner's "Collection of Scots Reels or Country Dances," oblong 8vo, published in London about the middle of last century, we find the old tune, "I'm o'er young to marry yet," from which is evidently derived the excellent strathspey called Loch-Eroch Side," which will be found in this volume united to the song, "The lass o' Gowrie." The following is the old tune as given by Bremner:—

KELVIN GROVE.

ARRANGED BY J. T. SURENNE.

Let us haste to Kel - vin grove, bon - nie las - sie, O, Through its

maz - es let us rove, bon - nie las - sie, O, Where the rose in all her

pride, Paints the hol - low din - gle side, Where the midnight fai - ries glide, bon - nie las - sie, O.

We will wander by the mill, bonnie lassie, O,
To the cove beside the rill, bonnie lassie, O,
Where the glens rebound the call,
Of the roaring waters' fall,
Through the mountain's rocky hall, bonnie lassie, O.

Then we'll up to yonder glade, bonnie lassie, O,
Where so oft beneath its shade, bonnie lassie, O,
With the songsters in the grove
We have told our tale of love,
And have sportive garlands wove, bonnie lassie, O.

(Though I dare not call thee mine, bonnie lassie, O,
As the smile of fortune's thine, bonnie lassie, O,
Yet with fortune on my side,
I could stay thy father's pride,
And win thee for my bride, bonnie lassie, O.)

Ah! I soon must bid adieu, bonnie lassie, O,
To this fairy scene and you, bonnie lassie, O,
To the river winding clear,
To the fragrant-scented brier,
Even to thee of all most dear, bonnie lassie, O.

For the frowns of fortune lower, bonnie lassie, O,
On thy lover at this hour, bonnie lassie, O,
Ere yon golden orb of day
Wake the warblers on the spray,
From this land I must away, bonnie lassie, O.

When upon a foreign shore, bonnie lassie, O,
Should I fall midst battle's roar, bonnie lassie, O,
Then, Helen! shouldst thou hear
Of thy lover on his bier,
To his memory shed a tear, bonnie lassie, O.

"KELVIN GROVE." The words of this song first appeared in "The Harp of Renfrewshire," a collection of songs and other poetical pieces, published in numbers, and of which William Motherwell was editor. They were afterwards inserted with the air in R. A. Smith's Scottish Minstrel, ii. (1821). In both cases the name of the writer was given as John Sim. This gentleman having died abroad, Mr. Robert Purdie, the publisher of the Minstrel, purchased the copyright of the song from his heirs in March 1823. Scarcely had this been done, than a new claimant for the authorship appeared in the person of Thomas Lyle, a college friend of Sim. In May 1823 he addressed to R. A. Smith a short quotation from which may be sufficient. He says, "This song was wrote by me . . . I sent a copy of it to Mr. Sim, to insert into The Harp of Renfrewshire, with strict (sic) injunctions that it should be published anonymously." This statement was at first received with considerable doubt. Motherwell having been appealed to, wrote thus to R. A. Smith :—"Lawrence" (the publisher) "has in his possession the MS. of the song as it came from Sim, in Sim's handwriting; which MS. is interlined, corrected, and otherwise amended, as the first MS. of an original composition generally is." After much more he adds, "The claim of this Mr. Lyle comes with a very bad grace. You will observe The Harp was published in 1819, and Sim given as the author of this very song ; Lyle never wrote to the publisher of the injustice done to him. He has remained silent till the grave has closed upon the only witness who could gainsay his assertions. In the face of the MS. which Sim has left, and of the uniform belief that he was the author thereof, they must be credulous indeed who place any faith in what Lyle now says." Eventually it was admitted, however, that while Lyle wrote the first draft of the song, Sim added much, and altered more. Mr. Purdie, a prudent sagacious man, put an end to further debate by purchasing the copyright of the song a second time. His own opinion of the merits of the case may be judged of by the fact that the name of John Sim was never removed either from the index or the page of the volume of the Minstrel where the song appeared.

The whole story of the song would fill many pages ; for besides the letters of Lyle, Motherwell, and R. A. Smith, there were incipient law proceedings regarding the copyright ; no fewer than four spurious editions having been brought out in London. So great was the success of the song, that the publisher was in the habit of saying that had the estate of Kelvin Grove been as near to Edinburgh as it was to Glasgow, he would certainly have tried to purchase it.

The version of the words given in this work is from The Harp of Renfrewshire, with the exception of the fourth stanza, which Sim showed his good taste by omitting. "Kelvin Grove, a picturesque and richly wooded dell, through which the river Kelvin flows, lies at a very short distance to the north-west of Glasgow, and will in all probability soon be comprehended within the wide-spreading boundaries of the city itself. At one part of it (North Woodside) is an old well, originally called the Three-Tree-Well, now corrupted into Pear-Tree-Well. This used to be, and still is to some extent, a favourite place of resort for young parties from the city on summer afternoons." The original name of the air was, "O the shearin's no for you," which was the first line of a song now deservedly forgotten.

MY COLLIER LADDIE.

ARRANGED BY T. M. MUDIE.

♩ = 84

MODERATO.

1. Where live ye, my bon - nie lass, And tell me what they ca' ye? My
3. Ye shall gang in cra - ma - sie, Weel busk - it up fu' gau - die; And

name, she says, is Mis - tress Jean, And I follow the col - lier lad - die.
ane to wait on il - ka hand, Gin ye'll leave your col - lier lad - die.

2. See ye not yon hills and dales, The
4. Though ye had a' the sun shines on, And the

* An octave lower in the original.

sun shines on sae braw - lie; They a' are mine, and they shall be thine, Gin ye'll
earth con - ceals sae low - ly, I wad turn my back on you and it a', And be

leave your col - lier lad - die.
true to my col - lier lad - die.

Luve for luve is the bargain for me,
Though the wee cot-house should haud me,
And the warld before me to win my bread,
Au' fair fa' my collier laddie.

"MY COLLIER LADDIE." Allan Cunningham, commenting on this song, says, "These words were transmitted to the Museum by Burns; he probably wished to pass them for verses of an older day,—they are chiefly, however, from his own mint. The last verse is a fine one. The poet, it must be admitted, was a skilful seeker of old songs; when an air wanted words, Johnson gave the Bard of Kyle a line or a chorus by way of sample, and a genuine old song to suit was soon found."

Scott Douglas—in what may well be styled the *editio princeps* of Burns—says, "This is one of those songs never seen or heard in the world before the poet picked it up, both words and music, from the singing of a country girl."

The air, by a very slight alteration, is here, for the first time, made accessible to singers with a very moderate compass of voice.

In estimating how much Scottish song owes to Burns, we are apt to think only of the excellent verses which he wrote for George Thomson's celebrated collection, to supersede the silly or indecorous words which often condemned a fine old melody to silence. We forget the numerous songs which he amended and sent to Johnson for the Scots Musical Museum. To one single volume of that work—the fifth, published after his death—he contributed no fewer than forty-three songs out of the hundred, and with sixteen of these he sent the airs, many of them picked up by himself, and not previously known.

PIBROCH OF DONUIL DHU.

ARRANGED BY A. LAWRIE.

Pi - broch of Do - nuil Dhu, Pi - broch of Do - nuil, Wake thy wild voice a - new,

Sum - mon Clan Co - nuil. Come a - way, come a - way, Hark to the sum - mons!

Come in your war ar - ray, Gen - tles and com - mons. Come a - way, come a - way,

Hark to the sum - mons! Come in your war ar - ray, Gen - tles and com - mons.

Come from deep glen, and
  From mountain so rocky,
The war-pipe and pennon
  Are at Inverlochy.
Come every hill-plaid, and
  True heart that wears one;
Come every steel-blade, and
  Strong hand that bears one
    Come every hill-plaid, &c.

Leave untended the herd,
  The flock without shelter;
Leave the corpse uninterr'd,
  The bride at the altar.
Leave the deer, leave the steer,
  Leave nets and barges;
Come with your fighting gear
  Broadswords and targes.
    Leave the deer, leave the steer, &c.

Come as the winds come, when
  Forests are rended:
Come as the waves come, when
  Navies are stranded.
Faster come, faster come,
  Faster and faster:
Chief, vassal, page, and groom,
  Tenant and master.
    Faster come, faster come, &c.

Fast they come, fast they come;
  See how they gather!
Wide waves the eagle plume,
  Blended with heather.
Cast your plaids, draw your blades,
  Forward each man set;
Pibroch of Donuil Dhu,
  Knell for the onset!
    Cast your plaids, draw your blades, &c.

"PIBROCH OF DONUIL DHU." The air was long known under the name of "Lochiel's March." The words were written by Scott in 1816, for A. Campbell's "Albyn's Anthology," in the first volume of which they were published. In the Dissertation prefixed to Patrick M'Donald's Collection of Highland Airs, we find the following passage:—"A very peculiar species of martial music was in the highest request with the Highlanders. It was sometimes sung, accompanied with words, but more frequently performed on the bagpipe. And, in spite of every change, a *pibrach*, or *cruineachadh*, though it may sound harsh to the ear of a stranger, still rouses the native Highlander, in the same way that the sound of the trumpet does the war-horse. Nay, it sometimes produced effects little less marvellous than those recorded of ancient music. At the battle of Quebec, in April 1760, whilst the British troops were retreating in great confusion, the General complained to a field-officer of Fraser's regiment, of the bad behaviour of his corps. 'Sir,' answered he, with some warmth, 'you did very wrong in forbidding the pipes to play this morning: nothing encourages Highlanders so much in a day of action. Nay, even now they would be of use.' 'Let them blow like the d—l then,' replied the General, 'if it will bring back the men.' And, the pipers being ordered to play a favourite *cruineachadh*, the Highlanders, who were broken, returned the moment they heard the music, and formed with great alacrity in the rear."

THERE ARE TWA BONNIE MAIDENS.

ARRANGED BY A. C. MACKENZIE.

1. There are twa bon-nie maidens and three bon-nie maidens Come o - ver the Minch aud come
2.   Flo - ra, my hon - ey, sae dear and sae bon-nie, And ane that is tall, and

o - ver the main, Wi' the wind for their way, and the cor-rie for their hame, And
hand - some with - al; Put the one for my king, and the oth - er for my queen, And

they are dear - ly wel - come to Skye a - gain. Come a - long, come a - long, wi' your
they are dear - ly wel - come to Skye a - gain. Come a - long, come a - long, wi' your

boatie and your song, My ain bon-nie maid-ens, my twa bon-nie maidens; For the
boatie and your song, My ain bon-nie maid-ens, my twa bon-nie maidens; For the

night it is dark, and the red-coat is gone, And ye are dear-ly wel-come to Skye again.
la-dy of Macou-lain she dwelleth her lane, And she'll wel-come you dear-ly to Skye again.

2d verse.   *concluding verse.*

2. There is
3. Her

Her arm it is strong, and her petticoat is long,
  My ain bonnie maidens, my twa bonnie maidens;
By the sea moullet's nest I will watch o'er the main,
  And ye are bravely welcome to Skye again.
Come along, come along, with your boatie, *etc.*
  My ain bonnie maidens, my twa bonnie maidens,
And saft sall ye rest where the heather it grows best,
  And ye are dearly welcome to Skye again.

There's a wind on the tree, and a ship on the sea,
  My ain bonnie maidens, my twa bonnie maidens;
On the lee of the rock shall your cradle be rock,
  And ye'll aye be welcome to Skye again.
Come along, come along, with your boatie, *etc.*
  My ain bonnie maidens, my twa bonnie maidens,
Mair sound sall ye sleep, as ye rock on the deep,
  And ye'll aye be welcome to Skye again.

"THERE ARE TWA BONNIE MAIDENS." In the Jacobite Relics (ii. 357), Hogg tells us that he took down this song "from the mouth of Betty Cameron from Lochaber; a character known over a great part of the lowlands for her great store of Jacobite songs, and her attachment to Prince Charles, and the chiefs who suffered for him, of whom she never spoke without bursting into tears. She said it was from the Gaelic; but if so, I think it is likely to have been translated by herself." It is almost unnecessary to say that the song alludes to the escape of the Prince to Skye, in the guise of a female attendant of Flora Macdonald, when he was so beset by enemies in the small island of South Uist, that all escape was thought impossible.
The air is a modified version of a dance tune which was much played about the beginning of the present century.

TAMMY.

ARRANGED BY T. M. MUDIE.

1. I wish I ken'd my Mag - gie's mind, If she's for me or
2. I've spier'd her ance, I've spier'd her twice, And still she says she

Tam - my; To me she is but pass - ing kind, She's cauld - er still to
can - na; I'll try her a - gain, an' that maks thrice, An' thrice, they say, is

Tam - my.   An'   yet she lo'es me   no that ill,   If
can - ny.   Wi'   him she'll ha'e a   chaise and pair,   Wi'

I be - lieve her gran - ny; O sure she maun be wond - rous nice, If she 'll
me she 'll ha'e shanks - naig - ie; He's auld an' black, I'm young an' fair, She 'll

p

neith - er ha'e me nor Tam - my.
sure - ly ne'er tak Tam - my.

f

But if she 's a fuil, an' lightlies me,
I 'll e'en draw up wi' Nancy ;
There 's as guid fish into the sea
As e'er cam' out, I fancy.
An' though I say 't that shou'dna say 't,
I'm owre guid a match for Maggie ;
Sae mak' up your mind without delay,
Are ye for me or Tammy?

"I WISH I KEN'D MY MAGGIE'S MIND." The tune appears in Macdonald's Highland Airs (1781), under the name of "Araidh nam badan," but it first became known as a song in R. A. Smith's Scottish Minstrel (i. 45), 1821. The words are initialed S. M.—in the third edition—and have been ascribed to Lady Nairne ; but as her acknowledged songs in that work are signed B. B., the probability seems to be that this was rather a joint production of the coterie of ladies who managed the literary department of the [S]cotish [M]instrel. Of these Lady Nairne was unquestionably the leading spirit, and no doubt originated some, and gave many a finishing touch to others, of the partnership ditties that appeared in the six volumes of the work.

Like many other good songs, this lay hidden away waiting the interpreter who should make the world feel that a really clever thing had been overlooked. In the present instance the interpreter was John Wilson, who did so much by his fine taste to redeem Scottish song from the charge of vulgarity, so often brought against it through the coarse style of not a few of our national singers and their imitators.

OF A' THE AIRTS THE WIND CAN BLAW.

ARRANGED BY J. T. SURENNE.

Of a' the airts[1] the wind can blaw, I dear-ly like the west; For there the bonnie lass-ie lives, The

lass that I lo'e best: Tho' wild woods grow, an' ri-vers row, Wi' mo-nie a hill be-tween, Baith

day an' night, my fancy's flight Is e-ver wi' my Jean. I see her in the dew-y flow'r, Sae

[1] *Airt*—direction, point of the compass.

love - ly, sweet, an' fair; I hear her voice in il - ka bird, Wi' mu - sic charm the air: There's

not a bon-nie flow'r that springs, By fountain, shaw, or green, Nor yet a bon-nie bird that sings, But

minds me o' my Jean.

dim. *p*

mf

O blaw, ye westlin winds, blaw saft	What sighs an' vows amang the knowes,
Amang the leafy trees;	Ha'e past atween us twa!
Wi' gentle gale, frae muir and dale,	How fain to meet, how wae to part,
Bring hame the laden bees;	That day she gaed awa'!
An' bring the lassie back to me	The powers aboon can only ken,
"Wi' her twa witchin' een;"	To whom the heart is seen,
Ae blink o' her wad banish care,	That nane can be sae dear to me,
Sae lovely is my Jean!	As my sweet lovely Jean!

"OF A' THE AIRTS THE WIND CAN BLAW." As to this air, see Note on "The Lowlands of Holland." The song is certainly one of Burns' best, so far as he wrote it. Captain Charles Gray, R.M., in his "Cursory Remarks on Scottish Song," says, that he believes "Burns did not write more than the first sixteen lines of this beautiful song." He also observes that the third and fourth stanzas were not found among Burns' MSS. after his death; and that none of his editors or commentators, except Allan Cunningham and Motherwell, have claimed them for Burns. Farther, that Dr. Currie in his edition of Burns, Mr. Stenhouse in "Johnson's Musical Museum," and Mr. David Laing in his additional notes to that work, do not mention these stanzas as of Burns' composition; and that Mr. George Thomson, in his "Melodies of Scotland," (edition of 1838,) has rejected them as spurious. By some they have been ascribed to William Reid, Bookseller, Glasgow; but Captain Gray is rather inclined to believe they were written by John Hamilton, Musicseller, Edinburgh.

OH, I HA'E BEEN ON THE FLOW'RY BANKS O' CLYDE!

AIR, "THE BLUE BELLS OF SCOTLAND."   ARRANGED BY T. M. MUDIE.

♩ = 60

MODERATO.

Oh,

I ha'e been on the flow - 'ry banks o' Clyde! And I ha'e seen Tay's

sil - ver wat - ers glide; I ken a bon - nie lad on

Seidlaw's heather brae; And, oh! in my heart wi' him I'd like to gae! He

colla voce. p

pu'd the fair-est blue-bells, and wreath'd them in my hair; And,   oh!   in my heart   I   maun
colla voce.

love   him   ev - er - mair!
colla voce.

His e'e is bright as the summer morn to me;
Its shade fa's light as the gloamin' on the lea:
It's no his manly bearing, it's no his noble air,—
But, oh! 'tis the soul that gives expression there!
We've wander'd 'mang the gowd-broom,[1] and by the river side,—
And, oh! in my heart, I think I'll be his bride!

1 Golden-broom.

"THE BLUE BELLS OF SCOTLAND." The words have been expressly written for this work, and presented to the publishers, by that talented lady, Miss Stirling Graham of Duntrune. We rejected the old words as very silly, and quite unworthy of the popular air to which they were adapted. The air given in Johnson's Museum is different from and inferior to that which we find in Mr. George Thomson's Collection, vol. iii. p. 135, adapted to Mrs. Grant's words, "O where, tell me where, is your Highland laddie gone?" We have, of course, chosen the most popular of the two airs, which appears to us to be of English composition, although hitherto claimed as Scottish. Mrs. Grant's song has evidently been suggested by the words, No. 548 of Johnson, or by words of a less delicate kind, given in Ritson's "North-country Chorister," beginning, "There was a Highland laddie courted a Lawland lass." It consists of seven stanzas, and Ritson adds the following note:—"This song has been lately introduced upon the stage by Mrs. Jordan, who knew neither the *words* nor the *tune.*" Charles Kirkpatrick Sharpe, Esq., says, in the Museum (vol. vi.), "but there is another set of words, probably as old, which I transcribed from a 4to collection of songs in MS. made by a lady upwards of seventy years ago." It begins, "O, fair maid, whase aught that bonny bairn?" and is of the same character as the song given in "The North-country Chorister." The allusion to the Parson and the Clerk in each of these songs shows their English origin.

It should be pointed out that the words mentioned by Mr. Kirkpatrick Sharpe require to be sung without a starting-note and with the accent on the O—"O, fair maid, wha's aught that bonny bairn?" This may possibly not be the original song, but it carries us back to the Spanish war of 1762, for its third line is, "It is a sodger's son, she said, that's lately gone to Spain," and it was copied from a MS. written seventy years before 1835-36. Everything about the song seems to denote a military origin. The quaint old air given by Johnson has a certain swing about it, with a dream of drums and fifes, as if it were the march tune of a regiment. Its opening phrase is emphasized by its re-iteration on the tone above, and is not a mere weak repetition of the same notes, as in the modern air. This very repetition, however, points it out as the original tune altered *by* or *for* Mrs. Jordan, and which Ritson complained that she did not know.

I LOVE THEE STILL.

AIR, "DONALD."

ARRANGED BY T. M. MUDIE.

I love thee still, al - though my path In life can no'er bo thine; And though thy heart, in ear - ly youth, Was fond - ly pledged to mine, Donald! Tho lovo of wealth, the pride of rank, Have bro - ken ma - ny a vow; But these, when we were first be - trothed, I

scorn'd, as I do now, Donald!

p

We once were equal in our love,
But times are changed for thee;
Now rich and great, while I am poor,
Thou art no mate for me—Donald!

I would not take thy offer'd hand,
Although it bore a crown;
Thy parents taunt me with thy wealth—
My poortith-pride's my own—Donald!

"I LOVE THEE STILL." Mr. George Thomson introduced the air called "Donald," as Scottish or Irish, into his Collection, with words written by Burns for the tune of "Gilderoy." The air appears again, with a different close, in R. A. Smith's Scottish Minstrel, vol. iv. pp. 46, 47, with Burns' words slightly altered, and also with other words. The additional words given by R. A. Smith in his Scottish Minstrel to the air "Donald," are nothing but a new version, with verbal alterations, of the third and fourth stanzas of the song published in the Orpheus Caledonius, and in William Napier's Second Collection, 1792, to the air, "Haud awa' frae me, Donald." In modern versions, such as those in William Napier's Collection, and in R. A. Smith's Scottish Minstrel, the words to "Haud awa' frae me, Donald," have been Anglified and altered; probably at the time when Scottish songs were much in fashion in England. Hence might originate the idea that the air was Scottish. It appears in Shield's opera, "The Highland Reel," 1788; but it is doubtful whether it is his own composition, for he frequently made use of airs which were popular at the moment. We are of opinion, however, that it is the production of some English musician of the days of Shield and Arnold; it has indeed a flavour of Barthelemon's once popular air "Durandarte and Belerma." With this caveat we give it, as it has appeared in several Scottish collections; admitting that it is not of Scottish growth, nor yet of Irish, though Moore has included it in his "Melodies" set to the words, "I saw thy form in youthful prime." The words given to the air in the present work are written by a friend of the publishers.

The following are the two altered stanzas as given by R. A. Smith to the air, "Donald," in the Scottish Minstrel, vol. iv. p. 46:—

When first you courted me, I own,
I fondly favour'd you;
Apparent worth and high renown
Made me believe you true, Donald.
Each virtue then seem'd to adorn
The man esteem'd by me—
But now the mask's thrown off, I scorn
To waste one thought on thee, Donald.

O, then, for ever haste away,
Away from love and me;
Go seek a heart that's like your own.
And come no more to me, Donald.
For I'll reserve myself alone,
For one that's more like me;
If such a one I cannot find,
I'll fly from love and thee, Donald.

YE BANKS AND BRAES O' BONNIE DOON.

ARRANGED BY J. T. SURENNE.

Ye banks and braes o' bon-nie Doon, How can ye bloom sae

fresh and fair; How can ye chant, ye lit-tle birds, And I sae wea-ry,

'u' o' care! Ye'll break my heart, ye warb-ling birds, That wan-ton through the *ritenuto.   a tempo.*

flow'-ry thorn; Ye mind me o' de-part-ed joys, De-part-ed ne-ver

to re-turn.

ritenuto.

Oft ha'e I roved by bonnie Doon,
To see the rose and woodbine twine;
And ilka bird sang o' its love,
And fondly sae did I o' mine.

Wi' lightsome heart I pu'd a rose,
Fu' sweet upon its thorny tree;
But my fause lover stole my rose,
And ah! he left the thorn wi' me.

"THE BANKS OF DOON; OR, THE CALEDONIAN HUNT'S DELIGHT." The story of the composition of this tune by a Mr. James Miller, a writer in Edinburgh, has been often told, and has been accepted, without further inquiry, as true in all its details. Mr. Miller, desirous of being the composer of a Scottish tune, was told that by keeping to the black keys of a pianoforte he would probably succeed. In this way he produced the first part of the tune, and submitted it to Stephen Clarke, the arranger of the music in Johnson's Museum, to be put into shape. We can scarcely suppose that Mr. Miller really knew that he had accidentally stumbled on a part of the melody of an English song, "Lost is my quiet for ever," which is almost identical with his own air. But when Stephen Clarke proceeded to add the second part of the English air to Mr. Miller's first part, it is no longer possible to admit want of knowledge. The first part is not exactly the same in both airs, but the second part is so, and includes, as part of the tune, what in the original is a mere instrumental echo, introduced to complete the rhythm. That others besides Clarke knew the English air is proven by the fact that George Thomson applied to Burns to write words for it, under the new name, however, of "The Caledonian Hunt's delight;" and that the poet, after completing one stanza, beginning, "Why, why tell thy lover?" gave up the attempt; for, said he, "Such is the peculiarity of the rhythm of this air, that I find it impossible to make another to suit it." And yet this is the air which, by the addition of a few extra notes, is made to suit perfectly the common rhythm of "Ye banks and braes o' bonnie Doon." There is, however, yet more to be said regarding the air. As early as 1690 we find in Playford's Apollo's Banquet "a new Tune," which in its first part bears so striking a resemblance to our modern air, that it is just possible it may have given rise to a statement alluded to by Burns when writing to Thomson in November 1794. He says, "I have heard it repeatedly asserted that this is an Irish air; nay, I met with an Irish gentleman who affirmed he had heard it in Ireland among the old women; while, on the other hand, a countess informed me that the first person who introduced the air into this country was a baronet's lady of her acquaintance, who took down the notes from an itinerant piper in the Isle of Man. How difficult, then, to ascertain the truth regarding our poesy and music!" We may remark, is it possible or probable that Playford's "New Tune" can have spread so widely over the British isles as to be claimed by each nationality as its own? or is the melody so obvious as to suggest itself to many individuals acting independently of each other?

There can be no doubt that Burns's beautiful song has had much to do with the popularity of the air, which indeed might have been otherwise lost sight of, for the English words, "Lost is my quiet," are too silly to have had more than an ephemeral existence.

Another and an earlier version of this song was found by Cromek among Burns's papers, and was admitted into the "Reliques." It is even more simple and touching than the altered version: and has often been pointed out as a fine specimen of Burns's natural powers. See Appendix for the English air and words.

WHAT'S A' THE STEER, KIMMER?

ARRANGED BY J. T. SURENNE.

were na worth a pluck.²

(*He.*) I'm right glad to hear't, kimmer,
I'm right glad to hear't;
I ha'e a gude braid claymore,
And for his sake I'll wear't.

(*Both.*) Sin' Charlie he is landed,
We ha'e nae mair to fear ;
Sin' Charlie he is come, kimmer,
We'll ha'e a jub'lee year.

¹ Disturbance; commotion.   ² Neighbour; Gossip. (*Commere.*—French.)   ³ The third part of a penny sterling.

"WHAT'S A' THE STEER, KIMMER." The air seems to be a strathspey. It was published, with anonymous words, in the Scottish Minstrel, 1821. We learn, however, from a receipt granted by the author, that it was one of thirty songs written by Robert Allan of Kilbarchan for that work. The words were probably suggested by verses published in Cromek's "Remains of Nithsdale and Galloway Song," 1810. These verses are given as expressing, roughly, the feelings of the peasantry of Scotland, on hearing the extraordinary escape of Lord Maxwell of Nithsdale from the Tower of London, on 23d February 1715, "dressed in a woman's cloak and hood, which were for some time after called *Nithsdales*." The veritable account of that escape is printed by Mr. Cromek, from a copy of the original MS. letter by the Countess of Nithsdale to her sister, dated 16th April 1718, from Rome, and in the possession of Constable Maxwell, Esq. of Terreagles, a descendant of the family of Nithsdale. Some verses of a similar tenor to those above alluded to are given by Allan Cunningham in the fourth volume of his edition of Burns' Works, London, 1834. Cunningham gives the word "Cummer" instead of "Carlin," which occurs in the verses quoted by Cromek.

The words and music here given are reprinted on account of the popularity which they obtained about twenty years ago by the public singing of Miss Stephens, afterwards Countess of Essex. Miss Stephens gave a long lease of popularity to this song, as well as to "We're a' nid noddin'," and other songs, all of which are still popular. Miss Stephens was one of the most admired of modern English singers. A notice of her, published in London in 1824, informs us that she was born in London, and received her first instructions in singing from Lanza, under whose tuition she remained for a considerable time. Lanza's slow and sure Italian method formed her power of voice and her intonation. While still under Lanza, she was brought out as a singer at the Pantheon. It appears that her father, getting impatient of the slowness of Lanza's process of tuition, put her under Mr. Thomas Welsh, who used all means to bring her rapidly forward with *éclat* before the public; and that she made her *début* at Covent Garden Theatre "with brilliant approbation," as the critics then expressed themselves. The quality of her voice was said to be then (1824) more rich and full than that of any other public English singer. "The peculiar bent of her talent seems to be towards ballads and songs of simple declamation; in a word, towards that particular style which is generally esteemed to be purely English, though the formation of the voice may have been conducted upon the principles of Italian teaching." The writer adds, that "there are no other" than the Italian principles of voice training. We must observe that the departure from these old principles, and the rapid *forcing* system generally produced in England, and NOW in Italy, are the very causes of our having so few good singers. Too often vox *et praterea nihil !* Voices totally untrained and untaught. The late ingenious Doctor W. Kitchiner, in his "Observations on Vocal Music, 1821," pp. 53, 54, speaks as follows of Ballad Music, and of Miss Stephens :—"The *chef-d'œuvre* of difficulty is A PLAIN ENGLISH BALLAD, which is, 'when unadorned, adorned the most,' and, indeed, will hardly admit of any ornament beyond an *Appoggiatura*. This style of song is less understood than any (other?); and though apparently from its simplicity it is very easy, yet to warble a Ballad with graceful expression, requires as much real judgment and attentive consideration of every note and every syllable, as it does to execute the most intricate *Bravura*—the former is an appeal to the heart—the latter merely plays about the ear, and seldom excites any sensation beyond. Who would not rather hear Miss Stephens sing an old Ballad than any *Bravura*?—although her beautiful voice is equally calculated to give every effect to the most florid song." Miss Stephens became Countess of Essex 19th April 1838.* To the honour of art, she is not the only female performer who has been raised by her own merits to the rank of nobility in Great Britain.

* George Capel Coningsby, fifth and late Earl of Essex, born 13th November 1757, died without issue 23d April 1839.—*See Lodge's Peerage,* 1844

O, WILLIE BREW'D A PECK O' MAUT.

ARRANGED BY FINLAY DUN.

$\text{♩} = 108$

ALLEGRO MODERATO.

O, Wil-lie brew'd a peck o' maut, And Rob and Al-lan cam' to prie;[1] Three blyther lads, that lee-lang[2] night, Ye wad-na fand in Christ-en-die. We are na fou', we're no that fou', But just a wee drap in our e'e; The cock may craw, the day may daw', But aye we'll taste the

bar - ley bree.[3]

Here are we met three merry boys,
Three merry boys I trow are we :
And mony a nicht we've merry been,
And mony mae we hope to be!

Wha first shall rise to gang awa',
A cuckold coward loon is he;
Wha last beside his chair shall fa',
He is the king amang us three.

It is the moon—I ken her horn—
That's blinkin' in the lift[4] sae hie;
She shines sae bricht to wyle us hame,
But by my sooth she'll wait awee.[5]

[1] To taste   [2] Livelong.   [3] Ale, beer—sometimes, whisky.   [4] The firmament.   [5] A short time—but here to be understood ironically.

"O, WILLIE BREW'D A PECK O' MAUT." In the autumn of 1789, Burns wrote this excellent convivial song, which his friend Allan Masterton, a writing-master in Edinburgh, set to music. Masterton died about the year 1800. The song was written on the occasion of a "house-warming" at William Nicol's farm of Laggan, in Nithsdale "We had such a joyous meeting," says Burns, "that Mr. Masterton and I agreed, each in his own way, that we should celebrate the business." William Nicol was one of the masters of the High School of Edinburgh. He was Burns' companion in his tour of the Highlands, and died in the summer of 1797. Dr. Currie, in his Life of Burns, gives an interesting account of Nicol. The air, as composed by Masterton, appears in Johnson's Museum, vol. iii. p. 301 ; but that set has long been superseded by the one here given, which is an improvement on Masterton's air, by some unknown singer or arranger.

Captain Charles Gray, R.M., in No. XIV. of his "Cursory Remarks on Scottish Song," when speaking of Burns as having "contributed no less than two hundred and twenty-eight songs" to Johnson's Museum, adds—"we take credit to ourselves for being the first to claim for him the merit of his collecting and preserving above fifty Scottish melodies. This labour of love alone would have entitled Burns to the thanks and gratitude of his countrymen, had he done nothing else; but it was lost in the refulgent blaze of his native genius, which shed a light on our national song that shall endure as long as our simple Doric is understood. In the lapse of ages even the lyrics of Burns may become obsolete, but other bards shall rise, animated with his spirit, and reproduce them, if possible, in more than their original beauty and splendour. We hold our national melodies to be imperishable. As no one can trace their origin, it would be equally futile to predict their end. Their essence is more divine than the language to which they are wedded."

U

ALASTAIR MACALASTAIR.

ARRANGED BY H. E. DIBDIN.

♩ = 100

CON
SPIRITO.

Oh, A - las - tair Mac - A - las - tair, Your chan - ter sets us a' a-steer, Get out your pipes, an' blaw wi' birr, We'll dance the High - land fling.

Now A - las - tair has tuned his pipes, An' thrang as bum - bees frae their bikes,¹ The lads an' lass - es loup² the dykes, An' ga - ther on the green. Oh, A - las - tair Mac - A - las - tair, Your chan - ter sets us a' a - steer, Then to your bags, an' blaw wi' birr, We'll

dance the High - land fling.

The succeeding verses begin at the sign :§:; those within brackets may be omitted.

The miller Hab was fidgin' fain
To dance the Highland fling his lane,
He lap, an' danced wi' might an' main,
  The like was never seen.
    Oh, Alastair, &c.

As round about the ring he whuds,[3]
An' cracks his thumbs, an' shakes his duds,[4]
The meal flew frae his tail in cluds,
  An' blinded a' their een.
    Oh, Alastair, &c.

[Neist rauchle-handed[5] smiddy Jock,
A' blacken'd o'er wi' coom an' smoke,
Wi' shauchlin'[6] blear-e'ed Bess did yoke,
  That harum-scarum quean
    Oh, Alastair, &c.]

[He shook his doublet in the wind,
His feet like hammers strak the grund;
The very moudiewarts[7] were stunn'd,
  Nor kenn'd what it could mean.
    Oh, Alastair, &c.]

Now wanton Willie was na blate,[8]
For he got haud o' winsome Kate,
"Come here," quo' he, "I'll show the gate
  To dance the Highland fling."
    Oh, Alastair, &c.

Now Alastair has done his best;
An' weary stumps are wantin' rest,
Forbye wi' drouth they're sair distress'd,
  Wi' dancin' sae, I ween.
    Oh, Alastair, &c.

[I trow the gantrees[9] gat a lift;
An' round the bicker flew like drift;
An' Alastair that very nicht,
  Could scarcely stand his lane.
    Oh, Alastair, &c.]

| [1] Bees from their hives | [2] Leap. | [3] Bounds. | [4] Ragged clothes. | [5] Strong-handed |
| [6] Shambling. | [7] Moles. | [8] Bashful. | [9] The trestle upon which barrels are placed |

"ALASTAIR MACALASTAIR." The author of this lively song has not been discovered. The air is a dance-tune, bearing considerable resemblance to "Mrs. Wemyss of Cuttle-hill's Strathspey," composed by Nathaniel Gow, and also to the "Marquis of Huntly's Strathspey," a tune said to have been composed by Mr. Marshall, butler to the Duke of Gordon

JEANIE MORRISON.

ARRANGED BY A. C. MACKENZIE.

dear, dear Jeanie Mor - ri - son, The thochts of by - gane years, Still
miud ye, luve, how aft we left The deav - in' din - some toun, To

fling their shad - ows o'er my path, And blind my een wi' tears. They
wand - er by the green burn-side, And hear its wa - ters croon? The

blind my een wi' saut, saut tears, And snir and sick I pine, As
sim - mer leaves hung o'er our heads, The flow'rs burst round our feet, And

mem'ry id - ly sum - mous up The blythe blinks o' lang - syne.
in the gloam - in' o' the wood The thros - tle whisslit sweet.

I've wander'd east, I've wander'd west,
  I've borne a weary lot ;
But in my wanderings, far or near,
  Ye never were forgot.
The fount that first burst from this heart
  Still travels on its way ;
And channels deeper as it rins
  The luve o' life's young day.

O dear, dear Jeanie Morrison,
  Since we were sunder'd young
I've never seen your face, nor heard
  The music of your tongue ;
But I could hug all wretchedness,
  And happy could I dee,
Did I but ken your heart still dream'd
  O' bygane days and me.

"JEANIE MORRISON." This is one of Motherwell's finest poems, but as it consists of twelve stanzas of eight lines each, it is much too long for a song. It is so beautiful, however, that it was thought a selection of these might be made without altogether destroying the fine feeling that pervades it. Original airs without number have been set to the words, but none of these settings have been even moderately successful with the public. It is here adapted to an old air,—Major Graham,—which Burns recommended for his words, "My love is like the red, red rose," though they are now always sung to a modernized version of "Low doun in the broom." This air, "Major Graham," was originally a dance tune, and required a few alterations to make it thoroughly vocal ; this has been both tastefully and effectively done by the arranger, Mr. A. C. Mackenzie.

I HEARD A WEE BIRD SINGING.

ARRANGED BY A. C. MACKENZIE.

$\bullet = 84$

NOT TOO
SLOW.

p

ped.   * ped.*   *

1. I   heard   a wee bird
2. He   heard   the wee bird

sing - ing, In my cham - ber as I lay,   The case - ment op - en
sing - ing, For its notes were wondrous clear,   As if wed - ding-bells were

mf   *mf*

swing - ing, As morn - ing woke the day ;   And the boughs around were
ring - ing Me - lo - dious to the ear ;   And still it rang that

mf   *mf*

We heard the wee bird singing,
After brief time had flown,
The true bells had been ringing,
And Willie was my own.

Oft I tell him, jesting, playing,
I knew what the wee bird was saying
That morn when he, no longer straying,
Flew back to me alone.

"I HEARD A WEE BIRD SINGING." These pretty words were written by William Jerdan, the well-known editor of the Literary Gazette (1782-1869). They are here united to music for the first time.

The tune is a ballad air, from which, however, the ornamental shakes and other peculiarities of the ballad singer have been removed. It is taken by permission from Dean Christie's Traditional Ballad Airs, where a note informs us that it has long been a favourite in the three north-eastern counties of Scotland. The Dean's handsome volumes contain many fine melodies not previously printed. Of these some are ancient, many are curious; others, again, are northern versions of well-known airs, such as "Gala Water," "Barbara Allan," "Leader haughs," and one called "Young Peggy" has been moulded on "The ewe-bughts" so strangely as almost to escape recognition. So large and varied a collection could only have been given to the world by a gentleman whose family had old musical traditions, for it evidently contains the gatherings of three generations, all enthusiasts in ballads and their melodies.

THY CHEEK IS O' THE ROSE'S HUE.

AIR, "MY ONLY JO AND DEARIE, O."   ARRANGED BY T. M. MUDIE.

= 84

MODERATO

Thy cheek is o' the ro-se's hue, My on-ly jo and

dear-ie, O; Thy neck is o' the sil-ler dew Up-on the banks sae brier-ie, O.

Thy teeth are o' the i-vor-y; O sweet's the twin-kle

o' thine e'e! Nae joy, nae plea - sure, blinks on me, My

colla voce.

on - ly jo and dear - ie, O.

The birdie sings upon the thorn
  Its sang o' joy, fu' cheerie, O,
Rejoicing in the simmer morn,
  Nae care to mak' it eerie,[1] O;
Ah! little kens the sangster sweet,
Aught o' the care I ha'e to meet,
That gars my restless bosom beat,
  My only jo and dearie, O.

When we were bairnies on yon brae,
  And youth was bliukin' bonnie, O,
Aft we would daff[2] the lee-lang day,
  Our joys fu' sweet and monie, O.
Aft I wad chase thee o'er the lee,
And round about the thorny tree;
Or pu' the wild flowers a' for thee,
  My only jo and dearie, O.

I ha'e a wish I canna tine,[3]
  'Mang a' the cares that grieve me, O,
A wish that thou wert ever mine,
  And never mair to leave me, O;
Then I would dawt[4] thee night and day,
Nae ither warldly care I'd ha'e,
Till life's warm stream forgat to play,
  My only jo and dearie, O.

[1] Timorous.   [2] Sport.   [3] To lose.   [4] Caress.

"MY ONLY JO AND DEARIE, O." "This beautiful song, which is another of the productions of the late Mr. Richard Gall, was written at the earnest request of Mr. Thomas Oliver, printer and publisher, Edinburgh, an intimate acquaintance of the author's. Mr. Oliver heard it sung in the Pantomime of Harlequin Highlander, at the Circus, and was so struck with the melody, that it dwelt upon his mind; but the only part of the words he recollected were—

     'My love's the sweetest creature
     That ever trod the dewy green;
     Her cheeks they are like roses,
     Wi' the op'ning gowan wet between.'

And having no way of procuring the verses he had heard, he requested Mr. Gall to write words to his favourite tune. Our young bard promised to do so; and in a few days presented him with this elegant song, in which the title of the tune is happily introduced at the close of every stanza." See Museum Illustrations, vol. vi., pp. 406, 407. In the Note upon "I ha'e laid a herrin' in saut," we have given a brief account of Richard Gall.

AND YE SHALL WALK IN SILK ATTIRE.

ARRANGED BY T. M MUDIE.

And ye shall walk in silk at - tire, And sil - ler ha'e to spare, Gin ye'll con - sent to be his bride, Nor think o' Don - ald mair. Oh! wha wad buy a silk - en gown Wi' a poor bro - ken heart? Or

what's to me a sil - ler crown, Gin frae my love I part!

The mind whase every wish is pure,
  Far dearer is to me;
And ere I'm forced to break my faith,
  I'll lay me down and dee;
For I ha'e pledged my virgin troth,
  Brave Donald's fate to share,
And he has gi'en to me his heart,
  Wi' a' its virtues rare.

His gentle manners wan my heart,
  He gratefu' took the gift;
Could I but think to see it back,
  It wad be waur than theft.
For langest life can ne'er repay
  The love he bears to me;
And ere I'm forced to break my troth,
  I'll lay me down and dee.

"AND YE SHALL WALK IN SILK ATTIRE." Very little seems to be known regarding this song, further than that the words were written by Miss Susannah Blamire. It was first published on a single sheet, and was then copied into Napier's first, and Johnson's third volume, both published in the same year, 1790. The versions are similar, but not identical; both are written in ¾ time, and both are faulty in rhythm. In George Thomson's great work (1798) the limping rhythm was corrected, and two syllables were added to the second and sixth lines of each stanza; for the air ought strictly to have three lines of eight, and one of six syllables in each quatrain. As these additional syllables weaken the verses, they have been generally rejected, but are here subjoined as an alternative mode of singing. 2d line—An siller *ay shall* ha'e to spare. 6th—To hide a *pining*, breaking heart. 10th—Is dearer far *than gold* to me. 14th—*My ain* brave Donald's fate to share. 18th—He gratefu' took the *willing* gift. 22d—The *well tried* love he bears to me.

GLOOMY WINTER'S NOW AWA.

ARRANGED BY T. M. MUDIE

Gloo - my win - ter's now a - wa, Saft the west - lin' breez - es blaw,

'Mang the birks o' Stanley shaw, The ma - vis sings fu' cheer - ie, O. Sweet the craw flow'rs ear - ly bell,

Decks Glen - if - fer's dew - y dell, Blooming like thy bon - nie sel', My young, my art - less dear - ie, O.

Come, my las-sie, let us stray O'er Glen-kil-loch's sun-ny brae, Blythe-ly spend the gowden day 'Midst joys that ne-ver wea-rie, O.

Tow'ring o'er the Newton woods,
Lav'rocks fan the snaw-white clouds ;
Siller saughs, wi' downy buds,
   Adorn the banks sae briery, O.

Round the sylvan fairy nooks,
Feath'ry breckans fringe the rocks,
'Neath the brae the burnie jouks,
   And ilka thing is cheerie, O.

Trees may bud, and birds may sing,
Flowers may bloom, and verdure spring,
Joy to me they canna bring,
   Unless wi' thee, my dearie, O.

"GLOOMY WINTER'S NOW AWA." The song was written by Robert Tannahill, about 1809, for a young lady who was very fond of the air. It is still a favourite, and would be much oftener sung, but for the extreme compass of the melody. To remedy this, small notes and other marks of substitution have been introduced in the present edition, so that any voice possessing the easy compass of a tenth can now sing it.

Neil Gow, in his Fourth Collection, gives the melody as "Lord Balgonie's favourite, a very old Highland tune." On the other hand, Alex. Campbell, of the Register House, Edinburgh, claims to have composed and published it as a strathspey in 1792. In disputed cases of this kind, it will generally be found that there is somewhat of truth on both sides. In Captain Fraser's Collection (1816) there is an old Highland air, "An dileacdhan" (The Orphan), which has many points of resemblance with "Gloomy Winter." In his early wanderings in the Highlands we may suppose Campbell to have heard this tune, and afterwards unwittingly reproduced a considerable portion of it, while Gow probably adopted Campbell's version, believing it to be the veritable old tune.

Alexander Campbell seems to have been an enthusiast in regard both to the poetry and music of his country. He was appointed by the Highland Society in 1815 to make a collection of airs floating about unpublished among the peasantry of the north and west of Scotland. This he did very successfully, laying before his patrons at the end of the year a collection of about two hundred melodies. From these a selection was made and published, along with a few border airs, under the name of Albyn's Anthology, the first volume in 1816, the second two years later ; a third was promised, but never appeared. Verses were written for the work by Sir Walter Scott, James Hogg, and others, and it had considerable success ; owing, however, to the arrangements of the airs having been made by the collector himself, whose musical knowledge was not equal to his zeal, it is now sought for only by the antiquary or by those who are fond of possessing a somewhat rare work.

LOUDON'S BONNIE WOODS AND BRAES.

AIR, "MARQUIS OF HASTINGS' STRATHSPEY."   ARRANGED BY A. LAWRIE.

Loudon's bon-nie woods and braes, I maun leave them a', las-sie;

Wha can thole¹ when Britain's faes Would gi'e Britons law, lassie? Wha would shun the field o' danger?

Wha to fame would live a stranger? Now when Freedom bids avenge her, Wha would shun her ea', lassie!

¹ Suffer; endure.

Lou-don's bon-nie woods and braes, Ha'e seen our hap-py bri-dal days, And gen-tle hope shall soothe thy waes, When I am far a-wa', lassie.

Hark! the swelling bugle rings,
Yielding joy to thee, laddie;
But the dolefu' bugle brings
Waefu' thochts to me, laddie.
Lanely I may climb the mountain.
Lanely stray beside the fountain,
Still the weary moments counting,
Far frae love and thee, laddie.
O'er the gory fields o' war,
Where Vengeance drives his crimson car,
Thou'lt maybe fa', frae me afar,
And nane to close thy e'e, laddie.

Oh, resume thy wonted smile,
Oh, suppress thy fears, lassie,
Glorious honour crowns the toil
That the soldier shares, lassie:
Heaven will shield thy faithfu' lover,
Till the vengeful strife is over;
Then we'll meet, nae mair to sever,
Till the day we dee, lassie:
Midst our bonnie woods and braes,
We'll spend our peacefu' happy days,
As blythe's yon lichtsome lamb that plays
On Loudon's flow'ry lea, lassie.

"LOUDON'S BONNIE WOODS AND BRAES." These verses were written by Robert Tannahill, and appear to have been very popular for ten or twelve years before the close of the last European war. Loudon Castle, in Ayrshire, was the seat of the Earl of Moira, afterwards created Marquis of Hastings, while Governor-General of India in 1816. This song is said to be commemorative of his parting, upon foreign service, from his young wife the Countess of Loudon.

Referring to many previous notes, we think we have shown satisfactorily that all ascriptions of the composition of Scottish melodies to Rizzio (or Riccio) are founded in error; and we now take leave of the subject by a short recapitulation of the facts.

1. Rizzio's name is not mentioned as a composer of music of any kind for a hundred and sixty years after his death. 2. He lived little more than four years in Queen Mary's household, and for much the greater part of that time in the capacity of a menial. 3. The Italian writer, Tassoni, makes no mention of Rizzio's pseudo-compositions. 4. Thomson, in his "Orpheus Caledonius," printed in London in 1725, was the first to ascribe seven Scottish airs to Rizzio; and, in the second edition of his work, 1733, ashamed of the imposture, entirely suppressed Rizzio's name. 5. James Oswald, a noted impostor, in his Second Collection of Scottish Airs, also printed in London, again resumed the ridiculous deception regarding Rizzio, while the contemporaneous Edinburgh Collections of Ramsay, Craig, and M'Gibbon, make no mention of Rizzio. Craig, 1730, states, that the airs are "the native and genuine product of the country." 6. We have shown Geminiani's opinions regarding Rizzio, and Scottish and other music to be absurdly erroneous; and the opinions of his blind and ignorant follower, Oliver Goldsmith, to improve greatly in error and absurdity upon those of Geminiani and others. If any Rizzio MSS. should turn up, like the Skene, and Straloch, and Leyden, we should welcome them heartily as very wonderful curiosities.

HERE'S A HEALTH TO ANE I LO'E DEAR.

ARRANGED BY J. T. SURENNE.

$\textbf{.} = 108$

Andantino Grazioso.

Legato.

Here's a health to ane I lo'e dear, Here's a health to ane I lo'e dear; Thou art sweet as the smile when fond lov-ers meet; And soft as their part-ing tear, Jes-sie! Al-though thou maun ne-ver be

mine, Al - though o - ven hope is de - nied, 'Tis sweet - er for thee de -
spair - ing, Than aught in the world be - side, Jes - sie!

colla voce. dim. a piacere.

I mourn through the gay gaudy day,
As hopeless I muse on thy charms;
But welcome the dream o' sweet slumber,
For then I am lock'd in thy arms, Jessie!

I guess by the dear angel smile,
I guess by the love-rolling e'e;
But why urge the tender confession,
'Gainst fortune's fell cruel decree?—Jessie!

"HERE'S A HEALTH TO ANE I LO'E DEAR." In Blackie's "Book of Scottish Song," p. 133, is the following Note:—"This exquisite little song was among the last Burns ever wrote. It was composed in honour of Jessie Lewars, (now Mrs. Thomson of Dumfries,) the sister of a brother exciseman of the poet, and one who has endeared her name to posterity by the affectionate solicitude with which she tended Burns during his last illness." Mr. Stenhouse, in vol. v. p. 371 of Museum, says that the air was communicated by Burns, but is not genuine. Mr. Stenhouse annexes a copy of the music in three-eight time, which he gives as correct, but does not say whence he derived it. The author of the tune is not known. It has little of a Scottish, and still less of an antique character; but seems to owe somewhat to "Kenmure's on and awa'."

Burns himself strenuously opposed any alterations in national Scottish melodies. In a letter to Mr. Thomson, April 1793, in which he sends the song beginning "Farewell, thou stream that winding flows," he writes thus:—"One hint let me give you—whatever Mr. Pleyel does, let him not alter one iota of the original Scottish airs; I mean in the song department; but let our national music preserve its native features. They are, I own, frequently wild and irreducible to the more modern rules; but on that very eccentricity, perhaps, depends a great part of their effect." In his answer to that letter, Mr. Thomson, 26th April 1793, says:—"Pleyel does not alter a single note of the songs. That would be absurd, indeed! With the airs which he introduces into the sonatas, I allow him to take such liberties as he pleases, but that has nothing to do with the songs."

WE'RE A' NODDIN'.

ARRANGED BY T. M. MUDIE.

$p = 104$

ALLEGRETTO
A
PIACERE

And we're a' noddin', nid, nid, noddin', And we're a' noddin' at our house at hame. Gude e'en to ye, kimmer, And are ye alane? O come and see how blythe are we, For Jamie he's cam' hame; And O, but he's been lang a-wa', And O, my heart was sair, As I sobbed out a lang farewell, May—

colla voce.

The succeeding verses commence at the sign :S:

O sair ha'e I fought,
  Ear' and late did I toil,
My bairnies for to feed and clead[1]—
  My comfort was their smile ;
When I thocht on Jamie far awa',
  An' o' his love sae fain,[2]
A bodin' thrill cam' through my heart
  We'd maybe meet again.
    Noo we're a' noddin', &c.

When he knocket at the door,
  I thocht I kent the rap,
And little Katie cried aloud,
  "My daddie he's cam' back!"
A stoun,[3] gaed through my anxious breast,
  As thochtfully I sat,
I raise—I gazed—fell in his arms,
  And bursted out and grat.[4]
    Noo we're a' noddin', &c.

| [1] Clothe. | [2] Fond. | [3] Pang. | [4] Wept. |

"WE'RE A' NODDIN'." Air, "Nid noddin'." The words are taken from page 31 of that copious and excellent Collection, "The Book of Scottish Song," published by Messrs. Blackie and Son, Glasgow, Edinburgh, and London, 1843. Messrs. Blackie give three different versions of "Nid noddin'."—1. The coarse verses published in Johnson's Museum, and evidently founded on the original words to "John Anderson, my jo," inserted in Bishop Percy's Reliques of Ancient English Poetry ; 2. Verses written by Allan Cunningham, for Mr. G. Thomson's Collection ; 3. The verses which we have adopted as the best, and of which the author is unknown. About thirty years ago the air was very popular, and was sung at public concerts by several of the fashionable singers of that time. It owes much of its present form to W. Hawes, gentleman of the Chapel Royal, who arranged many of our airs early in the present century. The original will be found in Johnson's Museum, No. 523.

WHA'LL BUY CALLER HERRIN'.

ARRANGED BY G. A. MACFARREN.

♩ = 120

MODERATO.

1, 2, & 3. Wha 'll buy cal-ler her-rin', They 're bonnie fish and halesome farin',

Wha 'll buy caller her - rin', New drawn frae the Forth?

When ye were sleepin' on your pillows,
O when the creel o' her-rin' passes,
O neighbour wives! now tent my tellin',

Dream'd ye aught o' our puir fellows Darkling as they faced the billows, A' to fill the woven willows?
La - dies clad in silk and la - ces, Gather in their braw pe-liss-es, Cast their heads and screw their faces,
When the bonnie fish ye 're sellin', At a word aye be your dealin', Truth will stand when a' thing's failin',

Wha'll buy caller herrin', They're bonnie fish and halesome farin', Buy my caller her - rin',

New drawn frae the Forth. Wha'll buy my caller herrin', They're no brought here without brave darin',

Buy my caller her - rin', Ye lit - tle ken their worth: Wha'll buy my cal - ler her - rin', O

ye may ca' them vulgar farin', Wives and mithers maist despairin', Ca' them lives o' men.

"CALLER HERRIN'." This air was composed early in the present century by Nathaniel Gow, the son of the celebrated old Neil Gow of Dunkeld, and father of young Neil, the composer of "Bonnie Prince Charlie," "The Lament of Flora Macdonald," and other modern airs. The opening bars of "Callor Herrin'" were suggested by the cry of the Newhaven fishwives, who to this day are accustomed to carry to town the fish caught over night. This they do in a large creel or basket resting on the back, and supported from the forehead by a broad leathern band. Thus accoutred they walk through even the best streets of Edinburgh, bringing their wares to the very door of the consumer. The second strain of the air is formed from the chimes of St. Andrew's Church, then recently erected in George Street. The song first appeared in R. A. Smith's Scottish Minstrel (v. 18). It was initialed B. B., and is now known to have been written by Lady Nairne. In the original there are other two verses; but they are not equal in merit to those selected, and have been omitted, as the song is quite long enough without them.

The following, copied from the original single sheet, is both rare and curious. It shows the composer's idea in the construction of the tune :—

"CALLER HERRING. Composed (from the original cry of the Newhaven fishwives selling their fresh herring in the streets of Edinburgh) by Nath[aniel] Gow."

THE ORIGINAL CRY OF THE FISHWOMEN.

Buy   my   cal - ler   her - ring.

A fishwoman in George Street going East.

George Street bells at practice.

Three different fishwomen in St. Andrew Square.

The woman from George Street arrives in the Square.

O HOW COULD YE GANG, LASSIE?

ARRANGED BY T. M. MUDIE.

1. O how could ye gang, lassie, how could ye gang; O how could ye gang sae to grieve me? Wi' your beau-ty and your art ye ha'e brok-en my heart, For I nev-er nev-er thought ye wad leave me.

2. O wha could ha'e thought that sae bon-nie a face Wad e'er wear a smile to de-ceive me? Or that guile could ev-er find in that bos-om a place, And that you wad break your vow thus and leave me?

3. Yet, Ma-ry! all faithless and false as thou art, Thy spell-bind-ing glan-ces, be-lieve me, So closely are entwined round this fond foolish heart, That death a-lone of them can be-reave me.

Fine.

"O HOW COULD YE GANG, LASSIE?" This song appeared for the first time in the Scottish Minstrel (iii. 98), 1821. The first stanza was written by Tannahill, the second and third by A. Rodgers. The air was composed by R. A. Smith.

O WHA'S AT THE WINDOW, WHA, WHA?

ARRANGED BY FINLAY DUN.

$\text{♩} = 132$

MODERATO
E
SEMPLICE.

O wha's at the win - dow,

wha, wha! O wha's at the win - dow, wha, wha! Wha but

blythe Jam - ie Glen, He's come sax miles and ten, To tak' bon - nie Jean - ie a -

wa, a - wa, To tak' bon - nie Jean - ie a - wa.

He has plighted his troth, and a', and a',	There's mirth on the green, in the ha', the ha',
Leal love to gi'e, and a', and a';	There's mirth on the green, in the ha', the ha',
And sae has she dune,	There's laughing, there's quaffing,
By a' that's abune,	There's jesting, there's daffing,
For he lo'es her, she lo'es him, 'bune a', 'bune a',	And the bride's father's blythest of a', of a',
He lo'es her she lo'es him, 'bune a'	And the bride's father's blythest of a'.
Bridal maidens are braw, braw,	Its no' that she's Jamie's ava, ava,
Bridal maidens are braw, braw;	Its no' that she's Jamie's ava, ava,
But the bride's modest e'e,	That my heart is sae eerie
And warm cheek are to me,	When a' the lave's cheerie,
'Bune pearlins and brooches, and a', and a',	But its just that she'll aye be awa', awa',
'Bune pearlins and brooches, and a'.	Its just that she'll aye be awa'.

"O WHA'S AT THE WINDOW?" The words were written by Mr. Alexander Carlile of Paisley; the air is by the late R. A. Smith. Early in the seventeenth century a *window* song of this kind seems to have been very popular in England. Some verses of it are sung in three of Beaumont and Fletcher's Plays. See also a parody in Wedderburne's "Godly and Spiritual Songs," 1578.

In Mr. Prior's edition of the works of Oliver Goldsmith, (London, Murray, 1837,) we find an "Essay on the different Schools of Music," upon which it is necessary to make some animadversions, as it contains most erroneous statements with regard to the music of Scotland. The Essay, indeed, as a whole, displays so much ignorance of the subject it professes to discuss, that, but for the deserved high reputation of the author in other respects, we would have passed it over as altogether unworthy of comment. After stating that the Italian school was founded by Pergolese, (!) and that of France by Lulli, Goldsmith says:—"The English school was first planned by Purcell. He attempted to unite the Italian manner that prevailed in his time with the ancient Celtic carol and the Scotch ballad, which probably had also its origin in Italy; for some of the Scotch ballads, 'The broom of Cowdenknows, for instance, are still ascribed to David Rizzio."—Vol. i. p. 175. In one of his Notes, Goldsmith writes:—"It is the opinion of the melodious Geminiani, that we have in the dominions of Great Britain no original music except the Irish; the Scotch and English being originally borrowed from the Italians. And that his opinion in this respect is just, (for I would not be swayed merely by authorities,) it is very reasonable to suppose; first, from the conformity between the Scotch and ancient Italian music.* They who compare the old French vaudevilles brought from Italy by Rinuccini, with those pieces ascribed to David Rizzio, who was pretty nearly contemporary with him, will find a strong resemblance, notwithstanding the opposite characters of the two nations which have pre served these pieces. When I would have them compared, I mean I would have their bases compared, by which the similitude may be most exactly seen. Secondly, it is reasonable, from the ancient music of the Scotch, which is still preserved in the Highlands, and which bears no resemblance at all to the music of the Low country. The Highland tunes are sung to Irish words, and flow entirely in the Irish manner. On the other hand, the Lowland music is always sung to English words."

As to the opinion of "the melodious Geminiani," (whose music, by the way, is very dry and unmelodious,) it is, like every other opinion, to be valued only so far as it is supported by evidence. We, therefore, point to the Collec tions of Martini, Paolucci, and Choron; in which are preserved specimens of ancient and modern Italian music— ecclesiastical and secular; in none of which can be found one single melody bearing the slightest resemblance to Scottish music. As to Rinuccini, who is said to have brought the "old *French* vaudevilles out of *Italy*," (!) the mention of him is evidently a mere subterfuge, for it is not pretended that his airs have any Scottish character. It is in their *bases* (!) that we are to seek for the pretended resemblance! This is almost too absurd for a serious answer. Every musician knows, that to any given simple bass may be written an air in the Italian or the Scottish, in the military or the pastoral styles; and every series of variations upon a given theme and bass by a skilful composer will afford examples of what may be done in this way. Goldsmith's absurdities regarding Purcell's style, as having been compounded of the Italian manner and the ancient Celtic carol and the Scotch *ballad*, we leave to be dealt with by Purcell's countrymen as they think proper.

* This subject has been already discussed in the Note to "Wilt thou be my dearie?"

JESSIE, THE FLOWER O' DUNBLANE.

ARRANGED BY T. M. MUDIE.

The

$\text{♩} = 100$

ANDANTE
SEMPLICE.

sun has gane down o'er the lof - ty Ben - lomond, And left the red clouds to pre-

side o'er the scene, While lone - ly I stray in the calm sim - mer gloamin', To

muse on sweet Jessie, the flower o' Dunblane. How sweet is the brier wi' its saft fauldin' blossom! And sweet is the birk wi' its mantle o' green; Yet sweeter and fairer, and dear to this bosom, Is

love - ly young Jessie, the flower o' Dunblane. Is love - ly young Jessie, Is love - ly young Jessie, Is

love - ly young Jessie, the flower o' Dunblane.

She's modest as onie, and blythe as she's bonnie;
  For guileless simplicity marks her its ain;
And far be the villain, divested o' feeling,
  Wha'd blight in its bloom the sweet flower o' Dun-
    blane.

Sing on, thou sweet mavis, thy hymn to the ev'ning,
  Thou'rt dear to the echoes of Calderwood glen;
Sae dear to this bosom, sae artless and winning,
  Is charming young Jessie, the flower o' Dunblane.

How lost were my days till I met wi' my Jessie!
  The sports o' the city seem'd foolish and vain;
I ne'er saw a nymph I could ca' my dear lassie,
  Till charm'd wi' sweet Jessie, the flower o' Dun-
    blane.

Though mine were the station o' loftiest grandeur,
  Amidst its profusion I'd languish in pain,
And reckon as naething the height o' its splendour,
  If wanting sweet Jessie, the flower o' Dunblane.

"JESSIE, THE FLOWER O' DUNBLANE." The words were written by Robert Tannahill. of whom some account has already been given in the course of this work. Tannahill's words were immediately set to music by the late Robert Archibald Smith, who indeed set most of that poet's best songs. Smith was brought to Edinburgh in 1823, by the late Rev. Dr. Andrew Thomson, and appointed by him precentor in St. George's Church. He died at Edinburgh on 3d January 1829. Not a few of the airs which Smith gave in his "Scottish Minstrel" as ancient Scottish melodies, were actually of his own composition, as could even now easily be proved. Whatever may be a man's ingenuity in committing musical or literary hoaxes upon the public, the principle of such doings will not bear the slightest examination.

THE YEAR THAT'S AWA'.

ARRANGED BY J. T. SURENNE.

Here's to the year that's a - wa'! We'll drink it in strong and in

sma'; And here's to ilk bon - nie young las - sie we lo'ed, While

swift flew the year that's a - wa'. And here's to ilk bon - nie young las - sie we lo'ed, While swift flew the year that's a - wa'.

Here's to the sodger who bled,
And the sailor who bravely did fa':
Their fame is alive, though their spirits are fled
On the wings of the year that's awa'.
    Their fame is alive, &c.

Here's to the friends we can trust,
When the storms of adversity blaw,
May they live in our song, and be nearest our hearts,
Nor depart like the year that's awa'.
    May they live, &c.

"THE YEAR THAT'S AWA'." This song was written by "Mr. Dunlop, late Collector at the Custom-House of Port-Glasgow, and father of Mr. Dunlop, author of The History of Fiction." So says Mr. Robert Chambers in his Scottish Songs, vol. ii. p. 437. We republish the words given by Mr. Chambers, seeing that in two or three editions of them set to music, several of the lines have been altered. A misprint of "friend" for "friends," in the first line of the last stanza, is here corrected. The history of the air, so far as we can learn, is as follows :—" Mr. Robert Donaldson, printer in Greenock, now in Glasgow, having been reading Dunlop's poems, thought the song so good as to be worthy of an air; and calling upon Mr. W. H. Moore, then organist there, (now in Glasgow,) hummed over to him what he considered might be a melody suited for it. This Mr. Moore remodelled considerably, and published, probably about the year 1820. It was afterwards taken up by some of the public singers, and became very popular. Indeed it is still sung about New-year time, though we cannot say much about either soldier or sailor fighting for their country in these days. Long may it continue so!"

There is another version of the air, which we subjoin on account of its being of less extensive compass than the original.

O SPEED, LORD NITHSDALE.

ARRANGED BY T. M. MUDIE.

speed, Lord Nithsdale, speed ye fast, Sin' ye maun frae your countrie flee, Nae

mer - cy mot fa' to your share; Nae pi - ty is for thine and thee.

Thy la - dy sits in lone - ly bower, And fast the tear fa's

frae her e'e ; And aye she sighs, O blaw ye winds, And bear Lord Nithsdale far frae me.

Her heart, sae wae, was like to break,
While kneeling by the taper bright ;
But ae red drap cam' to her cheek,
As shone the morning's rosy light.
Lord Nithsdale's bark she met na see,
Winds sped it swiftly o'er the main ;
"O ill betide," quoth that fair dame,
"Wha sic a comely knight had slain !"

Lord Nithsdale lov'd wi' mickle love ;
But he thought on his countrie's wrang ;
And he was doem'd a traitor syne,
And forc'd frae a' he lov'd to gang.
"Oh ! I will gae to my lov'd lord,
He may na smile, I trow, bot[1] me ;"
But hame, and ha', and bonnie bowers,
Nae mair will glad Lord Nithsdale's e'e.

[1] Bot, without ; as in the old motto, "Touch not the cat bot a glove."

"O SPEED, LORD NITHSDALE, SPEED YE FAST." These verses were written, about the year 1820, by Robert Allan, a poetical weaver of Kilbarchan, in Renfrewshire. Allan was a friend of R. A. Smith, for whom he wrote a number of songs, some of which appeared in the Scottish Minstrel and other musical publications. He died at New York, U.S., on 7th June 1841, eight days after his arrival there. The song alludes to the escape of Maxwell, Earl of Nithsdale, who was deeply involved in the rebellion of 1715. The first Earl of Nithsdale (or Nithisdale) was created in 1581. The last forfeited the title in 1715.

Sir Walter Scott thus describes Nithsdale's escape:—"Lady Nithisdale, the bold and affectionate wife of the condemned Earl, having in vain thrown herself at the feet of the reigning monarch, to implore mercy for her husband, devised a plan for his escape of the same kind with that since practised by Madame Lavalette. She was admitted to see her husband in the Tower upon the last day which, according to his sentence, he had to live. She had with her two female confidants. One brought on her person a double suit of female clothes. This individual was instantly dismissed, when relieved of her second dress. The other person gave her own clothes to the Earl, attiring herself in those which had been provided. Muffled in a riding-hood and cloak, the Earl, in the character of lady's maid, holding a handkerchief to his eyes, as one overwhelmed with deep affliction, passed the sentinels, and being safely conveyed out of the Tower, made his escape to France. So well was the whole thing arranged, that after accompanying her husband to the door of the prison, Lady Nithisdale returned to the chamber from whence her Lord had escaped, and played her part so admirably as to give him full time to get clear of the sentinels, and then make her own exit. We are startled to find that, according to the rigour of the law, the life of the heroic Countess was considered as responsible for that of the husband whom she had saved ; but she contrived to conceal herself."—*History of Scotland.*

The air was taken down by R. A. Smith from the singing of one of the ladies so often mentioned as having superintended the literary portion of the Scottish Minstrel. It is evidently a modern imitation of the antique, and bears some resemblance to "Waly, waly."

THOU BONNIE WOOD OF CRAIGIE-LEA.

ARRANGED BY J. T. SURENNE.

Thou bon - nie wood of Craig - ie - lea, Thou

bon - nie wood of Craig - ie - lea, Near thee I pass'd life's ear - ly day, And

won my Ma - ry's heart in thee. The broom, the brier, the birk - en bush, Bloom bon - nie o'er thy flow' - ry lea; And a' the sweets that ane can wish Frae

poco rall.

na - ture's hand, are strew'd on thee.

colla voce. *pp*

The following stanzas begin at the mark :𝕊:

Far ben thy dark green plantings' shade,
  The cushat croodles am'rously ;
The mavis, down thy bughted glade,
  Gars echo ring frae ev'ry tree.
      Thou bonnie wood, &c.

Awa', ye thoughtless, murd'ring gang,
  Wha tear the nestlings ere they flee !
They'll sing you yet a canty sang,
  Then, O in pity let them be !
      Thou bonnie wood, &c.

When winter blaws in sleety show'rs,
  Frae aff the Norlan hills sae hie,
He lightly skiffs thy bonnie bow'rs,
  As laith to harm a flow'r in thee.
      Thou bonnie wood, &c.

Though fate should drag me south the line,
  Or o'er the wide Atlantic sea,
The happy hours I'll ever mind,
  That I in youth ha'e spent in thee.
      Thou bonnie wood, &c.

"THOU BONNIE WOOD OF CRAIGIE-LEA." The words of this song were written by Robert Tannahill. The air, which has been very popular, was composed by James Barr, a professional musician in Kilbarchan, who afterwards went abroad. In a Bacchanalian song of Tannahill's, called "The Five Friends," James Barr is thus commemorated in the fourth stanza:—

> " There is blithe Jamie Barr, frae St. Barchan's toun,
>   When wit gets a kingdom, he's sure o' the crown;
>   And we're a' noddin, nid, nid, noddin,
>   We're a' noddin fu' at e'en."

In "The Poems and Songs of Robert Tannahill," edited by Mr. Philip A. Ramsay, Glasgow, 1838, we find that R. A. Smith says of this air,—"It is a very pleasing and natural melody, and has become, most deservedly, a great favourite all over the *West Kintra side*. I think this little ballad possesses considerable merit; one of its stanzas strikes me as being particularly beautiful :—

> When winter blaws in sleety show'rs,' &c.
>   ' *Harp*,' Essay, p. xxxvii.

The scenery here so finely described, lies to the north-west of Paisley. Since Tannahill's time its beauty has been sadly impaired by the erection of a most unpoetical object, the gas-work."

Y

MY NANNIE'S AWA'.

ARRANGED BY T. M. MUDIE.

in her green man - tle blythe Na - ture ar - rays, And lis - tens the lambkins that

bleat ower the braes, While birds war - ble wel'come in il - ka green shaw; But to

me its de - light - less, my Nannie's a wa'. But to me its de - light - less, my

Nan - nie's   a - wa'.

The snaw-drap and primrose our woodlands adorn,
And violets bathe in the weet o' the morn;
They pain my sad bosom, sae sweetly they blaw!
They mind me o' Nannie—and Nannie's awa'.

Thou laverock, that springs frae the dews of the lawn.
The shepherd to warn of the grey-breaking dawn,
And thou mellow mavis, that hails the night-fa';
Give over for pity—my Nannie's awa'.

Come, autumn, sae pensive, in yellow and grey,
And soothe me wi' tidings o' Nature's decay:
The dark, dreary winter, and wild-driving snaw,
Alane can delight me—my Nannie's awa'.

"MY NANNIE'S AWA'." Upon this song Captain Charles Gray, R.M., in his "Cursory Remarks on Scottish Song," gives the following Note. Before quoting it, we might perhaps venture to suggest, that Burns' admiration of Clarinda may find its remoter parallel in that of Petrarca, early in the fourteenth century, for the lady whom he has rendered so celebrated, in verse and prose, under the name of Laura. Petrarca, in his "Epistle to Posterity," calls his regard for Laura, "veementissimo, ma unico ed onesto." To say, that a very warm and sincere friendship cannot innocently subsist between a married woman and an unmarried man, is not only to contradict daily experience, but to utter a licentious libel upon human nature. Were such the case, many of the strongest heart-ties between friends and relatives must be at once torn asunder, never to reunite in this world.

" 'My Nannie's awa',' is one of the sweetest pastoral songs that Burns ever wrote. He sent it to Mr. Thomson in December 1794, to be united to the old melody of, 'There'll never be peace till Jamie come hame.' In this song the Bard laments the absence of Mrs. M'Lehose, (Clarinda,) who had left Scotland to join her husband in the West Indies, in February 1792. We may be pardoned, perhaps, for saying a word or two about the lady whose beauty and accomplishments had so captivated our Bard, and inspired him with this and some others of his most beautiful love-songs. Burns, having published the second edition of his poems in 1787, was just about to leave Edinburgh when he was introduced to Clarinda. One of our Poet's biographers alleges, that he was very tolerant as to the personal charms of his heroines; but as to the wit, beauty, and powers of conversation of Clarinda, there can be no doubt. She seems to have completely fascinated him at the very first interview. That Mrs. M'Lehose was no ordinary person is proved by her letters, now printed along with those of Burns; and it is saying much for her, that they do not suffer from being placed in juxtaposition with those of the Bard. This romantic attachment between the poet and poetess was not of very long duration; but while it lasted, as many letters passed between them as form a goodly sized octavo volume! The germ of 'Nannie's awa'' is to be found in one of Clarinda's letters, (see Correspondence, &c., p. 186,) written thirty-five days after they became acquainted. They were about to part, and she says:—'You'll hardly write me once a month, and other objects will weaken your affection for Clarinda; yet I cannot believe so. *Oh! let the scenes of Nature remind you of Clarinda! In winter, remember the dark shades of her fate; in summer, the warmth, the cordial warmth of her friendship; in autumn, her glowing wishes to bestow plenty on all; and let spring animate you with hopes that your poor friend may yet live to surmount the wintry blast of life, and revive to taste a spring-time of happiness!'* This passage, so beautifully descriptive, in the letter of his fair correspondent, was not overlooked by Burns. He says, in reply:—'There is one fine passage in your last charming letter—Thomson nor Shenstone never exceeded it, nor often came up to it. I shall certainly *steal it and set it in some future production,* and got immortal fame by it. 'Tis where you bid the scenes of Nature remind me of Clarinda.' The poet was as good as his word. Some months after Clarinda had left this country, Burns, reverting to the passage we have quoted from her letter, made it his own by stamping it in immortal verse, bewailing the absence of Clarinda in a strain of rural imagery that has seldom or never been surpassed."

The air to which we have here united the words, we believe to be modern; yet we have not been able to trace it to any composer. Like many other airs, it probably owes its present form to several individuals. It appears to have passed orally from one singer to another, until Mr. George Croall, a well-known musician in Edinburgh, rescued it a few years ago from threatened oblivion.

ROW WEEL, MY BOATIE, ROW WEEL.

ARRANGED BY FINLAY DUN.

♩ = 92

ANDANTE
CON
ESPRESSIONE.

weel, my boatie, row weel, Row weel, my mer-ry men a', For there's

dool and there's wae in Glen - fio - rich's bowers, And there's grief in my fa - ther's ha'.

animated.

And the skiff it danced light on the merry wee waves, And it flew o'er the wa - ter sae blue,   And the wind it blew light, and the moon it shone bright, But the boatie ne'er reach'd Al-lan-

dhu. O - hon! for fair Ellen, o - hon! O - hon! for the pride of Strath-

coo! In the deep, deep sea, In the salt, salt bree, Lord Reoch, thy El - len lies

low.

"Row weel, my boatie." The words were written by Walter Weir, house painter in Greenock, an intelligent man, and a learned Gaelic scholar. The subject is taken from an old Gaelic story which the author got from his mother. The air is by R. A. Smith. It was first published under the name of Ellen boideachd—Beautiful Ellen.

BONNIE MARY HAY.

ARRANGED BY T. M. MUDIE.

MODERATO.

1. Bonnie Ma - ry Hay, I will lo'e thee yet, For thine e'e is the slae, and thy
2. Bonnie Ma - ry Hay, will ye gang wi' me, When the sun's in the west, to the

hair is the jet. The snaw is thy skin, and the rose is thy check; O
haw - thorn tree? To the haw - thorn tree, in the bonnie ber - ry den, An' I'll

bonnie Ma-ry Hay, I will lo'e thee yet.
tell you, Ma-ry Hay, how I lo'e thee then.

dim. rall.

3. Bonnie Ma-ry Hay, it's hal-i-day to me When thou art couth-ie,
4. Bonnie Ma-ry Hay, thou maunna say me nay, But come to the bower by the

p

kind, and free; There's nae clouds in the lift, nor storms in the sky, My
haw-thorn brae, But come to the bower, an' I'll tell you a' that's true, How,

bon-nie Ma-ry Hay, when thou art nigh.
Ma-ry, I can ne'er lo'e ane but you.

dim. rall.

p   *p*

BONNIE MARY HAY.—Is the composition of Archibald Crawford (B. 1785, D. 1843). He was born in Ayr, was left an orphan in his ninth year, and had little education beyond what he acquired through his own energy. After being in various situations, he eventually settled down as an auctioneer in his native town. There he wrote for a provincial newspaper sketches founded upon tradition, which were afterwards collected and published in 1824, under the name of Tales of a Grandmother. The song was written in honour of a young Edinburgh lady, who had shown him much kindness during an attack of fever. It was set to music by R. A. Smith about 1823, was published as a single song, and deservedly became very popular. See Dr. Charles Rogers' most comprehensive volumes, "The Modern Scottish Minstrel."

WHEN THE KYE COMES HAME.

ARRANGED BY J. T. SURENNE.

♩ = 72

MODERATO.

Come all ye jol-ly shepherds that whistle through the glen, I'll tell ye of a se-cret That courtiers din-na ken. What is the greatest bliss That the tongue o' man can name I 'Tis to woo a bonnie las-sie When the kye comes hame. When the kye comes hame, When the kye comes hame, 'Tween the gloamin' and the mirk, When the kye comes hame.

'Tis not beneath the burgonet,[1]
　Nor yet beneath the crown,
'Tis not on couch of velvet,
　Nor yet on bed of down :
'Tis beneath the spreading birch,
　In the dell without a name,
Wi' a bonnie, bonnie lassie,
　When the kye comes hame.

There the blackbird bigs[2] his nest
　For the mate he loves to see,
And up upon the tapmost bough,
　Oh, a happy bird is he !
Then he pours his melting ditty,
　And love 'tis a' the theme,
And he'll woo his bonnie lassie
　When the kye comes hame.

When the bluart[3] bears a pearl,
　And the daisy turns a pea,
And the bonnie lucken gowan
　Has fauldit up his e'e,
Then the laverock frae the blue lift
　Draps down, and thinks nae shame
To woo his bonnie lassie
　When the kye comes hame.

Then the eye shines sae bright,
　The haill soul to beguile,
There's love in every whisper,
　And joy in every smile;
O, who would choose a crown,
　Wi' its perils and its fame,
And miss a bonnie lassie
　When the kye comes hame ?

See yonder pawky[4] shepherd
　That lingers on the hill—
His yowes are in the fauld,
　And his lambs are lying still ;
Yet he downa gang to rest,
　For his heart is in a flame
To meet his bonnie lassie
　When the kye comes hame.

Awa' wi' fame and fortune—
　What comfort can they gi'e ?—
And a' the arts that prey
　On man's life and libertie !
Gi'e me the highest joy
　That the heart o' man can frame ;
My bonnie, bonnie lassie,
　When the kye comes hame.

---

　‡ A kind of helmet.　　　　‡ Builds.　　　　§ The bilberry.　　　　‡ Sly, artful.

"WHEN THE KYE COMES HAME." In "Songs by the Ettrick Shepherd, now first collected, Blackwood, Edinburgh, 1831," James Hogg himself writes the following notes upon this song:—"In the title and chorus of this favourite pastoral song, I choose rather to violate a rule in grammar, than a Scottish phrase so common, that when it is altered into the proper way, every shepherd and shepherd's sweetheart account it nonsense. I was once singing it at a wedding with great glee the latter way, ('when the kye come hame,') when a tailor, scratching his head, said, ' It was a terrible affectit way that !' I stood corrected, and have never sung it so again. It is to the old tune of 'Shame fa' the gear and the blathrie o't,' with an additional chorus. It is set to music in the Noctes, at which it was first sung, and in no other place that I am aware of." . . . . . "I composed the foregoing song I neither know how nor when; for when the 'Three Perils of Man' came first to my hand, and I saw this song put into the mouth of a drunken poet, and mangled in the singing, I had no recollection of it whatever. I had written it off-hand along with the prose, and quite forgot it. But I liked it, altered it, and it has been my favourite pastoral for singing ever since. It is too long to be sung from beginning to end; but only the second and antepenult verses [stanzas] can possibly be dispensed with, and these not very well neither." As we do not think that Hogg improved his song by altering it, we adopt the earlier version. The air to which Hogg adapted his words is not a true version of "The Blathrie o't," but one considerably altered.

OH! WHY LEFT I MY HAME?

ARRANGED BY J. T. SURENNE.

Oh! why left I my hame? Why did I cross the deep? Oh! why left I the land Where my fore-fa-thers sleep! I sigh for Sco-tia's shore, And I gaze a-cross the sea, But I can-na get a

blink¹ O' my ain coun - trie.

poco rall.

colla voce   *mf*

The palm-tree waveth high,
  And fair the myrtle springs,
And to the Indian maid
  The bulbul sweetly sings;
But I dinna see the broom,
  Wi' its tassels on the lea,
Nor hear the lintie's² sang
  O' my ain countrie.

Oh! here no Sabbath-bell
  Awakes the Sabbath morn,
Nor song of reapers heard
  Amang the yellow corn:
For the tyrant's voice is here,
  And the wail of slaverie;
But the sun of freedom shines
  In my ain countrie.

There's a hope for every woe,
  And a balm for every pain,
But the first joys of our heart
  Come never back again.
There's a track upon the deep,
  And a path across the sea,
But the weary ne'er return
  To their ain countrie.

¹ Glimpse.   ² Linnet.

"OH! WHY LEFT I MY HAME?" In Johnson's Museum, vol. ii. No. 115, we find a tune called "The Lowlands of Holland," which remarkably resembles the tune here set to Mr. R. Gilfillan's words. Mr. Stenhouse says it was published by James Oswald in 1742, and was ascribed to him by his sister and daughter; but Mr. Stenhouse erred in making that statement, for the tune in Oswald's Second Collection is totally unlike that in Johnson. The original of Oswald's air is evidently No 17 of the Skene MS., a fact which demolishes his claim to the tune and his untrustworthiness, if he led his relatives to believe it to be his own composition. Johnson's air was altered into its present form by Mr. Peter Macleod, a musical amateur of Edinburgh. His compositions were numerous; one of the most popular being "Scotland yet," from the profits of which he placed a parapet and railing round the monument of Burns on the Calton Hill, Edinburgh.

HE'S O'ER THE HILLS THAT I LO'E WEEL.

ARRANGED BY T. M. MUDIE.

He's o'er the hills that I lo'e weel; He's o'er the hills we daur - na name; He's o'er the hills a - yont Dumblane, Wha soon will get his wel - come hame. My fa - ther's gane to fight for him, My bri - thers win - na bide at hame, My mi - ther greets and prays for them, And

'deed she thinks they're no' to blame. *Concluding Symphony.*

[The succeeding verses begin with the second part of the melody.]

The Whigs may scoff, the Whigs may jeer,
But, ah! that love maun be sincere
Which still keeps true whate'er betide,
An' for his sake leaves a' beside.
 He's o'er the hills, &c.

His right these hills, his right these plains
O'er Highland hearts secure he reigns;
What lads e'er did, our lads will do
Were I a lad, I'd follow him too.
 He's o'er the hills, &c.

Sae noble a look, sae princely an air,
Sae gallant and bold, sae young and sae fair;
Oh! did you but see him, ye'd do as we've done;
Hear him but ance, to his standard you'll run.
 He's o'er the hills, &c.

"HE'S O'ER THE HILLS THAT I LO'E WEEL." This is a modern Jacobite song, which appeared with its air in the Scottish Minstrel III., 1821. In the early editions it is anonymous, in the third it bears the signature S. M., and has been claimed for Lady Nairne, though some of the verses scarcely reach the high standard of her poetry. Probably it owes much to her, but I am inclined to believe that all the songs with this signature were altered, amended, or added to by the coterie of ladies who superintended the literary part of that work, and that no single individual could claim to be their author. This I believe to be the reason why ALL the songs which came afterwards to have the initials S. M. attached to them are, in the index to the early editions of the Minstrel, stated to be of *unknown* authorship. The new airs which appeared in the Minstrel are of uncertain origin. R. A. Smith confessed to having composed some of them himself; others he took down from the singing of the ladies mentioned above, while a few were re-modelled from very defective MSS. submitted to him.

Mr. George Alexander has pointed out (Irish Melodies, p. 151) that the air probably had the same origin as "Were I a clerk," to which Moore wrote his song, "You remember Ellen;" comparison will show that they resemble each other very considerably.

CAM' YE BY ATHOL?

ARRANGED BY A. LAWRIE.

Cam' ye by A - thol, lad wi' the phi - la - beg, Down by the Tum - mel, or banks o' the Ga - ry? Saw ye the lads, wi' their bon - nets an' white cock - ades, Leav - ing their mountains to fol - low Prince Char - lie! Fol - low thee, fol - low thee, wha wad-na fol-low thee? Lang hast thou loved an' trust-ed us fair-ly!

Char-lie, Char-lie, wha wad-na fol-low thee? King o' the Highland hearts,

colla voce.

bon-nie Prince Char-lie.

I ha'e but ae son, my gallant young Donald;
  But if I had ten, they should follow Glengarry;
Health to M'Donald, and gallant Clan-Ronald,
  For these are the men that will die for their Charlie.
    Follow thee, follow thee, &c.

I'll to Lochiel and Appin, and kneel to them;
  Down by Lord Murray and Roy of Kildarlie;
Brave Mackintosh, he shall fly to the field wi' them;
  These are the lads I can trust wi' my Charlie.
    Follow thee, follow thee, &c.

Down thro' the Lowlands, down wi' the whigamore,
  Loyal true Highlanders, down wi' them rarely;
Ronald and Donald drive on wi' the braid claymore,
  Over the necks of the foes o' Prince Charlie.
    Follow thee, follow thee, &c.

"CAM' YE BY ATHOL?" This song was written by James Hogg, the Ettrick Shepherd, was set to music by Neil Gow, Jun., and was published in "The Border Garland;" a work of which one number only was published. It seems to have been projected by Hogg to give publicity to his own musical as well as poetical compositions; but the work did not meet with much success, owing perhaps to its octavo form. Some years thereafter a folio edition was brought out with three additional songs, making twelve in all; the whole of the music having been re-arranged by James Dewar. Four of the songs, "The Lament of Flora Macdonald," "O Jeanie, there's naething to fear you," "The Skylark," and "Bonnie Prince Charlie," now came into notice, and were much sung.

FAR OVER YON HILLS.

AIR, "THE LAMENT OF FLORA MACDONALD." ARRANGED BY FINLAY DUN.

= 100

ANDANTE
ESPRESSIVO.

Far o - ver yon hills of the heather sae green, An' down by the Corrie that sings to the sea, The bon - nie young Flo - ra sat sighing her lane, The dew on her plaid an' the tear in her e'e. She look'd at a boat wi' the breez - es that swung, A - way on the wave, like a bird of the main; An' ay as it lessen'd she sigh'd an' she sung, "Fareweel to the lad I shall ne'er see a-gain; Fare-

con energia.

weel to my he-ro, the gallant an' young, Fareweel to the lad I shall ne'er see a-gain."

The moorcock that crows on the brows o' Ben-Connal,
He kens o' his bed in a sweet mossy hame;
The eagle that soars o'er the cliffs o' Clan-Ronald,
Unawed and unhunted his eyrie can claim;
The solan can sleep on the shelve of the shores;
The cormorant roost on his rock of the sea;
But, ah! there is one whose hard fate I deplore,
Nor house, ha', nor hame in his country has he;
The conflict is past, and our name is no more,
There's nought left but sorrow for Scotland an' me!

The target is torn from the arm of the just,
The helmet is cleft on the brow of the brave,
The claymore for ever in darkness must rust;
But red is the sword of the stranger and slave;
The hoof of the horse, and the foot of the proud,
Have trode o'er the plumes on the bonnet of blue:
Why slept the red bolt in the breast of the cloud
When tyranny revell'd in blood of the true?
Fareweel, my young hero, the gallant and good!
The crown of thy fathers is torn from thy brow.

"FAR OVER YON HILLS." James Hogg, in his second series of Jacobite Relics, gives this song and air as "The Lament of Flora Macdonald," with the following note:—"I got the original of these verses from my friend Mr. Niel Gow, who told me they were a translation from the Gaelic, but so rude that he could not publish them, which he wished to do on a single sheet, for the sake of the old air. On which I versified them anew, and made them a great deal better without altering one sentiment." In his "Songs," collected in 1831, Hogg reprints this under the title of "Flora Macdonald's Farewell," headed by the following note:—"Was composed to an air handed me by the late lamented Niel Gow, junior. He said it was an ancient Skye air, but afterwards told me it was his own. When I first heard the song sung by Mr. Morison, I never was so agreeably astonished,—I could hardly believe my senses that I had made so good a song without knowing it." In both these notes, the Shepherd's s complacency is very amusing.

COME O'ER THE STREAM, CHARLIE.

AIR, "MACLEAN'S WELCOME."   ARRANGED BY T. M MUDIE.

Come o'er the stream, Char - lie, dear Char - lie, brave Char - lie, Come
o'er the stream, Char - lie, and dine with Mac - Lean; And though you be wea - ry, we'll
make your heart chee - ry, And wel - come our Char - lie and his loy - al train.

Come o'er the stream, Charlie, dear Charlie, brave
  Charlie,
  Come o'er the stream, Charlie, and dine with
    MacLean;
And though you be weary, we'll make your heart
    cheery,
  And welcome our Charlie and his loyal train.
And you shall drink freely the dews of Glen-Sheerly,
  That stream in the star-light, when kings dinna
    ken;
And deep be your meed of the wine that is red,
  To drink to your sire and his friend the MacLean.

Come o'er the stream, Charlie, dear Charlie, brave
  Charlie,
  Come o'er the stream, Charlie, and dine with
    MacLean;
And though you be weary, we'll make your heart
    cheery,
  And welcome our Charlie and his loyal train.
If aught will invite you, or more will delight you,
  'Tis ready—a troop of our bold Highlandmen
Shall range on the heather, with bonnet and feather,
  Strong arms and broad claymores, three hundred
    and ten.

"COME O'ER THE STREAM, CHARLIE." In "Songs by the Ettrick Shepherd," 1831, we find the following Note by James Hogg:—"I versified this song at Meggernie Castle, in Glen-Lyon, from a scrap of prose, said to be the translation, *verbatim*, of a Gaelic song, and to a Gaelic air, sung by one of the sweetest singers and most accomplished and angelic beings of the human race. But, alas! earthly happiness is not always the lot of those who, in our erring estimation, most deserve it. She is now no more, and many a strain have I poured to her memory."

HEY THE BONNIE BREAST-KNOTS.

ARRANGED BY T. M. MUDIE.

Hey the bonnie, ho the bonnie, Hey the bonnie breast - knots; Blythe and merry were they a', When they got on the breast-knots.

1. There was a brid - al in this town, And till't the lasses a' were boun' Wi' mank - ie fac - ings on their gown, And some o' them had breast-knots.

2. At nine o'clock the lads convene, Some clad in blue, some clad in green, Wi' glanc - in' buckles in their sheen, And flow'rs up - on their waist - coats.

Hey the bonnie, ho the bonnie, Hey the bonnie breast-knots, Blythe and merry were they a', When

they got on the breast-knots.

Forth cam' the wives a' wi' a phrase,
And wish'd the lassie happy days,
And muckle thocht they o' her claise,
And specially the breast-knots.—Hey, *etc.*

When they'd tied up the marriage ban',
At the bridegroom's they neist did lan',
Forth cam' auld Madge wi' her split mawn,[1]
An' bread an' cheese a huist[2] o 't.—Hey, *etc.*

She took a quarter and a third,
On the bride's head she ga'e a gird,[3]
Till farls[4] flew across the yird,
Syne parted round the rest o 't.—Hey, *etc.*

Then a' ran to the barn in ranks,
Some sat on deals, and some on planks,
The piper lad stood on his shanks,
And dirl'd up the breast-knots.—Hey, *etc.*

[1] A basket.   [2] A heap.   [3] A slight blow sufficient to break the oat-cake.   [4] The quarter of a circular cake.

"THE BONNIE BREAST-KNOTS." This humorous song, written in the broad Buchan dialect, was sent to the editor of Johnson's Museum by an anonymous correspondent. Strange to say, the air which accompanied it, differing entirely from that which we here give, was an English morris-dance, still known in some parts of Derbyshire and Lancashire. The tune is found under the name of "The Breast-knot" in several collections of country dances of last century, and it may be a question whether the name suggested the writing of the song, or the song gave its name to the dance. In any case it seems singular that an English morris-dance should find its way to Aberdeenshire. That air has, however, long been discarded, and its place supplied by a sort of strathspey tune entirely modern, but regarding which nothing seems to be known with certainty.

In the original song there are fifteen stanzas, of which the 1st, 3d, 5th, 12th, 13th, and 15th, have been selected for this work. The 12th and 13th describe a curious Scottish marriage custom, now almost forgotten, of breaking a *farl* of shortbread or oaten-cake over the head of the bride when entering her new dwelling for the first time.

LUCY'S FLITTIN'.

ARRANGED BY T. M. MUDIE.

MODERATO.

1. 'Twas when the wan leaf frae the birk tree was fa'-in', And Mar-tinmas dow-ie had
2. She gaed by the sta-ble, where Ja-mie was stannin'; Right sair was his kind heart the
3. O what is 't that pits my puir heart in a flut-ter? An' what gars the tear come sae

wound up the year, That Lu-cy row'd up her wee kist wi' her a' in't, And left her auld master and
flit-tin' to see, .. "Fare ye weel, Lu-cy," quo' Ja-mie, an' ran in ; The ga-the-rin' tears trickled
fast to my ee?.. If I was na et-tled to be on-ie better, Then what gars me wish on-ie

nei-bours sae dear. For Lu-cy had serv'd in the glen a' the sim-mer; She
fast frae his e'e. As down the burn-side she gaed slow wi' her flit-tin', ...
bet-ter to be? I'm just like a lam-mie that los-es its mi-ther; Nor

cam there before the flow'r bloom'd on the pea, An orphan was she, an' they had been gude till her, Sure
"Fare ye weel, Lu-cy," was il - ka bird's sang; She heard the craw sayin't, high on the tree sit-tin', An'
mith-er nor frien' the puir lam-mie can see, I fear I ha'e tint my bit heart a' - the-gith-er, Nae

that was the thing brought the tear to her e'e.
ro - bin was chir - pin't the brown leaves amang.
won - der the tear fa's sae fast frae my e'e.

Wi' the rest o' my claes I hae row'd up the ribbon,
The bonnie blue ribbon that Jamie ga'e me ;
Yestreen when he ga'e me't, an' saw I was sabbin',
I 'll never forget the wae blink o' his e'e :
Though now he said naething but "Fare ye weel, Lucy,"
It made me I neither could speak, hear, nor see,
He cou'dna sae mair but just "Fare ye weel, Lucy,"
Yet that I will mind till the day that I dee.

The lamb likes the gowan, wi' dew when it's droukit,
The hare likes the brake an' the braird on the lea ;
But Lucy likes Jamie—she turn'd an' she lookit,
She thought the dear place she would never mair see.
Ah ! weel may young Jamie gang dowie an' cheerless !
An' weel may he greet on the bank o' the burn !
His bonnie sweet Lucy, sae gentle an' peerless,
Lies cauld in her grave, an' will never return.

"LUCY'S FLITTIN'." We need offer no apology, unless it be to Professor Veitch, for quoting his account of this song and its writer from that delightful work, The History and Poetry of the Scottish Borders (p. 524). "Lucy's Flittin' is the Lyric of the Borders which ranks next to the Flowers of the Forest. It was the production of William Laidlaw, the son of the farmer of Blackhouse, on the Douglas Burn, the early friend of Hogg, and the life-long friend and amanuensis of Sir Walter Scott. He was born in 1780, and died in 1845. Lucy's Flittin' could have been written only by one who had been brought up among the south country glens, who knew and felt the simplicity of rural life and manners there, and who, as a man of true lyrical soul, could for the time entirely forget himself, realise the feelings and speak the language of the breaking-hearted country lassie. The last eight lines of the song are by James Hogg."
The air is modern, and was written for the song ; but the author is not known.

HAME, HAME, HAME!

ARRANGED BY J. T. SURENNE.

$\boldsymbol{\rho} = 63$

ADAGIO
PATETICO.

Hame, hame, hame, O hame fain would I be, Hame, hame, hame, to my

ain coun-trie! There's an eye that ev-er weeps, and a fair face will be fain, As I

pass through Annan wa-ter with my bonnie bands again; When the flow'r is in the bud, and the leaf up - on the tree, The lark shall sing me hame in my ain coun - trie.

Hame, hame, hame, O hame fain would I be,
Hame, hame, hame, to my ain countrie!
The green leaf of loyalty's beginning for to fa',
The bonnie white rose it is withering and a',
But I'll water't with the blood of usurping tyrannie,
And fresh it will blaw in my ain countrie.

Hame, hame, hame, O hame fain would I be,
Hame, hame, hame, to my ain countrie!
There's nought now from ruin my countrie can save,
But the keys of kind heaven to open the grave,
That all the noble martyrs who died for loyaltie
May rise again and fight for their ain countrie.

Hame, hame, hame, O hame fain would I be,
Hame, hame, hame, to my ain countrie!
The great now are gane, a' who ventured to save;
The new grass is growing aboon their bloody grave;
But the sun through the mirk blinks blithe in my e'e,
I'll shine on ye yet in your ain countrie.

"HAME, HAME, HAME!" In vol. iii. pp. 246, 247, of The Songs of Scotland, edited by Allan Cunningham, we find a version of this song beginning, "It's hame, and it's hame." We have followed this version, omitting only the word "It's," which is an unmeaning word used by the country people in many parts of Scotland at the beginning of almost every song; and adopting from Blackie a better reading of the last line of the second stanza—that is, "And fresh it will blaw,"—instead of, "And green it will grow." As the "white rose" is the flower mentioned, the words, "green it will grow," are not applicable. The following is Cunningham's Note appended to the words :—"This song is noticed in the introduction to the 'Fortunes of Nigel,' and part of it is sung by Richie Moniplies. It is supposed to come from the lips of a Scottish Jacobite exile. The old song of the same name had a similar chorus, and one good verse against the British fleet, which was then—and may it ever continue!—master of the sea; the poet prayed for very effectual aid :—

'May the ocean stop and stand, like walls on every side,
That our gallant chiefs may pass, wi' heaven for their guide!
Dry up the Forth and Tweed, as thou did'st the Red Sea,
When the Israelites did pass to their ain countrie.'"

In the first volume of Hogg's Jacobite Relics, Song LXXX, we find verses nearly corresponding with those given by A. Cunningham, but beginning, "Hame, hame, hame, hame fain wad I be." Hogg's Note says :—"The air, to which I have heard it sung very beautifully, seems to be a modification of the old tune of *Mary Scott, the power of Yarrow*." The air given by Hogg to "Hame, hame," is a modification of "Dinna think, bonnie lassie, I'm gaun to leave you;" which again is borrowed from the air in triple time, "Mary Scot." The song is, in this work, adapted to a modern air which is evidently borrowed from "My love's in Germanie."

THE SUN RISES BRIGHT IN FRANCE.

ARRANGED BY T. M. MUDIE.

♩ = 92

SLOW
WITH
EXPRESSION.

1. The sun ris - es bright in France, And fair sets he, But he's tint the blythe blink he had In my ain coun - trie. It's nae my ain ru - in That meets aye my trie.

2. Fu' bienly low'd my ain . . . hearth, And smiled my sweet Ma - rie, O, I've left a' my heart be - hind In my ain coun - trie. O, I'm leal to high hea - ven, Which aye was leal to trie.

e'e; But the dear Ma - rie I left a - hin', Wi' sweet bair - nies
me And it's there I'll meet you a' soon Frae my ain coun - - -

three, And it's oh! waes me!
trie, And it's oh! waes me!

pp   *rall.*

"'THE SUN RISES BRIGHT IN FRANCE." In 1810 Cromek published this as a genuine Jacobite relic in his *Remains of Nithsdale and Galloway Song*. He gives it as if taken down from the singing or recitation of a Miss Macartney. In 1825, however, Allan Cunningham printed it, with his own name, in his *Songs of Scotland*, adding eight lines to it ; he likewise made several alterations in the first version of the words, but as these rather mar the original simplicity of the song, they have been generally rejected. The added lines are intercalated as a second and fifth quatrain, but they may be sung together as a second stanza, if the song be not thought long enough without them :—

O gladness comes to many,   The bud comes back to summer,
  But sorrow comes to me,   And the blossom to the bee ;
As I look o'er the wide ocean   But I win back—oh never !
  To my ain countrie.   To my ain countrie.

In 1821 Hogg included the song in his *Jacobite Relics*, as a "sweet old thing, very popular both in England and Scotland," but confessed it was uncertain to what period the song refers. The Ettrick Shepherd was, perhaps, not so well fitted by previous reading as might have been wished, to be the editor of a work which required antiquarian knowledge, and even research, to a considerable extent. Still he had a ready pen, had written some very good Jacobite songs from scraps of prose translation from the Gaelic, and was, above all, so general a favourite, that every collection was at once thrown open to him. He was thus put in possession of much information that another, possibly better fitted for the task, might have failed to obtain. With the music he ought to have done much better ; for in many cases the original tunes of the songs were indicated. He had, besides, the assistance of Mr. William Stenhouse, the annotator of Johnson's Museum, who had the reputation of possessing great knowledge of national music. Yet the airs are admittedly often taken at random, the versions are frequently uncouth, not to use a worse term, and the Shepherd shows a strange want of knowledge and appreciation of the pastoral airs of the south of Scotland : Sir Gilbert Elliot's "My sheep I neglected" is quite unknown to him, "Pinkie House" he entirely disowns. His own taste seems to have been towards the bagpipe tunes of the north, rather than the smoother-flowing melodies of the Ettrick and the Yarrow.

ANNIE LAURIE.

ARRANGED BY T. M. MUDIE.

Max - well - ton braes are bon - nie, Where ear - ly fa's the dew, And it's

there that An - nie Lau - rie Gi'ed me her pro - mise true; Gi'ed

me her pro - mise true, Which ne'er forgot will be, And for

bon - nie   An - nie   Lau - rie,   I'd   lay   me down   and   dee.

For first two verses.   :S: For last verse.

Her brow is like the snaw-drift,
Her neck is like the swan,
Her face it is the fairest
That e'er the sun shone on;
That e'er the sun shone on,
And dark blue is her e'e;
And for bonnie Annie Laurie
I'd lay me down and dee.

Like dew on the gowan lying,
Is the fa' o' her fairy feet;
And like winds in summer sighing,
Her voice is low and sweet.
Her voice is low and sweet,
And she's a' the world to me;
And for bonnie Annie Laurie
I'd lay me down and dee.

"ANNIE LAURIE." We give the more modern version of the song. With regard to the other version, said to have been written about 160 years ago, and which will be found in the Appendix, Mr. Robert Chambers says, "These two verses, which are in a style wonderfully tender and chaste for their age, were written by a Mr. Douglas of Fingland, upon Anne, one of the four daughters of Sir Robert Laurie, first baronet of Maxwellton, by his second wife, who was a daughter of Riddell of Minto. As Sir Robert was created a baronet in the year 1685, it is probable that the verses were composed about the end of the seventeenth or the beginning of the eighteenth century. It is painful to record that, notwithstanding the ardent and chivalrous affection displayed by Mr. Douglas in his poem, he did not obtain the heroine for a wife: she was married to Mr. Ferguson of Craigdarroch. See 'A Ballad Book,' (printed at Edinburgh in 1824,) p. 107."—*Chambers' Scottish Songs*, Edinburgh, 1829 vol. ii. p. 294. We must observe, however, that the second stanza of the song, ascribed to Mr. Douglas, beginning "She's backit like the peacock," is evidently borrowed, with modifications, from a stanza, not quotable, in an old version of "John Anderson, my Jo." The air of Annie Laurie is quite modern, having been composed by Lady John Scott. For the further satisfaction of our readers, we subjoin Allan Cunningham's Note upon "Annie Laurie," in his "Songs of Scotland," Edinburgh, 1825, vol. iii. pp. 256, 257. "I found this song in the little 'Ballad Book,' collected and edited by a gentleman to whom Scottish literature is largely indebted—Charles Kirkpatrick Sharpe of Hoddam. It is accompanied by the following notice:—'Sir Robert Laurie, first Baronet of the Maxwellton family, (created 27th March 1685,) by his second wife, a daughter of Riddell of Minto, had three sons and four daughters, of whom Anne was much celebrated for her beauty, and made a conquest of Mr. Douglas of Fingland, who is said to have composed the following verses under an unlucky star—for the lady married Mr. Ferguson of Craigdarroch.' I have only to add, that I am glad such a song finds a local habitation in my native place." Allan Cunningham quotes the song from Mr. Sharpe's "Ballad Book;" but we observe that that version differs in its readings from the one given by Mr. R. Chambers. The former reads—"Where I and Annie Laurie" —"I'd lay down my head and die"—"a peacock"—"a swan"—"may span;" while the latter reads—"Where me and Annie Laurie"—"I'll lay me down and die"—"the peacock"—"the swan"—"micht span."

CASTLES IN THE AIR.

ARRANGED BY A. C. MACKENZIE.

♩ = 80

Not too
Quick,
with
Heartiness.

1. The bonnie, bonnie bairn, who sits
2. sees muckle cas - tles tow-

poking in the asse,   Glow'rin' in the fire wi' his   wee round face;
or - ing to the moon;   He sees little sod - gers pu' - ing   them a' doun!

Laugh - ing at the fuffies' lowe, what sees he there?   Ha! the young dreamer's biggin'
Worlds whomling up and doun, bleezin' wi' a flare.   See how he loups! as they

castles in the air.   His wee chubby face, and his touz - ie cur -ly pow, Are
glimmer in the air.   For a' sae sage he looks, what can the laddie ken? He's

Sic a night in winter may weel mak him cauld,
His chin upon his buffy hand will soon mak him auld,
His brow is brent sae braid, O pray that daddy Care
Would let the wean alane wi' his castles in the air.
He 'll glow'r at the fire! and he 'll keek at the light,
But mony sparkling stars are swallow'd up by night;
Aulder e'en than his are glamour'd by a glare,
Hearts are broken, heads are turn'd, wi' castles in the air.

"CASTLES IN THE AIR." This clever song, written by James Ballantine, was one of about fifty which he contributed to David Robertson's excellent collection of Scottish songs by living authors called "Whistle-binkie." This work, begun in 1832, was so well received, that from time to time one series after another was called for, till in 1844 it was brought to a close by the appearance of the sixth, which consisted entirely of songs for children, and, among others, contained "Castles in the air." Some years thereafter it was set to a slightly altered version of an excellent old melody, "Bonny Jean," by a youthful amateur of Edinburgh. It is published here by permission of the proprietors of the copyright.

AULD JOE NICOLSON'S BONNIE NANNIE.

ARRANGED BY T. M. MUDIE.

MODERATO.

1. The dai - sy is fair, the day - li - ly rare, The bud o' the rose is
2. Ae day she came out, wi' a ro - sy blush, To milk her twa kye, sae
3. Her looks . . that stray'd o'er na-ture a - way, Frae bon-nie blue een sae

sweet as it's bon-nie; But there ne'er was a flower in garden or bower, Like
cou - thy and can - ny, I . . cower'd me down at the back o' the bush, . . To
mild . . . an' mellow, Saw . . naething sae sweet . . in Nature's ar-ray, . . . Though

auld Joe Nicolson's bon - nie Nannie. O, my Nannie! my dear lit-tle Nannie! My
watch the air o' my bou - nie Nannie. O, my Nannie! my dear lit-tle Nannie! My
clad in the morn - ing's gow - den yellow. O, my Nannie! my dear lit-tle Nannie! My

sweet lit-tle nid-dle-ty nod-dle-ty Nannie! There ne'er was a flower, in

colla voce.

garden or bower, Like auld Joe Nicolson's bon-nie Nannie.

f

My heart lay beating the flowery green,
In quaking, quivering agitation,
An' the tears cam' tricklin' down frae 'my een,
Wi' perfect love an' wi' admiration.
    O, my Nannie! my dear little Nannie!
    My sweet little niddlety noddlety Nannie!
    There ne'er was flower, in garden or bower,
    Like auld Joe Nicolson's bonnie Nannie!

There's mony a joy in this warld below,
An' sweet the hopes that to sing were uncanny,
But of all the pleasures I ever can know,
There's nane like the love of my bonnie Nannie.
    O, my Nannie! my dear little Nannie!
    My sweet little niddlety noddlety Nannie!
    There ne'er was a flower, in garden or bower,
    Like auld Joe Nicolson's bonnie Nannie!

"AULD JOE NICOLSON'S NANNIE." In the collected Songs by the Ettrick Shepherd (Blackwood, 1831) there is a very characteristic note regarding this song and its air :—"Auld Joe Nicholson's Nannie was written the year before last for Friendship's Offering, but has since become a favourite, and has been very often copied. I have refused all applications to have it set to music, having composed an air for it myself, which I am conscious I will prefer to any other, however much better it may be." The air here given is that which Wilson, the celebrated vocalist, introduced to the public about 1850; it is probably that already mentioned, for Wilson never made any claim to have composed it.

2 A

THE ROWAN TREE.

ARRANGED BY T. M. MUDIE.

1. Oh!
2. How

row - an tree, oh! rowan tree, thou'lt aye be dear to me, En -
fair wert thou in simmer time, wi' a' thy clus - ters white,

twin'd thou art wi' mo - ny ties o' hame and in - fan - cy. Thy
rich and gay thy autumn dress, wi' ber - ries red and bright. On

leaves were aye the first o' spring, thy flow'rs the sim - mer's pride; There
thy fair stem were mo - ny names, which now nae mair I see; But

was - na sic a bonnie tree in a' the countrie side. Oh! Row - an
they 're en - grav - en on my heart, for - got they ne'er can be. Oh! Row - an

tree.
tree.

We sat aneath thy spreading shade, the bairnies round thee ran,
They pu'd thy bonnie berries red, and necklaces they strang ;
My mither, oh ! I see her still, she smiled our sports to see,
Wi' little Jeanie on her lap, and Jamie at her knee.
                    Oh ! rowan tree.

Oh ! there arose my father's prayer in holy evening's calm ;
How sweet was then my mother's voice in the Martyr's psalm !
Now a' are gane ! we meet nae mair aneath the rowan tree,
But hallowed thoughts around thee turn o' hame and infancy.
                    Oh ! rowan tree.

"THE ROWAN TREE." This song is a fine specimen of the poetic feeling which Lady Nairne threw into all the memories of her youth. Though it was published about 1840, she was not known to be the author till after her death in 1845. Of the air little is known, but it is believed to owe its present form to Finlay Dun, who, during a quarter of a century, arranged so many modern Scottish airs from amateur sketches.

Lady Nairne was so very shy in regard to her writings, that there is really some doubt concerning a few of those first given to the world in the Scottish Minstrel. Though it is generally admitted that all those marked B. B. in that work are really by Lady Nairne, there are others, initialed S. M. (Scottish Minstrel), about which there is not the same certainty. For while the B. B. songs are all so marked in the first and every subsequent edition, the S. M. songs are, in the index of the first and second editions, stated to be of unknown authorship. In the third edition they first appear with the initials; it has therefore been suggested that these songs were probably the joint production of the ladies who edited the literary portion of the Minstrel ; of these, Lady Nairne was undoubtedly the leading spirit. Two of her most able coadjutors were Miss Hume, daughter of the Honourable Baron Hume of the Exchequer, and Miss Helen Walker ; it was from the singing of the latter that R. A. Smith took down the airs of Lord Nithsdale and Carlisle Yetts.

THE BONNETS OF BONNIE DUNDEE.

ARRANGED BY T. M. MUDIE.

1. To the Lords of Con - ven - tion 'twas Cla - ver - house spoke, Ere the King's crown go down there are
2. Dun - dee he is mount - ed, he rides up the street, The bells they ring backward, the

crowns to be broke; So each Ca - va - lier who loves hon - our and me, Let him
drums they are beat, But the Pro - vost (douce man) said, "Just e'en let it be, For the

fol - low the bon-nets of bon - nie Dun - dee. Come } fill up my cup, come
town is weel rid o' that deil o' Dun - dee." Come }

fill up my can, Come sad - dle my horses and call out my men, Un - hook the West Port, and

ff   *ff*

let us go free, For its up with the bonnets of bon-nie Dundee.

There are hills beyond Pentland, and lands beyond Forth,
If there 's Lords in the South, there are Chiefs in the North,
There are brave Duinewassals, three thousand times three,
Will cry " Hey for the bonnets of bonnie Dundee."
    Come fill up my cup, come fill up my can,
    Come saddle my horses and call out my men,
    Unhook the West Port, and let us go free,
    For its up with the bonnets of bonnie Dundee.

Then awa' to the hills, to the lea, to the rocks,
Ere I own a usurper I 'll crouch wi' the fox ;
And tremble, false Whigs, in the midst o' your glee,
Ye ha'e no seen the last o' my bonnets and me.
    Come fill up my cup, come fill up my can,
    Come saddle my horses and call out my men,
    Unhook the West Port, and let us go free,
    For its up with the bonnets of bonnie Dundee.

THE BONNETS OF BONNIE DUNDEE.—This lively modern tune is often erroneously called Bonnie Dundee, thus confounding it with a much finer slow air of the olden time, found in the Skene MS. (1635 ?), and now sung to Mary of Castlecary. Victor Hugo, in his "Travailleurs de la Mer," speaks justly of the "tristesse" of Bonnie Dundee, and has been blamed for not comprehending the character of the tune, by a corrector who evidently only knew this modern air under that name. The latter was known in Edinburgh about fifty years ago as "The band at a distance ;" it was much played by young ladies, the mode being to begin *pianissimo*, gradually increase the sound to *fortissimo*, and then die away as the band was supposed to recede into the distance. Many years afterwards a celebrated contralto of our time being in Scotland, heard the air, and adapted it to Sir Walter Scott's stirring words, to which it is admirably suited. The air is believed to be of Scottish parentage, but nothing more exact is known concerning it.

CAPTAIN PATON NO MO'E!

ARRANGED BY T. M. MUDIE.

1. Touch once more a   sober   measure,   And let punch and tears be   shed,   For a
2.   His   waistcoat, coat, and breeches,   Were all   cut off   the same   web,   Of a
6. Now and then up-on a   Sunday   He in - vit - ed me to   dine   On a
7.   Or   if   a bowl was mentioned,   The   Captain   he would   ring,   And bid

WITH
GRAVE
HUMOUR.

prince of good old   fel - lows, That,   a - lack - a - day, is dead! For a prince of worthy   fel-lows, And a
beau - ti - ful snuff col - our,   Or   a   mod-est genty drab;   The   blue stripe in his stocking, Round his
her - ring and a mutton-chop, Which his maid dress'd very fine; There was also a   lit - tle   Malm-sey And a
Nel - ly to the West-Port,   And a   stoup of water bring.   Then   would he mix the genuine stuff, As they

First and last stanzas only.

pret-ty man al - so,   That has left the Salt - mark - et   In   sorrow, grief, and woe—Oh! we
neat slim leg did   go,   And his   ruffles of the cambric fine, They were whiter than the
bot - tle of Bor - deaux,   Which be-tween me and the Cap - tain Passed   nimbly to and
made it long a - go,   With limes that on his property   In   Trin-i-dad did

The other stanzas.

	ne'er shall see the	like of	Captain	Pa - ton	no	mo'e !
snow— Oh !	we	ne'er shall see the	like of	Captain	Pa - ton	no	mo'e !
fro— Oh !	I	ne'er shall take pot - luck with	Captain	Pa - ton	no	mo'e !
grow— Oh !	we	ne'er shall taste the	like of	Captain	Paton's punch no	mo'e !

ff

Ritornel.　　　　*Last time.*

Sobbing.

3. His hair was curled in order,
  At the rising of the sun,
In comely rows and buckles smart,
  That about his ears did run ;
And before there was a toupee
  That some inches up did go ;
And behind there was a long queue,
  That did o'er his shoulders flow—Oh ! etc.
4. And whenever we forgather'd,
  He took off his wee three cockit,
And he proffer'd you his snuff-box,
  Which he drew from his side pocket ;
And on Burdett or Bonaparte
  He would make a remark or so,
And then along the plainstanes
  Like a provost he would go—Oh ! etc.
5. In dirty days he picked well
  His footsteps with his rattan,
Oh ! you ne'er could see the least speck
  On the shoes of Captain Paton !
And on entering the coffee-room
  About two, all men did know
They would see him with his " Courier "
  In the middle of the row—Oh ! etc.
8. And then all the time he would discourse
  So sensible and courteous,
Perhaps talking of the last sermon
  He had heard from Dr. Porteous ;
Or some little bit of scandal
  Of Mrs. So-and-so,
Which he scarce could credit, having heard
  The con, but not the pro—Oh ! etc.

9. Or when the candles were brought forth,
  And the night was (fairly) setting in,
He would tell some fine old stories
  About Minden-field or Dettingen ;
How he fought with a French major,
  And despatched him at a blow,
While his blood ran out like water
  On the soft grass below—Oh ! etc.
10. But at last the Captain sicken'd,
  And grew worse from day to day,
And all missed him in the coffee-room,
  From which now he stay'd away.
On Sabbaths, too, the Wynd Kirk
  Made a melancholy show,
All for wanting of the presence
  Of our venerable beau—Oh ! etc.
11. And in spite of all that Cleghorn
  And Corkindale could do,
It was plain, from twenty symptoms,
  That death was in his view ;
So the Captain made his testament,
  And submitted to his foe,
And we laid him by the Ram's-horn Kirk ;
  'Tis the way we all must go—Oh ! etc.
12. Join all in chorus, jolly boys,
  And let punch and tears be shed,
For this prince of good old fellows
  That, alack-a-day ! is dead ;
For this prince of worthy fellows,
  And a pretty man also,
That has left the Saltmarket
  In sorrow, grief, and woe !—For it, etc.

"CAPTAIN PATON NO MO'E !" This graphic description of a somewhat celebrated personage appeared in Blackwood's Magazine in September 1819, and is understood to have been written by J. G. Lockhart. In the Book of Scottish Song (Blackie), we are told that Captain Paton resided about the beginning of the century opposite the old Glasgow Exchange. Lockhart's description of him is said to be very accurate. The Wynd Kirk,—Wee Kirk in the original,—was at that time the most fashionable place of worship in the city. The air is believed to have been composed by Mr. William Mackean of Paisley.

THE NAMELESS LASSIE.

ARRANGED BY A. C. MACKENZIE.

SLOW
WITH
TENDERNESS.

Legato.

Calando.

1. There's nane may ev - er
2.   gen - tle as she's

guess or trow my bonnie lass - ic's name; There's nane may ken the humble cot my
bon - nie, an' she's modest as she's fair; Her vir - tues, like her beauties a', are

lass - ie ca's her hame; Yet though my lassie's nameless, an' her kin o' low de -
var - ied as they're rare. While she is licht and mer-ry as the lammie on the

colla voce.

gree, Her heart is warm, her thochts are pure, an' O she's dear to me; Her
lea; For hap-pi - ness and in - no - cence the - gith - er aye maun be; For

cres.   *f*   *rit.*   *p*

heart is warm, her thochts are pure, an' O she's dear to me.
hap - pi - ness and in - no - cence the gith - er aye maun be.

a tempo. mf

dim.   *pp*   *ped.*

2d verse.   *concluding verse.*

2. She's

cres.   *f*   *p*   *pp*

ped.   ✻   *ped.*   ✻   *ped.*   ✻   *ped.*   ✻

Whene'er she shows her blooming face, the flow'rs may cease to blaw,
And when she opes her hinnied lips, the air is music a';
But when wi' ithers' sorrows touched, the tear starts to her e'e,
Oh! that's the gem in beauty's crown, the priceless pearl to me.

Within my soul her form's enshrined, her heart is a' my ain,
And richer prize, or purer bliss, nae mortal e'er can gain;
The darkest paths o' life I tread wi' steps o' bounding glee,
Cheer'd onward by the love that lichts my nameless lassie's e'e.

"THE NAMELESS LASSIE." These verses were written by James Ballantine, one of the best and most prolific of our song writers since the time of Burns. Some of his earliest lyrics were contributed to Whistle Binkie, one of the most excellent collections of original Scottish song that has ever appeared. Between 1843 and 1872, he published "The Gaberlunzie's Wallet," "The Miller of Deanhaugh," "Lilias Lee," and "Malcolm Canmore," an historical drama, besides several editions of his collected songs. He was born in Edinburgh in 1808; died 1877.

The melody was composed by Alexander Mackenzie, a gentleman well known as a violinist all over Scotland; and whose rendering of our national melodies was quite a feature at the Theatre Royal, Edinburgh, in the golden days of William Murray. He was born at Montrose in 1819; showed so precocious a musical talent, that he appeared in Aberdeen at the early age of seven. He was connected with the Edinburgh Theatre from his eleventh year, under the successive managements of William Murray, Edmund Glover, and Robert Henry Wyndham, by all of whom he was held in much esteem. He wrote a good deal of melodramatic and dance music; and was very happy in his settings of several of Ballantine's songs:— Bonny Bonaly, The Grey Hill-plaid, and others. He died in 1857.

The song is published in this volume by the kind permission of Mr. John Blockley, Argyll Street, London, the proprietor of the copyright.

BONNIE BESSIE LEE.

ARRANGED BY T. M. MUDIE.

♩ = 88

ALLEGRETTO.

1. Bonnie Bessie Lee had a face fu' o' smiles, And mirth round her ripe lips was aye dancing slee; And light was the foot - fa', and win - some the wiles, O' the flower o' the par - och - in, Our ain Bessie Lee. Wi' the bairns she wad rin, and the school - laddies paik, And o'er the broomy braes like a fair - y wad

2. whiles she had a sweet - heart and whiles she had twa, A limmer o' a lassie; but a - tween you and me, Her warm wee bit heart - ie she ne'er threw a - wa', Though mony a ane had sought it frae bonnie Bessie Lee. But ten years had gane since I gazed on her last; For ten years had parted my auld hame and

3. Time changes a' things, the ill - natured loon; Were it ev - er sae right - ly, he'll no let it be; But I rubbit at my een, and I thought I would swoon, How the Carle had come round about Our ain Bessie Lee. The wee laughin' lassie was a gudewife growin' auld, Twa weans at her ap - ron, and ane at her

flee, Till auld hearts grew young again wi' love for her sake, There was life iu the blithe blink o'
me, And I said to my - sel', as her mother's door I pass'd, Will I ever get an - ither kiss frae
knee, She was douce too and wise - like, and wisdom's sae cauld, I would rather ha'e the ither ane than

bonnie Bessie Lee; Our ain Bessie Lee, our bonnie Bessie Lee, There was life in the
bonnie Bessie Lee; Our ain Bessie Lee, our bonnie Bessie Lee, Will I ever get an -
this Bessie Lee; Our ain Bessie Lee, our bonnie Bessie Lee, I would rather ha'e the

blithe blink o' bonnie Bessie Lee.
ither kiss frae bonnie Bessie Lee.   2. And
ither ane than this Bessie Lee.   3. But

"BONNIE BESSIE LEE" was written by Robert Nicoll,—"Scotland's second Burns" he has been called,—
who was the son of a small farmer in Perthshire; and who, notwithstanding a constant struggle for
existence, early connected himself with the press by writing many poems and a prose story, which appeared
in an Edinburgh magazine. Through the influence of his publisher, Mr. Tait, he was appointed editor of
the *Leeds Times* (1836), but only survived till the end of the following year, when he died at the early age
of twenty-three.

The air is modern, but the composer is unknown; John Wilson, the vocalist, probably helped to mould
it into its present form. As it requires stanzas of eight lines, it has been necessary to omit the following
four, which form the ninth to the twelfth lines in the original :—

> She grat wi' the waefu', and laughed wi' the glad,
> And licht as the wind 'mang the dancers was she ;
> And a tongue that could jeer, too, the little lassie had,
> Which keepit ay her ain side for bonnie Bessie Lee.

GOOD NIGHT. AND JOY BE WI' YE A'.

ARRANGED BY J. T. SURENNE.

Good night, and joy be wi' ye a', Your harm-less mirth has cheer'd my heart; May life's fell blasts out-o'er ye blaw! In sor-row may ye nev-er part! My spi-rit lives, but strength is gone, Tho moun-tain-fires now blaze in vain: Re-mem - ber, sons, the deeds I've done, And in your deeds I'll live a - gain!

Concluding Symphony.

When on yon muir our gallant clan
Frae boasting foes their banners tore,
Who show'd himsel' a better man,
Or fiercer wav'd the red claymore?
But when in peace—then mark me there,
When thro' the glen the wanderer came,
I gave him of our hardy fare,
I gave him here a welcome hame.

The auld will speak, the young maun hear,
Be canty, but be good and leal;[1]
Your ain ills ay ha'e heart to bear,
Anither's ay ha'e heart to feel;
So, ere I set, I'll see you shine,
I'll see you triumph ere I fa';
My parting breath shall boast you mine,
Good night, and joy be wi' you a'.

[1] Loyal: honest.

'GOOD NIGHT, AND JOY BE WI' YE A.'" These words were written by the late Sir Alexander Boswell, Bart., of Auchinleck, and published by him, anonymously, in a pamphlet containing some others of his songs, at Edinburgh, in 1803. The title of the song is "The old Chieftain to his sons." Of the air, Mr. Stenhouse says:—"This beautiful tune has, time out of mind, been played at the breaking up of convivial parties in Scotland. The principal publishers of Scottish Music have also adopted it, as their farewell air, in closing their musical works." There is a fragment of a song called "Armstrong's Goodnight," which Sir Walter Scott gave in his "Minstrelsy of the Scottish Border," with the following notice:—"The following verses are said to have been composed by one of the Armstrongs, executed for the murder of Sir John Carmichael of Edrom, Warden of the Middle Marches. The tune is popular in Scotland, but whether these are the original words will admit of some doubt:—

'This night is my departing night,
    For here nae langer must I stay;
There's neither friend nor foe o' mine
    But wishes me away.

What I have done thro' lack of wit,
    I never, never can recall;
I hope ye're a' my friends as yet,
    Goodnight, and joy be wi' ye all!'

Sir John Carmichael, the Warden, was murdered 16th June 1600, by a party of borderers, at a place called Raesknows, near Lochmaben, whither he was going to hold a Court of Justice. Two of the ringleaders in the slaughter, Thomas Armstrong, called *Ringan's Tam,* and Adam Scott, called *The Pecket,* were tried at Edinburgh, at the instance of Carmichael of Edrom. They were condemned to have their right hands struck off, thereafter to be hanged, and their bodies gibbeted on the Borough Moor; which sentence was executed 14th November 1601." See Border Minstrelsy, vol. i. p. 105, edition of 1802.

Scottish Airs

ARRANGED AS

PART-SONGS FOR FOUR VOICES

AS SUNG BY SPECIAL COMMAND AT BALMORAL BEFORE HER MAJESTY

THE QUEEN

BY

MR. H. A. LAMBETH'S SELECT CHOIR

CHARLIE IS MY DARLING.

Arranged by HENRY A. LAMBETH.

TREBLE. Oh! Char-lie is my dar-ling, My dar-ling, my dar-ling, Char-lie is my dar-ling, The

ALTO.

TENOR. Oh! Char - lie, Charlie is my dar - ling, Char-lie is my dar - ling, my

BASS. Oh! Char - - lie, Char - - lie, Char - - lie is my

ACCOMP.

young chevalier.

1. 'Twas on a Mon-day morn-ing, Right ear-ly in the year, When
2. As he cam' march-ing up the street, The pipes play'd loud and clear, An'
3. Wi' high-land bon-nets on their heads, An' bright clay-mores and clear, They
4. They've left their bon-nie high-land hills, Their wives and bairn-ies dear, To
5. Oh! there were mo-ny beat-in' hearts, An' mony a hope and fear; An'

dar - ling. Char - - - - - - - - - - lie, Oh!

dar - ling.

Char - lie cam' to our town, The young che - va-lier. Oh!
a' the folk cam' runnin' out To meet the che - va-lier. Oh!
cam' to fight for Scotland's right An' the young che - va-lier. Oh!
draw the sword for Scotland's lord, The young che - va-lier. Oh!
mo - ny were the prayers put up For the young che - va-lier. Oh!

Char - - lie,

Char - lie is my dar - ling, The young che - va - lier. Oh! Char - lie is my dar - ling, my

Marcato.

p

Char - - - - -

poco ritard. *fz*

Char - - lie, Char - - - lie is my dar - - ling.

poco ritard. *fz*

dar - ling, my dar - ling, Char - lie is my dar - ling, The young che - va-lier.

lie is my dar - - ling.

2 B

WANDERING WILLIE.

Written by Burns.

Arranged by HENRY A. LAMBETH.

1. Here a - wa', there a - wa', wan - der-ing Wil - lie, Here a - wa', there a - wa',
2. Rest, ye wild storms, in the caves of your slum - bers; How your dread howl-ing a

1. Here a - wa', there a - wa', wan - der-ing Wil - lie, Here a - wa', there a - wa',
2. Rest, ye wild storms, in the caves of your slum - bers; How your dread howl-ing a

haud a - wa' hame; Come to my bo-som, my ain on - ly dear-ie, Tell me thou bring'st me my
lov - er a - larms; Wau-ken, ye breezes, row gen - tly, ye billows, And waft my dear lad - die ance

haud a - wa' hame; Come to my bo-som, my ain on - ly dear-ie, Tell me thou bring'st me my
lov - er a - larms; Wauken, ye breezes, row gen - tly, ye billows, And waft my dear lad - die ance

Wil - lie the same. Win - ter winds blew loud and cauld at our part - ing,
mair to my arms. But oh, if he's faith - less, and minds na his Nan - nie,

Wil - lie the same. Win - ter winds blew loud and cauld at our part - ing,
mair to my arms. But oh, if he's faith - less, and minds na his Nan - nie,

rall. e p . . . . . .

Fears for my Wil - lie brought tears in my e'e ; Wel - come now sim - mer, and
Flow still be - tween us, thou wide roar-in' main ; May I never see it, may

rall. e p . . . . . .

Fears for my Wil lie brought tears in my e'e ; Wel - come now sim - mer, and
Flow still be - tween us, thou wide roar-in' main ; May I never see it, may

rall. e p . . . . . .

wel - come my Wil - lie, The sim - mer to na - ture, and Wil - lie to me.
I never trow it, But, dy - ing, be - lieve that my Wil - lie's my ain.

wel - come my Wil - lie, The sim - mer to na - ture, and Wil - lie to me.
I never trow it, But, dy - ing, be - lieve that my Wil - lie's my ain.

WAE'S ME FOR PRINCE CHARLIE.

Arranged by HENRY A. LAMBETH.

1. A wee bird cam' to our ha' door, He warbled sweet and clear-ly, An' aye the o'ercome o' his sang Was "Wae's me for Prince Charlie." Oh! when I heard the bonnie, bon-nie bird, The

1. A wee bird cam' to our ha' door, He warbled sweet and clear-ly, An' aye the o'ercome o' his sang Was "Wae's me for Prince Char-lie."

Oh! when I heard the bonnie, bonnie bird,

2. (Quoth I, " My bird, my bonnie, bonnie bird,
    Is that a sang ye borrow ?
Are these some words ye've learnt by heart,
    Or a lilt o' dule an' sorrow ?"
"Oh ! no, no, no," the wee bird sang,
    " I've flown sin' mornin' early,
But sic a day o' wind an' rain—
    Oh ! wae's me for Prince Charlie !")

3. " Dark night cam' on, the tempest roar'd
    Loud o'er the hills an' valleys ;
An' whare was't that your prince lay down,
    Wha's hame should been a palace ?"
" He row'd him in a Highland plaid,
    Which cover'd him but sparely,
An' slept beneath a bush o' broom—
    Oh ! wae's me for Prince Charlie !"

4. But now the bird saw some red coats,
    An' he shook his wings wi' anger ;
" Oh this is no a land for me,
    I'll tarry here nae langer !"
He hover'd on the wing a while,
    Ere he departed fairly ;
But weel I mind the fareweel strain
    Was, " Wae's me for Prince Charlie !"

* The last bar but one, observe the inflection in Soprano part ; Alto, Tenor, and Bass voices, wait on.

THERE WAS A LAD WAS BORN IN KYLE.

Words by Burns.   Arranged by Henry A. Lambeth.

TREBLE

Lively.

1. There was a lad was born in Kyle, But what na day o' what na style, I
2. Our monarch's hindmost year but ane Was five and twen - ty days be - gun, 'Twas
p 3. The gos - sip kee - kit in his lufe, Quo' she Wha lives will see the prufe, This
p 4. He'll hae mis - for-tunes great and sma', *f* But aye a heart a - bune them a'; He'll
5. But sure as three times three mak nine, I see by il - ka score an' line This

ALTO.

ACCOMPT.

doubt it's hard - ly worth my while To be sae nice wi' Ro - bin.
then a blast o' Jan - war win' Blew hand - sel in on Ro - bin.
wa - ly boy will be nae cuif; I think we'll ca' him Ro - bin.
be a cred - it to us a'; We'll a' be proud o' Ro - bin.
chap will dear - ly like our kin', Sae leeze me on thee, Ro - bin.

TREBLE. p e cre - - - - - - - - - - - - scen - - -
For Ro - bin was a ro - vin' boy, A ran - tin', ro - vin', ran - tin', ro - vin',
ALTO. p e cre - - - - - - - - - - - - scen - - -
For Ro - bin was a ro - vin' boy, A ran - tin', ro - vin', ran - tin', ro - vin',
TENOR. p e cre - - - - - - - - - - - - scen - - -
For Ro - bin was a ro - vin' boy, A ran - tin', ro - vin', ran - tin', ro - vin',
BASS. mf
A ran - tin', ro - vin', ran - tin', ro - vin',
- - - - - - - - - - do. riten - - u - - to.
Ro - bin was a rov - in' boy, O ran - tin', rov - in' Ro - bin.
- - - - - - - - - - do. riten - - u - - to.
Ro - bin was a rov - in' boy, O ran - tin', rov - in' Ro - bin
- - - - - - - - - - do. riten - - u - - to.
Ro - bin was a rov - in' boy, O ran - tin', rov - in' Ro - bin.
Ro - bin was a rov - in' boy, O ran - tin', rov - in' Ro - bin.

APPENDIX.

"Gala Water."—See page 50.

It is difficult to understand how so many fine airs, that are evidently ancient, should have escaped being copied into our early collections, and only been saved from oblivion by traditional singing until the second half of the eighteenth century. "Gala Water" was long thought to be modern, for it is not found in Allan Ramsay's Tunes for the songs in the Tea-Table Miscellany, nor in Craig's, nor even in Macgibbon's Collections. Oswald picked it up late (1760-65), but an examination of his version shows it to be pentatonic, and probably therefore a century earlier than his time. Notwithstanding the modern alterations—really improvements—made familiar by Johnson, George Thomson, and others, a pentatonic version continued to be sung so late as 1811, as one was then printed in the Caledonian Repository (Oliver & Boyd). Oswald's version, being curious as well as rare, is here given :—

"Gala Water."   (Pentatonic version.)

"Ye banks and braes o' bonnie Doon."—See page 300.

We give below the English original of the air which is now sung to "The Banks of Doon," and with it two sets of words. The upper line is the first stanza of the original English song ; the lower, in italics, is the single stanza which Burns wrote for George Thomson, telling him, when sending it, that he could not make a second, the measure being so cramp. It is evident that others besides Stephen Clarke were aware of the existence of the English tune, but were unwilling to hurt the feelings of Mr. Miller, by pointing out that his air was a mere reminiscence and not a new composition.

"Lost is my quiet for ever."   (The English original of the air "Ye banks and braes.")

"The broom o' the Cowdenknowes."—Pp. 14, 15.

We here give the old words to this air, which were displaced from the text to make way for the excellent verses by Mr. Gilfillan. They were originally published in the Tea-Table Miscellany, 1724, with the initials S. R. attached to them; the author's name, however, has not hitherto been discovered. The words to which the tune was originally adapted have been lost, with the exception of the burden or chorus—

" O, the broom, the bonnie, bonnie broom,
The broom o' the Cowdenknowes;
I wish I were at hame again,
Milking my daddie's ewes."

How blythe ilk morn was I to see
My swain come o'er the hill!
He skipt the burn, and flew to me,
I met him wi' good will.
O, the broom, the bonnie, bonnie broom,
The broom of the Cowdenknowes!
I wish I were wi' my dear swain,
Wi' his pipe, and my ewes.

I neither wanted ewe nor lamb,
While his flocks near me lay;
He gather'd in my sheep at night,
And cheer'd me a' the day.
O, the broom, &c.

He tuned his pipe and reed sae sweet,
The birds sat list'ning by;
Ev'n the dull cattle stood and gazed,
Charm'd wi' his melody.
O, the broom, &c.

While thus we spent our time by turns,
Betwixt our flocks and play,
I envied not the fairest dame,
Though e'er so rich and gay.
O, the broom, &c.

Hard fate! that I should banish'd be,
Gang heavily, and mourn,
Because I loved the kindest swain
That ever yet was born.
O, the broom, &c.

He did oblige me every hour,
Could I but faithfu' be?
He staw my heart; could I refuse
Whate'er he ask'd of me?
O, the broom, &c.

My doggie, and my little kit,
That held my wee soup whey,
My plaidie, broach, and crooked stick,
Maun now lie useless by.
O, the broom, &c.

Adieu, ye Cowdenknowes, adieu!
Fareweel a' pleasures there!
Ye gods, restore me to my swain,
It's a' I crave or care.
O, the broom, the bonnie, bonnie broom,
The broom of the Cowdenknowes!
I wish I were wi' my dear swain,
Wi' his pipe, and my ewes.

"Andro and his cutty gun."—Pp. 58, 59.

The old song to this air is full of humour, and though it has been banished from the drawing-room, is still welcome at the "ingle-side." Referring to it, Burns says, "This blythesome song, so full of Scottish humour and convivial merriment, is an intimate favourite at bridal-trystes and house-heatings. It contains a spirited picture of country ale-house, touched off with all the lightsome gaiety so peculiar to the rural muse of Scotland."

Blythe, blythe, and merry was she,
Blythe was she but and ben;
Weel she loo'd a Hawick gill,
And leuch to see a tappit hen.
She took me in, she set me doun,
And hecht to keep me lawin'-free;
But, cunning carline that she was,
She gart me birle my bawbee.

We loo'd the liquor weel eneuch;
But, wae's my heart, my cash was done,
Before that I had quench'd my drouth,
And laith was I to pawn my shoon.
When we had three times toom'd our stoup,
And the neist chappin new begun,
In startit, to heeze up our hope,
Young Andro wi' his cutty gun.

The carline brocht her kebbuck ben,
Wi' girdle-cakes weel-toasted brown;—
Weel does the canny kimmer ken,
They gar the scuds gae glibber doun.
We ca'd the bicker aft about,
Till dawnin' we ne'er jee'd our bun,
And aye the cleanest drinker out
Was Andro wi' his cutty gun.

He did like ony mavis sing;
And, as I in his oxter sat,
He ca'd me aye his bonnie thing,
And mony a sappy kiss I gat.
I hae been east, I hae been west,
I hae been far ayont the sun;
But the blythest lad that e'er I saw,
Was Andro wi' his cutty gun.

" TWEEDSIDE."—Pp. 92, 93.

THE high praise which has been bestowed, by various persons, upon the pastoral written for this air by Robert Crawford of Drumsoy, and which we give below, caused us hesitate not a little before displacing it from the text. Our estimate of the song was, that it had been much overrated—that it was stiff in versification, and affected in sentiment. Finding that this opinion of its merits was shared by many poets, as well as good judges of poetry, we induced a friend, who wishes to remain anonymous, to write the song which we have adapted to the air, and which will be found to possess much of the simplicity as well as the language of the olden time.

We may here remark, that in our opinion, there are many of our best old airs, such as " The yellow-haired laddie," " Peggy, I must love thee," " The boatman," " Allan Water," &c., still unsuited with words. The excellence of Burns has made us fastidious ; songs which in his day were highly lauded, now remind us of "men in buckram," or at best of Watteau's fine ladies and gentlemen playing at shepherds and shepherdesses. Their style is tame—their phraseology affected—and their sentiments, as they do not come from the heart, so they do not reach it. In looking over the lyrics of cotemporaries, we regret to see that many of their happiest efforts are never likely to be heard united to music ; as, from an unfortunate oversight, they have been written to airs which Burns or others have already made their own. We would offer this advice to aspirants for lyrical honours, to be more cautious in the selection of their airs ; and instead of vainly attempting to cope with Burns, and to dispossess him of what the world allows to be his own undisputed property, to remember that the " better part of valour is discretion ;" and that they are much more likely to hear their verses sung, if they prudently make choice of melodies still " unwedded to immortal verse."

What beauties does Flora disclose !
 How sweet are her smiles upon Tweed !
Yet Mary's still sweeter than those,
 Both nature and fancy exceed.
No daisy, nor sweet blushing rose,
 Not all the gay flowers of the field,
Not Tweed, gliding gently through those,
 Such beauty and pleasure does yield.

The warblers are heard in the grove,
 The linnet, the lark, and the thrush ;
The blackbird, and sweet cooing dove,
 With music enchant ev'ry bush.
Come, let us go forth to the mead ;
 Let us see how the primroses spring ;
We'll lodge on some village on Tweed.
 And love while the feather'd folk sing.

How does my love pass the long day ?
 Does Mary not tend a few sheep ?
Do they never carelessly stray
 While happily she lies asleep ?
Should Tweed's murmurs lull her to rest,
 Kind nature indulging my bliss,
To ease the soft pains of my breast,
 I'd steal an ambrosial kiss.

'Tis she does the virgins excel ;
 No beauty with her may compare ;
Love's graces around her do dwell ;
 She's fairest where thousands are fair.
Say, charmer, where do thy flocks stray ?
 Oh, tell me at morn where they feed ?
Shall I seek them on sweet-winding Tay ?
 Or the pleasanter banks of the Tweed ?

" SAW YE JOHNNIE COMIN'."—Pp. 86, 87.

WE are aware that this song of the olden time has long been looked upon as belonging to the humorous class, and has been sung as such by the popular singers of the day. We confess, however, that we have never viewed it in this light. Manners and customs have changed since the time the song was written ; maidens may have become more reserved ; duplicity, in some instances, may have taken the place of rustic simplicity, but human nature remains the same It appears to us that the intense love of the unsophisticated maiden for her Johnnie overcomes all her scruples, and the way in which she pleads with her thrifty father to fee him, has, to our minds, nothing offensive or indelicate in it. On the contrary, when she urges the good qualities of her lover—his being " a gallant lad, and a weel doin' "—as a reason that her hesitating father should not stand "upon a merk o' mair fee," nothing can be more natural. But when she throws the weight of her fond affection into the scale, no wonder that it turns the balance in her favour, for what father could refuse such an appeal made to him by a loving daughter ?

" For a' the work about the house,
 Gaes wi' me when I see him."

Surely there is nothing comic in this. It is one of those simple and happy touches, so true to nature, that it could only be thrown off by the pen of a poet.

Although the composer of the fine old melody to this song might not have been fully aware of the deep pathos which he had infused into it, yet he never could have so far mistaken his own intention, as to suppose that he had written a lively air. This discovery was left to the singers who came after him.

"O MY LOVE IS LIKE THE RED RED ROSE."—P. 72.

CAPTAIN CHARLES GRAY, R.M., that indefatigable inquirer into everything that bore upon the poetry or the life of Burns, learned from Mrs. Begg, Burns's sister, that these verses were partly founded on one of the many old songs sung by her mother. It was rather a long ditty, but she could still recollect sixteen lines of it, among which were those referring to the "seas," the "rocks," and the "ten thousand miles." Captain Gray says, "It is not very often that the first half of a stanza should be what is called the 'making of a song,' but so it is in this instance; the first four lines were undoubtedly written by Burns." This is now the generally received opinion, but Mr. Scott Douglas thinks otherwise; he says, "This sweet song, truly in the ancient style, and as truly Burns's own, every line, has produced a rush of 'traditioners,' who pretend to treat us to what they call the old words;" and so on. In this and in similar passages Mr. Douglas often seems to deny to Burns what many think one of his great merits; no one but himself ever succeeded in infusing new life into some old half-forgotten ditty, and this not more by what he added than by what he rejected. With him indeed the half was often much more than the whole.

"THE YELLOW-HAIR'D LADDIE."—P. 94.

BESIDES the songs already mentioned, this beautiful air has received the honour of Italian words. They were written for it by Sir Gilbert Elliot (1697-1766), second baronet of Minto, and a Senator of the College of Justice. His family inherited his poetical talent; his son, the third baronet, also Sir Gilbert, being the writer of the pastoral "My sheep I neglected, I lost my sheep crook," and his daughter Jane, that of the still more celebrated song, "I've heard them lilting at our ewes milking," set to the ancient melody the first in the present collection. It will be found that Sir Gilbert's Italian words to the "Yellow-haired Laddie" are smoother and more *singable* than those in our own tongue.

Veduto in prato	Al bosco, al monte,
Il mio pastor,	Lo cerco in van',
Il crin coronato	E presso al fonte
D'un serto di fior.	Non trovo ch'il can';
Il sol' negli occhi,	Ah! cane fedele
La fide nel sen',	Deh! dimmi perche,
Ah! dove s'asconde	Il mio crudele
Il caro mio ben'?	S'asconde di me?

"THE WEARY PUND O' TOW."—P. 158.

CAPTAIN CHARLES GRAY, R.M., has pointed out that a song bearing this name existed prior to the days of Burns. Strange to say, it escaped the researches of David Herd, who seemed to have an art of his own in finding curious old songs. It appeared however in Lawrie and Symington's edition of Herd, 1791. "It may possibly be of no great antiquity, but is certainly not devoid of the quaint humour peculiar to the Scottish Muse, as will be seen from the following stanza—

I lookit to my yarn knagg, and it grew never mair,
I lookit to my meal kist,—my heart grew wondrous sair;
I lookit to my sour-milk boat, and it wad never sour,
For they suppit at, and slaikit at, and never span an hour."

"JENNY DANG THE WEAVER."—P. 193.

WE quote from that curious work, "The Contemporaries of Burns," the following particulars regarding Sir Alexander Boswell, Bart.:—

"He was born on the 9th of October 1775, and was the eldest son of the well-known biographer of Dr. Johnson, and grandson of Lord Auchinleck, one of the Senators of the College of Justice. His mother, a daughter of Sir Walter Montgomery, Bart., of Lainshaw, was a woman in several respects the very opposite of his father, possessing a warmth of feeling and a soundness of judgment which at once rendered her manner dignified and agreeable. Alexander, together with his only brother, James, was educated in England, first at Westminster School, and afterwards at the University of Oxford; and on the death of his father in 1795 succeeded, ere he had completed his twentieth year, to the paternal estate. Having made the tour of Europe about this date, he subsequently resided chiefly at Auchinleck, and was early distinguished in the county of Ayr as a gentleman of much spirit, warmth of heart, and public enterprise. He inherited his father's fondness for literature, and amid the accumulated stores of the Auchinleck library—one of the most valuable private collections in the country—he had ample opportunities of gratifying his taste for antiquarian research. We willingly pass over the unhappy circumstances which led to his death in March 1822, from a pistol-shot received in a duel."

"JOHNIE COPE."—P. 214.

WE subjoin the vigorous song written for this air by Captain Charles Gray, R.M. :—

The blairin' trumpet sounded far,
And horsemen rode weel graithed for war,
While Sir John Cope rode frae Dunbar
Upon a misty morning.

Prince Charlie wi' his Highland host,
Lay westward on the Lothian coast,
But Johnie bragg'd wi' mony a boast
He 'd rout them ere neist morning.

Lang ere the cock proclaim'd it day,
The Prince's men stood in array ;
And, though impatient for the fray,
Bent low the knee that morning.

When row-dow rolled the English drum,
The Highland bagpipe gied a bumm,
And told the mountain clans had come,
Grim death and danger scorning.

Ilk hand was firm, ilk heart was true,
A shot ! and down their guns they threw ;
Then forth their dread claymores they drew,
Upon that fearfu' morning.

The English raised a loud huzza,
But durstna bide the brunt ava' ;
They waver'd—turn'd—syne ran awa',
Like sheep at shepherd's warning.

Fast, fast their foot and horsemen flew,
And caps were mix'd wi' bonnets blue,
And dirks were wet, but no' wi' dew,
Upon that dreadfu' morning.

Few stay'd—save ae devoted band—
To bide the blow frae Highland brand,
That swept around—and head and hand
Lopped on that bluidy morning.

What sad mishaps that few befell !
When faint had grown the battle's yell,
Still Gardiner fought—and fighting fell,
Upon that awesome morning !

Nae braggart—but a sodger he,
Wha scorn'd wi' coward loons to flee,
Sae fell aneath the auld thorn-tree
Upon that fatal morning.

"COME UNDER MY PLAIDIE."—P. 268.

WANT of space prevented the following stanzas from being given along with the air :—

" My father aye tell'd me, my mither an' a',
Ye 'd mak' a gude husband, and keep me aye braw,
It 's true I lo'e Johny, he 's gude and he 's bonny,
But waes me ! ye ken he has naething ava !
I ha'e little tocher, you 've made a gude offer,
I 'm now mair than twenty, my time is but sma',
Sae gie me your plaidie, I 'll creep in beside you,
I thocht ye 'd been aulder than threescore an' twa ! "

She crap in ayont him, beside the stane wa',
Whar Johny was list'nin', and heard her tell a' ;
The day was appointed, his proud heart it dunted,
And struck 'gainst his side as if burstin' in twa.
He wauder'd hame weary, the night it was dreary,
And thowless he tint his gate deep 'mang the snaw ;

The howlet was screamin', while Johny cried,
" Women
Wad marry Auld Nick, if he 'd keep them aye
braw ! "

" O the deil 's in the lassies ! they gang noo sae
braw,
They 'll lie down wi' auld men o' fourscore and
twa ;
The haill o' their marriage is gowd and a carriage,
Plain love is the cauldest blast now that can blaw !
But lo'e them I canna, nor marry I winna,
Wi' ony daft lassie, though fair as a queen ;
Till love ha'e a share o't, the never a hair o't
Shall gang in my wallet at morning or e'en."

"Logan Water."—Pp. 116, 117.

In the third volume of the Roxburgh Ballads, so ably edited by Mr. William Chappell for the Ballad Society, there is a Dialogue song beginning, "Bonny lass, I love thee well," to be sung to an excellent New tune, "The Liggan Waters." Mr. Chappell refers the name (Logan Water) to a stream near Drogheda, and presumably supposes the air to be Irish. To this several objections may be offered. 1. The tune has no Irish peculiarities whatever. 2. It is not found in Bunting's or in any other Irish collection that the present writer has examined. 3. On the other hand, it is quite Scottish in style; and the writer of the Ballad already mentioned would seem to have been of this opinion, by his having introduced many Scottish words into his verses, so as to be in keeping with the character of the music. Mr. Chappell has printed a copy of the air that is even more Scottish and more ancient in style than the version at present in use. Instead of the B flat which follows G in the first bar, the old set goes at once boldly down to F, the minor 7th, a peculiarity of the old tonality that would not have been found in a "New tune" of 1685-90, when this ballad was printed by Conyers. The tune could then only have been called *New* as being *unknown* to the English ballad-singers of the time.

"For a' that and a' that."—P. 278.

The original of this air has long been sought for, and without success until recently, when it was found in Bremner's Collection of Reels and Strathspeys (1758), under the name of Lady Macintosh's reel.

"The Blue Bells of Scotland."—P. 296.

We give below the original air of the song that Mrs. Jordan introduced on the stage under this name, and of which Ritson said "she knew neither the words nor the tune." It has all the appearance of having originally been the quick-step of a marching regiment. It is from Johnson's Scots Musical Museum, vol. vi. 1803.

"The Blue Bells of Scotland." (Original Air.)

O where and O where does your Highland laddie dwell? O where and O where does your Highland laddie dwell? He dwells in merry Scotland, where the blue bells sweetly smell, And all in my heart I love my lad - die well. He dwells in merry Scotland, where the blue bells sweetly smell, And all in my heart I love my lad - die well.

"Annie Laurie."—Pp. 364, 365.

In Mr. C. Kirkpatrick Sharpe's Ballad Book, privately printed (Edinburgh, 1824), the following is given as the original version of Annie Laurie :—

Maxwelton banks are bonnie,
  Whare early fa's the dew ;
Whare me and Annie Laurie
  Made up the promise true ;
Made up the promise true,
  And never forget will I,
And for bonnie Annie Laurie
  I 'd lay down my head and die.

She 's backit like a peacock,
  She 's breastit like a swan,
She 's jimp about the middle,
  Her waist ye weel may span ;
Her waist ye weel may span,
  And she has a rolling eye,
And for bonnie Annie Laurie
  I 'd lay down my head and die.

INDEX OF SUBJECTS,

WITH SLIGHT ADDITIONS TO THE NOTES.

PENTATONIC TUNES not now numerous, the early form of many of our melodies having probably been altered to suit modern notions and tastes. "Gala Water" an example of the change; Oswald alone giving the pentatonic form of the air, which might otherwise be thought quite modern, as it is not found in print before the middle of the eighteenth century. A simple pentatonic form of "Tweedside" is found in W. Graham's MS. Flute Book, 1694.

PERCY, BISHOP, 11, 251.

PETRIE, DR.—Irish airs, 227, 243. "The winter it is past."

PLAGAL CADENCE not infrequent in Scottish airs, 28, 30, 42, 64, 92, 162.

POSIE, THE, by Burns, preferred by Professor Wilson to Heliodora's Garland by Meleager, 183.

PRINGLE, THOMAS (1789-1834), 121.—Recovered "Why weep ye by the tyde, Ladie?" Completed Lady Grizel Baillie's song, "O the ewe-bughting's bonnie," 95.

REID, GENERAL JOHN, 275.—Established the Chair of Music in Edinburgh.

REMODELLING OF OLD AIRS, 90.

RIDDELL, REV. H. S., 101.

RIZZIO.—His having composed even one single Scottish air a mere fiction, 21. His style would be either Italian or French. Oswald frequently passed off his own tunes in private as compositions of Rizzio, 90. No traces of the Rizzio fiction for a century and a half after his death, 97. He was only four years in Scotland, 101. First heard of as a composer in 1725, 105. In 1742 Oswald ascribes four airs to him, 122. "Doun the burn, Davie," absurd fiction, 179. Geminiani, 1749. Recapitulation of facts, 319, 329.

ROSLIN CASTLE, 163.—Not composed by Oswald; early name "The house of Glammis."

ROY'S WIFE.—Gaelic name, Cog na Scalan, 139.

SACRED SONGS sung to popular tunes, 17.

ST. CRISPIN'S DAY.—Tune played at the annual procession on that day, 157.

SAW YE MY FATHER? 255.—An English air; even the old words probably altered from an English original.

SCOTT, SIR WALTER, 55, 289.

SCOTTISH CATCH OR SNAP, 191.

SCOTTISH COLLECTIONS infested with numerous indifferent amateur melodies, 105.

SCOTTISH MEASURE.—A dance, the figure of which is now totally unknown; it must have been very popular, as the number of tunes for it found in our collections is enormous; many of them have been set to words, though, from their extreme compass, they are but ill-suited for this purpose.

SIBBALD.—Chronicle of Scottish Poetry, 17, 73.

SKENE MS.—"Alas, that I cam' o'er the muir," 27; "Adieu, Dundee," 39. The MS. when presented to the Advocates' Library by Miss Skene of Hallyards, consisted of seven distinct parts, which are now bound together in a volume 6½ inches by 4½. It was written for or by John Skene of Hallyards (about 1635?) in tablature for the lute. It contains 115 airs; of these 85 were published by Mr. William Dauney, 11 were found to be duplicates, and the rest were rejected as being either unintelligible or uninteresting. The airs of Scottish origin appear to be about 45, of which 25 were previously unknown. As Part III. contains ten of the duplicate tunes, it may have belonged to some other member of the family; but from its being written in what is called the old tuning of the lute—C F A D G—there is no reason for believing it to be later than the rest. The other parts are in the new tuning—A D A D A. It must be noted, however, that these letters represent the intervals rather than the pitch of the notes.

SKINNER, REV. JOHN, 197-199.

SMITH, R. A. (1750-1829), 327, 328, 330, 334, 340, 342.

SOME TUNES end on the 6th, which have the feeling of a major key, all but the last bar, as in "The Lass of Ballochmyle" and "Cockle Shells." They ought not to be reckoned minor tunes, but simply as examples of an old Scottish practice of choosing some other rather than the key-note as a close.

SONG OF DEATH, THE, ORAN AN AOIG.—A wild Skye air, played by his piper to Cameron of Fassifern, mortally wounded and dying at Waterloo, 57.

SOUTERS OF SELKIRK, THE, 12.—Eighty men, headed by their town-clerk, joined James IV. on his way to Flodden, and were nearly all slain in the battle, 13.

STENHOUSE, W.—Scarcely ever quotes Playford's "Dancing Master" correctly; his own copy so late as 1718-21; cannot have known the early editions, 127. Almost equally incorrect in quoting the Orpheus Caledonius.

STEPHENS, MISS, 302.—Careful training by Lanza; our present forcing system the cause of the early ruin of voices. Appeared at Covent Garden, 1824; became Countess of Essex, 1838; died, 1882.

STIRLING-GRAHAM, MISS, 296.

STRALOCH MS., 1627, is lost; but a copy of it made by G. Farquhar Graham was presented by him to the Advocates' Library.

TAK' YOUR AULD CLOAK ABOUT YE, 11.—An English as well as a Scottish version of this ballad; the former found in Bishop Percy's ancient MS., and one stanza of it in Othello, but otherwise totally unknown. The latter printed by Allan Ramsay about 1728, nearly forty years before the Percy Reliques appeared.

TAM GLEN.—Written by Burns to a Cromwellian tune, picked up by him in Ayrshire. See air, 60.

TANNAHILL, ROBERT (1774-1810), 104, 281, 317, 319, 331, 339.

TASSONI ascribes to King James (I. or V. ?) the invention of a new style of music, "plaintive and mournful, differing from every other," 97, 187.

THE BLUE BELLS OF SCOTLAND.—An English air, brought into notice by the singing of Mrs. Jordan. Scottish words were written for it by Mrs. Grant (Anne MacVicar) of Laggan, also by Miss Stirling-Graham, 297.

THE WINTER IT IS PAST, 243.—Probably altered from an Irish original. A northern version given by Dean Christie.

THOMSON, JAMES (1700-1748).—"If those who live in shepherds' bowers," 179.

TODLIN HAME.—The air given in the Orpheus Caledonius, 1733, under this name, differs entirely from that in Johnson; it seems to have been a pipe-tune.

TRAIN, WILLIAM, 207.—Author of "The cauld cauld winter's gane."

TWEEDSIDE.—Dr. Petrie in his Ancient Music of Ireland gives a version of this air, which he had found with Irish words, under the name of "The banks of the Tweed." Singers always styled it "Fonn albanach," a Scottish tune. There is a very simple version of it in W. Graham's MS. Flute Book, 1694; the first, and probably only ancient, part of which is pentatonic.

UP IN THE MORNING EARLY, 67.—An English tune known as "Stingo," or "The Oyle of Barley," during the Commonwealth, afterwards as "Cold and raw," from words written to it by D'Urfey.

VENOSA, PRINCE OF.—His compositions, 187.

WEE WEE GERMAN LAIRDIE, THE (George I.), 173.

WHEN THE KING COMES OWRE THE WATER, 77.—Jacobite song, written to the "Boyne Water," or rather "The rashes," which is its earliest known name, "Boyne Water" being only a secondary and more recent name for the tune.

WILL YOU GO TO THE EWE BUGHTS, MARION? 6.—The earliest known version of the air (Orpheus Caledonius, 1733) is in a major key, and, like that in the present work, in rhythms of two bars. All the modern versions are in a minor key, and in rhythms of three bars. "The Duke of Gordon's three daughters" is a northern version of the tune. See Dean Christie's Traditional Ballad Airs, where both a major and minor form of it are given.

YE BANKS AND BRAES.—The air not composed by James Miller, but really English, having been originally set to the words, "Lost is my quiet for ever," 301.

INDEX TO THE SONGS AND AIRS.

INDEX TO APPENDIX.

PRINTED BY T. AND A. CONSTABLE, PRINTERS TO HER MAJESTY,
AT THE EDINBURGH UNIVERSITY PRESS.

www.ingramcontent.com/pod-product-compliance
Lightning Source LLC
Chambersburg PA
CBHW032314280326
41932CB00009B/809